World Yearbook of Education 2017

This latest volume in the World Yearbook of Education series examines the relationship between assessment systems and efforts to advance equity in education at a time of growing inequalities. It focuses on the political motives behind the expansion of an assessment industry, the associated expansion of an SEN industry and a growth in consequential accountability systems.

Split into three key sections, the first part is concerned with the assessment industry, and considers the purpose and function of assessment in policy and politics and the political context in which particular assessment practices have emerged. Part II of the book, on assessing deviance, explores those assessment and identification practices that seek to classify different categories of learners, including children with Limited English Proficiency, with special needs and disabilities and with behavioural problems. The final part of the book considers the consequences of assessment and the possibility of fairer and more equitable alternatives, examining the production of inequalities within assessment in relation to race, class, gender and disability.

Discussing in detail the complex historical intersections of assessment and educational equity with particular attention to the implications for marginalised populations of students and their families, this volume seeks to provide reframings and reconceptualisations of assessment and identification by offering new insights into economic and cultural trends influencing them. Co-edited by two internationally renowned scholars, Julie Allan and Alfredo J. Artiles, *World Yearbook of Education 2017* will be a valuable resource for researchers, graduates and policy makers who are interested in the economic trends of global education assessment.

Julie Allan is Professor of Equity and Inclusion and Head of the School of Education at the University of Birmingham, UK, and Visiting Professor at the University of Borås in Sweden.

Alfredo J. Artiles is Associate Dean of Academic Affairs and the Ryan C. Harris Professor of Special Education at Arizona State University's Mary Lou Fulton Teachers College, USA.

World Yearbook of Education Series
Series editors: Terri Seddon, Jenny Ozga and Gita Steiner-Khamsi

For a full list of titles in this series visit www.routledge.com/World-Yearbook-of-Education/book-series/WYBE

World Yearbook of Education 2017
Assessment Inequalities
Edited by Julie Allan and Alfredo J. Artiles

World Yearbook of Education 2016
The Global Education Industry
Edited by Antoni Verger, Christopher Lubienski and Gita Steiner-Khamsi

World Yearbook of Education 2015
Educational Elites, Privilege and Excellence: The national and global redefinition of advantage
Edited by Stephen Ball, Agnes van Zantén and Brigitte Darchy-Koechlin

World Yearbook of Education 2014
Governing Knowledge: Comparison, knowledge-based technologies and expertise in the regulation of education
Edited by Tara Fenwick, Eric Mangez and Jenny Ozga

World Yearbook of Education 2013
Educators, Professionalism and Politics:
Global Transitions, National Spaces and Professional Projects
Edited by Terri Seddon and John Levin

World Yearbook of Education 2012
Policy Borrowing and Lending in Education
Edited by Gita Steiner-Khamsi and Florian Waldow

World Yearbook of Education 2011
Curriculum in Today's World:
Configuring Knowledge, Identities, Work and Politics
Edited by Lyn Yates and Madeleine Grumet

World Yearbook of Education 2017
Assessment Inequalities

**Edited by Julie Allan
and Alfredo J. Artiles**

LONDON AND NEW YORK

First published 2017
by Routledge
2 Park Square, Milton Park, Abingdon, Oxon OX14 4RN

and by Routledge
711 Third Avenue, New York, NY 10017

Routledge is an imprint of the Taylor & Francis Group, an informa business

© 2017 selection and editorial matter, J. Allan and A.J. Artiles; individual chapters, the contributors

The right of the editors to be identified as the authors of the editorial material, and of the authors for their individual chapters, has been asserted in accordance with sections 77 and 78 of the Copyright, Designs and Patents Act 1988.

All rights reserved. No part of this book may be reprinted or reproduced or utilised in any form or by any electronic, mechanical, or other means, now known or hereafter invented, including photocopying and recording, or in any information storage or retrieval system, without permission in writing from the publishers.

The editors and publisher gratefully acknowledge permission to use reprints of the following:

'The power of numbers: The adoption and consequences of national low-stakes standardized tests in Israel' by Yariv Feniger, Mirit Israeli and Smadar Yehuda was published in *Globalisation, Societies and Education*, 13(4), 1–20. By permission of Taylor & Francis.

'The hunt for disability: The new eugenics and the normalization of school children' by Bernadette Baker was published in *Teachers College Record*, 2002, 104(4), 663–703. By permission of Teachers College, Columbia University.

'Untangling the racialization of disabilities: An intersectionality critique across disability models' by Alfredo Artiles was published in the *Du Bois Review*, 2014, 10(2), 329–347. By permission of Cambridge University Press.

'Culturally Responsive Experimental Intervention Studies:The Development of a Rubric for Paradigm Expansion' was published in *Review of Educational Research* 2016, 86(2), 319–359. By permission of Sage Publications.

Trademark notice: Product or corporate names may be trademarks or registered trademarks, and are used only for identification and explanation without intent to infringe.

British Library Cataloguing in Publication Data
A catalogue record for this book is available from the British Library

Library of Congress Cataloging in Publication Data
A catalogue record for this title has been requested

ISBN: 978-1-138-69922-9 (hbk)
ISBN: 978-1-315-51737-7 (ebk)

Typeset in Minion Pro
by Apex CoVantage, LLC

Printed and bound in Great Britain by
TJ International Ltd, Padstow, Cornwall

Contents

Contributors	vii
1 Introduction	1
JULIE ALLAN AND ALFREDO J. ARTILES	

PART I
The Assessment Industry
13

2 The Power of Numbers: The Adoption and Consequences of National Low-Stakes Standardised Tests in Israel	15
YARIV FENIGER, MIRIT ISRAELI AND SMADAR YEHUDA	
3 Special Educational Needs, Disability and School Accountability: An International Perspective	32
EMMA SMITH AND GRAEME DOUGLAS	
4 The Promise and Perils of Response to Intervention to Address Disproportionality in Special Education	47
WENDY CAVENDISH, BENIKIA KRESSLER, ANA MARIA MENDA AND ANABEL ESPINOSA	
5 Quality and Equity in the Era of National Testing: The Case of Sweden	68
ANETTE BAGGER	

PART II
Assessing Deviance
89

6 Risking Diagnosis? Race, Class and Gender in the Psychopathologization of Behaviour Disorder	91
JULIE ALLAN AND VALERIE HARWOOD	

vi   *Contents*

**7 Dis/ability as White Property: Race, Class and 'Special
    Education' as a Racist Technology**   104
DAVID GILLBORN

**8 The Right to Exclude: Locating Section 504 in the
    Disproportionality Debate**   120
NIRMALA EREVELLES

**9 The Hunt for Disability: The New Eugenics and the
    Normalization of School Children**   137
BERNADETTE BAKER

PART III
**The Consequences of Assessment and the Possibility of
Fairer and More Equitable Alternatives**   175

**10 Untangling the Racialization of Disabilities: An
    Intersectionality Critique across Disability Models**   177
ALFREDO J. ARTILES

**11 Examining Assessment for Students with Special Education
    Needs in Aotearoa New Zealand: Creating New Possibilities
    for Learning and Teaching for All**   198
MISSY MORTON AND ANNIE GUERIN

**12 The Refinement of the Idea of Consequential Validity within
    an Alternative Framework for Responsible Test Design**   218
ALBERT WEIDEMAN

**13 Culturally Responsive Experimental Intervention Studies:
    The Development of a Rubric for Paradigm Expansion**   237
AYDIN BAL AND AUDREY A. TRAINOR

Afterword   278
BETH HARRY
Index   281

Contributors

Julie Allan is Professor of Equity and Inclusion and Head of the School of Education at the University of Birmingham, UK. and Visiting Professor at the University of Borås in Sweden. Her work encompasses inclusive education, disability studies and children's rights and she has a particular interest in educational theory and the insights offered through poststructural and social capital analyses. Julie has been advisor to the Scottish Parliament, the Welsh Assembly and the Dutch and Queensland Governments and has worked extensively with the Council of Europe. She has published several books, including *Rethinking inclusive education: The philosophers of difference in practice*, published by Springer; *Social capital, children and young people: Implications for policy, practice and research*, with Ralph Catts and published by Policy Press; and *Psychopathology at school: Theorizing Mental Disorders in Education*, with Valerie Harwood and published by Routledge.

Alfredo J. Artiles is Dean of Graduate Education and Ryan C. Harris Professor of Special Education at Arizona State University's (ASU). His scholarship focuses on understanding and addressing educational inequities related to the intersections of disability with other sociocultural differences. His work aims to advance policies, personnel preparation programmes, and inclusive educational systems in diverse contexts. He directs the Equity Alliance and co-edits the *International Multilingual Research Journal* (Taylor & Francis) and Teachers College Press book series *Disability, Culture, & Equity*. He was Vice President of the American Educational Research Association (AERA) (2009–2011). Dr. Artiles is an AERA Fellow, a Spencer Foundation/National Academy of Education Postdoctoral Fellow (1998–2000), and a 2008–2009 Resident Fellow at Stanford's Center for Advanced Study in the Behavioral Sciences. He received the 2012 Palmer O. Johnson Award for best article published in an AERA journal. Dr. Artiles has held visiting professorships at Leibniz University (Germany), the University of Göteborgs (Sweden), the University of Birmingham (UK) and Universidad Rafael Landívar (Guatemala). He serves on President Obama's Advisory Commission on Educational Excellence for Hispanics and is the author of *Inclusive education: Examining Equity on Five Continents* (Harvard Education Press) (with Kozleski & Waitoller).

Anette Bagger is a senior lecturer and researcher at the University of Umeå at The Department of Applied Educational Science. Her research interests are

viii *Contributors*

found in the fields of special education, mathematics didactics and assessment. Bagger's dissertation *Is school for everyone?: the national test in mathematics at Grade three in Sweden* concerned students in need of special support and the national tests in mathematics in the third grade. Her research contributes to knowledge about discourses and the positioning of individuals in connection to assessment and raises questions regarding social justice, diversity, equity, equality and quality in mathematics education and learning. Anette is part of the research group *Umeå Mathematics Education Research Centre* (UMERC) and also involved in the network *Special Pedagogics Education* at Umeå University.

Bernadette Baker is Professor of Education Research at QUT. She has held appointments as Professor of Curriculum & Instruction, University of Wisconsin-Madison, USA; Professor of Sociology of Education, University of Turku, Finland; Honorary Professor of Humanities, University of Copenhagen, Denmark and Visiting Professor, ZheJiang University, China. Her research draws upon postfoundationalist approaches within philosophy, history, comparative cosmology and sociology as they intersect with and inform interdisciplinary curriculum studies, educational policy and debates over the nature of knowledge, child, and nation.

Aydin Bal is an assistant professor at the University of Wisconsin-Madison, Department of Rehabilitation Psychology and Special Education. Dr. Bal studies the racialization of psychological problems, racial disparities in behavioural outcomes, and systemic transformation in education. His recent studies focus on developing culturally responsive intervention methodologies to disrupt and transform the marginalisation of nondominant communities in education systems. Dr. Bal has developed the Culturally Responsive Positive Behavioral Interventions and Supports (CRPBIS) framework and the Learning Lab methodology. In Learning Labs, local stakeholders, specifically those who have been historically excluded from schools' decision-making activities, collectively examine exclusionary and punitive school discipline processes and design culturally responsive behavioural support systems in their schools. Dr. Bal has been leading a mixed-methods formative intervention study to implement CRPBIS Learning Labs in the state of Wisconsin.

Wendy Cavendish is an associate professor in the Department of Teaching and Learning at the University of Miami School of Education and Human Development. Her interdisciplinary research focus includes the practices and processes in schools and other social institutions (e.g., criminal justice system) that facilitate and support successful transition of youth both into and out of special education. Her work has been published in the *Journal of Learning Disabilities, Journal of Special Education, Journal of Youth & Adolescence, Journal of Emotional and Behavioral Disorders*, and *Journal of Adolescence* as well as numerous research reports and book chapters.

Graeme Douglas is Professor of Disability and Special Educational Needs in the School of Education, University of Birmingham. He is head of the Disability Inclusion and Special Needs (DISN) department which is the largest department of its kind in the UK and comprises over 25 academics researching and studying in the field of inclusion, SEN and disability. He is also the co-director of the Visual Impairment Centre for Teaching and Research (VICTAR) which is based within DISN. Graeme joined the School of Education as a researcher in 1993 having completed his PhD in the area of individual differences in learning and computer-based presentation (also at Birmingham). Graeme has been principal investigator and manager on many high-profile externally funded research projects in the area of visual impairment and SEN.

Nirmala Erevelles is Professor of Social and Cultural Studies in Education at the University of Alabama. Her research focuses on the unruly, messy, unpredictable and taboo body in the intersecting areas of disability studies, critical race theory, transnational feminism, sociology of education and postcolonial studies. Erevelles has published articles in the *American Educational Research Journal, Educational Theory, Studies in Education and Philosophy*, the *Journal of Curriculum Studies, Teachers College Record, Disability & Society, Disability Studies Quarterly* and the *Journal of Literary and Cultural Disability Studies*, among others. Her book, *Disability and Difference in Global Contexts: Towards a Transformative Body Politic* was published by Palgrave in November 2012.

Anabel Espinosa holds a PhD in Special Education and an M.S.Ed. in Early Childhood Special Education from the University of Miami. She is the Director of Research and Evaluation at the Early Learning Coalition of Miami-Dade/Monroe where she is committed to improving the quality of early learning for children of diverse cultural/ethnic backgrounds and diverse abilities. She is actively involved in programme development that addresses the needs of children with disabilities, as well as, the incorporation of inclusive programming in programmes that support children and families. Prior to joining the Coalition, Dr. Espinosa was Research Faculty at the Florida Center for Reading Research at Florida State University. Her research focuses on qualitative and quantitative research in the areas of tiered systems of support, disproportionality in special education, emergent literacy and teacher preparation, with a focus on the way these topics impact learners who are culturally and linguistically diverse.

Yariv Feniger is a senior lecturer in the Department of Education at Ben-Gurion University of the Negev, Israel. His main areas of interest include education policy, educational inequality, minority education and gender and education. His current research focuses on social inequality in higher education and on the effects of national and international standardised tests on learning, instruction and education policy.

Annie Guerin is an experienced practitioner who has worked across and within many communities on the West Coast of New Zealand's South Island. She is a Lecturer in the School of Educational Studies and Leadership the College of Education, Health and Human Development at the University of Canterbury. Annie's teaching includes undergraduate and postgraduate levels. Her research focuses on social justice, democracy and the concept of *manaakitanga* (care; nurture; respect; hospitality) in education. Annie models learning partnerships with schools, families and education providers. Her work privileges the narratives of disabled students to inform more inclusive practices.

x *Contributors*

David Gillborn is Professor of Critical Race Studies and Director of the Centre for Research in Race & Education (CRRE) at the University of Birmingham, UK. He is founding editor of the peer-reviewed journal *Race Ethnicity and Education* and twice winner of the 'Book of the Year' award by the Society for Educational Studies (SES). He is best known for his research on racism in educational policy and practice and, in particular, for championing the growth of Critical Race Theory internationally. David received the Derrick Bell Legacy Award from the Critical Race Studies in Education Association (CRSEA), for career accomplishments that demonstrate 'personal courage and professional commitment to supporting and advocating race equality in education,' and was recently named to the Laureate Chapter of the *Kappa Delta Pi* international honour society; membership is limited to 60 living educators who have made a significant and lasting impact on the profession of education. David is a Fellow of the Academy of Social Sciences and a Fellow of the Royal Society of Arts. His most recent books are *The Colour of Class* (co-authored with Nicola Rollock, Stephen J. Ball and Carol Vincent, 2015) and *Foundations of Critical Race Theory in Education* (co-edited with Edward Taylor and Gloria Ladson-Billings, 2016).

Valerie Harwood is Professor of Sociology of Education and Australian Research Council Future Fellow, University of Wollongong. Her research is centred on a social and cultural analysis of access and participation in educational futures and the relationships of educational justice to wellbeing. This research includes: work on educational disadvantage, imagination and educational futures; the production of knowledge on child and youth psychopathology; critical disability studies; and child and youth exclusion. Her current research includes: Getting an Early Start to Education: Understanding how to promote educational futures in early childhood (ARC Future Fellowship); and partnership with the Australian Indigenous Mentoring Experience (AIME), funded by the ARC and Australian Government Department of Education and Training.

Beth Harry is a professor of Special Education in the Department of Teaching and Learning at the University of Miami's School of Education and Human Development. A native of Jamaica, Beth received her Bachelors and Masters degrees from the University of Toronto, and her PhD from Syracuse University. Her teaching and research focus on issues of diversity and special education, the challenges of serving families of children with disabilities, and qualitative methods in educational research. She served on the National Academy of Sciences (2002) panel on ethnic disproportionality in special education and has published numerous articles and two books on that topic. Beth credits her passion for disability issues to her now deceased daughter, Melanie, whose condition of cerebral palsy was the initial impetus for Beth's entry into the field. Her memoir, *Melanie, bird with a broken wing*, chronicles that journey.

Mirit Israeli is a PhD candidate in the Department of Education at Ben-Gurion University of the Negev, Israel. In her master's dissertation, she explored the effects of standardised tests on primary schools in Israel. Her doctoral research focuses on distributed leadership and the role of coordinators in teacher collaboration.

Benikia Kressler is an assistant professor at California State University, Fullerton. She received her PhD in Teaching and Learning with a focus in Special Education and Diversity from the University of Miami. Dr. Kressler's work centers on bridging the research to practice gap in culturally responsive pedagogy and special education in teacher training and classroom instruction. To advance this research agenda she focuses on the intersection of culture, race, class and disability within urban schools and the role of educators as advocates for social justice for at-risk youth. In addition, Dr. Kressler's research and teaching interests include mentorship for social justice, qualitative/action research and culturally competent data-based decision making. Dr. Kressler has several years of experience in the field of special education teaching diverse high school students with mild/moderate disabilities in inclusive and resource classrooms as well as supporting teachers to become culturally responsive educators who advocate for their at-risk students of colour.

Ana Maria Menda holds a PhD in Special Education from the University of Miami and a Master's Degree with a focus in Bilingual/Bicultural Education from the University of Connecticut. Ana was born and raised in Rio de Janeiro, Brazil and is trilingual in Portuguese, Spanish and English. Ana is interested in qualitative research with a focus on the intersectionality of bilingualism and special education. Ana has 15 years teaching experience with students from the elementary to the doctoral level. Ana is also a parent to a child on the Autism spectrum and is involved with advocacy work for children with disabilities.

Missy Morton describes her work as sitting within Disability Studies in Education. Her current research interests include investigating approaches to curriculum, pedagogy and assessment that build and support cultures of belonging across educational settings (including teacher education). She is also interested in the ways tools of ethnography can be taken up in the everyday practices of educators, to help educators make sense of their own and others' understandings of learning and culture. She has worked on numerous research and development contracts with the New Zealand Ministry of Education, including leading the project on the development of narrative assessment for students with special education needs. Missy is the Head of School of Educational Studies and Leadership, and the Director of the Inclusive and Special Education Research Group in the College of Education, Health and Human Development, University of Canterbury, New Zealand.

Emma Smith is Professor of Education at the University of Leicester. She researches issues of educational equity and the role that educational policy can play in reducing inequalities and closing achievement gaps in both the national and international context. Recent and ongoing work has been in the following areas: special education and school accountability, inequalities in participation in post-compulsory science programmes, shortages in the STEM workforce xii *Contributors*

and school policy in England. She is a co-editor of the *BERA/SAGE Handbook of Education Research and Methodology* which will be published in 2017.

Audrey A. Trainor is an associate professor of special education at the NYU Steinhardt School of Culture, Education, and Human Development, Department of Teaching and Learning at the New York University. Her work, using both qualitative and quantitative methods, focuses on the transition to adulthood for adolescents with high incidence disabilities and multicultural issues in special education. A central focus of Dr. Trainor's work has been addressing the ongoing need for improved transition services and postschool outcomes for youth with high incidence disabilities who are also youth of colour, bilingual, living in poverty, or those who experience other types of marginalisation. She has also written about qualitative methods, with a special interest in research ethics, pertaining to issues of equity. She currently serves the department as special education programme leader and she is deeply committed to graduating highly qualified, dually certified teachers who will effectively meet the needs of students with and without disabilities. Dr. Trainor is a longstanding member of both the American Educational Research Association and the Council for Exceptional Children. In 2013–2014 she was President of the CEC Division on Career Development and Transition. She is currently an associate editor for Remedial and Special Education, and a consulting editor for *The Journal of Special Education*. Prior to her career in postsecondary education, she was a special education high school teacher working with students with high incidence disabilities for nearly a decade.

Albert Weideman is an expert language tester. The tests he has designed or helped to develop have been used in tertiary institutions in South Africa, Vietnam, Namibia, Singapore and the Netherlands. A former CEO of the Inter-institutional Centre for Language Development and Assessment (ICELDA), a formal partnership of four multi-lingual South African universities, he currently holds the positions of professor of applied language studies and senior research fellow at the University of the Free State. He holds postgraduate qualifications from the University of Essex and from the University of the Free State. His research focus is on assessing language ability, and on how this relates to developing a theory of applied linguistics, or what he calls a foundational framework for working responsibly within that discipline. He has published widely and is the author of several books. These include *Beyond expression: A systematic study of the foundations of linguistics* (2009) and *A framework for the study of linguistics* (2011), a joint publication of Paideia Press and Van Schaik. His *Responsible design in applied linguistics: Theory and practice* (2016) (Springer) is currently in production.

Smadar Yehuda is a middle school principal. She earned her master's degree from the Department of Education at Ben-Gurion University of the Negev, Israel. In her dissertation she examined variability in school principals' adjustment to the era of standardised tests. Currently, Yehuda is leading pedagogical interventions aimed at enhancing advanced writing skills among middle school students.

1 Introduction

Julie Allan and Alfredo J. Artiles

The volume examines the relationship between assessment systems and efforts to advance equity in education at a time of growing inequalities. It considers the political motives behind the expansion of an assessment industry (Lingard, Martino and Rezai-Rashti 2013; Stiggins 2002), the associated expansion of an SEN industry (Tomlinson 2012) and a growth in consequential accountability systems (Sahlberg 2007). The book examines in detail the complex historical intersections of assessment and educational equity with particular attention to the implications for marginalized populations of students and their families.

The assessment industry has grown at unprecedented rates in the last two decades. The main emphasis has been in the use of standardized tests to assess student learning, gauge teacher impact, and measure programme effectiveness. Generally, the impetus for this growth pattern has revolved around discussions about the changing nature of work in the 21st century that demands different skill sets, international competitiveness, and the need to use common standards (Darling-Hammond and Adamson 2010). The explosion of information production around the world – with the amount of new technical information doubling every two years (Darling-Hammond and Adamson 2010: 2) – also justifies the need to design educational programmes and assessments that enable learners to learn how to learn, use what they know in new situations, and make efficient use of ever changing technologies, information, and so on. Ironically, the skills needed for the future are not aligned with the traditional multiple choice tests that are typically used in a number of developed and developing nations.

International comparisons of educational achievement receive considerable attention and have a substantial influence on curriculum and assessment reforms, particularly in the Western world. The PISA and TIMSS tests are two prominent examples that dominate international discussions about student performance. Although the relatively low ranking of certain developed nations like the U.S. has prompted intense debates and reforms, a number of criticisms have been levelled against these international comparisons. For instance, questions have been raised about the comparability of samples across nations, the validity of the tests, and the error terms of test scores (Carnoy 2015). Carnoy (2015) has also raised questions about the meanings of these comparisons – e.g., low mathematics scores are not predictors of future economic growth (the U.S. being a good example); scores from

2   Julie Allan and Alfredo J. Artiles

international tests have limited value for a country's educational policies (see also Creswell, Schwantner and Waters 2015; Di Giacomo, Fishbein and Buckley 2013).

Despite such criticisms, these developments in the assessment industry influence the school curricula. In the U.S. and some European nations (e.g., UK), these changes have narrowed the curriculum and prompted negative consequences that include punitive measures against schools and teachers. In addition, researchers have shown that when teachers teach to the test, students are less likely to transfer what they know to items that assess the same knowledge in a different format (Darling-Hammond and Adamson 2010). However, other nations do not use these assessments for such purposes. In fact, some European and Asian nations have built curricula and assessment systems aligned with 21st century skills (Darling-Hammond and Wentworth 2010). Unfortunately, although criteria and guidelines have been produced to ensure fairness and quality in assessment systems (Darling-Hammond 2010; Darling-Hammond and Adamson 2013), the advent of the assessment industry, particularly efforts that rely on narrow and decontextualized measures, has had substantial negative implications for subgroups of learners across nations. We provide examples below of negative developments in the description of the first section of the book.

There is a growing recognition of the function of assessment practices in hunting down difference (Baker 2002) and in even generating recognition of new forms of deviance, such as mental disorder (Allan and Harwood 2014). The sustained overrepresentation of particular populations of students, especially black and Latino within special education (Artiles, Bal and King Thorius 2010; Waitoller, Artiles and Cheney 2010) partly arises from those tests of general achievement, with their cultural and experiential bias (Artiles et al, 2010; Ball and Harry 2010; Donovan and Cross 2002). Furthermore, there is a proliferation of diagnoses of SEN and disability (Allan 2010; Harwood 2006; Youdell 2011) that can be associated with more intensified assessment practices and with an 'explicit faith in assessment as a scientific gateway to special education' (Ball and Harry 2010: 105). The growth of institutional gaming practices legitimizes the systematic identification and exclusion of particular students (Cavendish, Artiles and Harry 2014). However, as Meekosha (2011) reminds us, there remain children within the Southern Hemisphere whose impairments go undetected and responded to and which may themselves have been produced through the colonizing practices of the global metropole of the 'North' (Connell 2007; Ghai 2002). More generally, there is increasing frustration with the failure of assessments to measure what is meaningful and to do so validly (Darling-Hammond 2014), whilst pursuing and evidencing deviance with increasing avidity.

Response To Intervention (RTI), within the United States, was intended as a superior system to the 'wait to fail' approaches (Ball and Harry 2010: 117) that have preceded it, by identifying those at risk of failure, systematic monitoring of performance and an alternative basis for eligibility for a diagnosis of learning disability to the pre-existing IQ/achievement discrepancy model. A key feature of RTI is its early and intensive screening, aimed at discovering students 'at risk' even before the teacher notices them having problems in the classroom (Ferri 2012). As Ferri and others (e.g., Gallagher 2010) have noted, there is a fuzziness behind RTI which

Introduction   3

arises from a discourse that 'speaks of fidelity, universal protocols and standardization on the one hand and [has] a glaring lack of consensus or research behind the model on the other' (Ferri 2012: 867). Alongside this fuzziness, however, observes Artiles (2011: 437), 'tiers of increasing intensity and individualization' are built into educational processes. Claims that RTI will reduce the overrepresentation of minority ethnic students in special education (Gresham 2007) have not, so far, been justified. Artiles et al. (2010; Artiles 2011) suggest that RTI does not take into account the institutional and social structures that give rise to inequalities in education. Thus, the framing of RTI as a technical intervention that neither acknowledges, nor promises to address, 'misrecognition injustices through more precise identification procedures' (Artiles et al. 2010: 252) introduces its own restrictions.

New economic trends and constraints appear to be influencing how assessment and identification practices are shaped (Allan and Youdell 2015), potentially creating an obligation on professionals to mark individual children in ways that guarantee a continuity of heterogeneity (Bogard 2000). There appear also to be new cultural practices that formalize the role of assessment and identification in recognizing, apprehending and measuring inherent learner differences associated with race and poverty. This includes forms of genetic determinism (Gillborn 2016; López 2014) and a 'new eugenics' of assessment (Gillborn 2010), which are more subtle but nevertheless function as a scientific discourse.

The political function that categories of deviance operate, within an education system that insists that 'everyone do better than everyone else' (McDermott 1993: 274) has been well documented (Ferri 2004; Sleeter 1986). Following Sleeter's (1986) seminal critique of the role of learning disability (LD) in enhancing the competitive status of the US whilst allowing some of the racist assumptions about ability to remain intact (Ferri 2004), several researchers have affirmed the political purpose of labels such as LD in 'keeping people in their place' (McDermott 1993: 271; Mehan 1992; Hood, McDermott and Cole 1980) and in serving institutional and organizational ends.

> LD exists as a category in our culture, and it will acquire a certain proportion of our children as long as it is given life in the organization of tasks, skills, and evaluations in our schools . . . moments are put aside for the discover, description and remediation of certain children who display particular traits.
> (McDermott 1993: 271)

The differential usage of categories, based on varied eligibility criteria has led Harry and Klinger (2006: 5–6) to conclude that the categories are highly subjective and 'influenced by social and political agendas of various states, groups and individuals'.

At the same time as the assessment of difference within education continues to be pursued enthusiastically, there is a growing interest, within popular culture, in the celebrity deviant. Hacking (2010: 632), for example, notes a significant growth, indeed a 'boom industry' in autism narrative, with fiction and non-fiction, as well as other media forms, specifically about individuals diagnosed as autistic. This genre promotes, through 'terrible psychology' (ibid: 654), understandings

4   *Julie Allan and Alfredo J. Artiles*

of autistic individuals as having special attributes neurotypicals lack and tells us, according to Hacking, less about autism itself but more about the times in which we live. This storytelling orientation also appears to feed the thirst, among the public and professionals, for knowing the autistic person and reinforces the 'morbid fascination for the odd' (Hacking 2010: 641).

There has been a lack of public and political concern for how culturally insensitive assessment disadvantages particular students or for how pedagogies that fail to recognize students' cultural competence actively produce failure among these students, that assessment merely confirms. Instead, attention has centred on the so-called achievement gap, a spurious construction that Ladson-Billings (2006: 3) notes has, like popular culture music stars, become a 'crossover hit', entering the discourse of politicians at both end of the spectrum and of the public, but with little debate over its meaning. Ladson-Billings (2006) argues for a replacement of a gap analysis with a consideration of educational 'debts', which are made up of a series of further debts. These are economic debt, through the disproportionately low funding given to schools with high proportions of ethnic minority students; socio-political debt, with the exclusion of minority groups from civic processes; and moral debt, the disparity between what is known to be the right thing to do and what is actually done.

Attention to the socio-historical contexts of assessment practices and to the precedents of educational debts that affect certain groups in society compel educators to raise questions about the consequences of assessment tools and systems. Given the unprecedented growth of the assessment industry worldwide, particularly for accountability purposes, and knowing that assessment tools and evidence can be used to create and reproduce deviance, validity questions – do tools assess what they purport to measure? – emerge to the forefront of educational reform and policy discussions. The growing inequities across the developed and developing worlds, with the attendant effects on the reduction of opportunities for certain groups, raise concerns about the validity of assessment systems and tools, particularly about the inferences drawn from assessment scores and the implications for actions derived from such assessment results. Messick (1989) introduced the idea of consequential validity and Shepard (1997), among others, refined the discussion to include intended/unintended as well as positive and negative consequences stemming from the inferences drawn from assessment results. Although the idea of consequential validity has been debated over time (Welner 2013), the equity concerns at the core of this construct is timely at this time in history.

The use of high-stake assessments in the last 20 years has heightened debates about the equity consequences of these practices. These measures tend to rely on traditional formats most often operationalized as standardized multiple choice tests. In the U.S., the No Child left Behind illustrates this trend. Welner (2013) explained this was a case of the use of measurement tools as policy levers. Specifically, standardized achievement test scores were used to evaluate teachers and programmes as a means to ensure accountability and educational equity. For this purpose, test reports disaggregated the evidence by student subgroups (e.g., race, disability). Ironically, although NCLB promised that the educational system would be accountable to all learners, inequities were produced and reproduced (Artiles

Introduction 5

2011). For instance, if Annual Yearly Progress (AYP) was not met, drastic consequences would be applied, including school closings, teacher dismissals and student
transfers to other schools. Darling-Hammond (2004) explained that a 'diversity
penalty' was created in this policy climate as schools and communities with fewer
resources were more likely penalized and got caught in a self-perpetuating cycle
of low performance and penalties. Another consequence of this assessment paradigm was that 'when quantitative measures such as test scores are used to make
key decisions, the measures themselves are subject to corruption pressures and, in
addition, the high stakes distort and corrupt teaching and student learning' (Welner 2013: 2). Thus, cases of cheating on test administration, scoring and reporting were documented (Nichols and Berliner 2007). Moreover, the curriculum was
impacted substantially as many schools stressed test preparation at the expense
of quality teaching. Again, schools serving the most disenfranchised students that
should have been benefiting from these policies were disproportionately affected.
If test scores from special education students did not have a direct impact on AYP,
incentives were implicitly created to place low-performing learners in these programmes; substantial proportions of such students were from racial and linguistic minority and low income groups (Artiles 2011). Changes in accountability and
assessment systems around the world have also had important equity consequences
for students living at the margins of societies (Artiles, Kozleski and Waitoller 2011).

More recently, efforts have been made to reorient these negative developments.
For instance, the Gordon Commission produced important syntheses and insights
on the future of assessment in education (Baker and Gordon 2014). Scholars critiqued the longstanding emphasis on 'the use of decontextualization in the interest of control and precision in measurement science . . . [and called for] a deeper
understanding of the interactive relationship between context, performance, and
their assessment' (Gordon and Campbell 2014: 2, 3). Specifically, this perspective
requires that assessments account for the interactions of the performing person and
his/her (social, cognitive, emotional, linguistic) toolkits, the assessment task, and
the assessment setting. The next generation of assessments should transcend the
traditional focus on 'basic skills' and must be grounded in a vision of XXI century
skills (Darling-Hammond and Adamson 2010; Gee 2010). In this regard, Baker and
Gordon (2014: 1) called for 'a transformation of assessment purpose and use, from
annual, time-controlled accountability assessments to more continuous assessments used in the course of a learner's acquisition of understanding, motivation for
learning, collaborations, and a deep application of knowledge in problem solving,
communication, and authentic settings' (see also Gorin 2014; Pellegrino 2014).

The Structure of the Book

The first part of the book is concerned with *The assessment industry*, and considers
the purpose and function of assessment in policy and politics and the political context
in which particular assessment practices have emerged. It explores the appetite and
demand from governments across the world for International test comparisons. Contributors to this part of the book make visible the consequences of contemporary trends
in the use of assessment for the stratification of student populations around the world.

6 *Julie Allan and Alfredo J. Artiles*

The power of numbers is illustrated vividly by Yariv Feniger, Mirit Israeli, and Smadar Yehuda, who show the unintended consequences of low-stakes testing, introduced in Israel with the purpose of enhancing assessment for learning. Feniger and colleagues report strong negative effects on learning, instruction, and school administration as well as significant variation across schools. In warning against an 'arms race' between assessment agencies and schools, they urge politicians to think more responsibly about the long-term consequences of governance by numbers, and of comparisons, and the systemic and behavioural changes that this provokes. This is vividly highlighted by a principal's comment, quoted by Feniger and colleagues: 'Once you publish test results . . . there is a serious problem. . . . Instead of concentrating on pedagogy we concentrate on public relations'. Their warnings about the cost inevitably paid by pupils, teachers, school prinicipals, and others are salutary.

Emma Smith and Graeme Douglas, in Chapter 3, offer an insight into the standards-driven accountability that is found in most industrialized countries and explain its importance to its key stakeholders, students, institutions, and policymakers. Smith and Douglas examine the way PISA operates in general and specifically show how different countries elect to 'remove' children from PISA although they point out that other children, such as non-native speakers and low-achievers may also be excluded. The within-school exclusion categories enable children to be legitimately placed outside the assessment and Smith and Douglas's comparisons of countries' use of these criteria is intriguing. Their argument for a balance between access by children with special needs to generic assessments such as PISA and assessments that are actually meaningful to individual or groups of students is as an extremely important one.

Wendy Cavendish, Benikia Kressler, Ana Maria Menda, and Anabel Espinosa offer a detailed analysis of the RTI, which includes scrutiny of its cultural responsiveness. Considering the requirement by States in which there was disproportionality to produce a development plan, Cavendish and colleagues found significant variance in the cultural responsiveness among the states, with some not addressing cultural and linguistic diversity at all within their RTIs. Furthermore, there were very few instructional materials available to teachers. The need for English-language-specific support is further understood with an illustration of the teachers' recourse to explanations of innate ability when such support is not in place. Furthermore, teachers' beliefs in the contingency of adequate parental support in student success limited their own capacity to take responsibility for assisting students' growth. Teachers' lack of understanding of RTI and its role in relation to equity, revealed by Cavendish and colleagues, is disconcerting, So too, was the threat of consequences to individual teachers of student failure. However, the most alarming was the tendency of teachers, under such threats, to fast track students into the safe haven of special education and to resort to the status quo of labelling. The importance of developing cultural sensitivity among teachers is underlined by this work.

Anette Bagger provides an analysis of the Swedish context in which testing, and the use of PISA, has become well established and 'normalized' and considers the consequences for quality and equity. Sweden is particularly challenged by this

Introduction 7

new orientation because of its longstanding commitment to the provision of high-quality education for all, but as Bagger points out, Sweden has not escaped the neoliberalist influences which privilege competition and choice. Bagger highlights some tensions that arise within the assessment of mathematics and how values of equity and accessibility are undermined through processes that allow for the systematic exclusion of children with special needs and children with a first language that is other than Swedish.

Part 2 of the book, *Assessing deviance*, explores those assessment and identification practices that seek to classify different categories of learners, including children with Limited English Proficiency, with special needs and disabilities and with behavioural problems. Contributors examine the production of inequalities within assessment in relation to race, class, and disability. The overrepresentation of particular groups of children, including certain cultural minorities in special education and children living in poverty, is given attention. The increased interest within neuropsychiatry in associating deviance with particular categories of difference, for example race, is also considered.

Allan and Harwood offer an analysis of the growth in diagnosis of mental disorder among even very young children. This, they argue, emerges through an increasing prevalence of a process that they identify as 'psychopathologization' within school (Harwood and Allan 2014) whereby children's behavioural problems are reassigned to categories of mental disorder. The authors examine the particular 'risks' associated with race, class, and gender and argue that belonging to certain minority groups puts children at risk of receiving a medical diagnosis in respect of their behaviour. The danger associated with the psychopathologisation of behaviour is that it obscures other interpretations of children and their behaviour. It also detracts from considerations of what is best, educationally, for individual children, by forcing attention instead on how to manage the child.

David Gillborn offers a stark autobiographical account of how race and racism probably saved him from remedial education, while he watched his less fortunate (Black) classmate disappear. Gillborn, reporting on a major research project on the intersections of race and class in education, reveals the systemic and systematic use of special educational needs assessments as a way of diverting attention from race and racism. Black parents, once forced into this system, found their own professional knowledge dismissed, received inadequate support, and encountered teachers' suspicion of their children's achievement. The fate for black children was bleak, and one psychologist described vividly how individual with prior attainment that was good to average simply gave up once he had become labelled as 'SEN' by a school that 'just brutalizes those children, unintentionally'. Gillborn reads into disability the operationalization of Cheryl Harris's concept of whiteness as property. By this he means that disability is controlled and regulated in ways that make it a White racial privilege.

Nirmala Erevelles takes the disproportionality debate further in an effort to end the 'incessant prattling' about individuals students and teachers' practices that deflect from considerations of the intensified oppression. Like Gillborn, Erevelles provides

8 *Julie Allan and Alfredo J. Artiles*

a personal narrative of her incursion into the history of slavery when she happened upon a museum commemorating the *Dred Scott v. Sandford* case in Missouri. She describes her affective response and goes on to offer a forensic account of the underuse by black parents of 504 plans. These plans protect students from discrimination and mandate schools to offer accommodations to support full inclusion. Yet, this seemingly emancipatory civil rights statute produces unintended, but dangerous consequences for black students in the form of exclusion and a consolidation of antiblackness and of whiteness as property (Harris 1993).

Bernadette Baker takes up issues of sameness, difference, equality and democracy within the current school system. She considers the processes of identification and classification from the perspective of eugenics as a means of 'quality control' of populations. Baker argues that disability becomes an 'outlaw ontology' which reinvests old eugenic discourse in a new discourse that maintains an ableist normativity. She offers some alternative ways of thinking about disability that might avoid 'sending the posse out in schools'.

The final part of the book considers the *consequences of assessment and the possibility of fairer and more equitable alternatives*. It examines the production of inequalities within assessment in relation to race, class, gender, and disability and the overrepresentation of particular groups of children, including certain cultural minorities in special education and children living in poverty among those diagnosed with mental disorder. This part of the book contains some critical challenges to these enduring problems and advances alternative approaches which seek to be fair and equitable and which offer 'intelligent accountability' (Sahlberg 2007: 155) to education systems.

Alfredo Artiles offers an intersectional perspective in the analysis of racial inequities in special education. He reminds us of the significant racial disproportionality in some disability categories and of the dire long-term consequences for the educational trajectories of these learners. Artiles critiques disproportionality research and its (lack of) attention to intersections of race and disability (and other markers of oppression). He offers a clear agenda for future research on racial disparities in special education that has regard for intersectional complexity.

The particular challenges posed by national level language assessments in the context of South Africa is scrutinized by Albert Weideman. His analysis of the 11 home languages, granted equal status in law, revealed a variation in average marking that show learners to be treated unfairly. Furthermore, Weidman shows how the tests become elevated to high stakes assessments. More significant concerns exist over the validity of the language tests. Weideman considers the source of the problem to lie with ambiguity in what constitutes home languages, with these not necessarily equating with the students' mother tongue nor with the language of instruction. Washback, whereby assessment drifts and acquires a life of its own, appears inevitable. Weideman's alternative model of consequential validity that challenges the orthodoxy of validity's dependence on interpretation. Weidman's responsible assessment design, empirically tested and validated, has at its core a technical ethics that is defined by care, consideration and compassion.

Missy Morton and Annie Guerin also offer a culturally responsive approach to assessment, as well as to curriculum and pedagogy within the New Zealand education context. Their narrative assessment, informed by core values concerned

Introduction 9

with understanding a Māori worldview, actively engages the learner through a structured system of noticing and of utilizing all the interactions of that learner in every situation. It also situates the teacher as a learner – both about the student and about themselves as teachers. Morton and Guerin describe the (lengthy) process of building trust with one student, Tom, his family, his teachers, and his peers in school and reveal the rewards as they all enhance their communication and understanding of one another. Opening up teachers to alternative ways of knowing, and alerting them to their responsibilities to provide students with multiple ways of showing what they know, allowed them to recognize Tom's achievement and skills.

Aydin Bal and Audrey Trainor offer a rubric, which is modelled on prior rubrics for quality indicators of special education research that identify criteria for culturally responsive research. They developed their rubric items following a systematic review of literature and after gathering feedback from experts. The 15-item rubric uses culture as a generative concept that mediates each aspect of experimental intervention research. Their model enables a new kind of thinking about validity – ecological validity – which is altogether more promising.

Beth Harry provides a touching personal note in the afterward to this volume, reflecting on her son's conundrum over racial identification between categories of 'black' and 'bi-racial'. Her wish for a future in which young people do not have to choose which part of themselves should represent their true identities, and for an education system that encourages 'full expression of their wholeness and the full range of their authentic selves' is one that we share.

References

Allan, J. (2010). The sociology of disability and the struggle for inclusive education. *British Journal of Sociology of Education*, 31(5), 603–619.

Allan, J., and Harwood, V. (2014). *Psychopathology at school: Theorizing mental disorder in school*. London: Routledge.

Allan, J., and Youdell, D. (2015). Ghostings, materialisations and flows in Britain's special educational needs and disability assemblage. *Discourse*. DOI: 10.1080/015936306.2015.1104853

Artiles, A.J. (2011). Toward an interdisciplinary understanding of educational equity and difference: The case of the racialization of ability. *Educational Researcher*, 40(9), 431–445.

Artiles, A.J., Bal, A., and King Thorius, K.A. (2010). Back to the future: A critique of response to intervention's social justice views. *Theory into Practice*, 49(4), 250–257.

Artiles, A.J., Kozleski, E., Trent, S., Osher, D., and Ortiz, A. (2010). Justifying and explaining disproportionality, 1968–2008: A critique of underlying views of culture. *Exceptional Children*, 76(3), 279–299.

Artiles, A., Kozleski, E. and Waitoller, F. (2011). *Inclusive education: Examining equity on five continents*. Boston: Harvard Education Press.

Baker, B. (2002). The hunt for disability: The new Eugenics and the normalization of school children. *Teachers College Record*, 104(4), 663–703.

Baker, E., and Gordon, E. (2014). From the assessment of education to the assessment for education: Policy and futures. *Teachers College Record*, 116(11), 1–24.

Ball, E. W. and Harry, B. (2010). Assessment and the policing of the norm. In C. Dudley-Marling and A. Gurn (eds.) *The myth of the normal curve*, (pp. 105–122). New York: Peter Lang.

Bogard, W. (2000). Smoothing machines and the constitution of society. *Cultural Studies*, 14(2), 269–294.

10 *Julie Allan and Alfredo J. Artiles*

Carnoy, M. (2015). *International test score comparisons and educational policy: A review of the critiques.* Stanford: National Education Policy Center.

Cavendish, W., Artiles, A.J., and Harry, B. (2014). Tracking inequality: Does policy legitimize the racialization of disability? *Multiple Voices*, 14(2), 30–40.

Connell, R. (2007). *Southern theory: Social science and the global dynamics of knowledge.* Sydney: Allen and Unwin.

Creswell, J., Schwantner, U., and Waters, C. (2015). *PISA: A review of international large-scale assessments in education: Assessing component skills and collecting contextual data.* Washington, DC: The World Bank/Paris: OECD.

Darling-Hammond, L. (2004). From "Separate but Equal" to "No Child Left Behind": The Collision of New Standards and Old Inequalities. In Deborah Meier and George Wood (eds.), Many Children Left Behind. NY: Beacon Press, 2004

Darling-Hammond, L. (2010). *The flat world and education: How America's commitment to equity will determine our future..* New York: Teachers College Press.

Darling-Hammond, L. (ed.). (2014). *Next generation assessment: Moving beyond the bubble test.* San Francisco, CA: Jossey-Bass.

Darling-Hammond, L., and Adamson, F. (2010). Beyond basic skills: The role of performance assessment in achieving 21st century standards of learning. Retrieved on 10 June from: https://scale.stanford.edu/system/files/beyond-basic-skills-role-performance-assessment-achieving-21st-century-standards-learning.pdf

Darling-Hammond, L. and Adamson, F. (2013). *Developing assessments of deeper learning: The costs and benefits of using tests that help students learn.* Stanford: Stanford Center for Opportunity Policy in Education.

Di Giacomo, T., Fishbein, B., and Buckley, V. (2013). International assessment: Broadening the interpretability, application and relevance to the United States. Retrieved on 10 June from: https://research.collegeboard.org/sites/default/files/publications/2013/6/researchin review-2012–5-international-comparative-assessments.pdf

Donovan, S.M., and Cross, C.T. (2002). *Minority students in special and gifted education.* Washington, DC: National Academy Press.

Ferri, B (2004). Interrupting the discourse: A response to Reid and Valle. *Journal of Learning Disabilities*, 37(6), 509–515.

Ferri, B. (2012). Undermining inclusion? A critical reading of response to intervention (RTI). *International Journal of Inclusive Education*, 16(8), 863–880.

Gallagher, D. (2010). Educational researchers and the making of normal people. In C. Dudley-Marling and A. Gurn (eds.), *The myth of the normal curve* (pp. 25–38). New York: Peter Lang.

Gee, J. P. Equity, literacy and learning in a digital world. Short biographical statement. Retrieved on 18 October 2016 from: https://coe.unm.edu/common/documents/2010-colloq-gee.pdf

Ghai, A. 2002. Disability in the Indian context: Post-colonial perspectives. In M. Corker and T. Shakespeare (eds.), *Disability/post-modernity* (pp. 88–100). London: Continuum.

Gillborn, D. (2010). Reform, racism and the centrality of whiteness: Assessment, ability and the 'new eugenics'. *Irish Educational Studies*, 29(3), 231–252.

Gillborn, D. (2016). Softly, softly: Genetices, intelligence and the hidden racism of the new geneism. *Journal of Education Policy*, 31(4), 365–388.

Gordon, E.W., and Campbell, E.B. (2014). Context and perspective: Implications for assessment in education. *Teachers College Record*, 116(11), 1–18.

Gorin, J. (2014). Assessment as evidential reasoning. *Teachers College Record*, 116(11), 1–26.

Gresham, F.M. (2007). Evolution of the response-to-intervention concept: Empirical foundations and recent developments. In S.R. Jimerson, M.K. Burns, and A.M.

Introduction   11

VanDerHeyden (eds.), *Handbook of response to intervention: The science and practice of assessment and intervention* (pp. 10–24). New York: Springer.

Hacking, I. (2010). Autism fiction? A mirror of an internet decade? *University of Toronto Quarterly*, 79, 632–655.

Harris, C. I. (1993). Whiteness as Property. *Harvard Law Review*, 106(8), 1707–1791.

Harwood, V. (2006) *Diagnosing disorderly children: A critique of behaviour disorder discourses*. Abingdon: Routledge.

Harry, B., and Klinger, J. (2006). *Why are so many students in special education? Understanding race and disability in schools*. New York: Teachers College Press.

Harry, B., and Klinger, J. (2006). *Why are so many students in special education? Understanding race and disability in schools*. New York: Teachers College Press.

Hood, L., McDermott, R.P., and Cole, M. (1980). 'Let's try to make it a good day' – Some not so simple ways. *Discourse Processes*, 3, 155–168.

Ladson-Billings, G. (2006). From the achievement gap to the educational debt: Understanding achievement in U.S. schools, *Educational Researcher* 35(7), 3–12.

Lingard, B., Martino, W., and Rezai-Rashti, G. (2013). Testing regimes, accountabilities and education policy: Commensurate global and national developments. *Journal of Education Policy*, 28(5), 539–556.

López, I. (2014). *Dog whistle politics: How coded racial appeals have reinvented racism and wrecked the middle class*. Oxford: Oxford University Press.

McDermott, R.P. (1993). The acquisition of a child by a learning disability. In C. Chaiklin and J. Lave (eds.), *Understanding practice: Perspectives on activity and context* (pp. 269–305). New York: Cambridge University Press.

Meekosha, H. (2011). Decolonising disability: Thinking and acting globally. *Disability and Society*, 26(6), 667–682.

Mehan, H. (1992). Understanding inequality in schools: The contribution of interpretive studies. *Sociology of Education*, 65, 1–20.

Messick, S. (1989). Meaning and values in test validation: The science and ethics of assessment. *Educational Researcher*, 18(2), 5–11.

Nichols, S. and Berliner, D. C. (2007) High stakes testing and the corruption of America's schools. *Harvard Education Letter*, 23(2), 1–2.

Pellegrino, J.W. (2014). Assessment in the service of teaching and learning: Changes in practice enabled by recommended changes in policy. *Teachers College Record*, 116(11), 1–10.

Sahlberg, P. (2007). Education policies for raising student learning: The Finnish approach. *Journal of Educational Policy*, 22(2), 173–197.

Shepard, L. A. (1997). The centrality of test use and consequences for test validity. *Educational Measurement: Issues and Practice*, 16(2), 5–8, 13–24.

Sleeter, C (1986). Learning disabilities: The social construction of a special education category. *Exceptional Children*, 53, 46–54.

Stiggins, R. J. Assessment crisis: The absence of assessment FOR learning. Phi Delta Kappan. Retrieved on 18 October from: http://www.electronicportfolios.org/afl/Stiggins-AssessmentCrisis.pdf

Waitoller, F., Artiles, A., and Cheney, D. (2010). The miner's canary: A review of overrepresentation research and explanations. *The Journal of Special Education*, 44(1), 29–49.

Welner, K.G. (2013). Consequential validity and the transformation of tests from measurement tools to policy tools. *Teachers College Record*, 115(9), 1–6.

Youdell, D. (2011). *School trouble: Identity, power and politics in education*. New York, NY: Routledge.

Part I

The Assessment Industry

2 The Power of Numbers

The Adoption and Consequences of National Low-Stakes Standardised Tests in Israel

Yariv Feniger, Mirit Israeli and Smadar Yehuda

Abstract

The use of standardised tests as a central tool in education policy has in recent decades become a common feature of many national education systems. In 2002, the Israeli Ministry of Education introduced new mandatory state tests for primary and middle schools. These low-stakes tests are intended, according to the Ministry of Education, to provide schools with 'assessment for learning.' The article describes the adoption of these tests in the framework of globalisation and 'policy borrowing' and assesses their impact on schools using quantitative and qualitative data. It shows that the tests have unintended negative consequences similar to those reported in studies on high-stakes tests in other countries. An explanation for these findings, based on the notion of 'power of numbers,' is proposed and discussed.

Introduction

The use of standardised tests as a central tool in education policy has in recent decades become a common feature of many education systems. State-administered standardised tests are seen by many policymakers as an important tool for raising student achievements and narrowing educational gaps, and as a basis for accountability and transparency in school systems. In an interview for a popular Israeli news website, Gideon Sa'ar, who was the Israeli Minister of Education between 2010 and 2013, clearly conveyed these notions: 'I do not believe it is possible in life, in any field, to manage systems, certainly not large systems, without measuring. It is not possible to achieve without measuring data according to standards' (*Ynet*, 14 August 2013). In this interview, Sa'ar harshly criticised his successor as Minister of Education, Shai Piron, for his decision to postpone and re-evaluate the national standardised tests for primary and middle schools in Israel, known as Meitzav (a Hebrew acronym for Growth and Effectiveness Measures for Schools[1]). Sa'ar, who had awarded the Meitzav tests considerable prominence during his tenure in office, argued that this is a very dangerous decision, asking: '[H]ow will we know if at a particular school, the level is deteriorating or not? How can we intelligently

16 *Yariv Feniger et al.*

allocate funds if we do not have such a database? How will we know what gaps there are in the education system?'

The Meitzav tests are state-administered tests targeted at the second, fifth and eighth grades. They cover four subjects: language literacy (Hebrew in Jewish schools and Arabic in Arab schools), mathematics, English (the main foreign language taught in Israel) and science. The tests also measure school climate and several pedagogical aspects. They were introduced into the education system in 2002 as part of a neoliberal shift in Israeli education policy towards a greater emphasis on educational standards and governmental control of school curricula (Yogev 2007; Yonah, Dahan and Markovich 2008). The Meitzav tests were presented to the education system and the wider public as a low-stakes accountability system. According to the Israeli National Authority for Measurement and Evaluation in Education (known by its acronym RAMA in Hebrew), which has been responsible for these tests since 2006, the purpose of the Meitzav tests is 'assessment for learning,' that is, to provide information that helps improve learning and instruction (Beller 2006). As this article shows, despite the goals proclaimed by the Ministry of Education, there is ample evidence attesting to the negative consequences of these tests to schools, teachers and pupils. These findings are similar to findings from countries which have adopted accountability systems based on high-stakes testing, such as increased pressure on teachers and pupils, learning to tests, narrowing of the curriculum, cheating and more (e.g., Abrams, Pedulla and Madaus 2003; Au 2007; Jennings and Beveridge 2009; Nichols and Berliner 2007; Perryman, Ball, Maguire and Braun 2011). Furthermore, as has happened in other countries (e.g., Lingard 2010), a public discourse that concentrates on test scores has rapidly evolved and educational comparisons between schools and neighbourhoods have flourished in the traditional media and the internet.

This article presents and discusses the case of the Israeli Meitzav tests, which challenges the common distinction in the literature on standardised tests between high-stakes and low-stakes testing. It is often claimed that high-stakes tests are more prone than low-stakes tests to have unintended negative consequences (e.g., Nichols and Berliner 2007). Yet the Israeli experience with national low-stakes testing suggests that such tests can have strong negative effects on learning, instruction and school administration. Using quantitative and qualitative data, we show that these effects are both pervasive and profound. We also acknowledge the fact that different schools may respond differently to measurement and that these responses are connected to characteristics of the student body, pressures from local actors and the pedagogical ideologies of school principals.

The article is structured as follows. First, we briefly review the recent literature on the use of standardised tests as a major tool in education policy, while also discussing the distinction between high-stakes and low-stakes testing. Second, we present the introduction of the Meitzav tests into the Israeli education system and the debates it has sparked. This section highlights the importance of globalisation and 'policy borrowing' as a theoretical framework for the understanding of the adoption of these tests. Third, findings from a mixed-method study that examined the influence of the Meitzav tests on Israeli primary schools are presented and discussed. We conclude by developing an argument about the 'power of numbers' in the education field. Following Lundahl and Waldow (2009), we argue that standardised tests are powerful because they offer a mode of communication that appeals to the common sense of policymakers, Ministry of Education officials, school personnel, parents and the media. The use of national standardised tests, in itself, causes a shift in the way actors in this field think and speak about education.

Accountability and National Testing Regimes

The use of standardised tests for educational accountability has become a global phenomenon in recent decades (Lingard, Martino and Rezai-Rashti 2013). It is part of a much broader process of quantification of social phenomena. This process is related to the growing demand from organisations such as private firms, hospitals, universities and schools for accountability, transparency and efficiency (Espeland and Sauder 2007; Espeland and Stevens 2008). However, as Espeland and Sauder (2007) remind us, 'people are reflexive beings who continually monitor and interpret the world and adjust their actions accordingly' (2). Measures of human actions are therefore reactive. Espeland and Sauder identify two mechanisms related to this kind of reactivity. The first is self-fulfilling prophecies, that is, 'processes by which reactions to social measures confirm the expectations or predictions that are embedded in measures or which increase the validity of the measure by encouraging behavior that conforms to it' (11). The second mechanism is commensuration, which is 'characterized by the transformations of qualities into quantities that share a metric' (16). Commensuration thus redefines the way people think about complex phenomena by reducing and simplifying them to rankings, cost-benefit ratios or standardised tests.

The history of standardised tests in the American education system reveals that their use has gradually intensified to the point of their becoming a major tool in education policy. Chapman (1988) suggests that developments in the science of cognitive testing in the late 19th and early 20th centuries contributed to practices of educational sorting in the face of growing ethnic heterogeneity in American schools. Lin (2000) identifies five waves of assessment that took place in the American education system during the second half of the 20th century. The first wave occurred in the 1950s and was related to tracking decisions. In the 1960s, standardised tests were mainly used to assess the progress of students participating in compensatory programmes. In the 1970s and early 1980s, minimum competency testing spread across the Unites States. Later in the 1980s, assessment came to be used increasingly for school and district accountability, and during the 1990s the concept of standards-based accountability gained prominence.

The enactment of the No Child Left Behind Act of 2001 (NCLB) marks the culmination of the trend of using standardised tests for accountability in the American education system. The Act requires all states to create apparatuses of school accountability based on high-stakes testing. Students should be tested annually from grades three through eight in order to monitor adequate yearly progress. For the purpose of observing inequality, scores are disaggregated according to

18 *Yariv Feniger et al.*

social lines such as ethnicity and poverty. Schools that do not meet the expected progress of all subgroups are subject to several sanctions, including replacement of the principal and staff (Ravitch 2010, Chapter 6). The NCLB and its implementation sparked heated debates over its effectiveness and unintended negative consequences (e.g., Gamoran 2007; Nichols and Berliner 2007; Ravitch 2010). Numerous American studies have demonstrated that high-stakes tests account for several major negative consequences. These include increased pressure on pupils, teachers, principals and education officials (e.g., Abrams, Pedulla and Madaus 2003; Nichols and Berliner 2007); narrowing of the curriculum and concentration on tested subjects (e.g., Au 2007; Diamond 2007); learning and instruction that focuses on testing skills and teaching to the tests (e.g., Jacob 2005; Koretz 2008); focusing on students near the proficiency level while exempting low achievers from the tests (e.g., Jennings and Beveridge 2009; Neal and Schanzenbach 2010); constraining teachers' professionalism (e.g., Wills and Haymore Sandholtz 2009); and various forms of cheating at all levels of the education system (e.g., Jacob and Levitt 2003; Nichols and Berliner 2007).

In England, high-stakes testing became an integral part of education during the 1980s and 1990s. The Thatcher government that steered the UK towards a neoliberal era in social and economic policy also paved the way for the pervasive use of standardised tests. As Ozga (2009) observes, '[t]he Conservative government project from 1979–97 became more and more focused on economy and efficiency as measures of educational performance; its associated measures were those of outputs and stressed managerial or consumer/contract based accountability' (151).

While the American policymakers who enacted NCLB focused on regulations and formal sanctions, the British policymakers put their trust in choice, competition and other market forces. The Education Reform Act of 1988 that introduced a new national curriculum also required the testing of pupils and, more importantly, the publication of comparisons of school performances. It took the English education system into an era dominated by the effects of 'league tables' that rank schools according to their pupils' achievements. This created competition that encouraged schools to compete for more able students (Gregory and Clarke 2010). Perryman and her colleagues (2011) use the metaphor of a pressure cooker in order to describe everyday life in English schools under the influence of league tables. In line with previous research, teachers in their study reported 'feeling frustrated at having to work to an externally imposed agenda, and feeling uncreative and deprofessionalised' (193). Numerous other studies have found negative consequences of the British testing regime that are similar to those found in the U.S. (e.g., Alexander 2009; Boyle and Bragg 2006; West 2010).

The new Australian testing regime is another case in which standardised tests are part of an accountability system. In the second half of the first decade of the 21st century, the Australian federal government introduced the National Assessment Program – Literacy and Numeracy (NAPLAN) and established the Australian Curriculum, Assessment and Reporting Authority (ACARA). ACARA's My School website provides online data on school performances. Lingard (2010) argues that 'despite claims to the contrary, the literacy and numeracy tests that underpin the website have quickly become high-stakes, with all the potentially negative effects on pedagogies and curricula as evidenced in other national systems' (130). In a recent Australian study, conducted after the launch of the My School website, Polesel, Rice and Dulfer (2014) found that although some teachers see it as a helpful tool to identify weaknesses in student learning, many others tend to see it 'as a means for "policing" and "ranking" schools . . . [that] undermines schools' reputations, parents' perceptions and staff morale' (652). In addition, as in the English case, the publication of school performances on this website rapidly resulted in league tables and the categorisation of schools as 'successful' or 'failed.' Similarly to the situation in England, this categorisation is offered without enough attention being paid to the social context in which the school operates.

The American, English and Australian cases of the use of standardised tests for school accountability share the common logic of 'policy as numbers' (Ozga 2009), but they also demonstrate that globalisation of education policy does not mean simply convergence. As Ball (1998) put it,

> National policy making is inevitably a process of bricolage: a matter of borrowing and copying bits and pieces of ideas from elsewhere, drawing upon and amending locally tried and tested approaches, cannibalising theories, research, trends and fashions and not infrequently flailing around for anything at all that looks as though it might work.
>
> (126)

While the American and the British testing regimes were deliberately designed, in different ways, to put pressure on schools, the Australian accountability system seems not to have been purposefully created as a high-stakes regime. What turned it into such a regime was the decision to publicise school performances and thus enable comparisons in the form of league tables (Lingard 2010).

The Israeli Meitzav Tests: A Low-Stakes Accountability Regime?

The Meitzav, a Hebrew acronym for Growth and Efficiency Measures of Schools, is an interesting case because it was deliberately designed to be a low-stakes testing regime. The Meitzav was introduced in 2002 as part of a shift in the Israeli education system from an emphasis on school autonomy and professional development of teachers to a policy that focuses on a core curriculum and assessment of pupil achievement (Yogev 2007). It includes student achievement tests for the second, fifth and eighth grades and questionnaires regarding school climate and other pedagogical aspects. Achievement is measured in four core subjects: language (Hebrew or Arabic), mathematics, English and science. The assessment reflects the Israeli curricula and is aimed at 'examining the extent to which school students in elementary and junior-high schools achieve the expected level required of them according to these curricula' (Beller 2010, 5). Following the recommendations of the National Task Force, better known as the Dovrat Committee, published in 2005, a new and independent National Authority for

20 *Yariv Feniger et al.*

Measurement and Evaluation in Education (RAMA in Hebrew) was established and assumed responsibility for the implementation of the tests (Yonah, Dahan and Markovich 2008).

The recommendations of the Dovrat Committee and the establishment of RAMA should be understood in light of globalisation processes and the concept of 'policy borrowing.' Cross-national policy attraction and policy transfer have been extensively studied in comparative education. But, as Steiner-Khamsi (2012) notes, in recent years the concept of policy borrowing (and lending) has received renewed attention due to new debates on 'how global governance affects national educational systems, beliefs, and practices' (5). The growing influence of transnational organisations such as the OECD, UNESCO and the World Bank on education policymakers, the media and public opinion has created a new context for policy borrowing. These organisations promote policy environments that seek to adopt 'best practices' and to learn from 'high performing systems.' Recent studies on policy borrowing demonstrate how local actors use such messages while adapting them to the local context of policymaking (for further theoretical discussions of policy borrowing and lending and diverse empirical studies based on this notion, see Steiner-Khamsi and Waldow 2012). In the Israeli context, Feniger, Livneh and Yogev (2012) analysed the influence of results from the OECD's PISA test on public debates and policymaking. They show how the low ranking of Israeli pupils in the PISA test served as an important justification for the appointment of the Dovrat Committee.

The report of the Dovrat Committee expressed a strong commitment to public education in Israel, but it also stressed the need for decentralisation on the one hand and accountability and measurement of educational standards on the other hand. Analysing the Committee's report, Yonah, Dahan and Markovich (2008) argue that 'despite Israel's unique political situation, the state nonetheless follows the same pattern by which other neoliberal states attempt to meet challenges to their legitimacy: it endeavours to meet these challenges through pedagogic reforms – formal as well as informal – rather than through social and economic policies aiming to reduce inequalities and pursue educational equality of opportunity' (201).

The Dovrat Report clearly conveys the well documented neoliberal ideology underlying the adoption of standardised tests in other countries (Lingard, Martino and Rezai-Rashti 2013). In line with other cases of policy borrowing, the Committee uses arguments about other countries' education systems to justify its recommendations. Thus, beneath the headline 'targets and outcomes oriented education,' it explains that in recent years policymakers in many countries have debated the traditional focus on educational investment and instead adopted a different view that focuses on outcomes. Following this explanation, the Committee recommends that clear educational targets be defined for all levels of the education system, and a measurement regime created to examine their attainment. Beneath the headline 'administrative decentralisation – accountability and transparency,' the report explains that measurement and assessment are crucial tools for the Ministry of Education in order to monitor local educational administrations and schools. The assessment, it is claimed, will serve schools, parents and policymakers (Ministry of Education 2005).

The Dovrat Report was submitted to the Israeli government in 2004 and was approved by the government at the beginning of 2005. However, teachers unions' strong opposition to the implementation of its recommendations prompted Labour Party ministers to prevent their enforcement through legislation (Zilbersheid 2008). Nevertheless, Resnik (2011) argues that the 'Dovrat Report has completely changed the picture [of Israeli education policy] and strongly encouraged the "evaluation, standards and measurement" social object' (260). This was clearly manifested in the establishment of a National Authority for Measurement and Evaluation in Education (RAMA) in 2005.

Professor Michal Beller was appointed as founder and director-general of the newly established authority. Beller, an expert in measurement and assessment, had previously served as director of the Israeli National Institute for Testing and Evaluation and a senior director of research and development at the Princeton-based Educational Testing Service (ETS), one of the biggest and most influential testing institutes. In addition to extensive knowledge in the theory and application of educational measurement, Beller brought to RAMA a cautious approach to the use of standardised tests. This approach is evident in the presentation of the Meitzav to the Israeli public, as well as in the decisions taken by RAMA and the Ministry of Education regarding these tests. In an official document that describes the Israeli testing project, entitled 'Assessment for Learning: From Theory to Practice,' Beller explains the dangers of attaching high-stakes to educational assessments:

> [A]long with the many benefits that may be reaped from these test systems, it has been acknowledged that over time there may also be negative consequences for the education system in general, and for the pedagogical procedures in school in particular. These negative consequences intensify as the tests become more central and important in the eyes of the system at all levels, and as the tests are perceived as 'high-stakes' or fateful by principals, teachers and students.
>
> (3)

Among these negative consequences, she lists the diversion of resources to subjects included in the tests, teaching to the tests, and 'illegitimate actions that harm test integrity' (3). She also acknowledges that '[b]esides harming the quality of the pedagogical process, turning the tests into "high-risk" may also impair the validity of the test results' (3).

In practice, RAMA and the Ministry of Education took several measures in order to minimise the negative consequences associated with large-scale assessment. First, despite pressures from parents, local authorities and other parties, the Ministry and RAMA refused for several years to publish the results of the tests. The debate over the publication of the results was eventually brought before the Israeli Supreme Court in 2012 by the Israeli Movement for Freedom of Information. The Ministry of Education attempted to defend its position that publication of the results might turn the Meitzav into high-stakes tests and that this would have negative consequences for the school system. The Supreme Court, however,

22 *Yariv Feniger et al.*

decided to oblige the Ministry to publish the results. This was apparently one of the reasons for the decision by the new Minister of Education, Piron, to postpone and re-evaluate the tests (Skop 2013). Second, the frequency of external testing was reduced after the establishment of RAMA and 'internal tests' (i.e., tests that are prepared by RAMA but administered and checked by the school) were introduced. Thus, as a rule, each school is required to be externally tested in each subject once every four years, and to administer the internal test when it is not externally tested (Beller 2010). (This held until the decision to postpone the external tests in 2013. New cycles of external testing were published for the 2014–2015 school year.) Third, RAMA has published on its website information about the rationale for the tests as 'assessment for learning' that encourages schools to avoid preparing their pupils for the tests.

The Israeli Meitzav tests, then, seem to be a clear case of a low-stakes testing regime that aims at improving learning and instruction through the use of data. It was not long after their introduction, however, that evidence of negative unintended consequences of these tests began to accumulate. In a presentation prepared by Professor Beller in 2006, she mentions the following negative consequences of the Meitzav tests that were observed in Israeli schools: diversion of resources to tested subjects, including the placing of 'best teachers' to teach these subjects in grades that take the tests; narrowing of the curriculum in order to cover tested subjects; teaching to the tests; teacher assistance to pupils during the tests; test anxiety among pupils; a popular discourse in the media that focuses on less important findings; and the drawing of inferences from wrong comparisons (Beller 2006, slide 24). The Israeli media has also extensively reported the negative consequences of these tests. For example, in a report headlined 'The Meitzav fever: schools lost their sanity,' Velner (2012a; 2012b) describes extensive preparations of pupils for these tests, and also reports that parents, pupils and experts are calling for a re-evaluation of the testing policy. In response to this report, the Ministry of Education declared that 'schools are not required to prepare their pupils for the tests. Any such preparation is contrary to the Ministry's policy' (2).

The Israeli testing regime therefore presents the intriguing puzzle of a low-stakes testing policy that has been accompanied by negative unintended consequences associated with high-stakes testing regimes. In the following sections of this article, we present findings from a mixed-method study that further explores these consequences both quantitatively and qualitatively. We focus on four types of negative consequences which have been widely reported in the research literature on high-stakes tests: (1) increased pressure on teachers and principals, (2) diversion of resources to tested subjects and grades, (3) teaching to the tests and (4) using 'educational triage' as a school policy that focuses efforts on pupils near the passing threshold (Booher-Jennings 2005). Following the concept of commensuration (Espeland and Sauder 2007), we examine Israeli principals' acceptance of the logic of standardised tests and how it has changed their perceptions of educational administration.

To the best of our knowledge, no previous Israeli study has directly examined the negative unintended consequences of the Meitzav tests, although the tests have been criticised from the psychometric and education policy perspectives (Cahan 2008). Kliger (2009) who interviewed teachers and principals found that most of them see the Meitzav tests as a tool for measuring student achievement and not as a tool for improving leaning and instruction, as stated by the Ministry of Education.

Data and Methods

In order to investigate the unintended negative consequences of the Meitzav tests, we conducted a mixed-method study, focusing on the effects of external Meitzav tests. The quantitative component of the study was a survey that collected information from principals of primary schools in Israel. In February 2012, an invitation to participate in this survey was sent to all principals of Israeli primary schools, except those of independent Jewish Ultra-Orthodox (Haredi) schools, many of which do not regularly participate in these tests. The letter of invitation, which was sent electronically via the internal communication system of the Israeli Ministry of Education, asked the principals to fill in an anonymous web-based questionnaire. After two more reminders, 177 principals decided to participate in the survey – a response rate of about 13%. While this is a relatively low response rate, it should be noted that response rates are lowest among executive respondents, in all types of surveys (Anseel, Lievens, Schollaert and Choragwicka 2010). The distribution of the respondents according to their school sector (Jewish, Jewish-religious and Arab) was similar to the corresponding distribution in the entire education system. In addition, despite the relatively low response rate, the sample generally reflects the diversity of the Israeli education system in terms of socioeconomic status and achievement levels.

In a series of preliminary analyses, we examined whether personal characteristics of the principals – gender, age, level of education and experience as a school principal – are related to their answers. These analyses showed no effect of these variables on the overall patterns that emerged from our data. In addition, we examined differences among different school sectors (Jewish, Jewish-religious and Arab) and among different levels of the school's student body's socioeconomic composition. The differences were in most cases small and statistically insignificant. In the Findings section, we refer to non-trivial differences that were found. A table showing the distribution of principals according to their personal characteristics and school sector is presented in the Appendix.

The second component of the study was based on qualitative research methods. It focused on five Jewish primary school principals. The five schools were chosen in order to examine the influence of the Meitzav tests in diverse social and educational contexts (i.e., socioeconomic status, different types of local authorities and different pedagogical ideologies). Each principal in these schools participated in two semi-constructed in-depth interviews over the 2012/2013 school year.[2] The interviews covered our main research questions, but also allowed principals to freely express their views on the Meitzav tests in their own terms. It is worth noting that recruiting principals for this study was unexpectedly a very difficult task. Several principals who were asked to be interviewed expressed their concern that the

24 *Yariv Feniger et al.*

information they shared with the researchers might harm them if published, even though strict confidentiality was promised. This concern should be understood in light of the findings that will be presented below about the pressure that principals experience in relation to the Meitzav tests.

Findings

Increased Pressure on Teachers and Principals

In our survey, about 80% of the principals reported that teachers in their school experience increased pressure before external Meitzav tests. About half of the principals (48%) reported that they themselves feel pressured before external tests. These findings were relatively constant across all schools' socioeconomic levels. Principals in Jewish-religious schools reported more pressure on teachers and themselves than principals in the other two school sectors. Our data did not reveal possible explanations for this difference. We hope that future research will further explore this interesting finding.

We next examined whether this pressure originates from the local authority to which the school belongs or from Ministry of Education officials. In Israel, schools are mainly financed by the central government, but they are administrated by and accountable to both the local authority and the Ministry of Education's district office. The findings clearly showed that the main source of pressure is the Ministry of Education. About 35% of the principals reported that they felt pressure from the local authority regarding Meitzav tests, while almost 70% reported pressure from Ministry of Education personnel. We also found that principals of schools that cater to students from less affluent families are more prone to pressure from the Ministry of Education. This is not surprising due to the fact that these schools have, on average, lower scores.

The in-depth interviews with principals further reveal the pressure felt by principals in relation to the Meitzav tests. A principal of a school that has a long tradition of progressive pedagogy (a school that mainly serves kibbutz children) said 'when I participate in principals' meetings I am shocked by what I hear about the pressure to achieve higher scores. Principals tell me that their pupils study during Easter vacation in order to prepare for the tests. We refuse to do that'. She further claimed that 'there is a wide gap between RAMA and the Ministry of Education. RAMA tells us not to prepare our pupils for the tests, but the Ministry's inspectors just keep pressuring us as if they see the principals as their subcontractors.' Ronit (note: all names are pseudonymous), whose school is located in an affluent suburb, expressed her own frustration with the pressure from inspectors: 'The main problem is the pressure on behalf of the Ministry's inspection . . . I was asked many times why my pupils, who come from good families, don't get better scores . . . The inspector constantly tells me: "You must do better on the Meitzav."' Rachel, whose school caters to lower middleclass families, adds: 'The test scores are sent to the inspector before they are sent to me. How can they tell me that the aim is not to measure and control us? . . . It is well known that principals are often required to explain what happened, why we failed . . . You find yourself giving excuses. . . . This is a very embarrassing situation.'

Diversion of Resources to Tested Subjects and Grades

According to our survey, primary schools in Israel devote, on average, about 70 school hours per year to preparing pupils for the Meitzav tests. Principals who reported pressure from the Ministry of Education devote, on average, 84 hours per year. Almost all of the survey respondents (94%) agreed with the statement that schools in Israel add school hours for tested subjects at the expense of other subjects. The principals who were interviewed in the qualitative study stressed that the Meitzav tests are taken into account when planning the school year. Ronit explained: 'Our fourth grade pupils will be tested in English and science next year. This is our focus . . . our curriculum is aligned with the tests and we invest more resources such as school hours, one-on-one instruction, and guidance for teachers. I cannot take the risk of waiting until next year.' Dorit was even more explicit: 'We use our fund of school hours according to the needs of the Meitzav. We invest more in grades that will be tested in the next two years.'

Teaching to the Tests

Teaching to the tests is one of most prevalent consequences of high-stakes testing (e.g., Koretz 2008; Stobart 2008). Both our survey and the in-depth interviews suggest that this practice is also prevalent in Israeli primary schools. About two thirds of the principals that participated in the survey reported that their schools have special preparation days for their pupils prior to the external tests. Almost 80% of them use previous Meitzav tests in order to prepare their pupils for the tests, and about the same percentage uses one-on-one instruction and learning in small groups for this purpose. Seventy-five percent of the principals confirmed that their schools teach strategies for coping with the tests.

Naama, who was very critical of the tests, mainly because of her belief in a more progressive type of education, explained that she prepares the pupils in her school for the tests because she wants to help them cope with the stressful situation. She explained that in previous years, pupils left the tests crying and that convinced her to invest in test preparations. Dorit, on the other hand, awards very high priority to the Meitzav tests. With financial assistance from the parents, her school bought a special preparation package for each pupil in the fifth grade in order to prepare them for the English test. She explained that many parents in this school are immigrants from the former Soviet Union who will cooperate with any effort intended to promote their children's achievement, including learning during school vacations.

Educational Triage

In her widely cited article, Booher-Jennings (2005) describes how accountability policies in Texas are associated with 'educational triage,' that is, the division of

26   *Yariv Feniger et al.*

pupils into three groups: safe cases, suitable for treatment and hopeless cases. This division of pupils leads to an unequal distribution of school resources, as schools prefer to invest more resources in the middle group, the 'bubble-kids' in the words of Booher-Jennings. While this is a rational response by schools to accountability pressures, it is undoubtedly a harmful policy for a school's weakest population. The practice of educational triage was revealed in our in-depth interviews. Four of the five principals who were interviewed said that they sort pupils according to their achievement and invest more in the middle group. Daniela, whose school mainly caters to pupils from a working class background, explained: 'We took the middle group and we endlessly invested in them for two years [before the test].' Dorit was much more explicit about practicing educational triage. Using the metaphor of a train, she explained that her school sorts the pupils into several 'wagons' and concentrates on those who are in the 'middle wagon.' She also admitted that she 'doesn't put the eggs' in the lowest wagon.

Accepting the Logic of Standardised Tests and Using Them for Decision Making

Although the two studies revealed criticism towards the Meitzav tests, they also found that the logic of the use of standardised tests is widely accepted by school principals. In the survey, we asked the principals to indicate whether they would have participated in the tests had the decision been theirs. About half of the principals (51%) answered that they would have chosen to participate in both external and internal tests, 22% indicated that they would have chosen to participate in the internal tests only and 6% would have chosen to participate in the external tests only. Only 21% replied that they would have chosen not to participate in any form of the tests. This suggests that most principals see the Meitzav tests not just as an external mode of control, but rather as a useful tool for them.

In the qualitative interviews, four of the five principals who were interviewed expressed the idea that the Meitzav tests provide valuable information. They said that they believe that the tests are 'professional', 'objective' and 'reliable', and that they help them to see where they stand vis-à-vis other schools. Rachel explained the gap between her positive attitude towards the tests and her criticism of the way the data are used: 'I think that the external tests are good. You can really see where you stand. . . . It's an important tool for the school. . . . On the other hand, RAMA's proclamations are misleading . . . unfortunately the tests are used [by the Ministry of Education] to threaten us.'

All the principals who were interviewed told us that they present the Meitzav scores to the school staff, and some of them also make them available to parents. During the interviews, they stressed that they were not trained to analyse this type of data and that the guidance they receive from RAMA and the Ministry of Education is very limited. When asked about action taken after analysing Meitzav data, in most cases the principals described practices associated with preparing pupils for the tests. In addition, an interesting paradox emerged from some of the interviews. Principals explained that when they analyse the data and use them for planning school activities, they focus on grades that will be tested in coming years. For example, in one school, the scores of fifth graders were relatively low, but the principal decided not to invest extra resources in this cohort because it would not be tested again (after the sixth grade, the pupils go to a middle school). Instead she took measures to ensure that younger cohorts in this school will be better prepared to meet the curricular requirements of the test aimed at the fifth grade. Thus, while the principals accept the logic of the tests and try to use them as leverage for improvement, the consequences of analysing and using the data can be harmful to many pupils.

Conclusions

The Israeli testing regime is part of a global movement towards the quantification of education and educational accountability. From a comparative perspective, this is an interesting project because it is attempting to create an accountability system that avoids the negative consequences associated with standardised tests. Being aware of these unintended consequences in other countries, the Israeli policymakers have been cautious regarding the implementation of the tests. They decided not to publish school outcomes (until this decision was changed in 2012 due to the ruling of the Supreme Court), and they have constantly emphasised that the main purpose of the tests is 'assessment for learning.' Yet the mixed-method study presented in this article, as well as reports published by RAMA and by the Israeli media, clearly shows that the Israeli standardised tests produce unintended negative consequences that are very similar to those found in countries in which the tests have high stakes.

In concluding this article, we attempt to offer an explanation for this seemingly paradoxical state of the Israeli testing regime. The explanation is based on the notion that numbers have power. The quantification of the educational field provides a mode of communication that reduces the complexity of the educational process. This 'quick language' (Lundhal and Waldow 2009), we argue, is related to two dimensions of the power of numbers. First, measurement of educational outcomes enhances the ability of inspectors and Ministry of Education directors to monitor and control school principals. It is not surprising, then, that shortly after the introduction of the Meitzav tests inspectors and district directors started using the test results as a quick language for communication with school principals. Although no formal sanctions were attached to test scores, they became a major source of pressure on principals. Thus, for example, instead of addressing the complexity of teaching mathematics in the fifth grade, the discussion between an inspector and a principal concentrates on the average score of fifth graders on the Meitzav mathematics test. As a consequence, principals consciously or unconsciously use the Meitzav as their frame of reference. In addition, as our studies show, principals are subject to overt direct pressure to achieve higher scores.

The second dimension of the power of numbers is the use of comparisons. Ozga (2009) argues that '[d]ata production and management were and are essential to the new governance turn; constant comparison is its symbolic feature, as well as

28 *Yariv Feniger et al.*

a distinctive mode of operation' (150). Schools are required to compare their outcomes with the national averages and with those of other schools. Here, again, the notion of quick language is useful. Comparisons of average scores are, in fact, 'a kind of shorthand communication among relevant groups of actors in the educational field' (Lundhal and Waldow 2009, 366). Comparisons are often used by inspectors and Ministry of Education directors as a justification for the requirement that schools present better results. Yet the influence of comparison on school personnel is much more profound. As Ball (2003) observes, '[i]ncreasingly, the day-to-day practice is flooded with a baffling array of figures, indicators, comparisons and forms of competition' (220). This description is apparently true for many Israeli schools in the era of Meitzav tests. The recent decision to publish the test results further aggravated this situation, as one principal told us: 'Once you publish test results . . . there is a serious problem. . . . Instead of concentrating on pedagogy we concentrate on public relations.'

The analysis of the Israeli testing regime suggests that low-stakes testing regimes can have consequences that are very similar to those of high-stakes testing regimes. The stakes themselves are only part of the picture. What lies at the basis of the unintended negative consequences of standardised tests is the power of numbers. The use of external standardised tests, in itself, causes a shift in the way actors in the educational field think and speak about education. The implications of this conclusion for education policy are quite straightforward. Policymakers in Israel and elsewhere should not be tempted to believe that standardised tests can be used without causing unintended negative consequences. When considering the benefits that might accrue from such tests, policymakers must also consider the inevitable price that pupils, teachers, principals and other actors will pay as a result of their implementation.

Beyond the immediate negative unintended consequences of standardised tests, policymakers should also consider the more profound influences of quantification of the educational arena. First, As Espeland and Sauder (2007, 35) nicely put it, 'reactivity limits the shelf-life of measures.' Over time, pupils, teachers and principals change their behaviours in ways that reduce the validity of the tests and therefore their value declines. This inevitable process might trigger an 'arms race' between assessment agencies, on the one hand, and schools on the other hand. Second, as we have demonstrated in this chapter, quantification tends to change the way teachers and principals think about education. An important example that emerged from our qualitative data is the adoption of comparisons between schools as a major lens through which principals look at their own school and accordingly make decisions.

Notes

1   In this article, we preferred the Hebrew term *Meitzav*. In some publications, the English acronym GEMS is also used.
2   The interviews were conducted in Hebrew. Excerpts from these interviews were translated by the authors to English for the purpose of this chapter.

References

Abrams, L.M., Pedulla, J.J., and Madaus, G.F. (2003). Views from the classroom: Teachers' opinions of statewide testing programs. *Theory Into Practice*, 42(1), 18–29.

Alexander, R. (ed.). (2009). *Children, their world, their education: Final report and recommendations of the Cambridge Primary Review.* London: Routledge.

Anseel, F., Lievens, F., Schollaert, E., and Choragwicka, B. (2010). Response rates in organizational science, 1995–2008: A meta-analytic review and guidelines for survey researchers. *Journal of Business Psychology*, 25(3), 335–349.

Au, W. (2007). High-stakes testing and curricular control: A qualitative metasynthesis. *Educational Researcher*, 36(5), 258–267.

Ball, S.J. (1998). Big policies/small world: An introduction to international perspectives in education policy. *Comparative Education*, 34(2), 119–130.

Ball, S. J. 2003. "The Teacher's Soul and the Terrors of Performativity." *Journal of Education Policy*, 18(2): 215–228.

Beller, M. (2006). Restructuring of the national assessment: Issues and challenges. [In Hebrew]. Presentation given in a seminar at the Israeli Center for Educational Technology, 13 November 2006. http://cms.education.gov.il/EducationCMS/Units/Rama/Maa gareyYeda/MaagareiYeda_Mazagot_heb.htm

Beller, M. (2010). Assessment in the Service of Learning: Theory and Practice. http://cms. education.gov.il/EducationCMS/Units/Rama/MaagareyYeda/MaagareiYeda_Mazagot_ heb.htm

Booher-Jennings, J. (2005). Below the bubble: "Educational Triage" and the Texas accountability system. *American Educational Research Journal*, 42(2), 231–268.

Boyle, B., and Bragg, J. (2006). A curriculum without foundation. *British Educational Research Journal*, 32(4), 569–582.

Cahan, S. (2008). The use of educational indicators in policy and decision making: The case of Meitzav tests. [In Hebrew] Background paper submitted to the Committee to Revise the System of Education Indicators in Israel.

Chapman, P. D. 1988. Schools as Sorters: Lewis M. Terman, Applied Psychology, and the Intelligence Testing Movement, 1890–1930. New York and London: New York University Press.

Diamond, J.B. (2007). Where the rubber meets the road: Rethinking the connection between high-stakes testing policy and classroom instruction. *Sociology of Education*, 80(4), 285–313.

Espeland, W.N., and Sauder, M. (2007). Rankings and reactivity: How public measures recreate social worlds. *American Journal of Sociology*, 113(1), 1–40.

Espeland, W.N., and Stevens, M.L. (2008). A sociology of quantification. *European Journal of Sociology*, 49(3), 401–436.

Feniger, Y., Livneh, I., and Yogev, A. (2012). Globalisation and the politics of international tests: The case of Israel. *Comparative Education*, 48(3), 323–335.

Gamoram, A. (ed.). (2007). *Standards-based reform and the poverty gap: Lessons for "No Child Left Behind."* Washington, DC: Brookings Institution Press.

Gregory, K., and M. Clarke. 2003. "High-Stakes Assessment in England and Singapore." *Theory into Practice*, 42(1): 66–74.

Jacob, B. (2005). Accountability, incentives and behavior: The impact of high-stakes testing in the Chicago Public Schools. *Journal of Public Economics*, 89(5–6), 761–796.

Jacob, B.A., and Levitt, S. D. (2003). Rotten apples: An investigation of the prevalence and predictors of teacher cheating. *Quarterly Journal of Economics*, 118(3), 843–877.

30 Yariv Feniger et al.

Jennings, J.L., and Beveridge, A.A. (2009). How does test exemption affect schools' and students' academic performance? *Educational Evaluation and Policy Analysis*, 31(2), 153–175.

Klieger, A. (2009). Perceptions of principals and teachers regarding the goals of the Meitzav. [In Hebrew] *Dapim*, 47, 142–184.

Koretz, D. (2008). *Measuring up: What educational testing really tells us*. Cambridge, MA: Harvard University Press.

Linn, R. L. 2000. "Assessments and Accountability." *Educational Researcher*, 29(2):4–16.

Lingard, B. (2010). Policy borrowing, policy learning: Testing times in Australian schooling. *Critical Studies in Education*, 51(2), 129–147.

Lingard, B., Martino, W., and Rezai-Rashti, G. (2013). Testing regimes, accountabilities and education policy: Commensurate global and national developments. *Journal of Education Policy*, 28(5), 539–556.

Lundahl, C., and Waldow, F. (2009). Standardisation and 'Quick Languages': The shape-shifting of standardised measurement of pupil achievement in Sweden and Germany. *Comparative Education*, 45(3), 365–385.

Ministry of Education (2005). *The National Task Force* ('The Dovrat Committee'). [In Hebrew]. Jerusalem: The Ministry of Education and Culture.

Neal, D., and Schanzenbach, D.W. (2010). Left behind by design: Proficiency counts and test-based accountability. *Review of Economics and Statistics*, 92(2), 263–283.

Nichols S.L., and Berliner, D.C. (2007). *Collateral damage: How high-stakes testing corrupts America's Schools*. Cambridge, MA: Harvard Education Press.

Ozga, J. (2009). Governing education through data in England: From regulation to self-evaluation. *Journal of Education Policy*, 24(2), 149–162.

Perryman, J., Ball, S., Maguire, M., and Braun, A. (2011). Life in the pressure cooker – School league tables and English and mathematics teachers' responses to accountability in a results-driven era. *British Journal of Educational Studies*, 59(2), 179–195.

Polesel, J., Rice, S., and Dulfer, N. (2014). The impact of high-stakes testing on curriculum and pedagogy: A teacher perspective from Australia. *Journal of Education Policy*, 29(5), 640–657.

Ravitch, D. (2010). *The death and life of the great American school system: How testing and choice are undermining education*. New York: Basic Books.

Resnik, J. (2011). The construction of a managerial education discourse and the involvement of philanthropic entrepreneurs: The case of Israel. *Critical Studies in Education*, 52(3), 251–266.

Skop, Y. 2013. "Israel Suspends Standardized Tests." [In Hebrew.] Haaretz, August 13. http://www.haaretz.com/misc/article-print-page/.premium-1.541140?trailing-

Steiner-Khamsi, G. (2012). Understanding policy borrowing and lending: Building comparative policy studies. In G. Steiner-Khamsi and F. Waldow (eds.), *World yearbook of education 2012: Policy borrowing and lending in education* (pp. 3–18). London: Routledge.

Steiner-Khamsi, G., and Waldow, F. (eds.) (2012). *World yearbook of education 2012: Policy borrowing and lending in education*. London: Routledge.

Stobart, G. (2008). *Testing times: The uses and abuses of assessment*. Abingdon: Routledge.

Velner, T. (2012a). The Meitzav fever: Schools lost their sanity. [In Hebrew] *Ynet*, 28 May. http://www.ynet.co.il/articles/0,7340,L-4235032,00.html

Velner, T. (2012b). The Meitzav: Mass cheating and dropping eighth grade scores. [In Hebrew] *Ynet*, 15 October. http://www.ynet.co.il/articles/0,7340,L-4292336,00.html

West, A. (2010). High stakes testing, accountability, incentives and consequences in English schools. *Policy and Politics*, 38(1), 23–39.

Wills, J., and J. H. Sandholtz 2009. "Constrained Professionalism: Dilemmas of Teaching in the Face of Test-Based Accountability." *Teachers College Record*, 111(4): 1065–1114.

Ynet, (2013). Sa'ar in Ynet exclusive: Canceling Standardized tests 'Dangerous.'" *Ynet*, 14 August. http://www.ynetnews.com/articles/0,7340,L-4417687,00.html

Yogev, A. (2007). Ideology, pedagogy and educational policy in Israel. [In Hebrew] In U. Aviram, J. Gal and Y. Katan (eds.), *The shaping of social policy in Israel: Trends and issues* (131–148). Jerusalem: Taub Center for Social Policy Studies in Israel.

Yonah, Y., Dahan, Y., and Markovich, D. (2008). Neo-liberal reforms in Israel's education system: The dialectics of the state. *International Studies in Sociology of Education*, 18(3), 199–217.

Zilbersheid, U. (2008). The Dovrat report: Transforming Israel's education system into a combination of public social assistance and privatization. *Israel Affairs*, 14(1), 118–134.

Table 2.1 Appendix

Descriptive statistics for the quantitative sample

Variable	Mean/Percent	SD
Age	48.5	11.1
Experience	9.1	7.6
Gender		
Female	61.8	
Male	38.2	
Level of education		
BA	23.5	
MA	72.6	
PhD	3.9	
School sector		
Jewish	48.3	
Jewish Religious	20.7	
Arab	31.0	

N = 177.

3 Special Educational Needs, Disability and School Accountability
An International Perspective

Emma Smith and Graeme Douglas

1 Introduction

Standards-driven accountability is now the norm in public schools in many industrialised countries (Department for Education 2016; OECD 2011). It involves holding schools accountable for the academic attainment of their students and, according to Hursh (2005: 609), is driven by 'a three-fold need to raise educational and economic productivity in an increasingly globalized economy, to decrease educational inequality and to improve the quality and objectivity of school-based assessment'. Arguably the key questions that increased levels of accountability have to answer are not only whether it leads to improved student performance but if it does, who benefits? It is well established that during compulsory education, academic success is predicated on success at the previous educational stage and that young people from less affluent social groups achieve at lower levels throughout schooling (Gorard et al. 2007; Smith 2012). Therefore the main challenges that face those concerned with both educational justice and school improvement involve unpacking the educational determinants of success in school (such as effective teaching) from the wider social and cultural influences; as well as understanding the ways in which accountability reform might mitigate against prior academic disadvantage.

This chapter will consider the relationship between test-based accountability reform and the education of students with special educational needs and disability (SEND)[1] with a particular focus on the role of international comparative tests of student attainment. The chapter begins by looking at the increased role of accountability-based reform and the extent to which high-stakes testing at the school level is able to effectively address the needs of students with SEND. In the second half of the chapter, we look at the role of international comparative tests of student attainment, specifically PISA, in informing accountability policies at the national level and the extent to which these assessments can include all students, particularly those with SEND. More specifically the chapter has the following aims:

- To consider the relationship between test-based accountability policies and the education of students with SEND.

An *International Perspective*   33

- To illustrate the issues around inclusion of students with SEND in national accountability-based reform.
- To examine the inclusion of students with SEND in international comparative assessments of student performance (specifically PISA).

We begin by providing a brief introduction to standards-based accountability policies and high-stakes testing in general, before considering some of their most widely rehearsed advantages and disadvantages.

2 Standards-Based Accountability Policies

The aim of test- or standards-based accountability policies is to identify a set of measurable performance standards across a number of core subject areas, to align the curriculum to these standards and to assess and scrutinise subsequent student attainment (Figlio and Loeb 2011). Evaluating learning against a common set of test scores will, in turn, provide policy makers, school administrators and members of the general public with an indicator of how well schools are performing relative to each other. The consequence of this is that schools that appear to be under-performing on this indicator might be subject to further sanctions and scrutiny that, in time, might lead to improvement. The use of these types of 'high-stakes' tests for holding schools accountable for the academic performance of their students have become the norm in many countries, particularly the United States and England. High-stakes tests are those in which the results have serious consequences for stakeholders. These include the student who achieves poorer results than expected in college entrance examinations and the institution using tests for accountability purposes, possibly linked to school funding or teacher tenure. Additionally, tests that might otherwise be low-stakes for the individuals who take them and their schools (such as the international comparative tests that we discuss here) can be high-stakes for policy makers and governments (Stobart and Eggen 2012).

This emphasis on academic attainment as the most tangible outcome of schooling makes the very premise of standards-based reform open to scrutiny, particularly because of concerns that this focus on testing may result in a side-lining of other aspects of education, such as citizenship, well-being and critical thinking (e.g. West, Mattei and Roberts 2011). Concerns about accountability driven reform are well rehearsed. Its critics argue that they result in a narrowing of the curriculum and an over-emphasis on the subjects that are tested (such as science and maths) at the expense of those that are not (such as music and social studies); they promote teaching to the test and emphasise low quality assessment such as multiple-choice responses at the expense of richer and more nuanced tasks; and they can also harm poor, disabled and minority students and increase the dropout rate (e.g., Darling-Hammond 2007; Haney 2000; Hout and Elliot 2011).

Alongside the apparent negative consequences of test-based accountability, there is also a body of evidence that suggests a positive relationship between such policies and student achievement (e.g., Dee and Jacob 2009; Hanushek 2005;

34   *Emma Smith and Graeme Douglas*

OECD 2011; Rockoff and Turner 2008). However, while there may be an 'emerging consensus that students whose scores are the most consequential for school accountability are those who gain the most' (Figlio and Loeb 2011: 411); evidence also suggests that not all student groups benefit equally from accountability-based reform. Hanushek and Raymond (2005), for example, find that while accountability policies in the United States have had some success in narrowing the achievement gap between Hispanic and White students, this is not the case for the Black–White achievement gap. In fact, one of the key issues for those who design accountability measures is in deciding which students should be included. Inclusively named policies such as No Child Left Behind and Every Student Succeeds in the USA and Every Child Matters in England and Wales, would suggest that measures to improve schools ought to include everyone. However, as Figlio and Loeb (2011: 394) argue, 'universal inclusion raises important questions about fairness and attribution' and, most pertinently here, 'should schools be held accountable for students for whom testing is more challenging, or potentially less reliable, such as students with disabilities?'

Whatever the arguments for and against school accountability policies, it is nevertheless the case that they are an integral part of the educational landscape in many nations. However the extent to which they can effectively and fairly include children and young people with SEND is a contentious matter. Indeed the role of accountability policies in ensuring a fair and equitable educational experience for students with SEND presents three key issues: first whether all students ought to participate in high-stakes testing, second the nature and effectiveness of the assessment tools used and third whether the assessments are in fact relevant and comprehensive for these students' needs. We consider these issues in the next section.

3 The Role of Accountability Policies in the Education of Students with SEND

Ensuring that schools are held accountable for the educational progress of students with SEND has generally been viewed positively by commentators and has, in part, been welcomed because of the disability community's concerns over the often poor educational performance of this group of young people (e.g. Center on Education Policy 2007; Cole 2006; McLaughlin and Thurlow 2003). For example, according to the National Council on Disability in the USA, the reauthorisation of the Individuals with Disabilities Education Act (IDEA) in 2004 has led to a 'palpable and positive change' (2008: 55) in the approach to including young people with disabilities in American schools and in state-wide testing. Indeed, one of the fundamental arguments in support of their inclusion in these tests is that because students with SEND now count in accountability-based assessments, due regard has to be paid to their progress:

> People teach what is tested and who is tested – so now that students with disabilities are included in the accountability system, they are being taught.
>
> (National Council on Disability 2008: 55)

An International Perspective 35

Perhaps unsurprisingly however, there are concerns about the negative consequences of an increased emphasis on testing and monitoring on the educational experiences of students with SEND. Many of these concerns stem from issues with the practicalities of assessing such a diverse group of learners, rather than an ideological objection to testing in its own right. Cole (2006) provides a number of examples of unintended consequences of standards-based accountability measures that are specific to students with SEND. First, students with SEND might be treated as scapegoats because if schools fail to meet accountability targets it is often (although not exclusively) because of the performance of students with SEND (Davidson, Reback, Rockoff and Schwartz 2015). Second, if students with SEND are considered to be one reason for a school's failure to meet their targets, then this might slow progress on inclusion. Finally, the need for schools to meet targets might lead to increased dropout and poor retention rates among students with SEND. Indeed, schools with large proportions of students with SEND might legitimately argue that holding them accountable for the performance of these students puts them at a disadvantage (Figlio and Loeb 2011). Additional areas of concern lie around the practice of grouping together different types of SEND rather than reporting on subgroups of disabilities (e.g. Altman *et al.* 2010; National Council on Disability 2008). Furthermore, the concept of primary disability can be problematic because many young people have a complex set of multiple conditions.

Possibly the most widespread area of concern is the amount of testing that these accountability-linked assessments often require. This increased emphasis on testing leads to a narrowly defined curriculum where, arguably, too much attention is paid to curriculum content that will feature in the tests. This, of course, is not a concern that applies only to students with SEND but is relevant for all young people in school. Nevertheless, the consequences for those with SEND are perhaps more profound. A focus upon the narrower and academic aspects of the curriculum may undermine those with learning disabilities for whom other areas of a balanced curriculum are of greater enjoyment, accomplishment or value (e.g., vocational topics, music, art, sport). Further, it may also detract from more nuanced (even disability-specific) aspects of the curriculum which are of particular value to students with SEND (e.g., mobility, access technology, independence skills, social communication). Such tests may result in them being held back for one academic year, subjected to 'humiliating' tests which they are unable to answer, or being denied entry to a particular school in the first place:

> Everything revolves around testing and the punitive nature of the system. It pervades everything, and kids pick up on it. And then you have the stress of the IEP [Individualized Education Program]. Teachers don't feel like they can just try something creative or different to help meet the needs of students with disabilities. There is no time to be creative – teachers are always planning for tests.
>
> (National Council on Disability study 2008: 75)

36   *Emma Smith and Graeme Douglas*

Lowrey, Drasgow, *et al.* (2007: 251) highlight this concern in relation to the use of alternate assessments in the USA for students with severe learning disabilities, noting that they may be at the expense of other 'meaningful targets that will improve a student's quality of life after leaving the public school system'.

Another argument against test-based accountability systems is that they may encourage schools to exclude low-performing students from assessments or even from the school itself (Banks et al. 2015; Holbein and Ladd 2015; McLaughlin and Rhim 2007; Wolf, Witte and Fleming 2012). Arguably, the exclusion of students with SEND from assessments is a particular issue for tests that are low-stakes at the school/student level, such as PISA, making it perhaps easier to exclude these students from the assessments. Associated with this is the concern that rather than sitting the general assessment, schools will reclassify students into SEND categories and they will then sit modified versions of the assessments, often with accommodations (such as extra time) that might potentially improve their performance (e.g. Figlio and Loeb 2011). For example, schools might improve their likelihood of raising test scores by selectively assigning students to SEND subgroups, perhaps by placing relatively high-achieving students with mild dyslexia into the disabilities subgroup.

In the next section, we look at the issues that arise when students with SEND are included in international assessments of student performance. While low stakes for the actual students, these tests are anything but low stakes for policy makers and for the architects of national education systems.

4 International Perspectives on SEND and School Accountability: The Role of PISA

One of the key drivers of school reform in many developed countries is their performance in international comparative tests such as the Programme for International Student Assessment (PISA) and the Trends in International Maths and Science Study (TIMSS). Here we focus specifically on PISA and consider the extent to which young people with SEND are included in this type of accountability-based assessment.

4.1 What Is PISA?

The Programme for International Student Assessment (PISA) is a series of assessments and questionnaires completed by 15-year-old students. They are designed to 'assess student performance and collect data on the student, family and institutional factors that can help explain differences in performance' (OECD 2001: 4). PISA is administered by the Organisation for Economic Cooperation and Development (OECD) and students are assessed in three subject domains: reading, mathematics and science. PISA runs in triennial cycles and while each domain is assessed in each cycle, only one domain is tested in detail, taking up nearly two thirds of the total testing time. The first wave of PISA took place in 2000, focused mainly on reading; subsequent cycles concentrated on mathematics and science

An International Perspective   37

before returning to reading in 2009. The most recent waves of PISA took place in 2012 and 2015 and focused on mathematics and science respectively (although findings from the 2015 wave were due to be published in late 2016). In 2012, around 510,000 students from 65 countries and economies took part. In addition to test score outcomes, PISA also gathers data on student perceptions of school, their demographic characteristics and other indicators of school climate. This enables the collection of data on the experiences of young people that extend beyond academic attainment. Further information on all waves of PISA can be found at: www.oecd.org/PISA.

PISA is typically administered to between 4,500 and 10,000 students in each country/economy. All students take pencil-and-paper tests, with assessments lasting a total of two hours for each student (with amendments made for students with SEND, see below). Test items are a mixture of multiple-choice items and questions requiring students to construct their own responses. The primary aim of the PISA assessment is to determine the extent to which young people have acquired the wider knowledge and skills in reading, mathematics and science that they will need in adult life (OECD 2014). In short, its aim is to 'measure how well 15-year-old students approaching the end of compulsory schooling are prepared to meet the challenges of today's knowledge societies' (OECD 2014: 22). PISA does not emphasise the taught curriculum. The test designers argue that a focus on curriculum content would restrict attention to curriculum elements common to all or most countries. This would result in many compromises with the item design and in an assessment that was 'too narrow to be of value for governments wishing to learn about the strengths and innovations in the education systems of other countries' (OECD 2009: 12).

4.2 The Political Influence of PISA

PISA is overtly political and is explicit in its aim 'to provide a new basis for policy dialogue and for collaboration in defining and implementing educational goals' (OECD 2007: 3). According to some critics, this leads to a distortion of education policies, which can result in policy making at the national level being heavily influenced by student performance at a single point in their educational careers (Figazzolo 2006; Hopmann and Brinek 2007; Jerrim 2011; Mortimore 2009; Sjøberg 2007). This in turn can result in a situation in which 'increasing emphasis is placed on standardisation and on comparison of student performance in order to measure the extent to which a country is meeting the international requirements' (Dolin 2007: 96). For example, PISA is quite explicit that systems with greater school autonomy coupled with stronger cultures of accountability are more likely to be associated with higher student performance (OECD 2011).

While not an accountability measure in its own right, the power of PISA and other similar assessments to influence national education policy (e.g., Dolin 2007; Rutkowski and Rutkowski 2010; Baird et al. 2011) is substantial. Indeed, the tests occupy a distinctive position in being low stakes for the test-takers and their schools (participants are not identified) and yet high stakes for politicians, whose

38   *Emma Smith and Graeme Douglas*

education policies will stand or fall on their outcomes (Stobart and Eggen 2012). The increasing popularity and sophistication of these tests has enabled nations to look critically at the performance of their schools in comparison with their international neighbours. This has led to many nations re-examining their education systems in light of perceived failings in these assessments (Ertl 2006). In several countries, this has been used to further justify dissatisfaction with the domestic school system and has led to accusations of falling academic standards and failing students, as well as calls for policy reform and increased levels of school accountability (e.g. BBC 2013; Mozihim 2014; Young 2010). For example, in the UK, the relatively poor performance of British 15 year olds in PISA 2009 and PISA 2012 (OECD 2010, 2014) simply served to reaffirm the dissatisfaction of policymakers with the current domestic school system (DfE 2016).

According to Gary Orfield (2000), policy makers' preoccupations with perceived mediocre performance in international tests such as PISA have contributed to a refocusing of educational priorities in many Western countries. This has resulted in a move away from policies that have attempted to resolve the inequities faced by poor and other disadvantaged children – for example by increasing access to high-quality education, desegregating schools and reducing achievement gaps – and towards ones concerned with more testing, more accountability and increasingly market-driven systems of school choice. In the United States context, this is reflected in systems of high-stakes testing and strict school accountability sanctions, epitomised by the 2002–2014 No Child Left Behind legislation. In England, an already highly regulated and highly accountable national school system has experienced further moves towards increased diversity of provision driven by choice and market-based policies.

4.3 The Inclusion of Young People with SEND in PISA

International assessments such as PISA are important processes for collecting comparative data on the academic attainment of different groups of students. However, while the physical and academic inclusion of students with SEND in schools and classrooms has steadily increased, their inclusion in this sort of standardised assessment has not kept pace (OECD 2007). While students may be excluded from PISA for a range of reasons, the most likely reason for exclusion is often linked to SEND. Therefore it is unsurprising that the exclusion of young people with SEND, as well as non-native speakers and low-achievers, from international comparative tests such as PISA has been controversial (Hopmann 2007; Schuelka 2013; Wuttke 2007). Since PISA 2003, attempts have been made to ensure that students with SEND are properly represented in the PISA sample. In addition to paper-based assessment material, there is also an optional test instrument UH (Une Heure) which provides an abridged version of the main assessment (plus financial literacy in 2012) for use in schools catering to students with SEND. The UH materials were used by 1,134 students in 11 countries in 2012 (OECD 2014).

The majority of countries/economies involved in PISA sample participants in a two-stage process. The first stage samples schools that have 15-year-old students

An International Perspective 39

registered and accounts for the size of the schools and the number of 15-year-olds who are enrolled. The second stage samples students *within* the school. Once the schools have been selected, a list of the 15-year-old students is prepared and around 35 students (depending on school size) are selected to participate in PISA. From PISA 2003 onwards, data on students' SEND status have also been collected and, within each sampled school, PISA co-ordinators are expected to identify students with SEND and decide whether or not they are to be included in the assessment (guidelines are provided to assist with this). Although PISA is explicit about the need to include students with SEND: 'the exclusion of special education students and students with insufficient assessment language experience is to be kept to a minimum' (OECD 2008: 24), there will be some students who are not able to participate for various reasons and there are five categories of student-based exclusion. Exclusion can take place at the school level (i.e., the whole school is excluded) or within a school (i.e., individual students are excluded). The five within-school exclusion categories are as follows:

i   Students with a mental, cognitive or emotional disability. The manual for PISA 2012 (OECD 2014: 67) uses the term 'Intellectual Disability' to describe this exclusion category.
ii   Students with a functional disability – applied if the student has a moderate to severe permanent physical disability. Functionally disabled students who could provide responses are included in the assessment.
iii Students with insufficient assessment language experience – this is applied if the student is not a native speaker of the assessment language and has limited proficiency in the assessment language and has received less than one year of instruction in the assessment language(s).
iv   Other (as defined by the national centres and approved by the international centre).
v   Students taught in a language of instruction for the main domain (e.g., mathematics in 2012) for which no materials were available.

Students can be excluded from participation in PISA on the basis of SEND or unfamiliarity with the language of instruction but cannot be excluded solely because of poor academic performance or common discipline problems. Additionally a school that was attended only by students who would be excluded for intellectual, functional or linguistic reasons could also be excluded from the PISA sample. In some countries this might include many special schools for children with SEND.

PISA stipulates that school-level exclusions for students in the first three SEND categories (listed above) should not exceed 2% and within-school exclusions should not exceed 2.5% of students (OECD 2014). The decision to use any of the above categories to exclude students from PISA is taken by the school PISA-coordinator following a set of OECD-approved guidelines and the details of all excluded students are recorded. Sampling for PISA is intended to ensure that there is a representative national sample of students included in the assessment. However, there is flexibility within the sampling frame to exclude certain types of schools including geographically remote schools, extremely small schools and those where the administration of PISA would be not feasible. This final criterion might include special schools. In England in PISA 2012, special schools and pupil referral units were excluded from the sampling frame (Wheater, Ager, Burge and Sizmur 2014). Table 3.1 shows the number of students excluded and included, the (OECD) category of SEND and the within-school exclusion/inclusion rate for a selection of the countries that participated in PISA 2009.

The exclusion and inclusion rates vary considerably. It is notable that some of the highest performing PISA nations (Finland, Shanghai-China and Australia) appear to exclude relatively small proportions of students with SEND within sampled schools. As might be expected, some countries have a high exclusion rate and a low inclusion rate (or vice versa), e.g., Canada, Finland. However, some countries have a different profile suggesting different levels of prevalence of SEND in the education system (or at least the sampled schools) which appears not to be explained by school-level sampling (e.g., the United States has relatively high exclusion and inclusion figures, while Shanghai-China and Japan have low). The zero score of Japan is particularly noteworthy and will be the focus of future research. Additionally, the categorisation of students with SEND is variable, e.g., Iceland and Finland making higher use of the 'other' category. It might be argued that there is little evidence to show that students with SEND are being routinely excluded from PISA in order to influence scores at the national level. However the absence of large-scale observational data on the administration and exclusion of young people with SEND from PISA means that it is difficult to draw any firm conclusions on this matter.

The issue of cross-national comparisons of the educational participation and attainment of young people with SEND is a complex one (Douglas, McLinden, Robertson, Travers and Smith 2016). It is certainly possible that some countries/ economies could exclude students with a particular need while others would include them. Another issue is that students taught in discrete special schools might be excluded from the process altogether (as happened in England and Ireland in 2009 and 2012). In addition, despite the efforts of organisations such as the OECD to develop common categories of SEND (OECD 2007), it is still the case that practice and categorisation of needs can vary widely. Indeed it is important to note that issues surrounding the inclusion of young people with SEND and PISA are relatively under-researched and there is a need for a more detailed examination of the area, including definitions and understanding of what is meant by SEN and differing approaches to inclusion.

5 Discussion

Writing about the UK context in 1985, Sally Tomlinson argued that the primary purpose of an expanding SEND sector was to respond to the dilemma of how to restructure the education-training system to deal with the 'increasing number of young people who are defined as being unable or unwilling to participate satisfactorily in a system primarily directed towards producing academic and technical

Table 3.1 Numbers of SEND students according to category of inclusion/exclusion in PISA 2009, selected countries

Country	All SEND		Cat. 1 Functional disability		Cat. 2 Intellectual disability		Cat. 3 Limited lang. proficiency		Cat. 4 Other SEND		Within-school exclusion rate**	Within-school inclusion rate**	Proportion of sample with SEND**
	Inc.	Exc.	Inc.	Exc.	Inc.	Exc.	Inc.	Exc.	Inc.	Exc.			
Australia	377	313	35	24	175	210	167	79	0	0	1.79	2.39	4.2
Belgium	607	30	40	3	486	17	81	10	0	0	0.24	7.61	7.9
Canada	118	1607	6	49	82	1458	30	100	0	0	5.47	0.66	6.1
Finland	312	75	5	4	143	48	53	12	111	11	1.15	4.46	5.6
France	142	1	49	1	59	0	34	0	0	0	0.04	3.53	3.6
Germany	78	28	18	6	57	20	3	2	0	0	0.47	1.72	2.2
Hong Kong-China	35	9	8	0	21	9	6	0	0	0	0.16	0.70	0.9
Iceland	252	183	5	3	75	78	25	64	147	38	4.10	6.52	10.6
Ireland	163	136	4	4	77	72	28	25	54	35	2.75	3.85	6.6
Japan	0	0	0	0	0	0	0	0	0	0	0.00	0	0
Korea	18	16	2	7	15	9	1	0	0	0	0.28	0.49	0.8
Mexico	24	52	6	25	15	25	3	2	0	0	0.15	0.14	0.3
Netherlands	42	19	5	6	33	13	4	0	0	0	0.35	1.10	1.5
New Zealand	102	181	8	19	42	84	52	78	0	0	3.15	2.26	5.4
Norway	95	207	4	8	59	160	32	39	0	0	3.79	1.87	5.7
Shanghai-China	27	7	2	1	14	6	11	0	0	0	0.13	0.52	0.6
Singapore	71	48	7	2	15	22	49	24	0	0	0.80	1.13	1.9
Sweden	254	146	160	115	0	0	94	31	0	0	2.89	5.59	8.5
United Kingdom*	-	318	-	40	-	247	-	31	-	0	2.44	-	-
United States	265	305	10	29	224	236	29	40	2	10	4.81	4.77	9.6

*No data available for SEND inclusions.
**Calculations made using weighted data.
Source: OECD 2010 tables A2.1 and A2.2 plus authors' own analysis.

42 Emma Smith and Graeme Douglas

elites' (Tomlinson 1985: 157). While much may have changed in the intervening years (with special education, and inclusive educational placement in particular, being now a key part of the education systems in many countries), the dilemma of how to prepare students with SEND for full and active citizenship in a high skilled, globalised economy still persists. As Tomlinson goes on to argue more recently:

> the ideology and practice of inclusive education has brought into mainstream schools and colleges large numbers of young people who would previously have been segregated in special schools or classes, joining their fellow students who were previously labelled slow, dull, retarded or remedial. The numbers of those variously regarded as having learning or behavioural difficulties and disabilities and unable to achieve required levels has increased, and pressures on public comprehensive schools and lower level schools in selective systems are intense.
>
> (2012: 275)

The economic imperative of higher levels of skills and training for all young people, including those with SEND, is a compelling driver of school reform in many industrialised countries. However, the question for governments is what to do with some young people with SEND in an economy where even low-skilled employment requires some level of qualification (Tomlinson 2012). One response to this has been to increase levels of engagement in education: in England, for example, since 2015 all young people have to remain in some form of education or training until they are 18. Another has been to urge school improvement for all students through systems of high-stakes testing that are linked to strict accountability policies that are aimed at raising standards.

While most will agree that some form of accountability for those teaching all pupils including those with SEND is desirable, the issue of what form that accountability should take and the impact of accountability policies on school reform are uncertain. While some evidence points to instances of improvement, there are concerns that not all students, in particular the most vulnerable, have benefited. For instance, research by the Civil Rights Project in the United States shows that rather than encouraging schools to become more inclusive, recent accountability policies are in fact moving schools towards greater inequalities and increased levels of segregation (Sunderman 2008). It is beyond the scope of this chapter to address all these issues. Instead we have examined the extent to which international comparative tests have a role in accountability measures that are inclusive of students with SEND. Our discussion shows that the prospects for including students with SEND in these assessments are mixed. For instance, in spite of PISA aiming to include students with SEND, variable definitions of SEND and sampling approaches in participating countries raise questions about their meaningful inclusion and about the comparison of PISA scores across countries more generally.

While accountability policies may well have changed the character of debate from excusing bad results because students were disadvantaged, to considering the education of a previously neglected group (Hanushek 2005), the issue of 'what form of accountability for what type of student?' remains. Including the most vulnerable students in stressful tests that may, or may not, measure the educational outcomes that are the most important for them has important implications for the fair treatment of these students in school; but arguably so does leaving them out of these assessments altogether. One way forward, according to Shippen, Houchins, Calhoon, Furlow and Sartor (2006: 327), is for schools to acknowledge that most students with SEND will never achieve at the 'average' levels demanded by most high-stakes tests and to establish appropriate standards and curriculum for these students. This recognises that the 'contention that *all* students with disabilities will attain average achievement is unrealistic'. However, such a proposal is likely to sit uncomfortably with those anxious to avoid a segregated 'special education' system in which different students experience different curricula. The inclusion of all children and young people with SEND in assessments related to accountability is an important aspiration. Considerable effort is required if such assessments are to be accessible, reliable and valid. Accommodated and alternative assessment approaches are important strategies in this regard and there are many examples of success from the considerable work in the United States. Nevertheless, young people with SEND vary enormously in terms of the challenges and dangers they face in relation to inclusion in assessment – 'lumping together' these groups and looking at averages across SEND as a whole has limited (if any) value when evaluating the efficacy of education. Therefore the collection of reliable and more detailed data in relation to student SEND characteristics would allow for more meaningful data analysis and disaggregation.

Overall, balance seems crucial. There should be a balance between performance in traditional attainment-focussed accountability tests and other relevant assessments which are meaningful to the given student and/or SEND subgroup. More recently we have conceptualised this balance within an 'inclusive assessment framework' in which assessment should: (1) include all, (2) be accessible and appropriate and (3) assess and report areas of relevance (Douglas et al. 2016). Finding such a balance is undoubtedly challenging – in addition to accommodated and alternative assessment approaches which increase assessment accessibility, assessment may also require additional sources of evidence which are relevant to student progress. For example, this might include evidence gathered through school inspection procedures or bespoke focussed studies (for example the United States–based National Longitudinal Transition Study-2 [NLTS2] gathers a broad range of progress and outcome data from over 8,000 students with disabilities). This requires considerable thought, but the imperative remains that systems for assessing student progress (with their associated use for accountability purposes) should seek to include and serve *all* students.

Note

1   Different countries use different terms to refer to students with 'special educational needs' (e.g. in United States 'disability' is used, while Scotland adopts the broader 'Additional Support Needs'). In this chapter, we use the term 'special educational needs and disability' (SEND) to avoid ambiguity.

References

Altman, J. R., Lazarus, S. S., Quenemoen, R. F., Kearns, J., Quenemoen, M., & Thurlow, M. L. 2010. 2009 survey of states: Accomplishments and new issues at the end of a decade of Dolinchange. Minneapolis: National Center on Educational Outcomes. http://www.cehd.umn.edu/NCEO/OnlinePubs/2009StateSurvey.pdf" www.cehd.umn.edu/NCEO/Online Pubs/2009StateSurvey.pdf

Baird, J.A., Isaacs, T., Johnson, S., Stobart, G., Yu, G., Sprague, T., and Daugherty, R. (2011). *Policy effects of PISA*. Oxford University Centre for Educational Assessment. http://oucea.education.ox.ac.uk/wordpress/wp-content/uploads/2011/10/Policy-Effects-of-PISA-OUCEA.pdf

Banks, J., Frawley, D., and McCoy, S. (2015). Achieving inclusion? Effective resourcing of students with special educational needs. *International Journal of Inclusive Education*, 19(9), 926–943.

BBC (2013). Pisa ranks Wales' education the worst in the UK, *BBC News*, 13 December 2013. http://www.bbc.co.uk/news/uk-wales-25196974

Center on Education Policy (2007). NCLB's accountability provisions for students with disabilities. Center on Education Policy Roundtable Discussion. www.cep-dc.org

Cole, C. (2006). Closing the achievement gap series: Part III what is the impact of NCLB on the inclusion of students with disabilities? Center for Evaluation and Education Policy. www.ceep.indiana.edu/projects/PDF/PB_V4N11_Fall_2006_NCLB_dis.pdf

Darling-Hammond, L. (2007). Race, inequality and educational accountability: The irony of "No Child Left Behind". *Race, Ethnicity and Education*, 10(3), 245–260.

Davidson, E., Reback, R., Rockoff, J., and Schwartz, H.L. (2015). Fifty ways to leave a child behind: Idiosyncrasies and discrepancies in states. *Implementation of NCLB, Educational Researcher*, 44(6), 347–358.

Dee, T., and Jacob, B. (2009). The impact of No Child Left Behind on student achievement. National Bureau of Economic Research. NBER Working Paper No. 15531.

Department for Education (2016). *Educational excellence everywhere, Cm9230*. London: HMSO.

Dolin, J. (2007). PISA: An example of the use and misuse of large-scale comparative tests. In S.T. Hopmann, G. Brinek and M. Retzl (eds.), *PISA according to PISA: Does PISA keep what it promises?* (pp. 93–126). Berlin and Vienna: LIT Verlag.

Douglas, G., McLinden, M., Robertson, C., Travers, J., and Smith, E. (2016). Including pupils with special educational needs and disability in national assessment: Comparison of three country case studies through an inclusive assessment framework. *International Journal of Disability, Development and Education*, 63(1), 98–121.

Ertl, H. (2006). Educational standards and the changing discourse on education: The reception and consequences of the PISA Study in Germany. *Oxford Review of Education*, 32(5), 619–634.

Figazzolo, L. (2009). Impact of PISA 2006 on the education policy debate, education international. http://download.ei-ie.org/docs/IRISDocuments/Research%20Website%20Documents/2009-00036-01-E.pdf

Figlio, D., and Getzler, L.S. (2002). Accountability, ability and disability: Gaming the system, Working Paper 9307. National Bureau of Economic Research. http://www.nber.org/papers/w9307

Figlio, D., and Loeb, S. (2011). School accountability. In E.A. Hanushek., S. Machin and L. Woessmann (eds.), *Economics of Education Vol. 3* (pp. 383–421). Amsterdam, The Netherlands: North-Holland.

An International Perspective   45

Gorard, S., Adnett, N., May, H., Slack, K., Smith, E., and Thomas, L. (2007). *Overcoming the barriers to higher education*. Stoke-on-Trent: Trentham Books.

Haney, W. (2000). The myth of the Texas miracle in education. *Education Policy Analysis Archives*, 8(41). http://epaa.asu.edu/ojs/article/view/432/828

Hanushek, E.A. (2005). Why the federal government should be involved in school accountability. *Journal of Policy Analysis and Management*, 24(1), 167–178.

Hanushek, E.A., and Raymond, M.E. (2005). Does school accountability lead to improved student performance? *Journal of Policy Analysis and Management*, 24(2), 297–327.

Holbein, J.B., and Ladd, H.F. (2015). Accountability pressure and non-achievement student behaviours, national center for analysis of longitudinal data in education research. Retrieved on April 2016 from: http://files.eric.ed.gov/fulltext/ED560678.pdf

Hopmann, S.T., and Brinek, G. (2007). Introduction. In S.T. Hopmann, G. Brinek and M. Retzl (eds.), *PISA according to PISA: Does PISA keep what it promises?* (pp. 9-20). Berlin and Vienna: LIT Verlag.

Hout, M., and Elliot, S.W. (2011). Incentives and test-based accountability in education. National Academies Press. http://www.nap.edu/catalog.php?record_id=12521

Hursh, D. (2005). The growth of high-stakes testing in the USA: Accountability, markets and the decline in educational equality. *British Educational Research Journal*, 31(5), 605–622.

Jerrim, J. (2011). England's "plummeting" PISA test scores between 2000 and 2009: Is the performance of our secondary school pupils really in relative decline? DoQSS Working Paper No. 11–09, London: Institute of Education.

Lowrey, K.A., Drasgow, E. et al., Renzaglia, A. and Chezan, L. (2007). Impact of alternate assessment on curricula for students with severe disabilities: Purpose driven or process driven? *Assessment for Effective Intervention*, 32(4), 244–253.

McLaughlin, M.J., and Rhim, L.M. (2007). Accountability frameworks and children with disabilities: A test of assumptions about improving public education for all students. *International Journal of Disability, Development and Education*, 54(1), 25–49.

McLaughlin, M.J., and Thurlow, M. (2003). Educational accountability and students with disabilities: Issues and challenges. *Educational Policy*, 17, 43.

Mortimore, P. (2009). Alternative models for analysing and representing countries performance in PISA, Paper commissioned by Education International Research Institute, Brussels.

Mozihim, A.K. (2014). PISA 2012 highlights deteriorating education performance in Malaysia. *Scientific Malaysian*, 18th April 2014. http://www.scientificmalaysian.com/2014/04/18/pisa-2012-deteriorating-education-performance-malaysia/

National Council on Disability (2008). The No Child Left Behind Act and the Individuals with Disabilities Education Act: A progress report. National Council on Disability. www.educationalpolicy.org/publications/pubpdf/NCD_2008.pdf

OECD (2001). Knowledge and skills for life: First results from PISA 2000. http://browse.oecdbookshop.org/oecd/pdfs/free/9601141e.pdf

OECD (2007). *Students with disabilities, learning difficulties and disadvantages: Policies, statistics and indicators*. Paris: OECD.

OECD (2008). PISA 2009 main survey, school co-ordinator's manual. https://mypisa.acer.edu.au/images/mypisadoc/sc_manual_ms09_v2_1.pdf

OECD (2009). PISA 2009 assessment framework: Key competencies in reading, mathematics and science. http://www.oecd.org/dataoecd/11/40/44455820.pdf

OECD (2010). PISA 2009 results: What students know and can do: Student performance in reading, Mathematics and Science (Volume I). http://dx.doi.org/10.1787/9789264091450-en

46 *Emma Smith and Graeme Douglas*

OECD (2011). PISA in focus, Issue 9. http://www.oecd.org/pisa/pisaproducts/pisainfocus/48910490.pdf

OECD (2014). PISA 2012, technical report. http://www.oecd.org/pisa/pisaproducts/PISA-2012-technical-report-final.pdf

Orfield, G. (2000). Orfield, G. (1999) Policy and equity: A third of a century of educational reforms in the United States Prospects 29(4), pp 579–594.

Rockoff, J., and Turner, L. (2008). *Short run impacts of accountability on school quality*. National Bureau of Economic Research. NBER Working Paper No. 14564.

Rutkowski, L., and Rutkowski, D. (2010). Getting it "better": The importance of improving background questionnaires in international large-scale assessment. *Journal of Curriculum Studies*, 42(3), 411–430.

Schuelka, M. (2013). Excluding students with disabilities from the culture of achievement: The case of the TIMSS, PIRLS and PISA. *Journal of Education Policy*, 28(2), 216–230.

Shippen, M., Houchins, D.E., Calhoon, M., Furlow, C., and Sartor, D. (2006). The effects of comprehensive school reform models in reading for urban middle school students with disabilities. *Remedial and Special Education*, 27(6), 322–328.

Sjøberg, S., (2007), PISA and "Real Life Challenges": Mission impossible? In S.T. Hopmann, G. Brinek, M. Retzl (eds.), *PISA According to PISA: Does PISA Keep What It Promises?* (pp. 203–225). Berlin and Vienna: LIT Verlag.

Smith, E. (2012). *Key issues in education and social justice*. London: Sage.

Stobart, G., and Eggen, T. (2012). High-stakes testing – value, fairness and consequences. *Assessment in Education*, 19(1), 1–6.

Sunderman, G. (2008). *Holding NCLB accountable: Achieving accountability, equity and school reform*. New York: Corwin Press.

Tomlinson, S. (1985). The expansion of special education. *Oxford Review of Education*, 2(2), 195–205.

Tomlinson, S. (2012). The irresistible rise of the SEN industry. *Oxford Review of Education*, 38(3), 267–286.

West, A., Mattei, P., and Roberts, J. (2011). Accountability and sanctions in English schools. *British Journal of Educational Studies*, 59(1), 41–62.

Wheater, R., Ager, R., Burge, B., and Sizmur, J. (2014). *Achievement of 15-year-olds in England: PISA 2012 national report*. London: HMSO.

Wolf, P.J., Witte, J., and Fleming, D.J. (2012). Special education and the Milwaukee parental choice program. SCDP Milwaukee Evaluation Report #35. http://www.uaedreform.org/SCDP/Milwaukee_Eval/Report_35.pdf

Wuttke, J. (2007). Uncertainties and bias in PISA. In S. T. Hopmann, G. Brinek, M. Retzl (eds.), *PISA according to PISA: Does PISA keep what it promises?* (pp. 241–264). Berlin and Vienna: LIT Verlag.

Young, T. (2010). British schoolchildren now ranked 23rd in the world, down from 12th in 2000. *The Daily Telegraph*, 7 December 2010.

4 The Promise and Perils of Response to Intervention to Address Disproportionality in Special Education

Wendy Cavendish, Benikia Kressler, Ana Maria Menda and Anabel Espinosa

In the United States, the disproportionate representation of students of color in special education has been noted for several decades (e.g., Artiles and Trent 1994; Deno 1970, 1994; Dunn 1968). Specifically, the U.S. Department of Education's Office of Civil Rights (OCR) and the Office of Special Education Programs (OSEP) has consistently reported that African American students are two to three times more likely to be identified in the categories of intellectual disability (ID) and emotional disturbance (ED). The reasons for disproportionate representation of youth of color in high incidence special education categories have been debated without consensus (Blanchett, Klingner and Harry 2009; Donovan and Cross 2002; Skiba et al. 2008). However, the relationship between overrepresentation in special education and testing bias has received attention in the literature. Skiba et al. (2008) examined the history of test bias and overrepresentation and reported that "the possibility of bias against minorities in standardized tests of intelligence and achievement was examined fairly extensively in the 1970s and 1980s" but that "extensive reviews of that literature have reached somewhat different conclusions" (271). Blanchett, Klingner and Harry (2009: 396) have cautioned that overrepresentation must be viewed as a "complex phenomenon that cannot be explained by simplistic views that focus narrowly on the role of poverty or students' presumed lack of intelligence or other deficits and that pay too little attention to the role of context" (396).

Accountability: Legal Changes and Tenets of Response to Intervention

Although there has been no consensus related to possible reasons for overrepresentation, policy has required that practitioners address the issue. Specifically, there has been national policy pressure for state education agencies (SEAs) in the United States to reduce disproportionate special education placement for youth of color in recent reauthorizations of the Individuals with Disabilities in Education Act (IDEA). In particular, the 2004 reauthorization of IDEA prioritized the issue of disproportionality in the federal statutes and required that 1) each state must develop and implement "policies and procedures" designed to "prevent the inappropriate over-identification or disproportionate representation" of youth in special education by race and ethnicity (20 U.S.C 1412[a] [24]); (2) states must monitor LEAs' disproportionate representation of racial and ethnic groups using quantifiable indicators (20 U.S.C. 1416 [a] [3] [C]); and (3) if significant disproportionality is reported, states must review and/or revise policies, practices and procedures used in special education identification and placement (20 U.S.C. 1418 [d] [2]).

As considerations of disproportionality in special education have led to speculation about possible bias in assessment procedures for some racial/ethnic groups (e.g., Hosp and Reschly 2003), the President's Commission on Excellence in Special Education (2002) and the Donovan and Cross (2002) reports both emphasized the importance of a contextualized assessment process that considered a child's opportunity to learn. This led to a de-emphasis on the IQ-achievement discrepancy identification model in the literature (e.g., Vaughn and Fuchs 2003; Vellutino, Scanlon and Lyon 2000) and ultimately to a change in policy with the introduction of Response to Intervention (RTI) models for identifying youth with disabilities as a means to ameliorate disproportionality in the 2004 reauthorization of IDEA. Based on these series of reports (e.g., President's Commission 2002), the reauthorization of IDEA (2004) recommended that state and local agencies adopt an alternative method to the discrepancy formula, like Response to Intervention (RTI). Section 1414(b)(6)(B) of IDEA specifically stated that "In determining whether a child has a specific learning disability, a local educational agency (LEA) may use a process that determines if the child responds to scientific, research-based intervention a part of the evaluation process." The option of RTI as a means to identify learning disabilities (LD) represented a shift in institutional priorities and was, as suggested by Johnston (2011), a response to four factors: problems with IQ-achievement discrepancy assessment, the growth in numbers of youth identified as LD, the overrepresentation of minority youth in special education and a growing research base documenting early intervention effectiveness.

RTI has been defined as a systematic general education model characterized by research-based, tiered interventions tailored to meet the needs of individual children (Mellard 2004). The National Research Center on Learning Disabilities (NRCLD 2004) recommended core features of RTI. These features were high-quality classroom instruction that produces research-based, universal screening; continuous progress monitoring of students' classroom performance; research-based interventions if progress is not being made; and the use of fidelity measures for instruction and interventions (Johnson, Mellard, Fuchs and McKnight 2006). The National Association of State Directors of Special Education (NASDSE 2005) articulated that RTI implementation should be based on the primary assumptions that 1) all students can learn in the general education classroom, 2) early intervention is critical to preventing problems from getting out of control, 3) the implementation of a multi-tiered service delivery model is necessary, 4) a problem-solving model should be used to make decisions between tiers, 5) research-based interventions should be implemented to the extent possible, 6) progress monitoring must be implemented to inform instruction and 7) data should drive decision making.

Policy Implementation

All U.S. states have responded to the IDEA (2004) policy change allowing Response to Intervention (RTI) models to be used as an alternative or supplement to discrepancy models for the identification of LD. The assumption and hope behind RTI was that the instructional methods found in empirically validated curriculum and interventions would address student learning needs prior to academic failure and reduce the disproportionate representation of minority students in special education. By 2008, all states had reported a timeline and state plan for RTI implementation (NCRI 2008). The U.S. Department of Education reported in July 2011 that 37 states reported using the IQ-achievement discrepancy model and RTI for LD identification, six states reported using the discrepancy model, but only with the inclusion of RTI data prior to IQ assessment, and seven states mandated RTI and disallowed the use of the discrepancy model for LD determination (NCEERA 2011).

Although features of RTI have been recommended, as with the lack of consensus related to the 'causes' of disproportionality, there is no federal guidance or consensus related to how to best implement RTI as a means of reducing disproportionality. Much of the research related to RTI effectiveness has been conducted through researcher-led interventions and not in naturalistic settings (Orosco and Klingner 2010). One component of RTI intervention that has been noted by researchers, but that has not been explicit in the federal guidelines, is the importance of the consideration of culturally and linguistically diverse learners throughout the process (Klingner and Edwards 2006; NCCREST 2005).

Culturally Responsive Instruction (CRI) and RTI

Response to Intervention models have been identified as having the potential to improve educational opportunities for culturally and linguistically diverse learners and reduce disproportionality (NCCREST 2005). Cartledge and Kourea (2008) noted that high-quality, research-based instruction and data-based decision making serve as foundational elements for effective RTI implementation and also represent instructional principles integral to culturally responsive classrooms. Classrooms in which data are used to guide instruction and where interventions are implemented that have been empirically validated with diverse populations should benefit all learners and would be expected to meet the needs of previously marginalized groups. It is this "quality . . . instruction in a supportive general education environment [that researchers] hope [will] decrease the number students who are inappropriately referred to and placed in special education" (Klingner and Edwards 2006: 108). However if quality instruction is to have the potential to decrease disproportionality it must be delivered with integrity and with consideration of culturally and linguistically diverse (CLD) learners. Thus, it has been suggested that if most students in a class "show limited growth" educators should assume that instruction was ineffective (Cartledge and Kourea 2008) rather than blaming community factors (e.g., poverty, family composition or home language).

50   *Wendy Cavendish et al.*

Klingner and Edwards (2006) noted that in cases where limited growth has persisted after the delivery of evidence based instruction, practitioners should look first to the contextual variables that contributed to the effectiveness of the approach. Klingner and Edwards also recommended that evidence based instruction should be "validated with students like those with whom it was applied" (Klingner and Edwards 2006: 109). If instruction and interventions are to have the potential to reduce disproportionality in special education referral, the process of assessment and instruction must be flexible enough to allow for contextual differences during delivery (Klingner and Edwards 2006).

Overview of RTI Implementation in the United States

Although the National Research Center on Learning Disabilities (NRCLD) is currently conducting large-scale longitudinal studies to determine how alternative approaches to identifying learning disabilities such as Response to Intervention may impact on who is ultimately identified as needing special education services, there have been no large-scale studies that have considered the relationship between disproportionality reporting, RTI development and processes and the inclusion of CLD youth in these processes. Berkeley, Bender, Gregg, Saunders and Saunders (2009) looked at the level of RTI development and implementation of RTI on a nation-wide scale. They reported that 47 out of 50 states had adopted a model of RTI, however great variance in the level of development and inclusion of components was found. Thus, we report data from a study that examined the ways in which states have utilized Response to Intervention models as a means to address disproportionality. Specifically, we examined the components of RTI models by states that note RTI as a means to address disproportionality as reported in their State Performance Plans. We then examined all states' level of RTI model development and the level of integration of culturally responsive practice provided in their RTI models and assessment and content area instructional guidance documents.

Response to Intervention Data Sources

The data sources include each state's IDEA Part B State Performance Plan for 2005–2010 submitted to the U.S. Department of Education Office of Special Education Programs and the National Center on Response to Intervention state level RTI model implementation matrix. We also reviewed each state's department of education RTI model training documents, RTI manuals for school districts/LEAs, all technical assistance papers related to RTI development and implementation, and all state documents relating to culturally responsive assessment and instruction in RTI materials and content area assessment and instruction documents.

States were in varying stages of RTI implementation; therefore, we selected multiple data sources for our review of RTI development. For each of the 50 states, two researchers reviewed RTI related information provided by the state department of education for the local districts. We accessed all states' RTI related training

Promise and Perils in Special Education   51

materials, including technical assistance papers, PowerPoint training documents, and web-based RTI modules. We then cross-checked all RTI related materials obtained through state department of education websites with the RTI implementation matrix provided through the National Center on Response to Intervention (NCRI). Research team members recorded information from all RTI materials for each state onto an adapted version of the RTI Model Screening Tool (Mellard and McKnight 2007). This screening tool was used by our research team to record and code information from each state related to: (a) the state's description of the RTI model; (b) the number of tiers and description of tiered interventions; (c) the state's description of the duration and frequency (if noted) for each tiered intervention and (d) the personnel identified to deliver the intervention(s). The RTI Model Screening Tool (Mellard and McKnight 2007) also included information related to each state's timeline or plan for professional development and the description of RTI training to be provided including web-based modules and links for technical assistance as well as nine dichotomously coded items related to general education practice, student assessment practice and intervention model practice. We used the data related to (a) through to (d) to create a data table for information related to the level of RTI model development.

Finally, in addition to the RTI materials, we examined each state's special education website links and their state reading plans for information provided to LEAs related to consideration of CLD learners in assessment and/or culturally responsive instructional delivery related to the LD identification process. We examined all guidance materials on inclusion of CLD youth and/or families related to assessment or instruction at any stage of the RTI process. Using all the RTI materials and assessment and instructional strategy documents, we recorded the descriptions provided for culturally responsive assessment and instruction for each state on an added section to the RTI Model Screening Tool termed Components of Cultural Responsiveness/Diversity. We sorted the descriptive information into categories that were dichotomously coded as yes (1) for present in materials or no (0) not present in materials. The seven categories were as follows: (1) definition of CLD students provided or noted presence of CLD students in the population; (2) consideration of CLD students in assessment and/or progress monitoring; (3) noted comparison of CLD students to true peers in assessment and progress monitoring; (4) noted CLD students and families involvement in the process; (5) mentioned differentiated instruction to meet the needs of CLD learners; (6) provided links and/or resources specific to instruction of CLD youth and (7) provided description of instructional strategies for CLD students.

States' Use of RTI to Address Disproportionality

States were required to designate an improvement plan if disproportionality was found in any district. The states that designated RTI as a means to address disproportionality in their State Performance Plans (SPP) between the years of 2005–2010 are presented in Table 4.1.

Table 4.1 Level of RTI Development by State

	RTI to address disproportionality	No description	Describes tiers	Frequency/ duration	Identifies delivery personnel
Alabama	X		√	√	√
Alaska	X		√	√	√
Arizona	X		√	√	√
Arkansas	X	√			
California			√		
Colorado	X		√		
Connecticut	X		√	√	√
Delaware	X		√	√	
Florida	X		√		
Georgia	X		√	√	
Hawaii			√		
Idaho	X		√	√	
Illinois	X		√		
Indiana	X		√	√	√
Iowa			√		
Kansas			√	√	√
Kentucky	X		√		
Louisiana	X		√		
Maine			√		
Maryland	X		√		
Massachusetts			√	√	√
Michigan	X		√		
Minnesota	X		√	√	√
Missouri	X		√	√	
Mississippi			√	√	√
Montana	X		√		
Nebraska	X		√		
Nevada			√	√	√
New Hampshire			√	√	
New Jersey		√			
New Mexico	X		√	√	√
New York	X		√	√	√
North Carolina	X		√		
North Dakota	X		√		
Ohio	X		√		
Oklahoma	X		√	√	√
Oregon			√	√	√
Pennsylvania	X		√		
Rhode Island	X		√		
South Carolina	X		√		
South Dakota	X		√	√	√
Tennessee	X		√	√	√
Texas	X		√	√	√
Utah	X		√	√	√

(Continued)

Promise and Perils in Special Education   53

Table 4.1 (Continued)

	RTI to address disproportionality	No description	Describes tiers	Frequency/ duration	Identifies delivery personnel
Vermont			√	√	
Virginia			√	√	
Washington	X		√	√	
West Virginia	X		√	√	√
Wisconsin	X	√			
Wyoming			√	√	√

√= Included in state Response to Intervention guidance materials

Table 4.1 shows that 72% (n = 36) of states outlined the use of RTI to address disproportionality reported in their State Performance Plan (SPP). The level of RTI model development was determined using information recorded on each state's RTI Model Screening Tool (Mellard and McKnight 2007) and is also reported in Table 4.1. Table 4.1 reveals variation between the states that listed RTI as an improvement activity for disproportionality on their SPP (n = 36) and those who did not list RTI as an improvement activity (n = 14). We reported on four categories of RTI development for each state: (1) no description of a state RTI model; (2) an RTI model which described tiers of instruction; (3) an RTI model which described instructional tiers along with frequency and duration of delivery at each tier and (4) an RTI model which described instructional tiers, frequency, duration and delivery personnel at each tier. As noted in Table 4.1, of the states that identified RTI as means by which to address disproportionality (n = 36), 38% (n = 14) had highly developed RTI Models and provided information to their LEAs that included a description of instructional tiers, details related to the frequency and duration of interventions and identified intervention delivery personnel at each tier and 14% (n = 5) described instructional tiers along with frequency and duration of delivery at each tier. Forty-two percent (n = 15) of states that identified RTI to address disproportionality provided a description of the RTI tiers of instruction and 5% (n = 2) had not provided a description of an RTI Model on state guidance documents.

Level of Inclusion of Cultural Responsiveness in RTI Models

Across the 50 states there was not only variation in degree of RTI development, there was considerable variation in the integration of cultural responsiveness within RTI and assessment/instruction guidance materials. State provided materials were coded for the inclusion of seven components related to provisions for CLD learners and culturally responsive instruction (see Table 4.2). These seven components were as follows: (1) mentions CLD learners in guidance documents by definition or presence in the population, (2) mentions CLD learners in reference to

Table 4.2 Guidance on CLD Learners by State

	RTI to address disproportionality	Definition	Assessment	True peer	Family	Differentiated instruction	Resources	Instructional strategies	Sum
Do not address CLD									
Hawaii									0
Iowa									0
Nebraska	X								0
New Hampshire									0
New Jersey									0
North Carolina	X								0
1–3 CLD Components									
Alabama	X					√			1
Arizona	X		√		√				2
Florida	X	√	√		√				3
Illinois	X	√							1
Louisiana	X							√	1
Maine		√	√			√			3
Maryland	X		√	√					2
Massachusetts			√						1
Michigan	X		√						1
Minnesota	X				√				1
Missouri	X	√							1
Mississippi					√	√		√	3
Montana	X		√						1
Nevada								√	1
New York	X		√	√		√			3
North Dakota	X		√						1
Ohio	X					√			1
Pennsylvania	X		√						1
Rhode Island	X		√			√	√		3
South Dakota	X		√				√		2
Tennessee	X	√	√					√	3
Texas	X		√						1
Utah	X		√						1

(Continued)

Table 4.2 Continued

	RTI to address disproportionality	Definition	Assessment	True peer	Family	Differentiated instruction	Resources	Instructional strategies	Sum
Virginia		√				√			2
Wisconsin	X					√	√		2
Wyoming			√						1
4–6 CLD Components									
Alaska	X	√	√		√	√	√	√	6
Arkansas	X	√	√		√	√		√	5
California		√	√	√	√	√			5
Colorado	X	√	√		√	√	√	√	6
Connecticut	X	√	√		√	√	√	√	6
Delaware	X	√			√	√	√	√	5
Georgia	X	√	√	√		√	√		6
Indiana	X	√	√		√	√			4
Kansas		√	√		√	√	√	√	6
New Mexico	X		√	√	√	√	√	√	6
Oklahoma	X	√	√	√	√	√	√		6
South Carolina	X		√	√	√	√	√		5
Vermont		√	√	√	√	√	√		5
West Virginia	X	√	√	√	√	√			4
7 CLD Components									
Idaho	X	√	√	√	√	√	√	√	7
Kentucky	X	√	√	√	√	√	√	√	7
Oregon		√	√	√	√	√	√	√	7
Washington	X	√	√	√	√	√	√	√	7

√ = Included in State guidance materials

56 *Wendy Cavendish et al.*

assessment, (3) mentions comparison of CLD learners to true peers, (4) mentions CLD learners in reference to diverse family and community needs, (5) mentions differentiated instruction to meet the needs of CLD learners, (6) provides links or resources specific to the instruction of CLD learners and (7) provides explicit directions for the instruction of CLD learners.

Only 8% of states (n = 4) included all seven of the CLD components in the state RTI guidance materials. Thirty-eight percent (n = 14) included 4–6 CLD components and 52% (n = 26) included 1–3 CLD components. Twelve percent (n = 6) did not address CLD student needs in their RTI materials at all. The states (n = 36) that identified RTI as an improvement activity to address disproportionality reported an average of 3.1 CLD components in their RTI materials. The states (n = 14) that did not designate RTI as a means to address disproportionality reported an average of 2.4 CLD components. A U.S. map that provides visual differentiation among the levels of CLD integration in RTI models across the states is provided in Figure 4.1.

As depicted in Figure 4.1, Hawaii, Iowa, Nebraska, New Hampshire and North Carolina did not include any reference to CLD learners or cultural response instruction in the RTI process. Also, of the 50 states, only Idaho, Kentucky, Oregon and Washington provided guidance for full integration of CRI to meet the needs of CLD learners in the RTI process.

RTI to Address Disproportionality

Our findings indicate variability across states in the level of development of RTI guidance materials to fully implement RTI. The findings demonstrate that 20 states have fully developed RTI models with duration and frequency of interventions as well as personnel identified for delivery of these interventions outlined. An additional seven states provided detailed intervention guidance. However, 19 states provided only descriptions of the tiers and RTI model without detail provided related to intervention delivery and two states have not provided any description of their RTI models. Unexpectedly, we also found that states that listed RTI as an improvement activity on their SPPs reported less developed RTI guidance for their LEAs as only 52% of those 36 states that identified RTI as an improvement activity provided fully developed RTI models with detailed intervention description and 71% of the states that did not cite RTI as an improvement activity provided fully developed RTI models and intervention description.

There has been limited research on RTI model development nationally, but our findings are congruent with the one previous study that examined national RTI development trends (Berkeley et al. 2009). Of concern is the continued finding of great variability across states related to their RTI implementation guidance. Berkeley et al. (2009) noted that the "lack of specificity in assessment, intervention implementation, selection of research based practices, and fidelity raise[d] concern about how consistently the [LD] eligibility process will be implemented both within and between states" and that this lack of specificity was also an issue raised related to the variability across states in use of the IQ-achievement discrepancy model (94). Our findings of state variability in development and guidance echo their concerns.

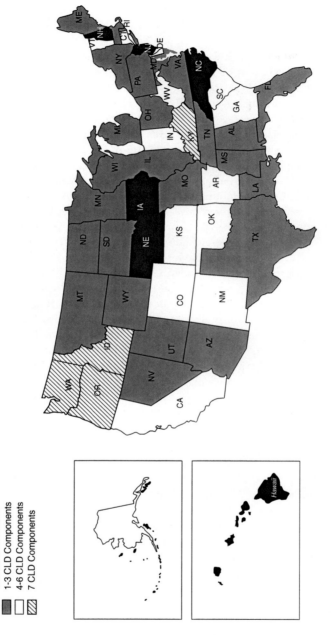

Figure 4.1 State Guidance on CLD Learners.

Inclusion of Cultural Responsive Instruction in RTI Models

Our examination of RTI guidance materials and content area assessment and instructional guidelines for the inclusion of CRI with CLD learners revealed that very few states incorporated detailed guidance to accommodate the needs of CLD learners. The widespread use of RTI in pre-referral intervention and assessment processes reflect a need for the inclusion of guidance for instruction of CLD learners if RTI is to be used (as noted by 36 states on their SPPs) to reduce disproportionality. The importance of culturally responsive instruction has been highlighted by many researchers (e.g., Artiles, Kozleski, Trent, Osher and Ortiz 2010; Artiles and Trent 1994; Harry and Klingner 2006; Klingner and Edwards 2006). Klingner and Edwards (2006) have noted that the use of research-based interventions in RTI models must include consideration of "with whom, by whom, and under what conditions" the intervention has been effective. Specifically, they recommended that RTI practitioners examine the ecological validity of assessments, progress monitoring tools and interventions that are utilized in the RTI process to ensure that they are appropriate for CLD learners. Klingner and Edwards cautioned that without consideration of these contextual factors in the RTI process, CLD youth will continue to be overrepresented in special education. Our findings that most states did not provide explicit guidance for instruction of CLD learners in their RTI materials or assessment and content area instructional guides indicate a need to refocus efforts to address the needs of CLD learners and provide culturally responsive instruction at all tiers of intervention. The increasing numbers of students who are culturally and linguistically diverse demand that educators take notice and proactively address education equity issues (Bakken and Smith 2011; Brown 2004; Cartledge and Kourea 2008). Klingner et al. (2005) noted that culturally responsive education systems must address disproportionality by "producing resources/tools and supporting stakeholders in the creation of educational systems that are responsive to culture and diversity" (8).

The Need for Context Specific CLD Guidance in RTI Models

We present two case study vignettes drawn from two larger qualitative studies (i.e., Menda 2014; Kressler 2014, respectively) that illustrate the need for the integration of culturally responsive instructional methods in RTI models if RTI implementation is to realize its promise in reducing disproportionality. The first case study (Menda 2014) provides an example of the need for explicit consideration of language acquisition processes for English language learners (ELLs) within RTI implementation.

Case Study A

This qualitative study examined the process used by a group of teachers in one urban elementary school as they made data-based decisions of RTI data for their ELL students. Semi-structured interviews with teachers (N = 9) along with observations (N = 4) of data decision-making meetings were analyzed through a grounded theory approach to learn more about the process. All teachers interviewed were ESOL certified and implementing RTI in their classrooms. According to the majority of the participants, ELL students' success and challenges as measured by progress monitoring assessments were tied to the teachers' perceived level of parental support, and not to the role of the teacher in student learning. A quote from an interview with a second grade teacher illustrates this point:

> I think one of the basic challenges is that at the house – at home, they don't have anybody that could give a good example how English is spoken, so they're non-English speaking and not very well educated. So I think that's one of the biggest challenges that they have. And their vocabulary is low, and they're not – especially in this area, they don't get exposed to a lot of different experiences.

Specifically, the following quote is an example of how the teachers perceived parents' lack of English proficiency as the culprit for the academic struggles of English Language Learners (ELLs):

> So [the] main challenge they're working with mainly is home language. Their parents, a lot of their parents, like my students, I can't even talk to the parents one on one at all. We have to get an interpreter because a lot of their parents don't speak English. So the main challenge is they have no one [at] home to assist them with their classwork.

For the majority of the teachers, the responsibility for ELLs' challenges in school rested on the parents' ability to support their child's education. For most teachers, the overarching belief was that parents were unsupportive because they did not speak enough English, their level of education was low and/or that they did not have the economic means to provide students with enriching experiences. The first grade teacher reinforced this notion of non-English speaking families as the problem with student's academic performance. She believed that the challenges for ELLs are inherent and that these students are born with a delay:

> But I think it's – has to do with the geographical makeup of this area, and the type of clientele we're serving. In the . . . population, I don't think that children have a lot of parental support and are not – you know, developmentally they're just behind, it seems, from birth.

Across all interviews, students' academic progress as measured by the RTI progress monitoring system was attributed to the level of parental input. By placing the condition of success on the home, teachers (indirectly) cast the home environment as the critical component for ELLs academic growth, instead of focusing on the teaching they are doing in the classroom. This perhaps unintentional removal of responsibility for both success and failure contributed to the teachers'

60   *Wendy Cavendish et al.*

lack of agency in the process. The focus of the study was to examine the relationship between teachers' knowledge of language development and its manifestation in RTI practice. Teachers' strong beliefs that their ELLs' success was contingent upon what they perceived to be adequate parental support mitigated their ability to take responsibility for students' academic growth and/or failures. The teachers in the study, for the most part, pointed towards external variables as the reason for their students' lack of academic success. Teachers' beliefs reflected how a rigid implementation of RTI limited their ability to make decisions and also influenced their beliefs about language and parents. The theme that emerged overall was that students' and parents' limited English was a hindrance to their ELLs' ability to succeed academically.

Case Study B

The second case study (Kressler 2014) examined urban high school teachers understanding and use of data to make educational decisions for CLD students within an RTI framework. The six teachers in this study were located in two diverse high schools within an urban school district in the Southeast. These schools and teachers were selected because of their self-selection of RTI support from the school district. They relied upon the district's personnel and school administrators to provide them with the training and understanding they needed to implement RTI and provide data-based decisions for their CLD students. Both high schools rolled out RTI in one department within their schools. The case study presented is from data collected at School A where they chose the English Speakers of Other Languages (ESOL) department to receive RTI. The student population at this high school was 84% Hispanic at the time of the study. The case study outlines the teachers' perceptions of RTI and data-based decisions for their CLD students.

Teachers in the study indicated that although they were part of the RTI team they were not quite sure what RTI was all about. In particular, teachers that were not appointed as the leaders of the RTI efforts (i.e., non-special education teachers) indicated that they had very little understanding of the concept of RTI. One teacher in the ESOL department stated, "I don't really like, I know that I do RTI, but like . . . that word, 'RTI', I don't use it, but I know that I use the strategies of RTI. It's just that I don't really know what RTI is all about, but I'm sure that I do use some of the strategies that are there." This quote illustrates that teachers didn't have a clear and focused understanding of RTI in general, not to mention for the purpose of equity for their CLD students. A reason for this limited understanding may be due to the minimal amount of district support these particular teachers received. The school was not receiving the ongoing feedback and support they needed to implement and understand RTI in a manner that would truly support CLD student achievement and instructional equity.

Nevertheless, teachers were still required to make data-based decisions despite the lack of training and support from the district and school administration. Given the current context of the accountability and value-added rating era (FLDOE 2016; USDOE 2011), teachers were incentivized to use data to identify students

Promise and Perils in Special Education   61

that were at risk of failing high stakes test. Teachers were acutely aware that if students did not perform well on high stakes standardized tests the consequences would land squarely on their shoulders. As one teacher stated, "It affects us. . . . It affects your grade as a teacher and your bonuses." Understandably, teachers were encouraged to focus their RTI efforts in a manner that would support a few struggling students but provide the most gains for teachers and the school. When asked about students targeted for Tier II intervention, one teacher explained why they chose ESOL students:

> ESOLs levels 1 through 4 [are the population we are working with]. Why? Because they are the learners who are struggling most in our school by population . . . at least the ESE (special education) kids have a shelter or an umbrella to catch them if they don't pass . . . or they don't meet graduation requirements on time. Because they are able to stay here additional years and they can waiver their FCAT [state test] if they don't pass it. But unfortunately, the ESOL kids don't have that window so that is who suffers the most because of their lack of success, in other words. So that's the effect, and they affect so many things. FCAT scores, retentions, graduation rates, they affect everything because if you don't pass the FCAT then they don't graduate. And so that not only affects their FCAT scores, they affect our retake scores and then they affect our graduation rate, so it's, you know, it's continuous whammy, whammy, whammy. We get hit with them three times in a row.

It's evident that teachers viewed RTI as Tier II interventions geared toward improving the test scores of a group of students that had the greatest impact on school and teacher ratings. Teachers also viewed RTI in strict terms of interventions (i.e., test prep) that should help students make the most gains on high stakes standardized assessments. Thus, accountability pressures created a situation in which teachers diverted their focus away from supporting all students through equitable access to high-quality instruction (i.e., Tier I settings) to the single focus on test preparation in Tier II settings.

Teachers were clearly concerned about providing safeguards for students that were not passing the state's high stakes exams. Because this is the high school setting, there was a sense of urgency to provide safeguards quickly. As the teacher earlier quoted explained, ESOL students did not have "a shelter or umbrella to catch them" if they didn't meet the demands of the high stakes exam. Consequently, they decided to look into referring these students to special education. She explains:

> with the ESOL population, we are going to focus this year on CELLA (Comprehensive English Language Learning Assessment) scores and FCAT scores at the end of the year. We will look at all 9th and 10th grades, and any 9th and 10th grader who did not increase an ESOL level and did not pass the FCAT in 10th grade, or 9th grade for that matter, will be um, looked at for possible referral . . . for the 11th grade year. Why? Because that will give us enough time to test and see if they are eligible. Why? Because that means that they

62 *Wendy Cavendish et al.*

have already gone through the RTI process, we've already you know, implemented the strategies, and we don't want to wait, because what's happening is that they are not graduating.

There was genuine concern about the graduation chances of students due to time constraints embedded in high school settings and the low passing rate of ELLs on high stakes tests. Interestingly, this teacher viewed special education as a safe haven for these students. Considering the fact that ELLs are overrepresented in special education in some states (Artiles, Rueda, Salazar and Higareda 2005), it's concerning that this school considered using RTI to fast track these students into the program. This approach, due to accountability pressures, contradicts the promise of RTI to reduce disproportionality in special education. Teachers reverted to the status quo of labeling at-risk students instead of re-examining instructional strategies to meet their needs.

Conclusions

In the United States, states that report disproportionate representation of students of color in special education are required to provide corrective actions. Our findings reveal that 72% of states that reported disproportionality designated RTI as an improvement activity. However, one of the intended foundational elements (as reported in H.R. 1350) of the RTI provision in IDEA (2004) was the inclusion of culturally responsive instruction for diverse learners. We hypothesized that those states that identified RTI as an improvement activity to address disproportionality would report more developed RTI models and would provide more guidance concerning CLD learners. Our findings indicated that although those states did not have more developed RTI models, they were more likely to provide guidance materials that addressed the needs of CLD learners. However, only four states provided in-depth guidance related to culturally responsive instruction. These findings suggest the need for greater federal guidance and continuing support be provided to states as they fully develop their RTI models for large-scale implementation. In particular, our findings indicate a need to refocus efforts to address the needs of CLD learners and provide culturally responsive instruction at all tiers of intervention. This may require states to develop additional guidance documents and training materials for teachers in order to make CRI for CLD learners a priority in the large-scale implementation of Response to Intervention systems.

Teachers are critical to the success of RTI's promise of equity and reduction of disproportionate representation of CLD students in special education. However, without funding, guidance and training from leadership, teachers cannot fulfill the promise of reducing disproportionality and creating more equitable outcomes for CLD students. There is evidence (e.g., Hartlep and Ellis 2012; Thorius and Sullivan 2013) that reveals the discrepancy between the promise of RTI to reduce disproportionality and the RTI models in implementation, as evidenced in the case studies presented (Kressler 2014; Menda 2014). We hold that this is partly due to the fact that teachers are not receiving meaningful and ongoing professional

Promise and Perils in Special Education 63

development that includes the necessary ongoing support for culture change that would lead to the fulfillment of the promise of RTI. As the case studies illustrate, teachers need support to embed CRI into their instructional delivery and meaningful professional development to address deficit-based perspectives. The focus on high stakes test scores in the high school implementing RTI and the lack of training on strengths based language acquisition for the elementary teachers of ELLs suggest that CLD students' needs are not being properly addressed in RTI models as implemented at these two schools.

Specifically, ELLs benefit from evidence-based explicit instruction that is delivered to small groups in a systematic way (Haager and Windmueller 2001; Kamps et al. 2007; Linan-Thompson, Vaughn, Prater and Cirino 2006; Solari and Gerber 2008). As RTI employs these methods, there is potential for ELLs to flourish in RTI systems. However, teachers must be able to understand and interpret their students' data in order to make informed decisions. The current recommendation in the literature calls for the adoption of a problem-solving approach that allows for flexibility, collaboration and discussion revolving around assessment use and the selection of adequate intervention for ELLs as a team based process (Haager 2007; Klingner, Hoover and Baca 2008; Richards-Tutor, Solari, Leafstedt, Gerber, Filippini and Aceves 2013; Rinaldi and Samson 2008). It is imperative for teachers to understand how positive language supports can influence academic growth. If ELLs are to be successful academically, teachers need to understand the importance of language trajectories, and be allowed to collaborate, discuss and advocate on behalf of adequate intervention and practices for ELLs that may be beyond the scope of standard protocol RTI systems. Further, RTI models include parent involvement for tier movement decisions and thus teachers and administrators should participate in collaborative interactions with parents in order to foster a mutual-learning environment in which parents are able to provide a voice instead of being cast as at fault for student failure.

If equity in outcomes for CLD students and a reduction of disproportionality are goals of RTI, there are several changes that need to be made. First, RTI efforts should be fully funded. Rolling out a comprehensive educational service delivery model with the goal of equity cannot be done without proper funding. Educators need training, materials and time for collaboration as well as time for the cultural shift to take place for the success of this endeavor. Further, district personnel and school administrators should be trained on the equity potential of RTI through CRI in order to better support and guide their teachers. Administrators are charged to set the culture of the school (Datnow and Park 2015). Currently, the school culture privileges standardized test score increases over the method used to increase scores. The case studies illustrate what other studies have indicated; teachers are more likely to focus on external factors as an explanation for student performance rather than instructional changes (Orosco and Klingner 2010; Thorius, Maxcy, Macey and Cox 2014). Therefore, teachers need training, ongoing support and modeling on how to modify their instruction to be culturally and linguistically responsive. If teachers were trained and coached on being culturally

64 *Wendy Cavendish et al.*

responsive they could provide instruction that is embedded in the socio-cultural realities of their students, thus increasing student engagement and academic achievement (Dee and Penner 2016). Furthermore, teachers would learn from their students and eradicate the deficit perspective that potentially cripples CLD student academic outcomes (Ladson-Billings 2014).

Finally, focusing on individual differences in student learning and modification of instruction is a goal of RTI that is missing in practice. Without focused attempts to remediate this misdirection, the status quo of CLD students disproportionately placed in special education will continue. By training teachers to become culturally responsive, providing time for feedback and collaboration as well as fully funding educational policies, students will have a better chance at receiving the support and responsive instruction they need to be successful.

References

Artiles, A., Kozleski, E., Trent, S., Osher, D., and Ortiz, A. (2010). Justifying and explaining disproportionality, 1968–2008: A critique of underlying views of culture. *Exceptional Children*, 76(3), 279–299.

Artiles, A. J., Rueda, R., Salazar, J., & Higareda, I. (2005). Within-group diversity in minority disproportionate representation: English Language Learners in urban school districts. Exceptional Children, 71, 283–300.

Artiles, A., and Trent, S. (1994). Overrepresentation of minority students in special education: A continuing debate. *The Journal of Special Education*, 27(4), 410–437.

Bakken, J., and Smith, B. (2011). A blueprint for developing culturally proficient/responsive school administrators in special education. *Learning Disabilities: A Contemporary Journal*, 9(1), 33–46. Retrieved on 23 January 2016 from: http://eric.ed.gov/?id=EJ925532

Berkeley, S., Bender, W., Gregg, L., Saunders, P., and Saunders, L. (2009). Implementation of response to intervention: A snapshot of progress. *Journal of Learning Disabilities*, 42(1), 85–95.

Blanchett, W., Klingner, J., and Harry, B. (2009). The intersection of race, culture, language, and disability: Implications for urban education. *Urban Education*, 44(4), 389–409.

Brown, C. (2004). Reducing the over-referral of culturally and linguistically diverse students (CLD) for language disabilities. *NABE Journal of Research and Practice*, 2(1), 225–243.

Cartledge, G., and Kourea, L. (2008). Culturally responsive classrooms for culturally diverse students with and at risk for disabilities. *Exceptional Children*, 74(3), 351–371. Retrieved on 23 January 2016 from: http://ecx.sagepub.com/content/74/3/351.short

Datnow, A., and Park, V. (2015). DATA USE – For equity. *Educational Leadership*, 72(5), 48–54.

Dee, T., and Penner, E. (2016). *The causal effects of cultural relevance: Evidence from an ethnic studies curriculum*. Cambridge, MA: National Bureau of Economic Research.

Deno, E. (1970). Special education as developmental capital. *Exceptional Children*, 37, 229–237.

Deno, E. (1994). Special education as developmental capital revisited: A quarter century appraisal of means versus ends. *The Journal of Special Education*, 27(4), 375–392.

Donovan, M., and Cross, C. (2002). *Minority students in special and gifted education*. Washington, DC: National Academy Press.

Dunn, L. (1968). Special education for the mildly retarded—is much of it justifiable? *Exceptional Children*, 35, 5–22.

Promise and Perils in Special Education   65

Florida Department of Education (2016). Performance evaluation. Retrieved 23 January 2016 from: http://fldoe.org/teaching/performance-evaluation/

Haager, D. (2007). Promises and cautions regarding using response to intervention with English language learners. *Learning Disability Quarterly*, 30(3), 213–218. Retrieved on 23 January 2016 from: http://eric.ed.gov/?id=EJ786244

Haager, D., and Windmueller, M. (2001). Early reading intervention for English language learners at-risk for learning disabilities: Student and teacher outcomes in an urban school. *Learning Disability Quarterly*, 24(4), 235.

Harry, B., and Klingner, J. (2006). *Why are so many minority students in special education?* New York, NY: Teachers College Press.

Hartlep, N., and Ellis, A. (2012). Just what is response to intervention and what's it doing in a nice field like education? A critical race theory examination of RTI. In J. Gorlewski, J. Porfilio and D. Gorlewski (eds.), *Using standards and high-stakes testing for students; exploiting power with critical pedagogy* 1st edn (pp. 87–108). New York: Peter Lang.

Hosp, J., and Reschly, D. (2003). Referral rates for intervention or assessment: A meta-analysis of racial differences. *The Journal of Special Education*, 37(2), 67–80.

H.R. 1350–108th Congress: Individuals with Disabilities Education Improvement Act of 2004. Retrieved on 23 January 2016 from: https://www.govtrack.us/congress/bills/108/hr1350

IDEA (2004) Individuals with Disability Education Act Amendments of 2004, retrieved 12th October 2016 from http://idea.ed.gov/

Johnson, E., Mellard, D., Fuchs, D., and McKnight, M. (2006). Responsiveness to intervention (RTI): How to do it. [RTI Manual]. National Research Center on Learning Disabilities. Retrieved on 23 January 2016 from: http://eric.ed.gov/?id=ED496979

Johnston, P. (2011). Response to intervention in literacy: Problems and possibilities. *The Elementary School Journal*, 111(4), 511–534.

Kamps, D., Abbott, M., Greenwood, C., Arreaga-Mayer, C., Wills, H., Longstaff, J., Culpepper, M., and Walton, C. (2007). Use of evidence-based, small-group reading instruction for English language learners in elementary grades: Secondary-tier intervention. *Learning Disability Quarterly*, 30(3), 153–168. Retrieved on 23 January 2016 from: http://eric.ed.gov/?id=EJ786240

Klingner, J., Artiles, A., Kozleski, E., Harry, B., Zion, S., Tate, W., Zamora Durán, G., and Riley, D. (2005). Addressing the disproportionate representation of culturally and linguistically diverse students in special education through culturally responsive educational systems. *Education Policy Analysis Archives*, 13(3), 8, 1–43.

Klingner, J., and Edwards, P. (2006). Cultural considerations with response to intervention models. *Reading Research Quarterly*, 41(1), 108–117.

Klingner, J., Hoover, J., and Baca, L. (2008). *Why do English language learners struggle with reading?* Thousand Oaks, CA: Corwin Press.

Kressler, B. (2014). High school teachers' perceptions of data driven decision making within a response to intervention framework. Open Access Dissertations, Paper 1250. Retrieved on 23 January 2016 from: http://scholarlyrepository.miami.edu/oa_dissertations/1250/

Ladson-Billings, G. (2014). Culturally relevant pedagogy 2.0: A.k.a. the remix. *Harvard Educational Review*, 84(1), 74–84.

Linan-Thompson, S., Vaughn, S., Prater, K., and Cirino, P. (2006). The response to intervention of English language learners at risk for reading problems. *Journal of Learning Disabilities*, 39(5), 390–398.

66 Wendy Cavendish et al.

Mellard, D. (2004). Understanding responsiveness to intervention in learning disabilities determination. National Research Center on Learning Disabilities. Retrieved 23 January 2016 from: http://www.nrcld.org/about/publications/papers/mellard.html

Mellard, D., and McKnight, M. (2007). Screening tool for well-described responsiveness-to-intervention models and comparison models. [Brochure]. National Research Center on Learning Disabilities, Lawrence, KS.

Menda, A. (2014). Understanding teachers' interpretation of progress monitoring data for English learners within response to intervention. Open Access Dissertations. Retrieved 23 January 2016 from: http://scholarlyrepository.miami.edu/oa_dissertations/1275/

National Association of State Directors of Special Education (2005). *Response to intervention: Policy considerations and implementation.* Alexandria, VA: NASDE.

National Center for Culturally Responsive Education Systems (2005). Cultural considerations and challenges to response-to-intervention models. Retrieved 23 January 2015 from: http://www.nccrest.org/PDFs/RTI.pdf?v_document_name=Culturally%20Responsive%20

National Center for Education Evaluation and Regional Assistance (2011). National assessment of IDEA overview. Retrieved 23 January 2016 from: http://ies.ed.gov/ncee/pubs/20114026/pdf/20114026.pdf.

National Center on Response to Intervention (2008). *Overview of technical assistance model. U.S. Department of Education: Office of special education programs,* Washington, DC.

National Research Center on Learning Disabilities (2004). Understanding responsiveness to intervention in learning disabilities determination. Retrieved 23 January 2016 from: http://www.nrcld.org/about/publications/papers/mellard.html

Orosco, M., and Klingner, J. (2010). One school's implementation of RTI with English language learners: Referring into RTI. *Journal of Learning Disabilities,* 43(3), 269–288.

President's Commission on Excellence in Special Education (2002). A new era: Revitalizing special education for children and their families, US Department of Education. Retrieved 23 January 2016 from: http://www2.ed.gov/inits/commissionsboards/whspecialeducation/reports/index.html

Richards-Tutor, C., Solari, E., Leafstedt, J., Gerber, M., Filippini, A., and Aceves, T. (2013). Response to intervention for English learners: Examining models for determining response and nonresponse. *Assessment for Effective Intervention,* 38(3), 172–184.

Rinaldi, C., and Samson, J. (2008). English language learners and response to intervention: Referral considerations. *TEACHING Exceptional Children,* 40(5), pp.6–14. Retrieved 23 January 2016 from: http://eric.ed.gov/?id=EJ852652

Skiba, R., Simmons, A., Ritter, S., Gibb, A., Rausch, M., Cuadrado, J., and Chung, C. (2008). Achieving equity in special education: History, status, and current challenges. *Exceptional Children,* 74(3), 264–288. Retrieved 23 January 2016 from: http://eric.ed.gov/?id=EJ817536

Solari, E., and Gerber, M. (2008). Early comprehension instruction for Spanish-speaking English language learners: Teaching text-level reading skills while maintaining effects on word-level skills. *Learning Disabilities Research and Practice,* 23(4), 155–168.

Thorius, K., Maxcy, B., Macey, E., and Cox, A. (2014). A critical practice analysis of response to intervention appropriation in an urban school. *Remedial and Special Education,* 35(5), 287–299.

Thorius, K., and Sullivan, A. (2013). Interrogating instruction and intervention in RTI research with students identified as English language learners. *Reading and Writing Quarterly,* 29(1), 64–88.

United States Department of Education (2011). No child left behind legislation and policies. Retrieved 4 May 2012 from: http://www2.ed.gov/policy/elsec/guid/states/index.html

Vaughn, S., and Fuchs, L. (2003). Redefining learning disabilities as inadequate response to instruction: The promise and potential problems. *Learning Disabilities: Research and Practice*, 18(3), 137–146. Retrieved 23 January 2016 from: http://eric.ed.gov/?id=EJ672967

Vellutino, F., Scanlon, D., and Lyon, G. (2000). Differentiating between difficult-to-remediate and readily remediated poor readers: More evidence against the IQ–Achievement discrepancy definition of reading disability. *Journal of Learning Disabilities*, 33(3), 223–238.

5 Quality and Equity in the Era of National Testing

The Case of Sweden

Anette Bagger

Introduction

This work considers quality and equity in mathematics education and addresses how discursive circumstances on national tests position students, particularly those in need of special support, at both the individual and group levels. Research on equity and quality in mathematics education often focuses on policy and the big picture, school governance, or personal stories. By contrast, the purpose of this text is to connect those perspectives, chiefly by exploring contradictions and connections as shown in discourses on equity and quality in Sweden. Sweden presents an interesting case given the tension between education's goal to promote social justice by providing 'high and equal education for all' and the neoliberal governance of schools where students' choice of school is central (Lundahl 2016). Finally, I offer some conclusions regarding equity in quality and quality in equity as those relationships inform national tests, as well as discussing challenges and possibilities that lie ahead.

Theoretical Underpinnings

In making my case, I draw heavily upon Foucault's theories on discourse and positioning (Foucault 1989, 1994). According to Foucault's thinking, discourse is understood as representations of knowledge and power, all of which govern what it is possible to talk about, for whom, and when, all as systems in which representations of truth become activated (Hall 2001). As such, discourses govern meaning making, practice, and ideas – that is 'the way that a topic can be meaningfully talked about. . . . It also influences how ideas are put into practice and used to regulate the conduct of others' (Hall 2001: 72). In being situated in cultures and spatiotemporal contexts, discourses are recreated and constructed as systems of representations of knowledge put to use by individuals (Hall 2001). Accordingly, positioning is understood as the socially accepted way of talking and acting (Gee 2008); discourse creates knowledge that individuals carry and that governs their positioning (Davies and Harré 2001). In that sense, positioning is understood as

> 'the discursive process whereby selves are located in conversations as observably and subjectively coherent participants in jointly produced story lines'.
>
> (Davies and Harré 2001: 264)

However, individuals can resist predominant discourses and positioning (Foucault, Rabinow and Hurley 1997) through expressions – in action, speech, or text – that are symbolic and can mediate discourse (Norris and Jones 2005). Walkerdine (1998) has contributed to current understandings of positioning as relational, as with Foucault's conceptualisation of power. The practice of national testing is thus understood as a discursive practice, in which systems of knowledge, power, and truth are put into play:

> Discursive practices are characterized by the demarcation of a field of objects, by the definition of a legitimate perspective for a subject of knowledge, by the setting of norms for elaborating concepts and theories. Hence, each of them presupposes a play of descriptions that govern exclusions and selections.
>
> (Foucault 1994: 11)

Foucault (1997) described the way that institutional discourses use power and knowledge to govern individuals as disciplinary power, which works through the examination. For Foucault, the examination is a system in which individuals know that they are being monitored for signs of what is undesirable or deviant, the discovery of which leads to correction by way of disciplinary power. When individuals have internalised that disciplinary power, it becomes self-governing (Foucault 1988).

Quality in Testing

National standardised testing is part of the governance of schools in many countries in recent decades, with international, large-scale testing, such as Trends in International Mathematics and Science Study (TIMSS) and the Programme for International Student Assessment (PISA). The results of these and other studies, in which countries are evaluated and sometimes ranked with other countries, are observed with great interest and concern. These monitoring international surveys, as Pettersson (2008) found, are used for argumentation, points of departure, goals for education, and the legitimisation of policy decisions. One example, PISA, was initiated in the 1980s and has often given rise to an interrogation of and adjustments to school policy (Martens, Knodel and Windzio 2014), including increased standardised testing to improve the quality of education and knowledge (Dreher 2012). The results of such tests are treated as measures of quality of education (Roth, Lundahl and Folke-Fichtelius 2010).

Several researchers have described the governance of schools in terms of achievement, decentralisation, and freedom of choice, particularly in relation to new public management (NPM) and neoliberalism (Antikainen 2006; Hudson 2011; Lundahl 2016; Mendick and Llewellyn 2011; Telehaug, Mediås and Aasen 2006). Hudson (2011) has dubbed the mechanisms in such governance 'soft governance', by which market values challenges the values of social justice and equality, especially in Nordic countries, yet are not so soft at all in reality. On the contrary, they are part of an international marketing trend in education in which

70   Anette Bagger

results, quality, and accountability are interconnected (Rönnberg 2011) and out of which quality becomes discussed in connection with the results of national standardised tests. In response, criticism of these tests, which are conceived to threaten democracy, equity, and diversity, has been expressed by professionals and researchers in Australia, the United States, and the United Kingdom (Dreher 2012). At the same time, monitoring surveys exemplify how measuring knowledge is also an exercise of power, for they form grounds for decisions that affect education goals and redistribute resources and action. Although such power might be difficult to identify, its identification is crucial. As Wrigley (2010: 136) states:

> Assessment is not just the articulation of knowledge about another, it is the assertion and exercise of power. Some of this is explicit, but, like other ways in which power is exercised, there is often a self-concealment.

In that sense, power is exercised in connection to tests when quality of education is connected with achievement, level of knowledge, and national prospects regarding welfare; as the above section states, tests and rankings of results are treated as a measure of the quality of education. In turn, that discourse affects the directions that schools take, that teachers take in mathematics classroom, and in the long run, that individual students make, especially those who do not contribute to the school's brand of quality in the form of high scores.

Equity in Mathematics Testing

Luke (2011) has criticised the kind of transnational governance of education described earlier, including testing practices, for not taking into account the cultural and national stances of educational practice and for affecting policy on equity, in which 'equity is couched in a new technical vocabulary of risk management, market choice, and quality assurance' (367). In a special issue on the equity and marketisation in Australian policy, Rizvi (2013) has noted a related shift in the meaning of the concept of equity, from equal treatment toward equal access to the market of education, which ultimately stresses that, for schools and teachers, such equity-oriented policies 'imply a lack of trust in teachers and schools' (278). The case is similar in Nordic counties, where educational policy has changed during the last half-century by diminishing 'the state's duty to provide equality of opportunity' to instead stress skills and 'output management' (Telhaug, Mediås and Aasen 2006: 279).

When skills and output management are the chief emphases, quality becomes connected to equity, especially for students in need of support. In a well-known example in a book by Hoeg (2003), Peter is a student living in Denmark during the 1950s who, along with this peers, is exposed to psychometric testing, which aims to separate students fit for higher education from ones who are not. Peter wonders

Quality and Equity: The Case of Sweden 71

about the discourse of assessment and its consequences for the children who do not succeed to prove their suitability:

> It's not with bad intent that you assess people; it's only because you have been tested so many times yourself. In the end, there's no other way of thinking. Maybe you don't see it as clearly if you've always managed to achieve what was expected. You see it best if you know that, throughout your whole life, you'll be on the line.
>
> (103)

What Peter experiences might be interpreted through Mendick and Llewellyn's (2011) arguments regarding which children count in mathematics education. Those authors have situated the concepts of quality and equity in a neoliberal framework to claim that it is exceptionally difficult to resist striving toward quality, though underlying values determine whether such an endeavour promotes or threatens equity. The argument resembles that made by Atweh (2011), who stresses that though equity and quality are common expressions in mathematics education policy, they are rarely defined or examined. For some researchers, equity in mathematics education means the right of all individuals to be able to demonstrate successful learning (Gates and Vistro-Yu 2003) with the responsibility of the school to afford such equity by giving all students opportunities to equally access high-quality education.

Lester (2007: 410) views the opportunity to learn in mathematics education as situated in mathematical educational contexts and systems. In that context, students' positioning is important, because opportunities might also be 'taken up by students as a function of their cultural and mathematical histories'.

At a personal level, equity contributes to student empowerment, development, and in turn, their ability and agency to learn (Cobb and Hodge 2007). Other researchers have discussed the use of equity primarily as a right to opportunities in mathematics education. Yet, when equity is narrowed to the opportunity to participate or progress, it hinders the discussion regarding structural inequalities (Mendick and Llewellyn 2011). In response, researchers have endeavoured to change their understandings of the concept of equity. As Mendick and Llewellyn (2011) have pointed out, values underlying a concept exert impact at the personal level, and they argue that the construct of equity determines what questions can be addressed and how students are approached in practice. Boaler (2006) uses the term *relational equity*, which refers to how a school teaches children to respect equality and other students in the mathematics classroom. In research on mathematics, so-called mathematics for all has become the consensus and, according to Valero (2013), relates to social, economic, and cultural progress for individuals and countries. Although mathematics for all emerged as a focus during the 2000s, the designation 'for all' has imposed a normative dimension that includes some but not others, the latter being primarily students of low socioeconomic status.

Exclusion and Testing

Just as students of low socioeconomic status are liable to be excluded from the concept of mathematics for all, exclusion in general has been identified in connection to standardised national tests that have been identified as counteracting social justice and equity in schools (Peters and Oliver 2009). Exclusionary practices related to national tests occur especially in tests with high-stakes elements and accountability and especially affect low-achieving students (Plank and Condliffe 2013; Rustique-Forrester 2005), yet are themselves affected by historical and societal factors (Lester 2007).

Contrary to the spirit of tests that claim to ensure equity by monitoring pupils' achievement and quality of education, tests exclude pupils. As with international monitoring tests such as PISA and TIMSS, students are excluded if their participation in and adaption to tests would threaten the validity of the test. Clausen-May (2007) has demonstrated the dynamic within the PISA and TIMMS, whereby individuals may be excluded on account of 'functional disability', 'intellectual disability', or 'limited assessment language proficiency' (155). Although a special version of the test was available, it has only been offered to students in special schools and not those in inclusive settings. The exclusion of low-performing pupils from tests, in an effort to maintain the schools' ratings (Rustique-Forrester 2005), has been evident in the United Kingdom. That tendency has also been reported in the United States, where testing accountability pressures teachers to focus on pupils who might make a difference to schools' statistics (Berliner and Nichols 2005).

The Case of Sweden: Quality and Equity in a School for All

In Sweden, as in many other countries, there is a worry, expressed in policy, research, and practice, about a decrease in knowledge and equity in the school at large but also specifically in the subject of mathematics. Reports from The Swedish Board of Education reveal that results are decreasing, more students are in need of special support and are not reaching the lowest grade at the same time as fewer students reach the highest grades at the end of school year nine (SIRIS, Skolverket 2012a; Skolinspektionen 2014). These circumstances also bear with them issues of equity since there are differences in achievement depending on gender, class, and ethnicity. A difference is also seen between classes within schools and between schools. Mathematics is the subject in which most students lack a grade at the end of compulsory school. In 2015, 20.4 % of the students lacked a grade in mathematics (SIRIS). A lacking of grade means that the student cannot apply to the public programmes at the secondary high school. These differences are also seen already in the third grade during national tests in mathematics (see for example Skolverket 2010a, 2011a) and a situation where segregation in knowledge between schools, groups of students, and classes is emerging (Skolinspektionen 2014, Skolverket 2012b).

This situation is challenging the vision of providing a school for all. The Swedish school system has long pursued this vision. Gadler (2011) has reviewed shifts in the meaning and heritage of the concept and sums up that the concept can be interpreted to uphold individual rights, ideal development, and the need of individuals and societies to enjoy appropriate socialisation. Generally, the vision centres on every child's right to equal education, though that goal has been interpreted in various ways. When the Swedish school system emerged in 1843, the vision was present, for schools were charged with providing society with competence and with making it possible for all individuals, regardless of class, to study. Yet, the concept of a school for all did not emerge in national curricula until 1980 (i.e., Skolöverstyrelsen 1980).

Bergh (2015) describes how the view of, and responsibility for, quality in Swedish education has changed over the last two decades and has precipitated contradictory expectations for education in the classroom. In referring to the shift in understanding toward new public management and total quality management, Bergh (2015) writes that 'Swedish education reforms of recent decades can be characterised as having created an education for a system, rather than a system for education' (591). Bergh (2015) adds that work related to quality is characterised by a tension between the autonomy and profession of teachers on one hand and, on the other, national control consisting of assessment, results, and a market orientation. The connection between individual results in mathematics and Sweden's future prospects became clear when Minister of Education Jan Björklund spoke about why the Swedish government has put so much money into improving mathematics education:

> Mathematics is much of the base of all science subjects and technology. That's why it's important for all Swedish and, yes, for Sweden's position as an industrial nation. That mathematics is decreasing so heavily in results in the last 20 years is very disturbing, and that's why we make such large investments in math.
>
> (Sveriges radio 2011)

Information about how pupils fare in national tests and schools' quality can be found in the Swedish Board of Education's database, SIRIS. This database is open to all and affords the possibility of making diagrams and comparisons among municipalities and schools. In response to how the database functions and is used, policymakers and school staff in Sweden have to reconcile the aim to promote high levels of knowledge with the service of informing individuals about making appropriate consumer choices. This, however, contrasts with authorities' stated efforts to make education equal and fair for all pupils, a goal that cannot be evaluated along with measures of quality, since they have no measures of experience or lived equality.

It is possible to ascertain, however, how many complaints the Office of the Child and School Student Representative (2016) has received regarding degrading treatment or discrimination, the frequency of cases in which schools have been found to deviate from rules, and claims about damages. Although it is not considered to be discrimination if special needs are not supported accordingly, in some cases

74   *Anette Bagger*

the Swedish Discrimination Act (Diskrimineringslag 2008) applies to insufficient special support. More generally, it protects individuals with disabilities against discrimination and a lack of access in school, as well as all individuals in terms of seven grounds for discrimination: disability, age, gender, gender identity or expression, ethnicity, religion or belief, and sexual orientation. Lack of access is also considered to constitute discrimination in this act. Between 2006 and 2015, the numbers of cases received have increased by 30%, and in 2015, the percentage of schools found to have not followed the rules regarding special support was 53%. That figure can be compared to cases concerning language, which are very few, as statistics from the Swedish Schools Inspectorate's website shows (Table 5.1).

There have been many commentaries on equity and quality in schools in Sweden. One teachers union, Lärarnas Riksförbund (2016), recently reported that teachers think that increased hours in mathematics education have affected teaching and learning. The argument is that teachers are overloaded with work and cannot perform their core assignment. A particular burden from which teachers are thought to need to be freed is pupils in need of support, with individuals ideally working with special education teachers. At the beginning of the report, Lärarnas Riksförbund states: 'Before PISA 2015 a series of measures have been launched to achieve the goal of teaching' (1). That statement implies that monitoring and international assessment are in fact important parts of the end-game of education, and that pupils who need support might be hindering the achievement of that goal. The Confederation of Swedish Enterprises has also recently investigated what is meant by equity in school, and the Research Institute of Industrial Economics

Table 5.1 Mistreatment cases on the grounds of special support and mother tongue in second-language learning, 2006–2015

	2006	2007	2008	2009	2010	2011	2012	2013	2014	2015
Complaints received about special support	297	285	273	331	610	747	779	922	922	994[e]
Shortcomings determined in educational support	104	60	109	258	332	332	432	450	473	528[e]
Complaints received about language	16	17	12	14	15	16	35	25	26	20
Complaints determined in Language	1	3	1	3	-	2	5	5	2	-

Note: e = Adapted in 2015, when schooling was added to the category of special support due to new rules in the Education Act (Skollag 2010).

recently published a policy paper on immigration and Sweden's declining results on PISA (Heller-Sahlgren 2015).

Organisation of the Swedish School System

In Sweden, education is regulated by a common curriculum determined by the government that provides directions in terms of fundamental goals and guidelines for each school. It also contains syllabuses for all subjects, with goals for teaching and for students' knowledge by the time they reach Grades three (age 9), six (age 12), and nine (age 15), all to direct students' development. The goals are to be interpreted and put into practice locally as to choice of method, material, or other contributing goals. The achievement of goals is measured by mandatory national tests in Grades three, six, and nine and throughout Grades six through nine. Although some tests and assessment practices are decided by the teacher and school, the forms for education and special support are regulated in the Education Act (Skollag 2010)), which was revised in 2015 regarding special support. The change was earlier suggested in a government proposal titled *Time for Education: Teachers Work With Support, Special Support and Individual Plans* (*Utbildningsdepartementet 2013*) and decided upon by the conservative government, which by that time had been in power for two terms. In effect, the change reduced the need to document special needs and support. A major argument for the change was that teachers had tremendous workloads stemming from, among other things, increased testing.

Multilingual Students at Risk

Along with many other countries, Sweden has received immigrant children from other countries. Between 2010 and 2015, students aged 5–14 years born abroad rose from 8.0% to 9.9% (Statistics Sweden 2016). Today, the concept of a school for all has been broadened to include all children's right to education regardless of birthplace or first language. In that sense, even if a child is not a Swedish citizen, he or she has the right to go to school, and it is the municipality's responsibility to arrange his or her education (i.e., the Swedish Migration Agency, 2016). Children's right to education is listed in the UN Convention on the Rights of the Child, and is proposed by the current social democratic government of Sweden to become national law (Utredningen om nationella prov 2016: 19). Since 1983, Sweden has maintained an agency tasked with monitoring and advocating children's rights (i.e., the Office of the Ombudsman for Children 2016), and the Swedish Schools Inspectorate also maintains the Office of the Child and School Student Representative (2016) that resolves issues and complaints regarding degrading treatment, harassment, and discrimination at school. Its tasks involve a scrutinising process in which the Swedish Schools Inspectorate can place pressure upon the school, impose a conditional fine, or revoke the licence required to run the school.

In a study in Sweden of how the market of school choice affected groups of students differently, Bunar and Ambrose (2016) detected a trend of segregation. In the

Swedish school system, segregation has been described repeatedly in recent years, in both national and international reports (Skolinspektionen 2014, 2016; Skolverket 2010a). Such a tendency, however, puts the tradition of inclusion and equity, as well as the vision of A school for all into question and even at risk. In response, Swedish municipalities have been encouraged to reverse the upward trend with incentives from the Swedish Schools Inspectorate, which, as mentioned earlier, can accompany fees and guidance from the Board of Education.

After the last social democratic government came into power, governmental decisions have been made to improve the situation for newly arrived pupils and pupils with mother tongues other than Swedish (Utbildningsdepartementet 2015), as well as to compensate with a redistribution of resources by allowing schools with greater needs to receive more resources (Regeringskansliet 2015). Sivenbring (2016) has shown how the focus on continued assessment and results has precipitated a process of student normalisation, in which, for example, students in Grade nine are disciplined by teachers charged with assessing them as part of a practice deemed serious and fair. Such means might provide students with opportunities to advance to upper secondary high school. Sivenbring (2016) further argues that the use of language in connection to assessment might promote exclusion if not adjusted to individual students' needs and prerequisites. Though the stakes of the Swedish system in terms of accountability for testing are not as great as in the United Kingdom and the United States, already in the third grade in Sweden, students with foreign-born parents are excluded from taking tests more often (Skolverket 2010b, 2011a).

It would appear, then, that the subject of mathematics in Sweden carries with it special forms of pedagogical segregation (Hansson 2011). Such segregation might be considered in the context of how pupils with other mother tongues are discussed in public debate, as well as how the Swedish-only discourse in mathematics books and in tests excludes pupils from fair test-taking (Norén 2010). Students with mother tongues other than Swedish talk about themselves as not having an equal opportunity to learn while drawing on the public conversation regarding them as a group (Björklund Boistrup and Norén 2015). Multilingual students' answers on tests are also disparaged during the re-evaluation of tests; research has shown that if their foreignness was displayed, it affected the scores negatively (Hinnerich, Höglin and Johannesson 2015). Such discourses are not unique to Sweden. In a study of Australian public debate concerning students' knowledge in mathematics, students were discussed as if they were products with different 'product values' depending on, for example, language skills and prerequisites for managing mathematics (Lange and Meaney 2014).

The Swedish findings run counter to the country's inclusive approach, with its goals of equity, fairness, and school for all. Furthermore, assessment discourses in mathematics act as gatekeepers regarding which pupils succeed in education or not (Björklund Boistrup, in press). That gatekeeping function might also inform national mathematics testing as early as the third grade, when schools and individuals begin to be sorted (Bagger 2015). Skolverket (2016a) has investigated how immigration affects goal achievement, in which grades are compared in terms of

Quality and Equity: The Case of Sweden   77

the amount of students born abroad. How well education is adapted to these pupils and carried out in regards to language and need for special support, however, is not taken into account. Further investigation of discursive patterns in relation to quality and equity and students' personal experiences in relation to national tests is necessary, especially that with a special focus on multilingual pupils.

Third-Grade National Mathematics Tests in Sweden

The official purpose of national tests is to evaluate the quality of education by measuring pupils' achievement (Björklund Boistrup and Skytt 2011; Ministry of Education and Research 2012). Accordingly, pupils' scores relate to quality of education, and high scores are associated with high-quality education. By the same token, poor achievement might call the school's legitimacy as an educational facility into question. Lundahl and Tveit (2015) discuss how this dual purpose of testing could threaten tests' legitimacy and the legitimacy of teachers as professionals. National tests in mathematics in students' third grade in school were reinstated in Spring 2010, and to date, third graders have taken national tests for seven years, something that might change given suggestions in a recent social democratic governmental investigation on national education assessment (SOU 2016: 25). In short, it is suggested that tests in third grade be eliminated, since the several purposes of national tests have been deemed incompatible. Specifically, the tests are intended to make grounds for grading only and thereby ensure equal assessment, not to evaluate the achievement of goals at the organisational level. Throughout national testing in mathematics in the third grade, a secondary purpose was cited as an important argument for tests and connected to the decreased levels of knowledge on the subject: to identify pupils in need of early support (Skolverket 2012a). Related to this, the following message was posted regarding an assignment given to the Board of Education by the government:

> The government believes that it is important, via early follow-up and other efforts, to provide all students with the possibility of meeting national targets and proficiency requirements. The school must have effective procedures for the continuous monitoring and early appraisal of students' knowledge in order to identify students with difficulties in achieving proficiency.
>
> (Regeringen 2011: 3)

In response, pertinent questions are how testing works, what it does other than test and in what ways tests function as gatekeepers for equity and quality. Moreover, it raises the question of what all of that means for pupils who need special education. A Swedish study of fifth graders' national tests during the previous curriculum (i.e., Lpo94, Skolverket 1994) revealed that the focus shifted from societal responsibility to afford just, equal education to the individual's responsibility to achieve (Lunneblad and Carlsson 2012). A Swedish sample of third graders who took the national tests of the current curricula (i.e., Lgr11, Skolverket 2015b) revealed similar consequences when the focus of testing shifts from learning to

78   *Anette Bagger*

controlling (Bagger 2016a). Another study that investigated reform regarding earlier grades and more testing by following classes of students through their fifth and sixth years revealed that enhanced focus on evaluation plays out in everyday classrooms in ways that cultivate negative pressure, limit teacher autonomy and sharpen the focus on achievement (Olovsson 2014).

Organisation of Third-Grade National Mathematics Tests in Sweden

National tests, administered during the third year of schooling, have been part of a policy reform that included extended and early testing of pupils' knowledge. Some parts of the curricula, but not all, are tested in assessments that evaluate whether pupils have achieved the goals and, in turn, measure the quality of mathematics education. The Swedish Board of Education provides instructions to teachers on how to administer the test and how to approach students. These instructions have a general introduction with key instructions and other special sections for each part of the test depending on information that should be given to students regarding, for example, mathematical content, difficult concepts, and special ways of writing answers or reading tasks. In 2010 and 2011, tests in mathematics consisted of seven parts taken over approximately two months. One part is a cooperative verbal test, whereas in others, tasks are often open-ended. Tests covering the Swedish language were taken during the same time, and nine year olds had to take approximately 17 national tests during the period (Skolverket 2010c, 2011b). Their teachers assess and evaluate the test – if possible, in collaboration with other teachers at the same school. Each test part commences with instructions from the teacher to students about how to act, what to remember, or what to pay attention to. Delivering the instructions can take from 5 to 10 minutes, while the time needed to complete each part can vary from 15 to 40 minutes (Bagger 2016a).

Students with Special Test-Taking Needs

To ensure testing equality, teachers are encouraged to follow the instructions. At the same time, teachers are obliged to adapt tests in appropriate ways so that all pupils can access the test. Compared to 2010 instructions, 2015 instructions stress the purpose of evaluating education, particularly tracking individuals' learning (Bagger, forthcoming). Teachers may translate words or tasks verbally, adapt test-taking times, divide test-taking occasions, explain words and concepts, and help students with reading, writing, and understanding tasks, and students may use a dictionary (Skolverket 2010c, 2015b).

Among third graders in 2010 and 2011, there was an over-representation of pupils with foreign-born parents not taking the mandatory test; this was the group that passed the test less often (Skolverket 2010b, 2011a). The test can be taken in Swedish or English, but newly arrived pupils are not allowed to take the test in a written translation in their language nor to use an explanatory lexicon (Skolverket 2016b). The emphasis of special support with the test language has become more

Quality and Equity: The Case of Sweden   79

concerned with categories of disability. However, that shifting interpretation does not align with changes made in the Education Act (SFS 2010: 800) regarding special support, in which a diagnosis of any kind is not grounds for special support. It is possible that the Discrimination Act (SFS 2008: 567) regarding disabilities and access has led to these changes (Bagger forthcoming).

Equity and Quality in National Testing in Sweden

In what follows, the discourse on equity and quality in connection with test-taking is illustrated with the example of an ethnographic study of third graders who took national tests in mathematics in Sweden 2010 and 2011. The study focused first on teachers' talk and test instructions regarding students in need of support (Bagger 2016a) and second on students' experiences with testing, their needs, and the support offered (Bagger 2016b).

In both studies, conducted during 2010–2011, 102 pupils, their teachers, principals, and special education teachers were filmed, observed, and interviewed. The schools varied in size, location, and socioeconomic standing in the living areas surrounding the schools (Bagger 2015), and the positioning of test takers in need of support and the discourse on support were investigated. In both studies, national tests and the special support given to students are understood as discursive practices. Students and teachers talk about the tests, and students' needs are not conceptualised as individual constructs, ideas, or opinions; rather they were understood as governed by discourses activated in the context, culture, and history of each classroom, school, and in the Swedish educational system in general (Skott, van Zoest and Gellert 2011).

One conclusion from the studies was that whether and how students get support depends on the positioning of the teacher and students, which in turn depends on the predominant discourses activated. Four discourses were identified – namely, a testing discourse, a competitive discourse, a caring discourse, and a supportive discourse. These reflect and strengthen each other by coexisting within the discursive practice of testing (see also Sjöberg, Silfver and Bagger 2015). Results also revealed teachers' positioning as test takers governed by the test, as well as test givers who discipline pupils and govern the testing situation. Both positions are connected to the dual purpose of the test: to evaluate the pupils' education and knowledge. As a test taker, the teacher might be accused of cheating if he or she gives too much help or inappropriate support, for too much help would make the quality of education look better than it is in reality. The supportive and caring discourses position teachers in a way that strengthens their agency to give students' support, whereas the testing and competitive discourses position teachers as people who should guard the tests' equality. Adjustments made beforehand were often but not always connected to those suggested in instructions and were made in order to help students to access the test (for example, enabling students to take the test in a small group with a teacher). This adjustment was made where students needed support with language or because they faced difficulties in reading, writing, or concentrating.

80 *Anette Bagger*

Discourse about how teachers were hindered, if not restricted, from giving support was contrasted with what the teacher felt that pupils might need. On those occasions, the testing discourse mostly represented the caring and supportive discourses. It was easier for the teacher to give support in situations when the caring discourse was stronger, such as when the testing time had expired and the teacher took a student aside to help him or her to complete the task. Nearly all teachers did this on one occasion or another. The caring discourse was also activated more acutely if a student showed a great deal stress or anxiety. The teachers criticised the means of measuring quality, a critique they put in relation to multilingual pupils, whose languages they could not translate. As one teacher said:

> Did the test constructors think about mathematics and second-language learners? How could I explain, because there are many who do not understand the language? Why can't the test be in all the major languages: Arabic, Persian, French, and Spanish?

Another teacher pointed out how students were denied access to mathematical content due to language and because of rules preventing students from helping each other out during a test: 'In an everyday situation, it is possible to use peers to, for example, explain the word *half*.

The testing and competitive discourses created knowledge among pupils about failure and future possibilities to learn and achieve, which positioned students as either winners or losers. Students did not talk about their needs in terms of special support or as an issue about accessing the test or achieving equity. Instead, they emphasised their needs in personal stories about feelings and fantasies about the future. Three positions of need were construed from pupils' discourse about the tests:

- *Position of fear*: Fear of not knowing mathematics, of retrieving knowledge, of losing social group membership, of losing educational progress in life, and of accessing the next grade;
- *Position of hurt*: Feelings of shame, sadness, and discomfort, of not passing the test, and of not having sufficient knowledge; and
- *Position of unfamiliarity*: Not knowing about the skills, mathematical content, or tests' appearance beforehand. (Bagger 2016b)

Although students rarely mentioned needs in the interviews, they talked about future possibilities, stressors, and losses. Their stories were about rather personal experiences, feelings, and notions that the test would affect them in terms of their progress, learning, and social life. Interestingly, every other multilingual student expressed negative pressure, though among native-speaking Swedish students, that concern affected only one in five.

Repositioning is a way of shifting or challenging the limits of discourse and changing power relations (Foucault 1994; Nealon 2008). Repositioning occurs when teachers move between discourses in their supportive actions, by which they

Quality and Equity: The Case of Sweden 81

act from the position of a supportive teacher or caretaker, not a test administrator. During tests, teachers are tasked with maintaining rules and disciplining students; at the same time, they are themselves disciplined by the governing documents and instructions for the test. In the testing situation, test equality is balanced against students' equity, thereby causing stress and frustration among both students and teachers. Resistance against discourse therefore takes place outside the test setting, by supporting students and helping them to finish tasks and thereby ensuring student equity. One conclusion is that when teachers can use their agency in supportive situations during tests and are guided by their professional knowledge about students' needs, both equity and quality in the testing situation can be achieved. Similar patterns in which teachers demonstrate loyalty to students have been shown in research from Australia (Connor 2008), England (Putwain, Connors, Woods, and Nicholson 2012), Finland (Kasanen and Räty 2007), and Norway (Mausethagen 2013).

Interviews with teachers and students revealed that they generally focused on efforts to obtain high scores and as few errors as possible, along with seriousness, individual responsibility, and achievement. The tests can therefore be said to shift the focus from learning to controlling. Participants were disciplined in testing situations, in which they strived to be loyal to the instructions and their common task to manage the test as best as possible and to be good test takers and test administrators. This dynamic might be explained in terms of Foucault's concept of the intensification of power (Nealon 2008), in which institutional disciplinary power is internalised so that individuals begin to strive to manage the test in the best interest of the school as an institution. A nine-year-old student's statement illustrates how the idea of quality as constituting high achievement represents an individual responsibility to the institution and even the country:

> Because there has been a lot of discussion on TV . . . that pupils have worse . . . what is it called . . . worse answers . . . how do you say it . . . worse answers on the tests, not right. The grades are beginning to be IG [i.e., fail] and G [i.e., pass] . . . and it should not need to be like that . . . so they might . . . the municipality might check up and such.
>
> (Bagger 2015: 79)

If test scores are equivalent to quality, then the means of measuring the scores will be guarded. In that sense, the tests can be described in terms of Foucault's (1980) concept of apparatus, in which the test is a system for evaluating and creating knowledge. For the apparatus to function, many technologies have to operate at different levels: for example, governmental decisions, work done by the Swedish Board of Education and test constructors in developing the test, test instructions, self-evaluations, assessment, reassessment, and that the test giver and test taker do their best during the test occasion. If some of those technologies do not work, then they need to be repaired; otherwise, the knowledge created is called into question and the legitimacy of the test threatened. If test takers do not succeed, then they may have to practise test-taking; if test administrators do not work, then it

82   *Anette Bagger*

could be necessary to implement external evaluations of the assessment; and if the test does not work, then another system for creating knowledge about students' learning and knowledge needs to be put in place. The investigation of national tests (Utredningen om nationella prov 2016) recommends that tests be omitted in the third grade in favour of some kind support for teachers in assessing students' knowledge and to computerise the tests and correct them externally, instead of by students' individual teachers. Support for teachers for assessment will be mandatory during students' first year (Skolverket 2016c)

The dual purpose of the test positions the teacher as a test taker, whose teaching is evaluated, and as a test administrator, with the responsibility to discipline test takers. The effects on pupil's scores, on the teacher's professional legitimacy and possibilities of being supportive in situations in which support is needed challenges equity. In practice, that dynamic is demonstrated in pedagogical dilemmas in testing situations in which teachers have tried to balance test equality with students' equity. That dilemma emerges especially among pupils in need of support and multilingual pupils with mother tongues other than Swedish. Among the conclusions that can be drawn, those pupils are disadvantaged and possibly hindered in their development in mathematics. A further interpretation is that both quality and equity are threatened. In other words, these students have low quality of equity and low equity within the quality measured. As such, it remains unclear whether both can be considered and negotiated in connection with the tests.

The Future of Quality and Equity in Testing in Sweden

The question of what a test does besides contribute to the ranking of schools and the assessment of pupils' levels of knowledge is connected to issues of quality and equity. For pupils in need of support as a group – even a heterogeneous group – quality as achievement creates a focus on how many students do not reach the lowest level and how much bigger that group of students is compared with last time or compared with other countries. The situation becomes a matter of equity when the needs of pupils within that group are considered. Tests can be important occasions for detecting inequalities in and between school systems, though the discourse on quality reflected in results also governs countries and schools by a process that is subtly forceful. As in the case of national testing in third-grade mathematics in Sweden (Bagger 2015), the competitive and testing discourses triumph over discourses of caring and support both between and within countries. How pupils who need support are affected on an indirect and personal level can thereby be foreseen.

Testing can also be understood as producing inequality by excluding individual pupils and groups of pupils (Berliner and Nichols 2005; Clausen-May 2007; Peters and Oliver 2009; Plank and Condliffe 2013; Rustique-Forrester 2005). I argue that the processes and systemic patterns prompting inequalities need to be evaluated at the local, national, and international levels. If the quality of equity and equity in quality are considered, then it might become possible to combine the educational goals of quality and equity. Atweh (2011) draws on Levinas's argument to posit that if equity and quality are considered to be ethical responsibilities,

Quality and Equity: The Case of Sweden   83

then both could be constructed as complementary and, in turn, both could be achieved. That possibility is especially viable since, as ethical responsibilities, they would complicate questions about what is good and, in fact, necessary to both consider in ethical decision making about policy and in the practice of mathematics education. Several researchers have considered equity and quality simultaneously, for example, Jurdak (2014) has investigated how socioeconomic and cultural aspects affect equity and quality in education. Although he points out that they are different constructs, he recognises them as intertwined and has created a framework for analysing equity in quality across and between countries. Moreover, Plank and Condliffe (2013) studied classroom quality in the context of testing with high stakes for accountability. Therein, emotional support was one of the aspects of quality – that is, something that affects scores in tests. As the authors suggest, what schools should be accountable for should be broadened, and a more holistic assessment system and accountability policy is needed. At the classroom level, Boaler and Staples (2008) have investigated Railside High's way of reducing inequalities while at once heightening achievement. Key in their work was the relational aspects of teaching and the equitable system achieved by, among other things, what Boaler (2006) labels *relational equity* promoted among students. Relational equity seems to be highly similar to what is labelled *likabehandling* ('equal treatment') in Sweden, which, though covered by the Discrimination Act, applies to grounds for discriminations and is not specific to students in need of special education or multilingual students.

It would seem desirable and perhaps also necessary to bring together the research on quality, in which also emotional support is considered as an aspect of classroom quality and research on equity, in which equity is not only about sameness but is also relational. In addition, it is important to consider both of these as ethical issues. I suggest that it is possible to combine the educational goals of quality and equity in order to promote the quality in equity and, at the same time, the equity of quality. To that end, I elaborate upon a new concept: reflecting on the qual(equ)ity of the test. The wording implies that quality and equity during tests with pupils in need of support can be considered simultaneously and as being intertwined. A model for evaluating the qual(equ)ity of testing would need to be adapted to specific settings of schools and countries, yet all models would be informed by research on critical aspects in test-taking regarding equity and quality. Questions regarding for whom tests are best suited and the purpose of tests also need to be posed. Some critical points from the Swedish example and from research referred to here are the students' experiences, accessibility, exclusion, and participation in connection with test-taking.

Test results might shed light on inequalities among groups regarding achievement that might reveal a lack of equity in school. Yet, what do they actually show? If groups of pupils do not receive appropriate adaptations in testing regarding language or supports, or if they are excluded, then do we really know whether they have less (or more) knowledge or if their education has a low (or high) quality? Or do we conclude that the test construction simply does not accommodate all pupils? Accessibility and participation then become core issues for judging the quality of

84 *Anette Bagger*

the equity, whilst evaluating equity in the measured quality. The qual(equ)ity of test-taking could lead to new approaches to national testing, their evaluation, and to how results are used in practice.

References

Antikainen, A. (2006). In search of the Nordic model in education. *Scandinavian Journal of Educational Research*, 50(3), 229–243.

Atweh, B. (2011). Quality and equity in mathematics education as ethical issues. In B. Atweh, M. Graven, W. Secada, and P. Valero (eds.), *Mapping equity and quality in mathematics education* (pp. 63–75). New York, NY: Springer.

Bagger, A. (2015). Is school for everyone? The national test in mathematics at grade three in Sweden (Doctoral thesis). Umeå University, Umeå, Sweden.

Bagger, A. (2016a). Pupil's equity vs the test's equality? Support during third graders National tests in Mathematics in Sweden. In L. Lindenskov (ed.), *Special Needs in Mathematics Education*, *CURSIV No18* (pp. 107–123). Copenhagen: Danish School of Education, Aarhus University.

Bagger, A. (2016b). Pressure at stake: Swedish third graders talk about national tests in mathematics. *Nordic Studies in Mathematics Education*, 21(1), 47–69.

Bagger, A. (forthcoming). The discourse regarding the multilingual student in need of support. MADIF10, Karlstad.

Bergh, A. (2015). Local quality work in an age of accountability: Between autonomy and control. *Journal of Education Policy*, 30(4), 590–607.

Berliner, D.C., and Nichols, S.L. (2005). *Test results untrustworthy: Point of view essay*. Education Policy Research Unit (EPRU), College of Education, Arizona State University.

Björklund Boistrup, L. (In press). Assessment in mathematics education: A gatekeeping dispositive. In N. Bohlmann, A. Pais and H. Straehler-Pohl (eds.), *The disorder of mathematics education*. Dordrecht, The Netherlands: Springer.

Björklund Boistrup, L., and Norén, E. (2015). *A school for all? Political and social issues regarding second language learners in mathematics education*. Proceedings of CIEAEM 67. Retrieved on 10 April 2016 from: http://math.unipa.it/(grim/quaderno25_suppl_2. htm

Björklund Boistrup, L., and Skytt, A. (2011). Ämnesprovet i årskurs 3. In G. Bergius, L. Emanuelsson, and R. Ryding. (eds.), *Matematik – ett grundämne*. (pp. 255–262) Göteborg: Nationellt centrum för matematikutbildning (NCM).

Boaler, J. (2006). Promoting respectful learning. *Educational Leadership*, 63(5), 74–78.

Boaler, J., and Staples, M. (2008). Creating mathematical futures through an equitable teaching approach: The case of Railside School. *Teachers College Record*, 110(3), 608–645.

Bunar, N., and Ambrose, A. (2016). Schools, choice and reputation: Local school markets and the distribution of symbolic capital in segregated cities. *Research in Comparative and International Education*, 11(1), 34–51.

Child and School Student Representative (2016). About the child and school student representative. Retrieved on 8 April 2016 from: http://beo.skolinspektionen.se/en/ English-Engelska/About-BEO-/

Clausen-May, T. (2007). International mathematics tests and pupils with special educational needs. *British Journal of Special Education*, 34(3), 154–161.

Cobb, P., and Hodge, L.L. (2007). Culture, identity, and equity in the mathematics classroom. In S.N. Nasir and P. Cobb (eds.), *Improving access to mathematics: Diversity and equity in the classroom* (pp. 159–164). New York, NY: Teachers College Press.

Quality and Equity: The Case of Sweden 85

Confederation of Swedish Enterprises (2016). *Förbättrad Välfärd. Likvärdighet i den Svenska Skolan.* Online HTTP: <http://www.svensktnaringsliv.se/migration_catalog/Rapporter_och_opinionsmaterial/Rapporter/likvardighet-i-svenska-skolanpdf_637909.html/BINARY/Likv%C3%A4rdighet%20i%20svenska%20skolan.pdf> (accessed 8 April 2016).

Connor, K.E. (2008). You choose to care: Teachers, emotions and professional identity. *Teaching and Teacher Education*, 24(1), 117–126.

Davies, B., & Harré, R. (2001). Positioning – The discursive production of self. In: M. Wetherell, S. Taylor, & S.J. Yates (eds), Discourse theory and practice: a reader (pp. 261–271). London: Sage.

Diskrimineringslag. (2008). SFS 2008:567. [Discrimination Act] Stockholm, Sweden: Kulturdepartementet.

Dreher, K. (2012). Tests, testing times and literacy teaching. *Australian Journal of Language and Literacy*, 35(3), 334–352.

Foucault, M. (1980). Prison talk. In C. Gordon (ed.), *Power/knowledge: Selected interviews and other writings 1972–1977* (pp. 109–133). New York, NY: Pantheon Books.

Foucault, M. (1988). *Technologies of the self: A seminar with Michel Foucault.* In L. H. Martin, H. Gutman, and P. H. Hutton (eds.). Amherst, MA: University of Massachusetts Press.

Foucault, M. (1989). *Power/knowledge: Selected interviews and other writings 1972–1977.* Brighton, East Sussex: Harvester Press.

Foucault, M. (1994). *Power.* London, UK: Penguin.

Foucault, M. (1997). *Discipline and punish: The birth of the prison.* Harmondsworth: Penguin, Peregrine Books.

Foucault, M., Rabinow, P., and Hurley, R. (1997). *Essential works of Foucault, 1954–1984. Vol. 1, Ethics: Subjectivity and truth.* New York, NY: New Press.

Gadler, U. (2011). En skola för alla – gäller det alla? Statliga styrdokuments betydelse i skolans verksamhet (Doctoral thesis). Växjö Universitet.

Gates, P., and Vistro-Yu, C.P. (2003). Is mathematics for all? In A.J. Bishop, M.A. Clements, C. Keitel, J. Kilpatrick and F.K.S. Leung (eds.), *Second international handbook of mathematics education* (pp. 31–73). Dordrecht, the Netherlands: Springer.

Gee, J.P. (2008). *Social linguistics and literacies: Ideology in discourses.* New York: Routledge.

Hall, S. (2001). Foucault: Power, knowledge, and discourse. In M. Wetherell, S. Taylor and S.J. Yates (eds.), *Discourse theory and practice: A reader* (pp. 72–81). London, UK: Sage.

Hansson, Å. (2011). Ansvar för matematiklärande: Effekter av undervisningsansvar i det flerspråkiga klassrummet (Doctoral dissertation). University of Gothenburg, Göteborg, Sweden.

Heller-Sahlgren, G. (2015). *Invandringen och Sveriges resultatfall i PISA.* IFN Policy Paper no. 71.

Hinnerich, B., Höglin, E., and Johannesson, M. (2015). Discrimination against students with foreign backgrounds: Evidence from grading in Swedish public high schools. *Education Economics*, 23(6), 660–676.

Hoeg, P. (2003). *De kanske lämpade.* Stockholm: Norsteds förlag.

Hudson, C. (2011). Evaluation: The (not so) softly-softly approach to governance and its consequences for compulsory education in the Nordic countries. *Education Inquiry*, 2(4), 671–687.

Jurdak, M. (2014). Socio-economic and cultural mediators of mathematics achievement and between-school equity in mathematics education at the global level. *ZDM*, 46(7), 1025–1037.

Kasanen, K., and Räty, H. (2007). "Do the very best you can": The third-grade class test. *Social Psychology of Education*, 11(2), 193–208.

86   Anette Bagger

Lange, T., and Meaney, T. (2014). It's just as well kids don't vote: The positioning of children through public discourse around national testing. *Mathematics Education Research Journal*, 26(2), 377–397.

Lärarnas Riksförbund. (2016). *Tid för matematik, tid för undervisning. Sveriges lärare om utökad undervisningstid och kompetensutveckling i matematik.* [Teacher Union Report]. Retrieved on 8 April from: http://mb.cision.com/Public/421/9903533/82793a58a1766d3e.pdf

Lester, F. K. (2007). Culture, race, power, and mathematics education. In F. K. Lester (ed.), *Second handbook of research on mathematics teaching and learning: A project of the National Council of Teachers of Mathematics, vol. 2.* (pp. 405–433). Charlotte, NC: Information Age.

Luke, A. (2011). Generalizing across borders. *Educational Researcher*, 40(8), 367–377.

Lundahl, C., and Tveit, S. (2015). Att legitimera nationella prov i Sverige och i Norge: En fråga om profession och tradition. *Pedagogisk forskning i Sverige*, 19(4–5), 297–323.

Lundahl, L. (2016). Equality, inclusion and marketization of Nordic education: Introductory notes. *Research in Comparative and International Education*, 11(1), 1–10.

Lunneblad, J., and Carlsson, M.A. (2012). Performativity as pretence: A study of testing practices in a compulsory school in Sweden. *Ethnography and Education, 7*(3), 297–310.

Martens, K., Knodel, P., and Windzio, M. (2014). Outcomes and actors' reactions on internationalization in education policy: A theoretical approach. In K. Martens, P. Knodel and M. Windzio (eds.), *Internationalization of education policy: A new constellation of statehood in education?* (pp. 1–34). Basingstoke, UK: Palgrave Macmillan.

Mausethagen, S. (2013). Talking about the test. Boundary work in primary school teachers interactions around national testing of student performance. *Teaching and Teacher Education*, 36, 132–142.

Mendick, H., and Llewellyn, A. (2011). Does every child count? Quality, equity and mathematics with/in with neoliberalism. In B. Atweh, M. Graven, W. Secada and P. Valero (eds.), *Mapping equity and quality in mathematics education* (pp. 49–62). Dordrecht, the Netherlands: Springer.

Ministry of Education and Research. (2012). *Fler nationella prov i vår.* Press release, 30 October 2008. Retrieved 1 September 2013 from The Ministry of Education and Research.

Nealon, J.T. (2008). *Foucault beyond Foucault: Power and its intensifications since 1984.* California: Stanford University Press.

Norén, E. (2010). Discourses and agency in a multilingual mathematics classroom. *Nordic Educational Research Working Paper Series*, 1, (1–16). Stockholm, Sweden. Stockholm University Press.

Norris, S., and Jones, R. H. (2005). *Discourse in action: Introducing mediated discourse analysis.* London, UK: Routledge.

Olovsson, T.G. (2014). The development of learner identities in relation to major reforms in the Swedish compulsory school. In A. Rasmussen, J. Gustafsson and B. Jeffrey (eds.) *Performativity in education: An international collection of ethnographic research on learners' experiences* (pp. 283–300). Painswick, UK: EandE.

Ombudsman for Children in Sweden (2016). *About the Ombudsman for children in Sweden.* Retrieved on 8 April 2016 from: http://www.barnombudsmannen.se/om-webbplatsen/english/

Peters, S., and Oliver, L.A. (2009). Achieving quality and equity through inclusive education in an era of high-stakes testing. *Prospects: Quarterly Review of Comparative Education*, 39(3), 265–279.

Quality and Equity: The Case of Sweden   87

Pettersson, D. (2008). *Internationell kunskapsbedömning som inslag i nationell styrning av skolan* (Doctoral thesis). Uppsala University, Uppsala, Sweden.

Plank, S.B., and Condliffe, B.F. (2013). Pressure of the season. *American Educational Research Journal*, 50(5), 1152–1182.

Putwain, D.W., Connors, L., Woods, K., and Nicholson, L.J. (2012). Stress and anxiety surrounding forthcoming standard assessment tests in English schoolchildren. *Pastoral Care in Education*, 30(4), 289–302.

Regeringen. (2011). Uppdrag om nationella prov, (U2011/6543/S). Stockholm: Utbildningsdepartementet. [Governmental assignment]. Retrieved on 11 February 2016 from: http://www.regeringen.se/contentassets/5a353eeaadc94d6c9abb1e0274865356/ uppdrag-om-nationella-prov

Regeringskansliet. (2015). PM. *Statsbidrag ska riktas till skolor med störst behov* [Governmental pressrelease]. Retrieved on 1 September 2015 from: http://www.regeringen.se/ pressmeddelanden/2015/07/statsbidrag-ska-riktas-till-skolor-med-storst-behov/

Rizvi, F. (2013). Equity and marketisation: A brief commentary. *Discourse: Studies in the Cultural Politics of Education*, 34(2), 274–278.

Rönnberg, L. (2011). Exploring the intersection of marketisation and central state control through Swedish national school inspection. *Education Inquiry*, 2(4), 695–713.

Roth, A.-C.V., Lundahl, C., and Folke-Fichtelius, M. (2010). *Bedömning i förskolans och skolans individuella utvecklingsplaner*. Lund: Studentlitteratur.

Rustique-Forrester, E. (2005). Accountability and the pressures to exclude: A cautionary tale from England. *Education Policy Analysis Archives*, 13(26), 2–41.

Sivenbring, J. (2016). *In the eye of the beholder: Young people on assessment in school* (Unpublished doctoral dissertation). University of Gothenburg, Göteborg, Sweden.

Sjöberg, G., Silfver, E., and Bagger, A. (2015). Disciplined by tests. *Nordic Studies in Mathematics Education*, 20(1), 55–75.

Skollag (2010). SFS 2010:800. [Education Act] Stockholm, Sweden: Utbildningsdepartementet.

Skolinspektionen (2014). *Rapport 2014:01 Kommunernas resursfördelning och arbetet med segregationens negativa effekter i skolväsendet*. [Report from The Board of Education regarding municipalities work against segregation]. Retrieved 10 April 2016 from: https://www.skolinspektionen.se/globalassets/publikationssok/granskningsrapporter/ kvalitetsgranskningar/2014/segregation/kvalgr-segregation-slutrapport.pdf

Skolinspektionen (2016). *Ökat fokus på skolor med större utmaningar*. Skolinspektionens erfarenheter och resultat 2015. Regeringsrapport 2016. Diarienummer: 01-2015:6905

Skolöverstyrelsen (1980). *Läroplan för grundskolan, Lgr80*. Stockholm: Liber.

Skolverket. (1994). *Läroplan för det obligatoriska skolväsendet, förskoleklassen och fritidshemmet Lpo94*. Stockholm: Skolverket: Fritzes.

Skolverket. (2010a). *Rustad att möta framtiden? PISA 2009 om 15 åringars läsförståelse och kunskaper i matematik och naturvetenskap* (Rapport 353). Stockholm: Fritzes.

Skolverket. (2010b). *Ämnesproven i grundskolans årskurs 3. En redovisning av genomförandet 2010*. Stockholm.

Skolverket. (2010c). *Provinstruktioner till det nationella provet i matematik i det tredje skolåret år 2010*. Stockholm: Skolverket.

Skolverket. (2011a). Ämnesproven i grundskolans årskurs 3. En redovisning av genomförandet 2011. Stockholm: Skolverket.

Skolverket. (2011b). Provinstruktioner till det nationella provet i matematik i det tredje skolåret år 2011. Stockholm: Skolverket.

Skolverket. (2012a). *15-åringars läsförståelse och skolans likvärdighet har försämrat*. Press release.

88 Anette Bagger

Skolverket. (2012b). *Likvärdig utbildning i svensk grundskola? En kvantitativ analys av likvärdighet över tid (Rapport 374)*. Stockholm: Fritzes.

Skolverket. (2015a). *Läroplan för grundskolan förskoleklassen och fritidshemmet 2011* (Reviderad 2015). Stockholm: Skolverket.

Skolverket. (2015b). *Provinstruktioner till det nationella provet i matematik i det tredje skolåret år 2015*. Stockholm: Skolverket.

Skolverket. (2016a). *Invandringens betydelse för skolresultaten: En analys av utvecklingen av behörighet till gymnasiet och resultaten i internationella kunskapsmätningar*. Skolverkets aktuella analyser 2016. Stockholm, Sweden: Skolverket.

Skolverket. (2016b). *Genomföra nationella prov med nyanlända elever* [Information on the Board of Education's website for national tests for newly arrived pupils]. Retrieved on 10 April 2016 from: http://www.skolverket.se/bedomning/nationella-prov/genomforande/nyanlanda-elever-1.193063

Skolverket. (2016c). *Bedömningsstöd i matematik*. Retrieved on 10 April 2016 from: http://www.skolverket.se/bedomning/bedomning/bedomningsstod/matematik

Skott, J., van Zoest, L., and Gellert, U. (2011). Theoretical frameworks in research on and with mathematics teachers. *ZDM*, 45(4), 501–505.

SOU (2016:19) *Barnkonventionen blir svensk lag*. [Governmental investigation]. Retrieved on 8 April 2016 from: https://riksdagen.se/sv/Dokument-Lagar/Utredningar/Statens-offentliga-utredningar/sou-2016–19-_H4B319/.Stockholm, Sweden: Government Press.

SOU (2016:25) *Likvärdigt, rättssäkert och effektivt – ett nytt nationellt system för kunskapsbedömning*. [Governmental investigation], Stockholm, Sweden: Government Press.

Statistics Sweden (2016). *Foreign born persons by region, age in ten year groups and sex. Year 2001–2015*. Retrieved on 8 April 2016 from: http://www.statistikdatabasen.scb.se/pxweb/en/ssd/START__BE__BE0101__BE0101E/UtrikesFoddaTotNK/?rxid=d6b41824-b4e8–40dc-858f-15f56083e9a5> (accessed 8 April 2016).

Sveriges radio (6 september 2011). Utbildningsministern intervjuas om satsningen.

Swedish Migration Agency (2016). *School. Can I go to School?* Online HTTP: <http://www.migrationsverket.se/English/Private-individuals/Protection-and-asylum-in-Sweden/Children-seeking-asylum/With-parent-/After-registration/School.html> (accessed 8 April 2016).

Telhaug, A.O., Mediås, O.A., and Aasen, A. (2006). The Nordic model in education: Education as part of the political system in the last 50 years. *Scandinavian Journal of Educational Research*, 50(3), 245–283.

Utbildningsdepartementet (2013). *Tid för undervisning – lärares arbete med stöd, särskilt stöd och åtgärdsprogram*. (Prop. 2013/14: 160). [Governmental proposition]. Stockholm: Sweden.

Utbildningsdepartementet (2015). *Uppdrag att genomföra insatser för att stärka utbildningens kvalitet för nyanlända elever och vid behov för elever med annat modersmål än svenska*. (U2015/3356/S). [Governmental assignment], Stockholm: Sweden.

Utredningen om nationella prov (2016). Betänkande. *Likvärdigt, rättssäkert och effektivt – ett nytt nationellt system 2016 för kunskapsbedömning* (SOU 2016:25). [Governmental decision], Stockholm: Utbildningsdepartementet.

Valero, P. (2013). Mathematics for all and the promise of a bright future. In B. Ubux, C. Haser and M.A. Mariotti (eds.), *Proceedings of the European society for research in mathematics education* (pp. 1804–1814). Ankara, Turkey: Middle East Technical University Press.

Walkerdine, V. (1998). *Counting girls out*. London, UK: Falmer.

Wrigley, T. (2010). The testing regime of childhood: Up against the wall. In D. Kassem, L. Murphy and E. Taylor (eds.), *Key issues in childhood and youth studies: Critical issues* (pp. 136–148). New York: Routledge.

Part II
Assessing Deviance

6 Risking Diagnosis?

Race, Class and Gender in the Psychopathologization of Behaviour Disorder

Julie Allan and Valerie Harwood

Introduction

Much of the scientific and educational literature on childhood and youth behavioural disorders appears to ignore, or give cursory attention to, the racialized, classed and gendered aspects of diagnosis of children with behavioural disorders. Minority groups and children from disadvantaged circumstances are over-represented in diagnostic categories relating to behaviour, such as Attention Deficit Hyperactivity Disorder (ADHD) and boys are significantly more likely to be diagnosed with ADHD than girls. In this chapter, we examine the 'risks' associated with 'race', class and gender and detail how these affect diagnosis and the medicalization of behaviour.

Our analysis is drawn from the literature on ADHD and childhood mental disorders, and from statistics from the UK, U.S., Australia and Brazil. We offer critical perspectives on patterns and trends within these contexts. We examine the risk factors of 'race', class and gender and, taking each of these 'oppressions' in turn, we consider what we call a process of psychopathologization that goes on within these arenas through, and as a consequence of, risk. We explore the specific patterns of diagnosis within each of the risk factors and the subsequent practices of spatialization that arise. At one level, following Soja (1996), spatialization concerns all social relations, but here it appears to have very specific – and often segregated – outcomes for the individuals concerned. We draw upon our own work as well as on theoretical perspectives from Disability Studies, Critical Race Theory and sociological analyses of social class to analyse these practices.

'Race': The Risk of Colour

Symonds (1998: 951) suggests that certain groups, for example young Black men in England, may have 'elevated perceptions of dangerousness' attributed to them while Bean, Bingley, Bynoe and Faulkner (1991) note higher rates of emergency detention of Afro-Caribbeans than for white and higher proportions of the former group at each point within the mental health system. 'Race' appears to be associated with a high risk of diagnosis of special educational needs, with particular racial groups at a particularly high risk (Artiles et al. 2010). It is precisely the

92 *Julie Allan and Valerie Harwood*

attention to the dangerousness associated with being Black and failing that both encourages a diagnostic gaze and diverts attention from the role of schools and society in producing inequality (Brantlinger 2006). This attention involves, first, processes of naming trouble at the intersection of 'race' and behaviour and, second, a series of spatializing practices that protect both the individual and others and, in so doing, separate them. We explore these naming and spatializing practices but before doing so, examine some of the available figures on prevalence relating to the diagnosis of special needs and behaviour disorder among minority ethnic groups.

Government figures for England (Department for Education 2014) indicate that in 2014, 27% of Black Caribbean children of compulsory school age were diagnosed with special educational needs (with an additional 4.1% having statements of special educational needs); 21% of Black African children had special needs diagnoses, with a further 3.2% being given a statement. This is compared with 16.5% of White British children with special needs (with a further 3.2% with statements). Gypsy/Roma children and children categorized as Travellers of Irish heritage feature significantly among the special needs population, with 38.9% of Gypsy/Roma children diagnosed with SEN (and 3.6% with a statement) and 49.3% of Travellers of Irish heritage (and 4.9% with statements). Proportions of Indian and Chinese children were much lower at 9.5% (plus 1.8% with statements) and 8.9% (and 2.1% with statements). These relatively recent data provide more nuanced detail on the particular minority groups and their levels of diagnoses of special needs, but do not specify levels of children from each group diagnosed with behavioural difficulties. However, earlier government figures (DFE 2011a & b) suggest a racialized pattern. The greatest 'at risk' group appear to be children of mixed 'race', of whom 34.3% were deemed to have emotional and behavioural difficulties, even though this group did not figure prominently as having a high proportion of SEN diagnoses. An eye-watering 32.2% of Black children were diagnosed with SEN; 39.9% of Black Caribbean children also had this label. Yet 26.6% of Black African children had been diagnosed which is lower than the 27.2% of White children within this population. Asian children again numbered fewer among the population diagnosed with emotional and behavioural difficulties (15.7%) as did Chinese at 13%.

Diagnosis of ADHD among minority ethnic groups is a mixed and indeed changing picture. In the U.S., ADHD prevalence increased from 1998–2000 to 2007–2009 for non-Hispanic white children (from 8.2% to 10.6%) and for non-Hispanic Black children (from 5.1% to 9.5%). In 2007–2009, ADHD prevalence was similar among non-Hispanic white, non-Hispanic Black and Puerto Rican children. ADHD was lower among Mexican children compared with children in the three other racial and ethnic groups (Akinbami, Liu, Pastor and Reuben 2011). Children of mixed 'race' were considered to be at high risk of an ADHD diagnosis with between 8.9 and 14.1% being accorded this status (Centers for Disease Control and Prevention 2011). More recent figures suggest a further increase with 14.6% of non-Hispanic white and 10.6% of non-Hispanic Black children aged 7–12 more likely to be diagnosed with ADHD (National Center for Health Statistics 2015).

Risking Diagnosis? 93

In Australia, national draft guidelines (Royal Australasian College of Physicians 2009) on ADHD admit to not having accurate data on ADHD among Australian Indigenous peoples but indicate that people with ADHD are over-represented in the criminal justice system and that rates of incarceration for Aboriginal and Torres Strait Islander peoples are high. The draft guidelines, advising on cultural sensitivity in the diagnosis of ADHD, point out that it is common for Indigenous children to move around the classroom, checking on one another and advise that this should not be viewed as an indicator of impulsivity. It should be noted, however, that these guidelines have never been formally endorsed following the identification of a conflict of interest violation by one of the U.S. authors whose work was heavily cited. The individual, a psychiatrist, failed to disclose the huge sums of money he had received from drug companies. Rates of diagnoses of Indigenous children from the Brazilian Amazon are cited as 24.5% (Azevedo, Caixeta, Andreda and Bordin 2010), although the difficulty in accessing remote populations to estimate prevalence was acknowledged, as was the case in Australia.

The National Collaborating Centre for Mental Health (2009) suggests that the differential rates among different ethnic groups may reflect different levels of tolerance within cultures for the symptoms of ADHD. This is a conclusion also reached by Tamimi and Taylor (2004), who found vastly different levels of diagnosis of ADHD across different cultures and regarded these as reflecting parental perceptions of what constituted 'normal' behaviour. This cultural distinction was underlined by Rohde (2002) in a study of ADHD in Brazil in which he pointed out that children and adolescents from Latin America are more likely to exhibit emotional distress and to be more talkative and active than their counterparts from Anglo-Saxon cultures and that such tendencies must be taken into account by physicians making assessments. Dwivedi and Banhatti (2005) also point to inconsistency in the way in which assessment criteria are applied and, reviewing several studies, all of which used the Connors rating scale, found diagnosis rates ranging from 16.6% in the UK, 16% in Spain, 15% in New Zealand and 12% in Australia to 3% in China, 4.5% in Scotland and 5.8% in both Brazil and Canada.

Racialized patterns of naming are so entrenched that, according to Walker (2006), who spent four years at the Yakama Indian Health Clinic, there was a 75% probability of children presenting with behavioural problems emerging with an ADHD diagnosis and prescribed stimulants. This pattern is particularly problematic because the deficit ADHD trajectory is at odds with the strength-based perspective of American Indian cultures and fails to acknowledge the importance of intergenerational and family contexts and to recognize that difficult behaviours may be part of 'an individual's and family's life path' (Simmons, Novins and Allen 2004: 61). This is a point also made by Rohde (2002), who, in his study of Brazilian diagnosis of ADHD is critical of the lack of regard for culturally specific behaviours as part of what constitutes normal. Walker (2006: 78) is not overstating in claiming that the indiscriminate translation of ADHD across culture without regard for that culture amounts to a form of colonization of the mind, 'with concepts about themselves and their children quite foreign to their culture' (78).

94   *Julie Allan and Valerie Harwood*

Within the school spaces occupied by special education there are distinctive sites of the psychopathologization of ethnicity. The overrepresentation of ethnic minorities within special education has been well documented (Artiles, Trent and Juan 1997; Graham 2012) and suspicion has turned on special education and its role in preserving education in the face of ever-increasing diversity (Dudley-Marling 2001). In spite of the convincing empirical evidence of the problem of overrepresentation of particular groups of students, Artiles (2004) questions the appropriateness of the focus on 'representation' of any group, the result of which, he argues, is that, 'these students are seen as the passive carriers of categorical markers of difference (e.g., 'race', class, gender) and their assumed nefarious consequences (e.g., low achievement, dropout, delinquent behaviour)' (552). This reductive tendency and the obsession with the physical presences and essences of students generates 'myopic understandings of the role of culture and history' (Artiles 2004: 552) and ensures that agency is denied.

Mind the (Achievement) Gap: Spatializing 'Race'

Paperson's (2010) notion of the ghetto is a helpful way of understanding the particular spatialization of minority groups. The ghetto, according to Paperson, is not, 'a fixed sociological space . . . [but rather] a dislocating procedure' (10) that draws on the, 'apparatus of empire' (21) to justify the separation, through diagnosis, of children from minority ethnic groups. Pathology, according to Paperson, becomes a valuable legitimizing device:

> Pathology generously rewrote us as anticolonialists. Our colonial complicity erased, pathology also erased the violence of this pushout. Thus, the ghettoed subject appears fleetingly as a problem, then vanishes as a person from the official record.
>
> (Paperson 2010: 9)

Cartography, which Paperson describes as a key technology in colonialism, allows for a kind of space shifting which is 'trickster magic' (2010: 10) and which leads to the eradication of those who do not fit: '[t]he trickster is shape shifting again, producing new regions of displacement and mapping these cartographies of nowhere onto bodies' (10). The diagnosis of children and young people from minority ethnic groups with a mental disorder maps both them and their ethnic identity as distinctive, and subsequently distances, dislocates and differentiates them from their peers. This cartographic practice is promoted as benign and as functioning in the best interests of children and young people and their peers.

School failure among minority ethnic groups is spatialized as a gap, yet Ladson-Billings (2006: 3) is critical of the 'achievement gap' that has become part of our common parlance, 'invoked by people on both ends of the political spectrum' and with 'few argu[ing] over its meaning or its import' (ibid). The achievement gap is 'often characterized as a single unyielding gap between white students and . . . minority students' (Ream, Ryan and Espinoza 2012: 37) but is more accurately conceived

Risking Diagnosis? 95

'as multiple gaps that fluctuate between racial, social class, and linguistic groups'. Gillborn (2008: 65) argues that 'Gap Talk' serves a particular strategic and political purpose in enabling a sense of incremental progress to be conveyed through messages about narrowing or reducing the gap and calls it 'a deception' (68). Gillborn suggests that the achievement gap is more of an 'educational debt' (2008: 44) which is persistent. Ladson-Billings and other scholars, particularly those writing within the U.S. have pointed to an impossibility of ever recovering this debt because of the 'locked in' (Roithmayr 2003: 38) nature of racialized inequalities. These are so deep rooted, historically and culturally, and so institutionalized that they become almost inevitable. Furthermore, as Gillborn (2008) argues, attending to the narrowing of the achievement gap obscures the real systemic problems that need to be tackled.

Class and Socio-Economic Striations

> The class struggle exists; it exists more intensely.
>
> (Foucault 1989: 18)

Children and young people living in poorer circumstances are four times more likely to be diagnosed with borderline to abnormal social, emotional or behavioural difficulties (Barnes, Chanfreau and Tomaszewski 2010; Goodman and Gregg 2010; HM Treasury and DfES 2007), have increased likelihood of school suspension and exclusion and have high rates of behaviour disorders and medication (Harwood 2006). Children are at greater risk of ADHD as a result of deprivation and this is mediated by both social class and ethnicity (Bauermeister et al. 2005). Here, we suggest that children and young people of low socio-economic status experience a naming of their chaotic lives and of the lack in their lives, not just of material goods but also of self-control. The naming of these omissions generates a moral obligation and leads to further spatial practices that situate the children and young people and their families as on the end of professional concern, support and control. These practices produce plural disadvantage (Wolff and De-Shalit 2007), whilst creating a '*positional* flexibility which puts [the professional] in a whole series of possible relationships with [the child and family] without ever losing him (sic) the upper hand' (Said 2002: 1009, emphasis added).

Confirmation has been sought from neuroscience that poverty and disadvantage affects children physically. Whilst in opposition, the UK MP Ian Duncan Smith studied the findings of research on the neural development of children from 'neglected and deprived' families compared with 'normal' families (Tomlinson 2012: 282) and the UK Parliamentary Strategy Office produced a paper contrasting a normal brain with an 'emotionally deprived brain' (Cabinet Office 2008: 87). Similarly, in Australia, during a sitting of the federal parliament in March 2001, Dr. Louise Newman, the then head of the child and adolescent faculty of the Royal Australian and New Zealand College of Psychiatrists, compared projected images of a healthy and a 'neglected' eight-year-old brain. Media coverage of this event

96   *Julie Allan and Valerie Harwood*

records Dr. Newman calling for awareness of the 'forgotten epidemic of child mal-treatment' and inferring poor parenting as potentially brain damaging (Ellingsen 2001: 1). As Tomlinson notes, this is not very far away from eugenics theories and from medical textbooks showing the 'warped brains of criminals and the mentally retarded' (Tomlinson 2012: 282). Schram (2000: 92), in his critique of the medicalization of welfare, argues that 'poverty can be an important cause of psychological problems, but correcting those psychological conditions will not necessarily correct the poverty that produced those conditions in the first place'. More broadly, this points to the need for medicalized treatment in poorer communities to be given careful scrutiny.

The UK study *Poorer Children's Educational Attainment: How important are attitudes and behaviour?* (Goodman and Gregg 2010) identifies the markedly lower levels of educational attainment reached by children from poorer families, pointing to behavioural problems as a key contributing factor. A Scottish study found one in four persistently poor children (aged three to four and five to six) rated as having social, emotional or behavioural difficulties (Barnes et al. 2010). Children in these circumstances experience multiple social, health and behavioural problems, with rates of 22 and 23% for five to six year olds living in short-term and persistent poverty, and a sharp increase of 28% for three to four year olds living in persistent poverty (Barnes et al. 2010). Research has predicted that young people aged 14 living in poverty have an increased likelihood of school suspension and exclusion as the number of family problems increases (HM Treasury and DfES 2007) and Gorard's analysis (Gorard 2010; Gorard and Smith 2010) highlights the confounding effects of children from poor families, from particular ethnicities and with additional learning needs clustering in specific schools. U.S. National statistics show that from 1998 through to 2009, ADHD prevalence increased to 10% for children with family income less than 100% of the poverty level and to 11%% for those with family income between 100% and 199% of the poverty level (Akinbami, Liu, Pastor and Reuben 2011). Patterns of higher diagnostic rates in low socio-economic areas are evident in Australia, a country which has rates of diagnosis of 11.2% and which has the third highest use of stimulant medication for ADHD, after the U.S. and Canada (Harwood 2010). The rates of medication are highest within disadvantaged communities in Australia, among unemployed families (Sawyer et al. 2002) and among children in care (Graham 2008). Concerns have been raised in Australia about the risk of paediatricians, 'medicating for social disadvantage' (Isaacs 2006: 44). The implication of social class and disadvantage as a risk factor has been recognized in urbanized Brazil where lower class young people were more likely to be identified for behavioural diagnoses by both clinicians and school staff (Béhague 2009), and where distinct socio-economic inequalities have been recorded between Black and white Brazilians (Gradín 2007).

Several researchers have discerned classed and racialized parental strategies that determine particular outcomes for their children. Gillies (2005), for example, comparing Scotland and England, distinguished between middle class parents who emphasize the individuality and competences of their children and working class parents who stress characteristics such as social skills, working hard and staying out of trouble. Similar differences were observed in the U.S. by Lareau (2003) who also distinguished between the intensive cultivation by middle class parents of their children and the concern to provide adequately for the physical needs of children by working class parents. A UK study by Vincent et al. (2012) found subtle differences among a group of middle class Afro-Caribbean parents in terms of their strategies for involvement and support and identified a continuum with parents doing whatever it took, including employing tutors, to get the best for their children at one end; parents merely hoping for the best at the other end and those in between who were described as 'watchful and circumspect' (347) and being guided by what was deemed to be appropriate parental involvement. Whilst these studies appear to show the value of an intersectional analysis, Strand (2010) warns that social class has limitations in accounting for ethnic-based differences. His UK research found that Pakistani, Bangladeshi, Black Caribbean and Black African children achieve, at the age of 14, three points behind their white peers and he suggests that these differences are better explained by pre-existing effects of ethnicity at age 11 than by factors relating to socio-economic status.

Chaos and Lack

Children and young people living in poor circumstances were especially marked by the manner in which problems were explained, with depictions of the chaos of their lives and of what they lacked, both in material terms and in their capacity for self-control. Depictions of poverty and 'the poor' as chaotic and lacking organization are recognizable characterizations. We suggest that the practices that medicalize poverty and child behaviour territorialize social class in new ways.

Territorializing the Home

The classed thematic becomes a tell-tale characteristic of the way in which classed-medicalization produces the behaviour assemblages of children from poorer backgrounds and territorializes the family and the home as a site for support. Following Fox and Ward (2011: 1015), we view behaviour assemblages as 'confluences of relations that *pattern* the psychic landscape of a subject and establish the boundaries of "what a body can do"'. Behaviour assemblages can result in limits that pathologize poverty. The salience of this consideration is made clear in Schram's (2000: 99) analysis of the medicalization of poverty:

> [The medicalization of poverty is] [P]otentially even more dangerous than medicalising welfare dependency. It creates the prospect of subordinating all low-income people to the terms of expert discourses designed to diagnose conditions as primarily or exclusively allopathically treatable.

One consequence of the depiction of parents as 'erratic' in the administration of medication is that it can serve as a rationale for services to focus concern onto the amelioration of inconsistent medication regimes and medicalized engagement.

98 *Julie Allan and Valerie Harwood*

The idea that parents need to be supported to engage productively with medication serves to compound identification of social classes with specific medical problems – and thereby medicalizes their experiences of poverty. Being poor and working class can therefore mean child behavioural issues fit neatly into striations that have the twofold effect of both creating and bolstering classed and medicalized modalities. The danger is that the problem becomes one of engagement with this classed-medicalized striation and, in so doing, risks missing other ways of conceptualizing the issues involved with child behaviour problems.

Gender: The Danger of Being a Boy

> Boys' behaviour at school is still more challenging than that of girls, but the behaviour of both is getting worse.
>
> (Association of Teachers and Lecturers 2011)

A salutary reminder is given by Roberts (2011) of the way in which attention to extremes of behaviour and achievements, in particular boys' underachievement, leads to 'ordinariness' (McDowell 2003: 204) being overlooked. Much of this appears to be associated with intense media interest in 'bad boys' and even though, as Ashley (2009: 181) points out, gender is a smaller risk factor than 'race' or class, 'it is boys to whom media often turn first for good stories'. At the same time as it can lead to the less dramatic, but nevertheless troubled, behavioural disorders exhibited by girls being missed, it can lead to an over-dramatizing and intensified regard for the behavioural problems that boys may present with.

Boys outnumber girls in diagnoses of ADHD by three to one, and this is the case in most neuropsychiatric conditions, but Cantwell (1996) notes a referral bias, whereby boys are more frequently referred than girls because of their aggressive behaviour, which takes the ratio of boys to girls within mental health clinics or hospitals to between six and nine to one. Girls are considered more likely to exhibit the characteristics of the less prevalent attention deficit disorder, which include sluggishness and anxiety, but because, by its nature, it does not involve hyperactivity, they may not be referred or may be misdiagnosed (Myttas 2001).

Whilst ADHD prevalence is increasing across the board, this is markedly higher among boys than girls and is noted as a worldwide phenomenon (Skounti et al. 2007). Also consistent across countries are the higher rates of prevalence where there is a clinical referral, going from a ratio of 3:1 to as much as 9:1, for example in New South Wales, Australia (NSW Department of Health 2002). Skounti et al. 2007 suggest that variation between countries may be due to cultural factors, reflecting, as in relation to ethnicities, different levels of tolerance of hyperactive behaviour, but these are not gender specific. Indeed, reporting on ADHD in Brazil, Rohde (2002) notes similarities in the male–female ratio, the prevalence of the combined type of ADHD, and the pattern of comorbid disorders with those reported in the U.S. As O'Dowd (2012) points out, reflecting on Australian statistics, most of the studies of ADHD are biased towards males. The presentation of other subgroups (girls, adolescents and adults) with atypical features suggests flaws in these studies and a need for more systematic scrutiny of evidence.

A major UK teachers union (Association of Teachers and Lecturers 2011) named boys' behaviour as still remaining more challenging than that of girls, but identified girls' behaviour as becoming increasingly problematic over recent years. A survey conducted with its own teacher members also identified gender differences in the problem behaviour, noting the boys as exhibiting aggressive behaviour, which teachers experienced as more challenging. Girls, according to the teachers, undertook more subtle forms of disruption, but this was nevertheless still challenging and the recent increases in forms of cyber-bullying using social media, which often spilled over into the classroom, had been most prevalent among girls.

Taking Boys Out

Department for Education figures, which cover England and which report 3,020 suspensions and 40 expulsions of five year olds during 2010, show boys were three times more likely to be suspended than girls and four times more likely to be expelled (Department for Education 2011). O'Regan (2010) notes that school exclusion impacts disproportionately on children with special educational needs and although the relationship between ADHD, boys and exclusion has been under-researched, Daniels and Porter (2007) suggest that rates of exclusion are higher among children with ADHD. The Attention Deficit Disorder Information and Support Service (ADDISS) (2006) documented rates of 11% of exclusion among children with ADHD, over 10 times higher than the average in 2006. O'Regan suggests that the significantly lower proportion of girls than boys with ADHD being excluded may reflect an under-diagnosis of girls' ADHD rather than anything else. Being excluded from school has clear 'knock on effects' (CALM 2010) on educational attainment for the obvious reason that children who are not in school will be not participating in lessons (although they may well be learning).

At the same time as there have been concerns that insufficient attention is given to behavioural disorders in the discipline practices within schools, leading to their physical exclusion, there has also been an intensification of regard for troubled boys and of spatialization practices. These practices are *inclusive* and therefore retain boys within the school, but mark them as both troubled and troublesome, either actually or potentially, and territorialize them as objects for special attention by specialist staff and for particular intervention programmes that may be gendered or that at least try to take account of masculinity.

The Risks of Diagnosis

'Race', class and gender heighten the risk of psychopathologically related diagnosis, while at the same time the very process of such diagnosis deflects attention from racialized discrimination or poverty in the lives of children and young people. The psychopathologization of behavioural problems, both in discourse and practice, is itself dangerous because it obscures other interpretations of children and their

100   *Julie Allan and Valerie Harwood*

behaviour. It also detracts from considerations of what is best, educationally, for individual children, by forcing attention instead on how to *manage* the child (Harwood and Allan 2014). The alternative is to find ways of privileging pedagogy over pathology, to seek to change the conversation through public discourse and debate and to help beginning teachers to engage more constructively with difference. This will mitigate the need for diagnostic assessment of behavioural problems and thereby reduce the numbers of children captured by the ADHD label.

References

Akinbami L. J., Liu, X., Pastor, P. N., and Reuben, C. A. (2011). Attention deficit hyperactivity disorder among children aged 5–17 years in the United States, 1998–2009. NCHS data brief, no 70. Hyattsville, MD: National Center for Health Statistics. 2011. Retrieved on 2 March from: http://www.cdc.gov/nchs/data/databriefs/db70.pdf

Artiles, A. (2004). The end of innocence: Historiography and representation in the discursive practice of LD. *Journal of Learning Disabilities*, 37(6), 550–555.

Artiles, A., Trent, S., and Juan, L. (1997). Learning disabilities empirical research on ethnic minority students: An analysis of 22 years of studies published in selected refereed journals. *Learning Disabilities Research and Practice*, 12, 82–91.

Artiles, A. J., Kozleski, E., Trent, S., Osher, D., and Ortiz, A. (2010) Justifying and explaining disproporitonality, 1968-2008: A critique of underlying views of culture. *Exceptional Children,* 76(3), 279–299.

Ashley, M. (2009). Time to confront Willis's lads with a ballet class? A case study of educational orthodoxy and white working-class boys. *British Journal of Sociology of Education*, 30, 179–191.

Association of Teachers and Lecturers (2011). Boys' behaviour at school is still more challenging than that of girls, but the behaviour of both is getting worse. Press Release. Retrieved on 30 July 2012 from: http://www.atl.org.uk/Images/15%20April%202011%20 -%20Boys%20behaviour%20still%20more%20challeging%20than%20girls%20but%20 behaviour%20of%20both%20is%20getting%20worse%20-%20ATL%20annual%20 conf%20final.pdf

Attention Deficit Disorder Information and Support Service (ADDISS) (2006). *Families survey August 2006.* Retrieved July 15, 2010 from: http://www.addiss.co.uk/

Azevedo, P., Caixeta, L., Andreda, L., and Bordin, I. (2010). Attention deficit hyperactivity disorder symptoms in indigenous children from the Brazilian Amazon. *Arquivos de neuro-psiquiatria*, 68(4), 541–544.

Barnes, M., Chanfreau, J., and Tomaszewski, W. (2010). *Growing up in Scotland: The circumstances of persistently poor children.* Edinburgh: National Centre for Social Research.

Bauermeister, J., Matos, M., Reina, G., Salas, C., Martinez, J., Cumba, E., and Barkley, R. (2005). Comparison of the DSM-IV combined and inattentive types of ADHD in a school-based sample of Latino/ Hispanic children. *The Journal of Child Psychology and Psychiatry*, 46, 166–179.

Bean, P. T., Bingley, I., Bynoe, A., and Faulkner, A. (1991). *Out of harm's way.* London: MIND.

Béhague, D. (2009). Psychiatry and politics in Pelotas, Brazil: The equivocal quality of conduct disorder and related diagnoses. *Medical Anthropology Quarterly*, 23(4), 433–482.

Brantlinger, E. (2006). Winners need losers: The basis for school competition and hierarchies. In E. Brantlinger (ed.), *Who benefits from special education? Remediating [fixing] other people's children* (pp. 197–232). Mahwah, NJ: Lawrence Earlbaum.

Risking Diagnosis? 101

Cabinet Office (2008). *Getting on, getting ahead: A discussion paper analyzing the trends and drivers of social mobility.* London: The Cabinet Office Strategy Unit.

Campaign Against Living Miserably (CALM) (2010). Exclusion – A boys problem. Retrieved on 9 August 2012 from: http://www.thecalmzone.net/2010/11/exclusion-a-boys-problem-around-80-of-students-permanently-excluded-from-schools-are-boys/

Cantwell, D. (1996). Attention deficit disorder: A review of the past 10 years. *Journal of the American Academy of Child Adolescent Psychiatry*, 35, 978–987.

Centers for Disease Control and Prevention (2011). Increasing Prevalence of Parent-Reported Attention-Deficit/Hyperactivity Disorder Among Children – United States, 2003 and 2007 Retrieved on 6 July from: http://www.cdc.gov/mmwr/preview/mmwrhtml/mm5944a3. htm?s_cid=mm5944a3_w#tab1

Daniels, H., and Porter, J. (2007). Learning needs and difficulties among children of primary school age: Definition, identification, provision and issues. *Primary Review Research Survey 5/2.* Retrieved 9 August, 2012, from: http://www.primaryreview.org.uk/downloads/ Int_Reps/4.Children_development-learning/Primary_Review_5-2_briefing_Learning_ needs_difficulties_071214.pdf

Department for Education (2011). Permanent and Fixed Period Exclusions from Schools in England 2009/10. Retrieved on 30 July 2012 from: http://www.education.gov.uk/rsgateway/DB/SFR/s001016/index.shtml; https://www.gov.uk/government/uploads/system/ uploads/attachment_data/file/362704/SFR26–2014_SEN_06102014.pdf

Department for Education (2014). Statistical First Release Special educational needs in England. Retrieved on 8 June 16 from: http://www.education.gov.uk/rsgateway/DB/SFR/ s001007/index.shtml

Dudley-Marling, C. (2001). Reconceptualizing learning disabilities by reconceptualizing education. In L. Denti and P. Tefft-Cousin (eds.), *New ways of looking at learning disabilities* (pp. 39-70). Denver: Love.

Dwivedi, K., and Banhatti, R.G. (2005). Attention deficit hyperactivity disorder and ethnicity. Archives of Disease in Childhood. Retrieved on 6 July from: http://adc.bmj.com/ content/90/suppl_1/i10.full.pdf

Ellingson, P. (2001) Drugging away the pain of youth. *The Age,* 12, March, 1.

Foucault, M. (1989). *Foucault live: Interviews.* Trans J. Johnson. Ed. S. Lotringer. New York: Semiotext(e).

Fox, N.J., and Ward, K.J. (2011). What are health identities and how may we study them? *Sociology of Health and Illness*, 30(7), 1007–1021.

Gillborn, D. (2008). *Racism and education: Coincidence or conspiracy?* Abingdon: Routledge.

Gillies, V. (2005). Raising the 'meritocracy': Parenting and the individualization of social class. *Sociology*, 39(5), 835–53.

Goodman, A., and Gregg, P. (2010). *Poorer children's educational attainment: How important are attitudes to behaviour?* Institute for Fiscal Studies. Joseph Rowntree Foundation.

Gorard, S. (2010). Education can compensate for society – A bit. *British Journal of Studies in Education*, 58(1), 47–65.

Gorard, S., and Smith, E. (2010). *Equity in Education: An international comparison of pupil perspectives.* London: Palgrave.

Gradín, C. (2007). *Why is poverty so high among Afro-Brazilians? A decomposition analysis of the racial poverty gap.* Bonn: Institute for the Study of Laboro.

Graham, L.J. (2008). Drugs, labels and (p)ill-fitting boxes: ADHD and children who are hard to teach. *Discourse: Studies in the Cultural Politics of Education*, 29(1), 85–106.

Graham, L.J. (2012). 'Disproportionate over-representation of Indigenous students in New South Wales government special schools. *Cambridge Journal of Education*, 42(2), 163–176.

102 Julie Allan and Valerie Harwood

Harwood, V. (2006). *Diagnosing 'disorderly' children: A critique of behaviour disorder discourses*. Oxford: Routledge.

Harwood, V. (2010). The new outsiders: ADHD and Disadvantage. In L. J. Graham (ed.), *(De)Constructing ADHD: Critical guidance for teachers and teacher educators* (pp. 119–142). New York: Peter Lang.

Harwood, V., and Allan, J. (2014). *Psychopathology at school: Theorizing mental disorders in education*. London: Routledge.

HM Treasury and DfES (2007). *Policy review of children and young people: A discussion paper*. Norwich: HMSO.

Isaacs, D. (2006). Attention-deficit/hyperactivity disorder: Are we medicating for social disadvantage? *Journal of paediatrics and child health*, 42, 544–547.

Ladson-Billings, G. (2006). From the achievement gap to the educational debt: Understanding achievement in US schools, *Educational Researcher*, 35(7), 3–12.

Lareau, A. (2003). *Unequal childhoods: Class, race, and family life*. Berkeley, CA: University of California Press.

McDowell, L. (2003). *Redundant masculinities? Employment change and white working class youth*. London: Blackwell.

Myttas, N. (2001). Understanding and recognizing ADHD. *Practice Nursing*, 12(7), 278–280.

National Center for Health Statistics (2015). Association Between Diagnosed ADHD and Selected Characteristics Among Children Aged 4–17 Years: United States, 2011–2013. Retrieved on 10 June from: http://www.cdc.gov/nchs/data/databriefs/db201.htm

National Collaborating Centre for Mental Health (2009). *Attention Deficit Hyperactivity Disorder: Diagnosis and management of ADHD in children, young people and adults*. Leicester/London: The British Psychological Society and the Royal College of Psychiatrists.

New South Wales Department of Health (2002). Trends in the prescribing of stimulant medication for the treatment of Attention Deficit Hyperactivity Disorder in children and adolescents in NSW. Retrieved on 30 July 2012 from: http://www.health.nsw.gov.au/pubs/2002/pdf/ADHD2002sup.pdf

O'Dowd, C. (2012). ADHD guidelines: Flaws in the literature and the need to scrutinise evidence. Retrieved on 30 July 2012 from: http://www.racgp.org.au/afp/201203/201203odowd.pdf

O'Regan, F. (2010). Exclusion from school and attention deficit/hyperactivity disorder. *The International Journal of Emotional Education*, 2(2), 3–18.

Paperson, L. (2010) The postcolonial Ghetto: Seeing her shape and his hand. *Berkeley Review of Education*, 1(1) (5–34).

Ream, R.K., Ryan, S.M., and Espinoza, J.A. (2012). Reframing the ecology of opportunity and achievement gaps: Why "no excuses" reforms have failed to narrow student group differences in educational outcomes. In T.B. Timar and J. Maxwell Jolly (eds.), *Narrowing the achievement gap: Perspectives and strategies for challenging times* Cambridge, MA: Harvard Education Press.

Rohde, A.L. (2002). ADHD in Brazil: The DSM-IV criteria in a culturally different population. *Journal of the American Academy of Child Psychiatry*, 14(9), 1131–1133.

Roithmayr, D. (2003). Locked in inequality: The persistence of discrimination. *Michigan Journal of Race and Law*, 9, 31–75.

Royal Australasian College of Physicians (2009). *Draft Australian Guidelines on Attention Deficit Hyperactivity Disorder (ADHD)*. Sydney: Royal Australasian College of Physicians.

Said, E. (2002). Excerpt from *Orientalism*. In C. Harrison and P. J. Wood (eds.), *Art in theory 1900–2000: An anthology of changing ideas*, 2nd edn (pp. 1005-1012). Wiley-Blackwell.

Sawyer, M.G., Rey, J., Graetz, B.W., Clark, J.J., and Baghurst, P.A. (2002). Use of medication by young people with attention-deficit/hyperactivity disorder. *Medical Journal of Australia*, 177(1), 21–25.

Risking Diagnosis? 103

Schram, S. F. (2000). The medicalisation of welfare. *Social Text*, 18(1), 81–107.

Simmons, T., Novins, D., and Allen, J. (2004). Words have power: (Re)-defining serious emotional disturbance for American Indian and Alaska Native children and their families. *American Indian and Alaska Native Mental Health Journal*, 11(2), 59–64.

Skounti, M., Philalithis, A., and Galanakis, E. (2007). Variations in prevalence of attention deficit disorder worldwide. *European Journal of Pediatrics*, 166(2), 117–123.

Soja, E. (1996). *Thirdspace: Journeys to Los Angeles and other real-and-imagined places.* Oxford: Blackwell.

Strand, S. (2010). The limits of social class in explaining ethnic gaps in educational attainment. *British Educational Research Journal*, 37(2), 197–229.

Symonds, B. (1998). The philosophical and sociological context of mental health care legislation. *Journal of Advanced Nursing*, 27, 946–954.

Tamimi, S. and Taylor, E. (2004). ADHD is best understood as a cultural construct. *British Journal of Psychiatry*, 184, 8–9.

Tomlinson, S. (2012) The irresistible rise of the SEN industry. *Oxford Review of Education*, 38, 267–286.

Vincent, C., Rollock, N., Ball, S., and Gillbourn, D. (2012). Being strategic, being watchful, being determined: Black middle-class parents and schooling. *British Journal of Sociology of Education*, 33(3), 337–354.

Walker, D. (2006). ADHD as the new "feeblemindedness". In G. Lloyd, J. Stead and D. Cohen (eds.), *Critical new perspectives on ADHD* (pp. 66–82). London: Routledge.

Wolff, J., and De-Shalit, A. (2007). *Disadvantage.* Oxford: Oxford University Press.

7   Dis/ability as White Property
Race, Class and 'Special Education' as a Racist Technology

David Gillborn

Introduction

This chapter argues that dis/ability is a contested and changing social category that is shaped by raced and classed dynamics of exclusion and oppression.[1] Drawing on the tenets of Critical Race Theory (CRT), I argue that dis/ability is a White property right, i.e., the construction and deployment of particular dis/ability labels operate to grant advantage to White middle class people while further marginalizing and excluding Black children and young people.

Context and Outline

Disability studies has exposed and resisted the social construction of dis/ability for decades (Allan 2010; Shakespeare 2014; Slee 2011). Pioneering attempts to combine a *race* and dis/ability focus (Artiles and Trent 1994; Artiles, Trent and Palmer 2004; Sleeter 1987; Tomlinson 1981, 2014) have been strengthened by the parallel growth of CRT (Bell 1992, Crenshaw et al 1995, Delgado and Stefancic 2000; Ladson-Billings and Tate 1995) and generated hugely important developments in recent years, such as the formulation of Dis/ability Critical Race Theory (DisCrit) (Connor, Ferri and Annamma 2016). This chapter draws on and feeds into these developments by using a CRT perspective to explore the dynamic interplay of oppressions around race, class, and dis/ability.

The chapter is in three parts. *First, a story about the construction of dis/ability.* Some of the most striking CRT uses the format of fictionalized accounts (drawing on real-world processes and examples) to throw into relief the racialized assumptions and actions that shape the everyday world but which typically evade critical scrutiny (Delgado 1989). These 'chronicles' stand among the most influential CRT scholarship to date (Bell 1992; Delgado 1995).

Second, an analysis of empirical data that explores the educational experiences and strategies of middle class Black parents. The data arise from a major two-year study that is the largest-ever qualitative inquiry into the education of the English Black middle class. In particular, I explore the struggles and battles fought by middle class Black parents who are either (a) resisting official attempts to label their children as emotionally and behaviorally disturbed (a label that typically leads to

Dis/ability as White Property   105

exclusion from mainstream opportunities); or (b) trying to mobilize their class capitals in order to have schools recognize and act upon what they see as the legitimate additional learning needs of their children.

Third, and finally, the chapter concludes with a reflection on the status of dis/ability as a racist technology in society. In particular, building on the foundational research of CRT legal scholar Cheryl Harris (1993) I argue that dis/ability is a White property right, i.e. dis/ability labels can act to facilitate or hinder educational support and achievement (depending upon the label and the associated institutional reactions). In short, dis/ability labels around emotional disturbance are deployed to put Black children beyond the reach of mainstream schooling (justifying further exclusion from mainstream education) but dis/ability labels that might bring additional resources and support (such as dyslexia and autism) are withheld from Black students who are seen as bogus claimants to these potentially positive resources.

The Personal and the Political: A Story about Race and Dis/ability

Critical Race Theory accords a particular weight to the experiential knowledge of people of color (Tate 1997). I have argued elsewhere that, while this explicitly speaks to the radical political aims of CRT, it also echoes the very best sociological practice in terms of trying to understand how institutions operate, especially institutions – like schools – that are structured by power inequities and operate to further create and legitimize social injustice (Becker1967; Gillborn 2008: 30–31). Much critical research also calls attention to the importance of acknowledging how we are each positioned at particular junctures of time/space and within the myriad intersections of inclusion/exclusion, power and identity (Dei 2011). The following CRT chronicle, narrated by a White author, considers one example of the construction and negotiation of dis/ability labels.

The woman in white: The chronicle of David and Stuart

'Is that correct?'

The young White woman asking the question is wearing a white lab coat and is seated uncomfortably on a chair designed for small children. Opposite her a young boy, aged around six or seven, moves his gaze between the woman and a series of cards laid out in front of him on the low children's table. They are the only two people in the classroom; usually full of life and noise, the room is silent and deserted except for these two figures. Both stare at the cards. In the room next-door David's classmates wait anxiously for their turn to see the mysterious 'lady' who, in the words of their class teacher, 'will ask you some questions'.

'Is that right?'

The woman repeats her question, phrasing it a little more simply in case the boy hasn't understood.

106   *David Gillborn*

The boy understands but is unsure how to answer.

He's been shown a picture in a book and asked to duplicate the image by rearranging a series of patterned cards on the table. He has moved them around and come *close* to an answer but he knows it isn't quite correct. Unfortunately, no matter how long he stares at the cards, he simply cannot see how to make the image right.

He looks at the woman.

She smiles.

David knows that in class his teacher will often ask the same question, even when they know the children haven't quite solved something. It's a kind of game. The child says 'yes' and then the teacher offers a clue. They say something like, 'Well, is *this one* in the right place? What about *this one*?' They'll point to where you've gone wrong and help you to find the answer.

David returns the woman's smile and plays his role correctly: 'Yes, miss'.

But something is wrong.

Instead of pointing to the misplaced card, the woman writes something on her jotter and gathers together the cards.

As the woman begins to organise the next part of the test David looks on in stunned silence. Doesn't she know how this works? Why isn't she helping me?

Two weeks later

David sits quietly in the same classroom. School finished about ten minutes ago and the only other people in the room are David's mother and his class teacher, an elderly woman who usually has a smile on her lips.

But neither David's mum nor his teacher are smiling. The grown-ups are having a serious conversation – about *him*.

Mrs Johnson is explaining that David did very badly in a test and there's talk of him going into the 'remedial' class. The 'remedial' class is a group of children who are taught away from everyone else; they have a 'special' teacher (who only teaches *them*) and they never mix with normal kids. David doesn't know what *remedial* means but he knows he doesn't want to be in there! He's starting to feel scared. One of his friends, Stuart, was moved to remedial last week. Stuart was the only Black boy in the class and he used to love sharing the building blocks with David.

David's mum is biting her lip – she looks upset – but Mrs Johnson touches mum's arm and smiles; 'It's partly *my* fault,' his teacher says. 'You see he's so quiet in class, I'm afraid that I haven't really given him much attention. He'll play with the wooden bricks all day if you let him. He's no problem at all.'

The grown-ups both look at David. They smile. He returns their smile but feels awkward. Has he been *naughty*? He *does* like the bricks. Is that *bad*?

'I'm sure he's got a brain underneath all that cotton-wool', Mrs Johnson states firmly, 'And I'm going to find it!'

On the way home Mum explains that, although he didn't do very well in a certain test, David will be allowed to stay in Mrs Johnson's class for another year. He won't have to go into 'remedial' because Mrs Johnson has said she'll make sure that he does more work next year. David is relieved but feels angry; this is all that woman's fault. The woman in the white coat. She was a *rubbish* teacher. If she'd known what to do – and helped him like a normal teacher – none of this would have happened.

Forty years later

'I've never done a *professor* before.'

David is about to take another test.

After a lifetime of hiding his problems with reading, things have finally become unmanageable. It's not that he *can't* read; he has a PhD, has written books, edits a peer-reviewed journal and became one of the youngest professors ever appointed at his University. David *can* read but he reads very slowly. *Very* slowly. His friend (and PhD student) Gregg – a disabilities activist – has encouraged him to get a dyslexia assessment for years. But David has refused. Partly, he's uneasy about laying claim to a disabled identity that he doesn't feel he has a right to. He's never really suffered because of his reading – he's bluffed his way through life using a variety of strategies – but now those strategies are failing him. His university is enforcing a 'workload management plan' that will credit him with one day's work when he examines a doctorate. But it takes David more than a week to read a thesis. The workload model is going to expose him. He won't cope. He's read around the internet and discovered that his story – which *feels* so unique – is very common. Lots of people go through life covering up but then something happens – there's a change (a new job is one of the most common triggers) – and suddenly the façade crumbles.

Once again the psychologist is a White woman, but this time she is dressed casually – no lab coat – and they sit at a desk designed for adults.

'I've had a few doctors but you're the first professor.'

'Your email said something about a full *cognitive abilities* profile.' He says uneasily. 'I'm not very comfortable about taking an IQ test. I don't believe in them.'

'Yes, I've read some of your work. But I won't hold it against you.'

The woman laughs and David feels as small and stupid as he did when the grown-ups were going to put him in 'remedial'. He'd like to leave but he can't think of an excuse. Fifteen minutes into the test he is asked to rearrange some cards in order to duplicate a picture in the tester's manual.

The chronicle of David and Stuart is autobiographical. Stuart (a pseudonym) was the only Black boy in my elementary school class and he was moved to the remedial group – away from the mainstream school – following the assessments conducted by the mysterious woman in the white coat. I've come to suspect that race and racism were vitally important in saving me from a similar fate. I don't know what kind of 'condition' the testers thought they had discovered in the two of us but it's clear from the adults' disposition that it was not positive.

108　*David Gillborn*

Like all stories, this one can be read in multiple ways. Personally I draw two major conclusions from the events; first, despite the scientific façade of psychometric testing (the tester really did wear a white lab coat) the tests, their administration and interpretation, are social constructions that are inseparable from wider social relations. My peers and I had been given no prior explanation about the nature of the test nor how we were meant to respond. I vividly remember my shock when the tester – whom I assumed to be a teacher – failed to follow the usual 'rules of the game' for teachers in the school. I knew my answer was wrong; why didn't she help me? The answer, of course, is that we were playing a different 'game.' In this game there are no clues, no help is offered. A few years later my classmates and I took another IQ test, this time it was a national assessment (the '11-plus') meant to identify those with the ability to enter high-status *grammar* schools rather than the artisan technical and 'modern' schools (Lowe 1997). Once again we were given no warning about the style and content of the assessments. In my small, largely working-class, elementary school there was no sign of the detailed coaching and preparation that middle class parents expect (and buy) from their elite schools and personal tutors.

The second key issue in the chronicle is racism. My fascination with the building blocks was viewed kindly by Mrs Johnson (a pseudonym). Indeed, she took responsibility for my failed test:

> he's so quiet in class, I'm afraid that I haven't really given him much attention. He'll play with the wooden bricks all day if you let him. He's no problem at all.

I wasn't present for the discussions about Stuart but I imagine it to have gone something like:

> he's so quiet in class. He'll play with the wooden bricks all day if you let him. Now I understand why; he's remedial.

Racism, Dis/ability and the Black Middle Class

The empirical data in this chapter are drawn from a two-year project funded by the Economic and Social Research Council (ESRC) and conducted with my colleagues Stephen J. Ball, Nicola Rollock and Carol Vincent.[2] The project began with an explicit focus on how *race* and *class* intersect in the lives of Black middle class parents. This focus arose from a desire to speak to the silences and assumptions that have frequently shaped education research, policy and practice in the UK where middle class families are generally assumed to be White, and minoritized families – especially those who identify their family heritage in Black Africa and/ or the Caribbean – are assumed to be uniformly working class (see Rollock et al. 2013). By interviewing Black parents employed in higher professional and managerial roles, we hoped to gain a more nuanced and critical understanding of race-class intersections.

The project sample was limited to parents who identify as being of Black Caribbean ethnic heritage. This group was chosen because the Black Caribbean community is one of the longest established racially minoritized groups in the UK, with a prominent history of campaigning for social justice, and yet they continue to face marked educational inequalities in terms of achievement and expulsion from school (Gillborn 2008; John 2006; Sivanandan 1990; Warmington 2014). At the time of the interviews, all the parents had children between the ages of 8 and 18, a range that spans key decision-making points in the English education system. As is common in research with parents, most interviewees were mothers, but the project team also wanted to redress common deficit assumptions about Black men (McKenley 2005; Reynolds 2010) and so we ensured that fathers were also represented in the sample (a fifth of the total). All the parents are in professional/managerial jobs within the top two categories of the National Statistics Socio-Economic Classification (Office for National Statistics 2010) and most live in Greater London (although we also included parents from elsewhere across England). Parents volunteered to take part by responding to adverts that we placed in professional publications and on the web. Once our initial round of 62 interviews had been completed, utilizing a technique that has proven successful in the past, we then re-interviewed the 15 parents chosen to facilitate greater exploration of the key emerging themes and questions. In total, therefore, 77 interviews provide the original data for the project.

Our interviews explored parents' experiences of the education system (including their memories of their own childhood and their current encounters as parents), their aspirations for their children and how their experiences are shaped by race/racism and social class. The project team comprised three White researchers and one Black researcher; respondents were asked to indicate in advance whether they preferred a Black interviewer, a White interviewer, or had no preference, and those preferences were met accordingly. Following the interviews, around half (55%) felt that interviewer ethnicity had made a difference and almost all of these felt that rapport with a Black researcher had been an advantage. The team is split evenly between men and women, and two of us have a declared dis/ability.

'Special Education' and the Intersection of Race, Class, Gender and Disability

The terms 'race' and 'disability' have a lot in common: both are usually assumed to be relatively obvious and fixed, but are actually socially constructed categories that are constantly contested and redefined. Historically, both have operated to define, segregate and oppress. Received wisdom views both 'race' and 'disability' as individual matters, relating to identity and a person's sense of self, but a critical perspective views them as socially constructed categories that actively re/make oppression and inequality (Annamma et al 2013; Beratan 2008; Leonardo and Broderick 2011). In the U.S., for example, Christine Sleeter (1987) has argued that the category 'learning disabilities' emerged as a strategic move to protect the children of White middle class families from possible downward mobility through low school achievement. Whereas *some* labels might be advantageous, for example by securing additional dedicated resources, it is clear that certain other dis/ability

110   *David Gillborn*

labels are far from positive. In both the U.S. and the UK, there is a long history of Black youth being over-represented in segregated low status educational provision, usually disguised beneath blanket terms like 'special' or 'assisted' education (Tomlinson 2014). Some of the earliest critical research on race inequities in the English educational system focused on the intersection of race and dis/ability (Coard 1971; Tomlinson 1981) and, despite the decades that have passed since those pioneering studies, the issue emerged as a key element in our interviews with contemporary Black middle class parents. Fifteen of our interviewees (around a quarter) mentioned dis/ability or related issues during their interviews and some important and disturbing patterns became clear. In the following sections, I review our key findings in relation to three simple questions: first, what processes lead to a 'special needs' assessment being made? Second, what happens after the assessment? Finally, whose interests are being served by the schools' reactions to, and treatment of, Black middle class parents and children in relation to the question of dis/ability? My concern, therefore, is to understand the experiences of Black middle class parents and their children as they encounter labels being used against them or alternatively how they attempt to use labels to access additional resources; I am interested in how racism intersects with other aspects of oppression (especially class and gender) in the processes that *make, assert* and *contest* the meaning of dis/ability in schools.[3]

Assessing 'Special' Needs

The British government's advice for parents of children with disabilities (DCSF 2009) describes a series of stages that should lead to a child's needs being assessed and met:

- The parents and/or school identify that the child is having problems;
- An assessment is arranged through the school or the local authority;
- The nature of the child's needs is identified and adjustments are recommended;
- The school then acts on these recommendations and the student is better able to fulfill their potential.

In our data there is only a single case that comes close to this model; where the school expressed concern to the parent, and they worked together harmoniously throughout the process. In every other case it was the parent – not the school – who identified a problem and sought an assessment. This involves parents drawing on both their *economic* capital (to finance expensive specialist assessments) and their *cultural* and *social* capital (often using friendship and professional networks to help negotiate the system). In each of these cases, the school seemed content to assume that the students' poor performance was all that could be expected: here Rachel[4] describes how her son was criticized for not paying attention:

> I took [my son] to get him educationally assessed and they said that he had dyslexia (. . .) I took him up to Great Ormond Street [Hospital] to get his

Dis/ability as White Property   111

hearing tested and they said he can't hear half of what's going on. So when the teachers are always saying 'he's distracted and not paying attention', he can't hear. (. . .) they were just very happily saying [he] doesn't pay attention, [he] doesn't do this, [he] doesn't do that, but, you know, *he can't hear.*

(Rachel, Senior Solicitor, Private Sector)

According to official guidance, where there is a sharp discrepancy between a student's performance on different sorts of task, this can be seen as indicating a possible learning difficulty (DANDA 2011). In our research, where Black children's performance was at stake, schools seemed happy to assume that the lowest level of performance was the 'true' indicator of their potential:

a discrepancy was emerging, in that she would get a B for a piece of work that she had spent time doing [at home] and then she would get a D or an E even [for timed work in class]. So I then contacted the school and said, 'look there's a problem here'. And they just said 'well, she needs to work harder'. So they were actually not at all helpful and I ended up having a row with the Head of Sixth Form because she accused me of being '*a fussy parent.*' And what she said was that my daughter was working to her level, which was the timed essay level, she was working to a D.

(Paulette, Psychologist)

Paulette was shocked that her professional knowledge could be dismissed so easily by the school. In a further manifestation of the low expectations that characterize so much of Black parents' experience of the system (Crozier 2001; Gillborn et al 2012) she discovered that the school viewed her daughter's *higher* levels of achievement as at best anomalous, at worst suspicious:

I felt really frustrated and actually very angry that they wouldn't listen. Because I could see that, yes, ok in a class of thirty you could overlook that, but if someone's actually pointing out to you the difference [between timed classwork and homework] and you are still saying, 'well actually, you know, we don't see that', and 'is someone actually helping her with her homework?' Which is what I was asked, because she is getting better grades when she is producing work from home, so it got really unpleasant.

(Paulette, Psychologist)

Following an independent assessment (that revealed dyslexia) and a move to a private institution (that made the recommended adjustments), Paulette saw a dramatic improvement in her daughter's attainment. In her 'A level'(Advanced) examinations at age 18, Paulette's daughter went from gaining two passes at grade E and one ungraded (fail) result, to three passes, all at grade B.

The low academic expectations that Black parents and students encounter almost routinely within schools (despite their middle class status) take numerous forms. For example, in many ways, Vanessa's son was well liked by his teachers but

112   *David Gillborn*

their lack of academic ambition for him meant that they were unconcerned by his passivity in class. She feels that *years* have been wasted:

> each time I went to school, or if I passed the window, [he] would be sitting looking out the window and I was convinced that he was somewhere on the autistic spectrum (. . .) but because [he] could sit for an entire lesson silent and not be disruptive, all they ever said was [in a patronizing tone] 'he's so handsome' and 'he's so quiet' and I said 'Yes, but that's not normal is it?' (. . .) So when he actually saw the psychologist he was just about to leave junior school – so he was about 11. So all the support that he could have had, the learning plan, *nothing* was done at all. So we wasted a lot of time that he could have been supported.
>
> (Vanessa, Community Development Officer)

In our interviews there were two cases where the school made the first move to initiate a formal assessment for special educational needs in a way that shocked and angered the students' parents. In both cases, the school's action served to divert attention from crude racism in the school and refocus attention on a supposed individual deficit in the Black child. For example, when Felicia told her son's school about him being violently bullied by White peers the reaction was initially encouraging:

> the Head of Year was quite shocked and quite encouraging in terms of our conversation; calling and saying, you know, 'Really sorry. We've let you down; we've let [your son] down; we didn't know this was happening' (. . .) But nothing happened. (. . .) My son's class teacher had said to my son that I'm asking *too much* but not to tell me (. . .) I got this telephone call out of the blue one Sunday afternoon, from his class teacher, suggesting that he have some *test* – I can't remember exactly how this conversation went because it was such a shock; it was five o'clock on Sunday afternoon – that there might be some reason for his under-performing: not the racism at the school that I told them about, but there might be some reason, that he might have some *learning difficulties.*
>
> (Felicia, Senior Solicitor)

Similarly, Simon described how his son was expelled for reacting violently to racist harassment. In a situation that directly echoes previous research on the overrepresentation of Black students in expulsions (Blair 2001; Communities Empowerment Network 2005; Wright et al 2000) the school refused to take account of the provocation and violence that the young man had experienced at the hands of racist peers and, instead, chose to view his actions in isolation. Simon's son was labeled as having 'behaviour and anger management' problems:

> someone called him a 'black monkey' and he responded by beating him up. (. . .) I just don't think the school really understood the impact, or how isolated

Dis/ability as White Property 113

pupils can feel when they stand out physically, and that's just something that I don't think they get.

(Simon, Teacher)

On two occasions in our data, therefore, Black middle class parents complained that schools had wrongly taken the initiative in seeking a SEN assessment as a means of shifting the focus away from racism in their institution and onto a supposed individual deficit within the Black child. In both instances the child was male. In contrast, schools proved reluctant to support an assessment in every case where Black middle class parents themselves felt that their child might have an unrecognized learning difficulty.

Schools' Reactions to SEN Assessments

Having used their class capitals to access formal SEN assessments, despite the inaction of their children's schools, Black middle class parents in our research then faced the task of making the schools' aware of the assessments and seeking their cooperation in making any reasonable adjustments that had been suggested. In a minority of cases, the school simply refused to act on the assessment; in most cases, the school made encouraging noises but their actions were at best patchy, at worst non-existent. For example, when Nigel's son was diagnosed with autism, the recommended adjustments included the use of a laptop in class. Nigel was prepared to buy the machine himself, but the school refused to allow its use:

we thought it would be a *fait accompli*, we thought we would get the laptop. We were going to buy the laptop, the school wouldn't have to *buy* it, you know, we would do all of that, and they said no. So we had a long conversation with the head, who we were very friendly with, and they said that it would set a precedent.

(Nigel, Human Resources Manager)

Although disappointing, the school's reaction to Nigel's request was at least clear; Linda's experiences were more typical. She found that, although adjustments were agreed with a senior teacher (the 'Year Head' in charge of the relevant age cohort) and the specialist SEN coordinator, not all teachers knew about them or accepted them. In several cases, the school's lack of action started to look like deliberate obstruction (despite their kind words). Lorraine feels that she lost two years of education struggling to get her daughter's school to deliver on their promises:

I have a daughter who now has been diagnosed with autism, I actually do want to get much more involved in the school and how they deal with her. But I think for the school it's easier if they don't get involved with me. So, for instance, going in and having meetings; her Head of Year says 'oh, you know, I understand now, we'll do this, we'll do that' and then that just doesn't happen (. . .) there were *constant* visits to try to get them to take some kind of action to

114   *David Gillborn*

> help. (. . .) You know, at first I thought it was me not being forceful enough, but as I said, I was accompanied by a clinical psychologist who tried to get them to help as well and *they* failed.
>
> (Lorraine, Researcher, Voluntary Sector)

Our data suggest, therefore, that Black parents – even *middle class* ones who are able to mobilize considerable class capitals (both social and economic) – have an extremely difficult time getting their children's needs recognized and acted upon. In contrast, schools appear much more ready to act on more negative dis/ability labels. As Beth Harry and Janette Klingner (2006: 2) note, in relation to the U.S., Black (African American) students face much higher levels of labeling (what they term 'risk rates') in SEN categories 'that depend on clinical judgment rather than on verifiable biological data.' These patterns have a long history and they continue today: the most recent comprehensive study of SEN demographics in the UK (Lindsay, Pather and Strand 2006) revealed that rates of Black overrepresentation are especially pronounced in the category defined as 'Behavioural, Emotional and Social Difficulties'; where Black students are more than twice as likely to be labeled as their White peers.[5] This category of student are often removed from mainstream provision and placed in segregated units. One of our interviewee parents visits such units as part of her work. She reported her distress at witnessing what she described as the 'brutalization' of Black boys in segregated provision within a state-funded secondary (high school): here we can see the intersection of gender (the all-male grouping) alongside race, class and dis/ability:

> I don't know for what reason [but] they were in a kind of different [part of the school] (. . .) they weren't in the main school building (. . .) The class was predominantly Black, not many students but they were really unruly, and I was really shocked at how unruly they were. (. . .) the SenCo [special needs coordinator] said to me, she said, 'well, that's what you get.'
>
> (Paulette, Psychologist)

In a direct parallel to the racialized impact of tracking in the U.S. (Oakes 1990; Oakes et al 2004; Watamabe 2012), in the UK as students move through high school they are increasingly likely to be taught in hierarchically grouped classes (known as '*sets*') which are known to place disproportionate numbers of Black students in the lowest ranked groups (Araujo 2007; Ball 1981; CRE 1992; Gillborn 2008; Gillies and Robinson 2012; Hallam 2002; Hallam and Toutounji 1996; Tikly et al 2006). Paulette was in no doubt that the cumulative impact of these processes had a dramatically negative impact on the Black boys she observed:

> the boys are in sets from the time they come in and those boys are in the bottom sets. And the bottom set has been written off as boys who are just not going to get anywhere. And literally they kind of turn into animals, they really had, because of the way that they had been treated and because of the expectations. (. . .) And I just felt that there was something that that school – you know

Dis/ability as White Property 115

it sounds crazy – but something that that school did, actually *did*, to particular Black boys. (. . .) And I just think, I just thought that what it is, is that maybe the school just brutalises those children, *unintentionally*. Am I making sense?

(Paulette, Psychologist)

Paulette went on to describe the fate of a Black student whom she had known for some time. Despite prior attainment in primary school that was 'good' to 'average,' the high school interpreted the SEN label as automatically signaling a generic and untreatable deficit:

because he had dyslexia they had put him in bottom sets for everything, even though he was an able student. So from year seven [aged 11], what do you do? He just became completely de-motivated, completely disaffected. He had completely given up. And that was such a shock to me, it was such a shock.

(Paulette, Psychologist)

This boy's fate is particularly significant. Many young people achieve highly despite dyslexia; indeed, it is exactly the kind of learning disability Sleeter (1987) views as an explicit part of attempts to protect the educational privilege of White middle class America. Under the right circumstances (with sensible adjustments to pedagogy and through the use of simple assistive technologies), the student might have had a very different experience. But in this school, the combination of SEN and race seemed to automatically condemn the student to the very lowest teaching groups where his confidence and performance collapsed.

Conclusion: Dis/ability as a White Property Right

[Whiteness] meets the functional criteria of property. Specifically, the law has accorded 'holders' of whiteness the same privileges and benefits accorded holders of other types of property. The liberal view of property is that it includes the exclusive rights of possession, use, and disposition. Its attributes are the right to transfer or alienability, the right to use and enjoyment, and the right to exclude others.

(Harris 1993: 1731)

Cheryl Harris' analysis of Whiteness as property is one of the single most important and influential contributions to critical race theory. She highlights how, in the words of Delgado and Stefancic (2012: 174), 'whiteness itself has value for its possessor and conveys a host of privileges and benefits.' Whiteness operates in numerous and complex ways (cf. Leonardo 2009). In practice – though not in principle – those who are deemed by society to be White (to *possess* Whiteness) enjoy numerous rights that are not available to 'non-Whites' (cf. Ladson-Billings and Tate 1995). In this chapter, I have outlined an analysis that views dis/ability as a *White property right*; that is, *dis/ability operates as a category that is regulated and controlled in ways that support White racial privilege.*

116   *David Gillborn*

To recap on the evidence; when it comes to assessment, we have seen that typically Black parents had to make their own arrangements for specialist needs assessment in the face of school indifference or outright opposition. The exception was where – following racist incidents – schools suggested an assessment and shifted the focus onto the supposed deficits of the individual Black child and away from institutional racist failings.

Schools see low achievement for Black students as the norm regardless of class background. Remember that the Black parents interviewed as part of the empirical study all work in highly trained professional occupations. These are people with confidence, who know how to navigate institutions and can draw upon specialist networks and understandings. And yet these class capitals seemed to lose their value in the face of White expectations and understandings. For example, a sharp discrepancy in performance on different tasks *can* be seen as an indicator of some forms of learning disability; but for *Black* students, the school is content to see the *lowest* performance as the '*true*' level of the child's potential.

When parents' produced independent expert assessments the most common reaction from schools was to *sound* welcoming and interested, but to respond in ways that are at best patchy, at worst obstructive and insulting. But when the school itself mobilized dis/ability labels in relation to Black students, the effects were usually disastrous, leading to segregation from the social and academic mainstream and decimated academic performance.

Despite the official rhetoric from government, and despite schools' encouraging words, in practice, the regulation of dis/ability labels appears to put the interests of the racist status quo ahead of the needs of the Black child. Hugely negative and damaging labels, such as 'emotional and behavioural' disorder, are used as a pseudo-medicalized excuse to segregate Black children and condemn them to academic failure. But for middle class students who are White – as Christine Sleeter famously argued almost 30 years ago – certain labels (like dyslexia and autism) can operate to secure a second chance.

Contrary to the public façade of dis/ability as a 'natural' and obvious state of being, dis/ability is socially constructed within a matrix of cross-cutting oppressions. Dis/ability is a contested and regulated field that operates as a White property right. White professional elites assume an absolute right to determine who may be allowed to possess dis/ability and what form that dis/ability assumes. In practice, dis/ability operates to further secure White racial and class advantage while Black students, regardless of class capitals, find themselves excluded and demonized.

Acknowledgements

This chapter draws on empirical research data collected and analyzed as part of an Economic and Social Research Council funded project (ESRC RES-062-23–1880) that I jointly conceived and executed with Stephen J. Ball, Nicola Rollock and Carol Vincent. Parts of the analysis presented here build upon an unpublished presentation 'The Wrong Kind of Special? The Black Middle Class and Dis/Ability' (AERA annual meeting, 2015) and earlier explorations of the data in Gillborn (2015) and

Rollock et al (2015). I take sole responsibility for the particular interpretations of the data in this chapter.

Notes

1 I follow Annamma, Connor and Ferri (2013: 24) in using 'dis/ability' to highlight the way in which the traditional form (disability) 'overwhelmingly signals a specific inability to perform culturally-defined expected tasks (such as learning or walking) that come to define the individual as primarily and generally "unable" to navigate society. We believe the "/" in disability disrupts misleading understandings of disability, as it simultaneously conveys the mixture of ability and disability.'
2 'The Educational Strategies of the Black middle classes' was funded by the Economic and Social Research Council (ESRC RES-062-23-1880): Professor Carol Vincent was Principal Investigator.
3 I am *not* asking questions of over- and under-representation, as if there were some objective *real* notion of dis/ability into which Black middle class students should gain rightful admittance or avoid wrongful categorization. See Annamma et al 2013.
4 All interviewee names are pseudonyms.
5 The most recent major study of these issues found that, relative to White British students, Black Caribbean students are 2.28 times more likely, and 'Mixed White and Caribbean' 2.03 times more likely, to be categorized as BESD: Lindsay, Pather and Strand 2006.

References

Allan, J. (2010). The sociology of disability and the struggle for inclusive education. *British Journal of Sociology of Education*, 31(5), 603–619, DOI: 10.1080/01425692.2010.500093
Annamma, S.A., Connor, D., and Ferri, B. (2013). Dis/ability critical race studies (DisCrit): Theorizing at the intersections of race and dis/ability. *Race Ethnicity and Education*, 16(1), 1–31.
Araujo, M. (2007). 'Modernising the comprehensive principle': Selection, setting and the institutionalisation of educational failure. *British Journal of Sociology of Education*, 28(2), 241–257.
Artiles, A., and Trent, S.C. (1994). Overrepresentation of minority students in special education: A continuing debate. *Journal of Special Education*, 27(4), 410–437.
Artiles, A., Trent, S.C., and Palmer, J.D. (2004). Culturally diverse students in special education: Legacies and prospects. In J. A. Banks and C. A. McGee Banks (eds.), *Handbook of research on multicultural education* (pp. 716–735). San Francisco: Jossey-Bass.
Ball, S.J. (1981). *Beachside comprehensive: A case-study of secondary schooling*. Cambridge: Cambridge University Press.
Becker, H.S. (1967). Whose side are we on? In H. S. Becker (ed.) (1970), *Sociological work: Method and substance* (pp. 123–134). New Brunswick: Transaction Books.
Bell, D. (1992). *Faces at the bottom of the well: The permanence of racism*. New York: Basic Books.
Beratan, G. (2008) The song remains the same: Transposition and the disproportionate representation of minority students in special education. *Race Ethnicity and Education*, 11(4), 337–54.
Blair, M. (2001). *Why pick on me? School exclusions and black youth*. Stoke-on-Trent: Trentham.

118   *David Gillborn*

Coard, B. (1971). *How the West Indian child is made educationally subnormal in the British School System.* London: New Beacon Books, reprinted in B. Richardson (ed.) (2005) *Tell it like it is: How our schools fail Black children* (pp. 27–59). London: Bookmarks.

Commission for Racial Equality (CRE) (1992). *Set to fail? Setting and banding in secondary schools.* London: Commission for Racial Equality.

Communities Empowerment Network (2005). Zero Tolerance and School Exclusions. *Special Issue of the CEN Newsletter*, 5(6).

Connor, D.J., Ferri, B.A., and Annamma, S.A. (eds.) (2016). *DisCrit: Disability studies and critical race theory in education.* New York: Teachers College Press.

Crenshaw, K., Gotanda, N., Peller, G., and Thomas, K. (eds.) (1995). *Critical race theory: The key writings that formed the movement.* New York: New Press.

Crozier, G. (2001). Excluded parents: The deracialisation of parental involvement. *Race Ethnicity and Education*, 4(4), 329–341, DOI: 10.1080/13613320120096643

Dei, G.S. (2011). *Indigenous philosophies and critical education.* New York: Peter Lang.

Delgado, R. (1989). Storytelling for oppositionists and others: A plea for narrative. *Michigan Law Review*, 87, 2411–2441.

Delgado, R. (1995). *The Rodrigo chronicles: Conversations about America and race.* New York: New York University Press.

Delgado, R., and Stefancic, J. (eds.) (2000). *Critical race theory: The cutting edge*, 2nd edn. Philadelphia: Temple University Press.

Delgado, R., and Stefancic, J. (2012). *Critical race theory: An introduction.* New York: New York University Press.

Department for Children, Schools and Families (DCSF) (2009). *Special Educational Needs (SEN) – A guide for parents and carers.* Nottingham: DCSF.

Developmental Adult Neuro-Diversity Association (DANDA) (2011). What is neuro-diversity? Retrieved on 28 September 2012 from: http://www.danda.org.uk/pages/neuro-diversity.php

Gillborn, D. (2008). *Racism and education: Coincidence or conspiracy?* New York: Routledge.

Gillborn, D. (2015). Intersectionality, critical race theory, and the primacy of racism: Race, class, gender, and disability in education. *Qualitative Inquiry*, 21(3), 277–287. DOI: 10.1177/1077800414557827

Gillborn, D., Rollock, N. Vincent, C., and Ball, S.J. (2012). 'You got a pass, so what more do you want?': Race, class and gender intersections in the educational experiences of the Black middle class. *Race Ethnicity and Education*, 15(1), 121–139. http://dx.doi.org/10.1080/13613324.2012.638869

Gillies, V., and Robinson, Y. (2012). 'Including' while excluding: race, class and behaviour support units. *Race Ethnicity and Education*, 15(2), 157–174.

Hallam, S. (2002). *Ability grouping in schools: A literature review.* London: Institute of Education, University of London.

Hallam, S., and Toutounji, I. (1996). *What do we know about the grouping of pupils by ability? A research review.* London: Institute of Education, University of London.

Harris, C.I. (1993). Whiteness as property. *Harvard Law Review*, 106(8), 1707–1791.

Harry, B., and Klingner, J.K. (2006). *Why are so many minority students in Special Education? Understanding race and disability in schools.* New York, NY: Teachers College Press.

John, G. (2006). *Taking a stand: Gus John Speaks on education, race, social action and civil unrest 1980–2005.* Manchester: The Gus John Partnership.

Ladson-Billings, G., and Tate, W.F. (1995). Toward a critical race theory of education. *Teachers College Record*, 97(1), 47–68.

Leonardo, Z. (2009). *Race, whiteness, and education.* New York, NY: Routledge.

Leonardo, Z., and Broderick. A. (2011). Smartness as property: A critical exploration of intersections between Whiteness and Disability Studies. *Teachers College Record*, 113(10), 2206–2232.

Lindsay, G., Pather, S., and Strand, S. (2006). *Special educational needs and ethnicity: Issues of over- and under-representation*. Research Report RR757. London: Department for Education and Skills.

Lowe, R. (1997). *Schooling and social change 1964–1990*. London: Routledge.

McKenley, J. (2005). *Seven Black Men: An Ecological Study of Education and Parenting*. Bristol: Aduma Books.

Oakes, J. (1990). *Multiplying inequalities: The effects of race, social class, and tracking on students' opportunities to learn mathematics and science*. Santa Monica: Rand Corporation.

Oakes, J., Joseph, R., and Muir, K. (2004). Access and achievement in mathematics and science: inequalities that endure and change. In J. A. Banks and C. A. M. Banks (eds.), *Handbook of research on multicultural education*, 2nd edn (pp. 69–90). San Francisco: Jossey-Bass.

Office for National Statistics (2010). SOC2010 Volume 3 NS-SEC (Rebased On SOC2010) User manual. Retrieved 27 May 2011. http://www.ons.gov.uk/about-statistics/classifications/current/soc2010/soc2010-volume-3-ns-sec – rebased-on-soc2010 – user-manual/index.html

Reynolds, T. (2010). Lone mothers not to blame. *Runnymede Bulletin*, (361), 11.

Rollock, N., Gillborn, D., Vincent, C., and Ball, S.J. (2015). *The colour of class: The educational strategies of the Black middle classes*. London: Routledge.

Rollock, N., Vincent, C., Gillborn, D., and Ball, S. (2013). Middle class by profession: Class status and identification amongst the Black middle classes. *Ethnicities*, 13(3), 253–275. DOI: 10.1177/1468796812467743

Shakespeare, T. (2014). *Disability rights and wrongs*, 2nd edn. London: Routledge.

Sivanandan, A. (1990). *Communities of resistance: Writings on black struggles for socialism*. London: Verso.

Slee, R. (2011). *The irregular school: Exclusion, schooling and inclusive education*. London: Routledge.

Sleeter, C. (1987). Why is there learning disabilities? A critical analysis of the birth of the field in its social context. In T. S. Popkewitz (ed.), *The formation of school subjects: The struggle for creating an American institution* (pp. 210–237). New York: Falmer Press.

Tate, W.F. (1997). Critical race theory and education: History, theory, and implications. In M. W. Apple (ed.), *Review of Research in Education, Vol. 22*. (pp. 195–247). Washington, DC: American Educational Research Association.

Tikly, L., Haynes, J., Caballero, C., Hill, J., and Gillborn, D. (2006). *Evaluation of aiming high: African Caribbean achievement project*. Research Report RR801. London: DfES.

Tomlinson, S. (1981). *Educational subnormality: A study in decision-making*. London: Routledge and Kegan Paul.

Tomlinson, S. (2014). *The politics of race, class and special education: The selected works of Sally Tomlinson*. London: Routledge.

Warmington, P. (2014). *Black British intellectuals and education: Multiculturalism's hidden history*. London: Routledge.

Watamabe, M. (2012). Tracking in US schools. In J.A. Banks (ed.), *Encyclopedia of diversity in education*, vol. 4 (pp. 2182–2184). Los Angeles, CA: Sage Reference.

Wright, C., Weekes, D., and McGlaughlin, A. (2000). *'Race', class and gender in exclusion from school*. London: Routledge.

8 The Right to Exclude
Locating Section 504 in the Disproportionality Debate

Nirmala Erevelles

> We have the wolf by the ears and we can neither hold him, nor safely let him go. Justice is on one scale and self-preservation, the other.
> (Thomas Jefferson to John Holmes, a letter of April 22, 1820.)

> [Slaves] are in truth a species of property sui-generis, to be held, disposed of and regulated according to the laws of each particular state where slavery exists. In all slave-holding states, colour raises the presumption of slavery, and until the contrary is shown, a man or woman of colour is deemed to be a slave.
> (Opinion of Justice William Scott, Missouri Supreme Court, *Rennick v. Chloe*, 1841.)

Walking into History: Reflections on *Dred Scott's* Legacy in Contemporary Times

On a breezy afternoon in April, after presenting a draft of this chapter at the Annual Meeting of the Council for Exceptional Children (CEC) in St. Louis, Missouri, I crossed the street to the Old Courthouse across from my hotel. Mounting the steep stairs and pushing open the heavy door, I found myself staring upward at the magnificent rotunda, its surrounding wings housing a museum of sorts detailing the history of the city. On speaking with the Park Ranger stationed in the rotunda, I learned that one of the exhibits in the museum memorialized the site where the notorious *Dred Scott v. Sandford* case took place. In 1846, Dred Scott, a slave, sued his owner Mrs. Emerson for his and his wife Harriet's freedom by taking advantage of a certain legal rule of the time – 'freedom by residence'. According to this rule 'if a slave lived for a time on free soil, where the bonds of slavery were banned, that residence freed the slave and changed the person's status unalterably, such that, if the slave again entered a jurisdiction where slavery was legal, the irreparably broken bonds would not reattach' (Vandervelde 2015: 263).

A personal servant of Dr. Emerson, a medical officer, Scott followed his master to Fort Snelling in Wisconsin, where slavery was illegal. When Dr. Emerson died, Scott became the property of his wife, Eliza Emerson, who now lived in St. Louis, Missouri, where slavery was legal. Mrs. Emerson then sold the Scotts to her brother John Sanford from New York, even while the Scotts still lived in

The Right to Exclude   121

St. Louis. But the Missouri courts refused to apply the 'freedom by residence' rule to the Scotts' case and after a series of appeals, it reached the U.S. Supreme Court. Finally, on March 1857, in a 7-to-2 decision, the United States Supreme Court ruled against Dred Scott on the grounds that a slave could never be considered a citizen (Powell and Menendian 2008).

Dred Scott was the first time a case reached the Supreme Court where a slave was pitted against his master (Vandervelde 2015). Its significance rested on the simple but potent refusal of the Court to recognize free Blacks as ever becoming members of an imagined community of U.S. Citizens by constituting 'whiteness as a salient feature of citizenship' (Powell and Menendian 2008: 1163). A similar refusal of recognition justified segregation under Jim Crow laws by drawing on the problematic mantra that 'separate was [indeed] equal', upheld by another notorious court case, *Plessy v. Ferguson*. This occurred despite the existence of the Fourteenth Amendment that guaranteed equal protection under the law to all its citizens including African Americans. Such practices that structure community along racial lines continue today as observed in 'our hyper-segregated and highly impoverished urban areas and coincident White suburban enclaves [where] . . . [r]esidential segregation curtails the experience of community for people of different races and is the most important factor contributing to racial inequality today' (Powell and Menendian 2008: 1164).

I argue in this chapter that structuring community along racial lines is also a contributing factor in the continued segregation in public schools in the United States. More than 50 years after *Brown v. Board of Education*, the everyday practices of racial segregation in public education are still indicative of the staunch conviction that Blackness is, in fact, inferior to Whiteness, echoing the *Dred Scott* decision more than 150 years earlier. This legacy of racialization enshrined 'whiteness as property' (Harris 1993) in the intimate interstices of legal discourse such that black bodies continue to remain second-class citizens in the country of their birth. In fact, this naturalized recognition of whiteness, as 'the attribute of free human beings' (1721) with the unquestioned 'right to exclude' (1714) non-whites has become the cornerstone on which most educational policies rest and has continued to reproduce the 'separate and unequal' doctrine that the *Brown* decision sought to overturn.

One example of structuring community along racial lines in public schools is evident in the racial disproportionality observed in special education programmes where white students dominate gifted programmes and inclusive classrooms while black students are overwhelmingly relegated to segregated classrooms and alternative schools (Annamma, Connor, and Ferri 2013; Ferri and Connor 2005; Artiles, Kozelski, Trent, Osher, and Ortiz 2010; Erevelles 2014; Holt 2003; Skiba, Poloni-Staudinger, Gallini, Simmons, and Feggins-Aziz 2006). In this chapter, I focus specifically on Section 504 of the Rehabilitation Act of 1973, a civil rights statute that requires that the needs of disabled students be met as adequately as the needs of nondisabled students in the regular classroom. However, while white students with labels of Attention Deficit Hyperactivity Disorder (ADHD) or Emotional Disabilities (ED) and with 504 plans are included in regular education settings, most black

122 Nirmala Erevelles

students with similar labels do not have 504 plans and are therefore often dislocated to segregated special education classrooms and alternative schools. I therefore suggest that, in a manner similar to the *Dred Scott* decision, it could be argued that Section 504 privileges 'whiteness as a salient feature of [educational] citizenship' with the unquestioned 'right to exclude' black students who have historically been perceived as undesirable in public education classrooms.

That April afternoon, I marvelled at this coincidence. Here, I was, a participant on a panel delineating how educational policies continue to propagate segregation at the intersections of race, class, and disability on the very day I serendipitously walked into the courthouse where the citizenship of racialized others had been passionately debated and then dismissed. Reading about this history as I wandered through the exhibition hall, I turned a corner only to confront the actual chamber where the *Dred Scott* decision was presumed to have taken place. I stood stock still, soaking in the historical significance of that moment, feeling the hairs on my skin stand straight up, and my heart pound loudly. I recognized then that I was witness to a momentous act of dehumanization that had occurred within these walls when race was located at the very centre of (in)justice in U.S. law. The *Dred Scott* decision was not an act of villainy. Nor was it an act of actual violence. Rather, in the casual everyday functioning of a U.S. courthouse focused on precedents and their mind-numbing technicalities, a monstrous act was perpetrated without it ever appearing as such. It could be argued that they were just doing their job by following the law to the letter. But this is exactly what the U.S. Supreme Court has always done in its (infamous) history of court decisions -*Plessy, Brown, Miliken, Bakke* – and that we continue to witness in in the lower courts in Florida, in Ferguson, in Baltimore, in New York . . . a legacy where 'antiblackness' (Dumas and Ross 2016) is enshrined as the usable logic on which to build one's case. This act of antiblackness did not summon as its protagonists men in white sheets, but rather the mundane intricacies of the legal system. I realized, then, that I had inadvertently stumbled into the pages of a history book filled with narratives of exclusion and I would now add yet another page to that sordid trail of injustice.

Where Are All the Black Students with 504 Plans?

At a public magnet elementary and middle school that offers an International Baccalaureate (IB) programme in the small college town located in the southeastern United States, the top 7% of the students identified from each of the public schools in the district are admitted to the school. Admissions to the school are based on the following assessment criteria: Student Performance (report cards) 25%; State Assessments (K–2 DIBELS, 3–7 ARMT +): 25%; Universal Screener: 25%; Learner Profile Screening Device: 25%. Though the philosophy of school chafes at standardization by opting for a curriculum that has an Arts focus and uses Project Based Learning (PBL) as a pedagogical practice, it nevertheless only admits students (as early as the first grade) who score at or above the 40th percentile on standardized tests. These admissions criteria appear contrary to the educational philosophy of the school that celebrates a non-traditional curriculum while at the same time

The Right to Exclude   123

inexplicably excluding non-traditional learners. Once admitted, students who do not make a C average or whose 'behaviour is disruptive to the extent that it interferes with the student's learning and indicates a lack of self-discipline or respect for others' are sent back to their home school according to the 'magnet school procedures' posted on the school's website.

Unable to meet these standardized criteria, many disabled students with an Individualized Educational Plan (IEP) are not admitted into the programme. The argument that the admissions committee makes is that such students will not be able to cope with the rigours of an IB programme. However, the school does admit disabled students (most of whom may not identify as such) who have a 504 plan. I was, however, made aware that almost all the students admitted to the magnet school with a 504 plan were mostly white children from upper middle class educated families (it is a university town after all) with labels such as anxiety disorder, unspecified learning disabilities, ADHD, and ED. As per the regulations of Section 504 of the Rehabilitation Act of 1973, students qualified for coverage under this plan cannot be discriminated on account of their disability and the school is mandated to offer them accommodations to support their full inclusion in the regular classroom with their peers. In sharp contrast, I also learned that there were very few if any black students with a 504 plan in the magnet school. And in an interesting twist, the only students who were required to return to their home school on account of low grades and unacceptable behaviours as outlined in the exit policy for the school were black students.

Noting this disproportionality in the magnet school, I wondered if a similar discrepancy existed in other schools in the district. I raised this issue with an assistant principal placed over special education in a Title I middle school that was majority black and where more than 80% of the students were entitled to free and reduced lunch. When I asked the administrator about the racial makeup of students with a 504 plan in this middle school, the administrator paused for a moment and then admitted with a dawning incredulity that he could not remember a single non-white student with a 504 plan in the last six years in this school. Why was there this discrepancy? Were black parents aware of the benefits of this civil rights legislation? Was the school forthcoming in informing parents about the educational possibilities enabled by 504 plans written for their children? In what ways was a seemingly progressive legislation structuring the school community along racial lines?

At around the same time, I became aware via social media about a blog in *Education Week* written by Christina Samuels (August 20, 2014) entitled, 'Students with "504 plans" More Likely to Be White, Enrolled in Non-Title I Schools'. This blog drew on the research of Perry Zirkel and John Weathers (2014) who analyzed data pertaining to students with 504-only plans obtained from the federal government's 2009–2010 Civil Rights Data Collection (CRDC). In her blog, Samuels (2014) summarized Zirkel and Weathers' (2014) findings as follows:

- White students are more than twice as likely (1.26 percent) to have a 504 plan compared to their Black (0.57 percent) or Hispanic (0.5 percent) classmates.

124   *Nirmala Erevelles*

- Male students were almost twice as likely to have a 504-only plan (1.27 percent) compared to female students (0.76 percent).
- A little less than 1 percent of children in Title I schools, or 0.84 percent, had 504 plans only. That compares to 1.23 percent of students in schools that do not receive Title I funds.

Intrigued by this data that now corroborated what I had suspected all along, in this chapter, I return to Zirkel and Weathers's research in an attempt to foreground the material and discursive practices that enable the spatial dis-placement of black (disabled) students in public education who are not under the protection of Section 504 of the Rehabilitation Act of 1973. I argue that their exclusion from access to a 504 plan results in their eventual dis-placement from the public education classrooms of their peers and is rooted in the same historical legacy of structuring community along racial lines that fueled the *Dred Scott* decision more than 150 years ago. I therefore ask the following questions: Why are black students with labels like ADHD and ED underutilizing Section 504? How do educational policies support these disproportionalities? What are the implications of these disproportionalities on students located at intersections of race, class, and disability? How do these dis-locations represent spatial injustices for students located at these intersections?

I begin this chapter with a brief overview of Section 504 legislation, its key characteristics and the educational protections it offers to disabled students in public schools. Then, moving on to Zirkel and Weathers's research paper, I discuss the significance of their findings using the conceptual framework of DisCrit. Finally, I discuss the implications of this intersectional analysis for assessment and other identification practices that continue to reproduce educational inequalities along the axes of race, class, gender, and disability.

Who Is Eligible under Section 504?

The history of the struggle for civil rights for disabled citizens derived its impetus from the civil rights struggle for racial equality in the United States. However, in educational contexts, this 200-year-long history of struggle for disability rights has seldom been conceived of within the trifecta of educational rights, civil rights, and residential rights for disabled people (Schraven and Jolly 2010). In fact, the sole emphasis in public education rests on ensuring educational access for disabled children as promised by the Individuals with Disabilities Education Act (IDEA). This singular focus on IDEA in educational contexts fails to recognize the significance of Section 504 of the Rehabilitation Act of 1973 – 'an important piece of civil rights legislation . . . intended to prevent discrimination while leveling the "playing field" for all students with disabilities' (Schraven and Jolly 2010: 420).

The passing of Section 504 of the Rehabilitation Act of 1973 came after nearly two decades of struggle post *Brown* in order to protect the civil rights of several minority groups including those excluded from public education. In the early 1970s, cases such as *Diana v. Board of Education, Lau v. Nichols* (both cases

The Right to Exclude 125

instrumental in extending educational rights to non-native speakers of English) and *Larry P. v. Riles* (the case that ruled that educational placement of students on the basis of one's intelligence was unlawful) served as precursors to the passing of Section 504 (Schraven and Jolly 2010). And lest one assumes that passing Section 504 was easy, Walker (2006) reminds us that

> although the Rehabilitation Act was passed in 1973, it took another four years and a twenty-five-day sit-in at the San Francisco regional office of the U.S. Department of Health, Education, and Welfare – the longest such occupation ever of a federal building by political protestors – before Section 504's implementing regulations were promulgated in 1977.
>
> (1588)

It should also be noted that this sit-in included 'an occupation army of cripples', who were supported by a 'very disparate group, a very wild and divergent community' (Corbett O'Toole as cited in Schweik 2011). This disparate group included the "Butterfly Brigade, 'a group of gay men who patrolled city streets on the lookout for gay violence', who smuggled walkie-talkies into the occupied building; Glide Church; local and national labour organizations; members of Delancey Street, the famous grassroots rehab programme for substance abusers and former felons, who brought breakfast into the building each day; the Chicano group Mission Rebels, who also provided food; and the Black Panthers, who publicly endorsed the action and provided hot dinners for the duration of the sit-in" (Mary Breslin as cited in Schweik 2011).

The original intent of Section 504 was to protect employees from discrimination on the basis of their disability, but it was soon broadened to prevent discrimination in educational settings that received federal funds. According to Section 504:

> No otherwise qualified individual with a disability in the United States . . . shall, solely by reason of her or his disability, be excluded from the participation in, be denied the benefits of, or be subjected to discrimination under any programme or activity receiving federal financial assistance.
>
> (Section 504 Regulations, 29 U.S. C. § 794 as cited in
> Schraven and Jolly 2010: 426)

While IDEA is a federal law that supports special education services in public schools, Section 504 is a civil rights statute (Schraven and Jolly 2010). Thus, for example, while IDEA's focus is on access to a Free Appropriate Public Education (FAPE), Section 504 emphasizes equal treatment for disabled citizens participating in federally funded programmes (Walker 2006). However, unlike IDEA, Section 504 is an unfunded mandate (Schraven and Jolly 2010; Zirkel and Weathers 2014), which perhaps can explain the seemingly lackadaisical attention it receives in public schools. Weber (2010) however, disagrees, claiming that rather than being considered an unfunded federal mandate, Section 504, instead, places conditions on receiving federal funding – conditions that states and schools districts are under no obligation to accept.

126 *Nirmala Erevelles*

That Section 504 has a broader reach than IDEA in its protection of the civil rights of disabled students is apparent in some of its key features that I will now explain:

a   Section 504 defines *a person with a disability* as '[a]ny person who has a physical or mental impairment that substantially limits one or more of that person's major life activities, or a person who has a record of such impairment, or a person who is regarded as having such impairment' (Section 504 Regulations, 29 U.S. C. § 794 as cited in Schraven and Jolly 2010: 426). Stated in this way, Section 504's mandate is much broader than IDEA because it covers students who may not be classified under the thirteen specific disability labels covered by IDEA (Schraven and Jolly 2010; Zirkel and Weathers 2014; Walker 2006; Weber 2010). Moreover, amendments to the American with Disabilities Act made in 2008 also impacted Section 504 by recognizing impairments that are episodic or are in remission (Zirkel and Weathers 2014).

b   The reference to *major life activities* in Section 504 includes functions such as caring for one's self, performing manual tasks, walking, seeing, hearing, speaking, breathing, learning, and working. The determination of the extent the impairment limits a major life activity is based on individually based assessments (Schraven and Jolly 2010; Walker 2006; Weber 2010).

c   When discussing *mitigating measures*, Section 504 is referring to those measures used by students to correct for or reduce the effects of their individual mental or physical impairment, like the use of eyeglasses for improving vision, or medications for anxiety, etc. With the 2008 expansions to the ADA, Section 504 instructs school districts to not consider any 'mitigating measures' used when assessing whether a student is eligible for a 504 plan (Schraven and Jolly 2010; Weber 2010). Ultimately, though the school has the final authority to include/exclude students from having a 504 plan based on a series of assessments that despite their attempts for objectivity, unfortunately fail to uphold these claims.

d   Additionally, Section 504 defines 'supplementary/related aids and services' as accommodations that include changes in the educational setting, materials, and/or strategies that while not significantly altering the content of the curriculum or level of expectation for a student's performance, nevertheless allow the student access to the general education curriculum in inclusive settings (Walker 2006; Walker 2010). Examples of such accommodations include seating the student in front of the room, providing extended time for testing, and providing behaviour supports in the classroom itself.

There are several benefits to disabled students having a 504 plan. The most important benefit is that Section 504 is an anti-discrimination statute and so protects the student. Another benefit is that a 504 plan follows a student all the way from public schooling to postsecondary education, unlike IDEA that ceases to cover students after the age of 22 years (Weber 2006). Additionally, students covered under IDEA are also eligible under Section 504, though many are unaware of this dual coverage.

The Right to Exclude   127

This lack of knowledge about the benefits of having a 504 plan is fairly widespread especially in underserved communities (Walker 2006). School administrators also find themselves in a similar situation of not knowing enough. In fact, Schraven and Jolly (2010) report that 65% of teachers claimed that they had no training on how to meet the needs of students with 504 plans in their classrooms. Perhaps, Section 504's relative obscurity in educational contexts can be attributed to the fact that for more than 30 years, it has been seen as only 'paper compliance' rather than as a legal mandate for services to help disabled students have equal access to the same educational opportunities as their nondisabled peers.

Section 504 Takes on the Disproportionality Debate

Since Section 504 has not garnered much attention in educational contexts, discussions of disproportionality have not taken centre stage as they have in reference to IDEA. This is surprising because given the history of failures of the civil rights legislation beginning with *Brown*, Section 504 cannot be immune to analogous disproportionalities at the intersections of race, class, gender, and disability. In fact, it would not be a far cry to claim that disproportionalities are endemic to U.S. public education. For example, according to the Civil Rights Project at Harvard University, while only 18 percent of white students and 30 percent of Asian students attend high-poverty schools, more than 60 percent of black and latino/a students attend high-poverty schools (Orfield and Lee 2005). Additionally, many of these high-poverty schools are also under-performing – an expected outcome of racially segregated schools. In fact, Logan, Minca, and Adar (2012) were able to provide empirical data to support *Brown*'s assertion that separate is inherently unequal, notwithstanding all the attempts post *Brown* directed towards addressing these inequalities.

It is in this context, I argue that given this dismal scenario, the promise of Section 504 to protect the civil rights of disabled children in U.S. public education continues to be jeopardized by the permanence of the colour line. Here, I invoke the still relevant quote by African American scholar, W.E.B. Du Bois when he wrote that '[t]he problem of the twentieth century is the problem of the colour line'. Recognizing the same challenges that Dred Scott was faced with in his failed claims to citizenship, Dubois (1999: 66) wrote:

> Since then a new adjustment of relations in economic and political affairs has grown up . . . which leaves still that frightful chasm as the colour-line across which men pass at their peril. Thus, then and now, there stand in the South [and elsewhere] two separate worlds; and separate not simply in the higher realms of social intercourse, but also in church and school, on railway and street-car, in hotels and theatres, in streets and city sections, in books and newspapers, in asylums and jails, in hospitals and graveyards.

More than 100 years later, the ubiquity of the colour line persists today in U.S. public schools. This colour line is most keenly noted in the disproportionality

128   *Nirmala Erevelles*

discourses pertaining to IDEA, but there is evidence that the colour line is also deployed when determining which students have access to protection under Section 504. I argue here that the colour line is maintained through assessment procedures and other practices that are enmeshed in the age-old assumption that 'whiteness as the attribute of free human beings' has the unquestioned 'right to exclude'. I, now, turn to Zirkel and Weathers's (2014) research study on disproportionality in the context of students with 504-only plans in order to illustrate how a civil rights mandate such as Section 504 continues to structure community along racial/colour lines in public education.

In their article entitled 'Section 504-Only Students National Incidence Data', Zirkel and Weathers analyze data that has seldom been cited in discussions of disproportionality. Using data from the U.S. Department of Education Office of Civil Rights (OCR), Zirkel and Weathers calculated the percentage of children receiving services under Section 504 only, paying close attention to the demographics of race, gender, and type of school (e.g., Title I/Non-Title I schools). The data were obtained from the 2009–2010 Civil Rights Data Collection (CRDC), drawn from a national sample of U.S. schools that included differential information for students with IEPs and students with 504-only plans. Approximately 7,000 school districts encompassing approximately 70,000 schools and representing 85% of all public school students were included in this data set. The authors offer a caution that, because the data was self-reported by school districts, they could not rule out inadvertent or deliberate inaccuracies.

One of the most significant findings of this study was that only 1.02% of students were identified as having a 504-only plan – a surprising fact given that the 2008 ADA amendments expanded the eligibility requirements under Section 504. Zirkel and Weathers explain that the effects of these expansions may not have been reflected in the analyses because the data were collected too soon after the expansions occurred. The authors also corroborated other researchers' (Schraven and Jolly 2010; Walker 2006; Weber 2010) claims that school districts have seldom paid much attention to Section 504 and as a result would not have been aware of these expansions. Further, the authors recognized that revisions in district policy are usually a cumbersome process, and as a result, district policy may not have reflected these expansions.

The second significant finding that Zirkel and Weathers reported was that white students were twice as likely to have a 504-only plan than their black and Latino classmates. Also, students in Title I (high-poverty) schools were significantly less likely to receive a 504-only plan than those in non-Title I schools. These findings demonstrate a reverse trend in disproportionalities in race and class for students served under IDEA. Ziegler and Weathers attribute this reverse racial and class disproportionality under Section 504 to the interaction between pressures against over-identification of students with IEPs in general (i.e., regardless of race) under IDEA and the litigiousness of white parents in upper-income suburbs of major metropolitan centres. Since Section 504 is a civil rights statue, privileged parents aware of the protections under this legislation have been able to use this knowledge to demand rights for their disabled children in public schools. The authors allege that parents from upper-income suburbs purportedly 'game' the system by using 504 plans to obtain SAT/ACT accommodations for their children in both high school and college/university classrooms. Additionally, they speculate that districts in litigious areas tended to provide a 504 plan as a 'consolation prize' in an effort to persuade parents not to resort to legal action.

While the authors' attempts to explain the reverse racial disproportionality apparent under Section 504 are plausible, it was disconcerting to note that they appeared to take a 'colour-evasive' (Stubblefield 2005) approach when addressing this issue. By a 'colour-evasive' approach, I am implying that they appear to deliberately de-center the politics of race at the intersections of class, gender, and disability. Therefore, the authors seek out individual, local, and administrative explanations to explain away these disproportionalities by assuming that their existence is a rational outcome of liberal educational policy. Such an approach obscures the insidious ways in which the colour line, sustained by racist structural practices, constitutes these disproportionalities in the first place. When discussing similar disproportionalities under IDEA, Artiles et al. (2010) reject more simplistic and individualistic explanations that pathologize historically underserved communities (e.g., culture of poverty-like explanations) and instead argue that assessment criteria and labelling procedures that contribute to racially disproportionate placement patterns are impacted by structural factors such as funding and skilled teachers, school policies such as discipline, high stakes testing, and cultural factors such as teacher and administrator values, attitudes, and organizational climate. Thus, responding to the call by Artiles et al. (2010) to make 'complexity transparent' (280) in discussions of disproportionality in U.S. public education, I propose an alternative analysis drawing on two conceptual frameworks: Disability Studies and Critical Race Theory or Dis/Crit (Annamma et al. 2013) to explore how the colour line justifies racial segregation at the intersecting axes of class, gender, and disability.

On the Other Side of the Colour Line: DisCrit, Disproportionality and Section 504

When explaining the existence of disproportionalities in the context of IDEA, Artiles et al. (2010) draw on cultural-historical explanations to foreground the unintended consequences of seemingly progressive legislation such as *Brown* and IDEA that sought to end the historical exclusion of students from public education on the basis of race and disability while ironically contributing to this very exclusion (Ferri and Connor 2005) Explaining disproportionality occurring under Section 504 requires a similar analysis. Like Artiles et al. (2010), I intend to move the discussion beyond our incessant prattling about the individual practices of students, parents, teachers, and administrators as well as beyond the simple urge to 'mathematize social problems with deep structural roots because such calculations are unable to unearth the historical precursors and ideologically laden processes that constitute them' (296–297). Rather, I am committed to an analysis that will expose how seemingly emancipatory policies are maintained by racially

130   *Nirmala Erevelles*

structured and ableist practices that are so naturalized that that they become justifiable as normative with a historical stake in maintaining the most privileged/pernicious conditions on either side of the colour line.

Because Section 504 is a civil rights statute that protects disabled students but has unintended but nevertheless dangerous implications for black students, the conceptual frameworks that are useful for this analysis are the intersecting fields of Disability Studies and Critical Race Theory, otherwise known as DisCrit (Annamma et al. 2013). Scholars working at the intersections of race and disability have described how oppressive discourses of disability have historically been used to justify the dehumanization of racialized bodies in the contexts of slavery, settler colonialism, educational and residential segregation, and the institutionalization and incarceration of racialized and disabled bodies (Annamma et al. 2013; Artiles et al. 2010; Ben-Moshe Chapman and Carey 2014; Erevelles 2014; Ferri and Connor 2005; Harry and Klinger 2006; Watts and Erevelles 2004). Thus, DisCrit urges us to explore the violent every day practices by which race and disability coalesce at the intersections of gender identity, sexuality, and class to enable the casual dis-location of certain marked bodies as 'matter out of [white] [normative] place' (Douglas 2003; 36).

DisCrit scholars have a critical stake in foregrounding the overrepresentation of students from non-dominant cultural groups in segregated special education classes based on dubious labels like mild mental retardation, emotionally disturbed/behaviourally disordered and linguistically disabled (Artiles 2013; Blanchett 2010; Erevelles 2014; Harry and Klinger 2006). Much of this research exhaustively highlights the complicated ways in which disability is attributed to racialized bodies to ensure their segregation in educational settings. Particularly relevant to this discussion is the simultaneous process of 'becoming black' AND 'becoming disabled' (Erevelles 2012) that is usually uncritically defined as 'natural' deviance or dis/respectability, and is used to justify the pathologization and criminalization of racialized and disabled bodies in educational contexts (Adams and Erevelles 2015).

The mutually constitutive event of simultaneously 'becoming black' and 'becoming disabled' is apparent in the ways in which race and disability are deployed under Section 504. The eligibility of those who qualify under Section 504 with the official designation of 'person with a disability' is presumably based on objective criteria supported by the medical model of disability where claiming a disability is assumed to be rooted in irrefutable biological fact. However, according to the data presented by Zirkel and Weathers (2014) (that echoes some of the concerns in the disproportionality debates under IDEA), we know that 'person with a disability' is an elastic category that can be expanded and contracted to include and exclude certain populations within particular historical and material contexts. In the specific context of Section 504, I argue that a 'person with a disability' is a historical construct imbued with dangerous implications for black (disabled) students.

When Zirkel and Weathers (2014) claim that upper-class white parents in non-Title I schools are apparently 'gaming' the system in order reap the benefits derived from a 504 plan, what the authors are essentially describing is the deployment of white upper-class privilege that provides white (disabled) students access

The Right to Exclude 131

to private economic and medical resources that are necessary for classification as 'a person with a disability' according to Section 504 guidelines. Now, I do not agree with Zirkel and Weathers that many of these parents are actually 'gaming' the system. That would be akin to accusing parents of committing disability fraud and demanding that their disabled children PROVE that they are actually disabled, whatever that actually means. Rejecting this premise, on the other hand, I foreground Zirkel and Weathers's argument to highlight the complex ways by which race and disability coalesce such that 'whiteness as property' anchored in class privilege is leveraged in order to claim a disability identity for the protection of the educational (and civil) rights of (white) disabled students under Section 504. Failure to seek this protection under Section 504 will result in the educational exclusion of (white) disabled students from regular classrooms, and often their mandatory segregation in special education ghettoes. And it is precisely the bleak experiences of disabled students in these special educational ghettoes that black (disabled) students without 504 plans do not have the privilege to avoid.

One of the questions that kept haunting me when discussing disproportionality was why black students were underutilizing Section 504 even if their labels met the criteria of 'person with a disability'. Here, in a fascinating reversal of the customary racial logic in the disproportionality debates around IDEA, Zirkel and Weathers's findings indicate that black students were *underrepresented* under the category 'person with a disability'. This would indicate that for students with possible labels of ADHD or ED, the 'mitigating measures' used to mediate their impairments were not considered applicable criteria for equipping them with a 504 plan. One of the explanations offered for this underrepresentation are economic costs. Since Section 504 is an unfunded mandate, Zirkel and Weathers point out that there are no monetary remunerations to ensure its mandate is carried out. Compared with the focus on assessment procedures to identify students under IDEA, there is a tangible neglect of attention paid to the identification of students under Section 504 that is further complicated by unclear regulations for grievance procedures that would ensure impartial hearings. This, coupled with a general lack of information from the school district regarding how to qualify for a 504 plan, has left many parents living in historically underserved communities in the dark. Additionally, if a parent is aware of the benefits of a 504 plan, the economic costs of obtaining a private medical diagnosis to challenge the school's refusal to consider one's child 'a person with a disability' under Section 504 guidelines makes obtaining a 504 plan for their child out of their reach.

While many of the hurdles parents from historically underserved communities face in attaining a 504 plan are mostly procedural, one particular hurdle is mired in oppressive ideologies mutually constituted at the intersection of race, class, gender, and disability. This hurdle draws its existence from a seemingly innocuous but potentially damaging practice called the 'manifestation review' that deals with a school's ability to invoke a set of disciplinary procedures on account of a disabled student's misconduct. A manifestation review offers significant protection under Section 504. Thus, students with a 504 plan have a right to a manifestation review where a team of educational professionals decides whether their misconduct is a

132   *Nirmala Erevelles*

manifestation of their disability, and if so, then the school is 'necessarily entailed by the duty not to discriminate on the ground of a disability' (Weber 2010: 23). This ensures that students with a 504 plan are protected against expulsion even if they are charged with misconduct and 'the burden is on the school to make the manifestation determination even if the student does not demand it' (23). Here, expulsion refers to 'any change of placement invoking the procedural protections of Section 504' (23). Thus, a manifestation review stands in sharp contrast with the lack of similar protections under IDEA, where some disciplinary removals may take place 'irrespective of whether the child's behaviour was a manifestation of the disability and [where] the definition of what is a manifestation of the disability is quite limited' (23).

It is through the 'manifestation review' or the lack of its applicability to black students who do not qualify for a 504 plan that the mutually constitutive practice of 'becoming black' and 'becoming disabled' gets materialized. One of the problematic touchstones of the disproportionality debate is the overrepresentation of black students in disciplinary procedures that include recommendations to attend alternative schools, out of school suspensions, and expulsions (Aul IV 2012; Erevelles 2014; Farmer 2010; McWilliams and Fancher 2010; Skiba, Michael, Nardo, and Peterson 2002). McWilliams and Fancher (2010) have identified the failure to evaluate for disabilities (or in this case a 504 plan) while in school as contributing to a demonstrated racial 'suspension gap' that negatively impacts communities of colour, especially the black community. Thus, for example, in affluent school districts, without access to a 'manifestation review,' black students with behavioural and/or emotional challenges, are denied the support that a 504 plan could have provided them (McWilliams and Fancher 2010). Unprotected by a 504 plan, a racist logic now comes into play when, for example, often the predominantly white administration assumes that these students are *choosing* to act out. The matter is further complicated by the tendency of teachers and school officials to define disruptive white youth with a 504 plan as in need of behavioural interventions/supports rather than suspension. This occurs in a context where social class, insurance coverage, and race are key indicators of who has a 504 plan and receives interventions and who does not have a 504 plan and is disciplined. In this context, race, class, and disability intersect to deny low-income students of colour with disabilities not only corrective and educational supports but also enable schools to exclude these 'troubled' black students from access to education with their peers (Erevelles 2014).

When black students are excluded from regular schools and exiled to alternative schools or the juvenile criminal system, they experience a kind of 'civic death' (Wacquant 2009). In other words, without protection under Section 504, black (disabled) students are denied their rights to full citizenship based on the same racist logic that was used to deny Dred Scott his rights to citizenship more than 150 years ago. This racist logic is concealed by the so-called objective assessment procedures that determine the eligibility of students under Section 504. What is concealed is that these assessment procedures constitute white (disabled) students and black (disabled) students as two sides of the same coin, held together and yet

The Right to Exclude   133

separated by an oppressive yet contradictory logic. According to this contradictory logic, black students are denied eligibility for protection under Section 504 because they are conceived of as naturally dangerous (Alexander 2010), foregrounding a dangerous biological determinism that is absurdly couched in a language of choice (i.e., they choose to act out). On the other hand, a white student's eligibility for a 504 plan is justified on the grounds of having a 'natural' deficiency also deploying a different form of biological determinism that is outside the realm of 'choice' (i.e., they cannot help their poor choices), and is, therefore eligible for protection under Section 504. It is in this context where absurd contradictions abound that the mutually constitutive practices of 'becoming black' AND 'becoming disabled' are materialized.

Conclusion: The Right to Exclude

In this chapter, I have identified procedural barriers and as well as racialized discourses and ableist practices to explain why black (disabled) students seldom qualify for protection under Section 504. I have described particular racialized discourses and ableist practices that contribute to the historical conditions that have created racial disproportionalities under Section 504. I have also described some of the oppressive and punitive consequences for black (disabled) students when they are excluded from protection under Section 504. Now, in the final section of this paper, I reflect on the broader social and political implications that arise from these conditions of disproportionality and the ensuing dis-location of black (disabled) students from [white] normative space as a result of their exclusion from protection under Section 504.

The differential access of black (disabled) students and white (disabled) students to 504 plans also results in differential outcomes. White (disabled) students with 504 plans have the privilege of being supported within inclusive educational contexts. Black (disabled) students with behavioural and/or emotional challenges with no access to 504 plans seldom experience support in inclusive classrooms are pathologized on account of their (non-normative) behaviours and are often expelled from inclusive spaces to segregated prison-like settings like the alternative school and the juvenile justice system (Erevelles 2014). When the intersecting discourses of race and disability as pathological deviance are deployed in a broader social context, black bodies (even the bodies of black children) failed to be seen as vulnerable and come to be feared so terribly that their very presence in large numbers in (white) classrooms creates 'moral panic'. Farmer (2010) defines 'moral panic' as 'the means of orchestrating consent by actively intervening in the space of public opinion and social consciousness through the use of highly rhetorical and emotive language which has the effect of requiring that something be done about it' (Farmer 2010: 372). This 'something be done about it' is exclusion – plain and simple – exclusion carried out via dubious standardized test cut-offs and zero-tolerance policies where no supports (504 forms) are offered to the children whose resistance against this exclusion only exacerbates this panic until their complete ejection from these (white) spaces is accomplished. Dumas and Ross (2016) call

134 *Nirmala Erevelles*

this experience of exclusion – 'antiblackness', which they define as 'a social construction, . . . an embodied lived experience of social suffering and resistance, and perhaps most importantly, . . . an antagonism, in which the Black is a despised thing-in-itself (but not person for herself or himself) in opposition to all that is pure, human(e), and White' (416–417).

Antiblackness was entrenched in the carefully selected admissions criteria with its codified assessment procedures and unstated behavioural norms that monitored who could be successful in the magnet school I described earlier. Antiblackness was entrenched in the lack of behavioural and academic supports offered to black students with no 504 plans who were forced out or chose to leave the school eventually. Antiblackness existed in the support groups of liberal white parents who shared trade secrets among themselves to encourage other white (disabled) children to obtain 504 plans but failed to connect with black parents whose children quietly and suddenly disappeared from those (white) classrooms. Antiblackness was quite simply the colour line drawn in the sand separating those (white) disabled children with 504 plans and those (black) disabled children without.

Recognizing the ubiquity of antiblackness and in the spirit of committed critique, I will end this chapter by making some polemical (truth) claims. First, I argue that the maintenance of the colour line as observed through the disproportionalities that have surfaced when analyzing data on students with 504-only plans is a deliberate act. It is a deliberate act because the protections offered under Section 504 cast 'whiteness as property' (Harris 1993) as a valued commodity while simultaneously casting black students as unwanted and unworthy citizens in public education settings. The refusal to grant protection under 504 to black students represents a deliberate act of antiblackness that mimics exactly the very same material and discursive practices that denied Dred Scott the right to his freedom more than 150 years ago. By maintaining the 'right to exclude' that inheres from the privilege invested in 'whiteness as property', the structuring of community along racial lines (the colour line) is maintained by drawing on contested and oppressive concepts of disability to justify these disproportionalities as natural and/or accidental outcomes of seemingly emancipatory statutes. I call these practices that maintain disproportionality under Section 504 'educational red-lining' in order to foreground the systematic denial of 504 plans to black children in public education (Velez and Solarzano, in press) – an exclusion that does not bode well for black students who find themselves exiled to alternative schools and eventually the school-to-prison pipeline. In that way, the problem in public education notwithstanding its stated claims to more objective and sophisticated assessment and labelling procedures is quite simply, in fact, the problem of the colour line.

References

Adams, D. L., and Erevelles, N. (2015). Shadow play: DisCrit, dis/respectability and carceral logics. In D. Connor, B. Ferri and S. Annamma (eds.) *DisCrit: Disability studies and critical race theory in education* (pp. 131–144). New York: Teachers College Press.

The Right to Exclude   135

Alexander, M. (2010). *The new Jim Crow: Mass incarceration in the age of colourblindness.* New York: The New Press.

Annamma, S.A., Connor, D., and Ferri, B. (2013). Dis/ability critical race studies (DisCrit): Theorizing at the intersections of race and dis/ability. *Race Ethnicity and Education,* 16(1), 1–31.

Artiles, A. J. (2013). Untangling the racialization of disabilities. *Du Bois Review: Social Science Research on Race,* 10(02), 329–347.

Artiles, A.J., Kozleski, E.B., Trent, S.C., Osher, D., and Ortiz, A. (2010). Justifying and explaining disproportionality, 1968–2008: A critique of underlying views of culture. *Exceptional Children,* 76(3), 279–299.

Aul IV, E. (2012). Zero Tolerance, Frivolous juvenile court referrals, and the school-to-prison pipeline: Using arbitration as a screening-out method to help plug the pipeline. *Ohio State Journal of Dispute Resolution,* 27, 180–206.

Ben-Moshe, L., Chapman, C., and Carey, A. (eds.). (2014). *Disability incarcerated imprisonment and disability in the United States and Canada.* Basingstoke: Palgrave Macmillan.

Blanchett, W.J. (2010). Telling it like it is: The role of race, class, and culture in the perpetuation of learning disability as a privileged category for the white middle class. *Disability Studies Quarterly,* 30(2), 1230–1277.

Douglas, M. (2003). *Purity and danger: An analysis of concepts of pollution and taboo.* New York: Routledge.

Du Bois, W.E.B. (1999). *Souls of black folk.* New York, NY: W.W. Norton and Company (Originally published in 1903).

Dumas, M.J., and Ross, K. J. (2016). "Be Real Black for Me"; Imagining BlackCrit in Education. *Urban Education,* 15(4), 415–442.

Erevelles, N. (2012). *Disability and difference in global context: Towards a transformative body politic.* New York: Palgrave.

Erevelles, N. (2014). Crippin'Jim Crow: Disability, Dis-Location, and the School-to-Prison Pipeline. In A.Carey, L. Ben-Moshe, & C. Chapman , (eds). *Disability Incarcerated* (pp.81-99). New York: Palgrave Macmillan.

Farmer, S. (2010). Criminality of Black Youth in inner-city schools: 'Moral panic,' moral imagination, and moral formation. *Race Ethnicity, and Education,* 13(3), 367–381.

Ferri, B.A., and Connor, D.J. (2005). In the shadow of brown special education and over-representation of students of colour. *Remedial and Special Education,* 26(2), 93–100.

Harris, C.I. (1993). Whiteness as property. *Harvard Law Review,* 106 (8), 1707–1791.

Harry, B., and Klingner, J. (2006). *Why are so many minority students in special education?* New York: Teachers College.

Holt, L. (2003). (Dis)abling children in primary school micro-spaces: Geographies of inclusion and exclusion. *Health and Place,* 9(2), 119–128.

Logan, J.R., Minca, E., and Adar, S. (2012). The geography of inequality why separate means unequal in American Public Schools. *Sociology of Education,* 85(3), 287–301.

McWilliams, M., and Fancher, M.P. (2010). Undiagnosed students with disabilities trapped in the school-to-prison pipeline. *Michigan Bar Journal,* 89 (8), 28–33.

Orfield, G., and C. Lee. 2005. *Why segregation matters: Poverty and educational inequality.* Cambridge, MA: Civil Rights Project at Harvard University.

Powell, J.A., and Menendian, S. (2008). Little Rock and the Legacy of Dred Scott. *Louis ULJ,* 52, 1153–1189.

Samuels, CA. (2014, August, 20). Students with '504 Plans' more likely to be white, enrolled in non-title I schools [Web log post]. http://blogs.edweek.org/edweek/speced/2014/08/students_with_504_plans_more_l.html

136 Nirmala Erevelles

Schraven, J., and Jolly, J.L. (2010). Section 504 in American public schools: An ongoing response to change. *American Educational History Journal*, 37(1/2), 419.

Schweik, S. (2011). Lomax's matrix: Disability, solidarity, and the black power of 504. *Disability Studies Quarterly*, 31(1). http://dsq-sds.org/article/view/1371/1539

Skiba, R.J., Michael, R.S., Nardo, A.C., and Peterson, R.L. (2002). The colour of discipline: Sources of racial and gender disproportionality in school punishment. *The Urban Review*, 34(4), 317–342.

Skiba, R.J., Poloni-Staudinger, L., Gallini, S., Simmons, A.B., and Feggins-Azziz, R. (2006). Disparate access: The disproportionality of African American students with disabilities across educational environments. *Exceptional Children*, 72(4), 411–424.

Stubblefield, A. (2005). Ethics along the color line. Ithaca, N.Y.: Cornell University Press.

Vandervelde, L. (2015). The Dred Scott case in context. *Journal of Supreme Court History*, 40(3), 263–281.

Velez, V.N. and Solarzano, D.G. (in press). Critical Race Spatial Analysis: Conceptualizing GIS as a Tool for Critical Race Research in Education. In D. Morrison, S. Annamma and D. Jackson, (eds.), The *spatial search to understand and address educational inequality to inform practice*. New York: Stylus.

Wacquant, L. (2009). *Punishing the poor: The neoliberal government of social insecurity*. Durham, NC: Duke University Press.

Walker, C.J. (2006). Adequate access or equal treatment: Looking beyond the IDEA to Section 504 in a post-Schaffer public school. *Stanford Law Review*, 58(5) 1563–1622.

Watts, I.E., and Erevelles, N. (2004). These deadly times: Reconceptualizing school violence by using critical race theory and disability studies. *American Educational Research Journal*, 41(2), 271–299.

Weber, M.C. (2010). A new look at Section 504 and the ADA in special education cases. *Texas Journal on Civil Liberties and Civil Rights*, 16, 1–27.

Zirkel, P.A., and Weathers, J.M. (2014). Section 504-only students national incidence data. *Journal of Disability Policy Studies*, 26(3), 184–193.

9 The Hunt for Disability
The New Eugenics and the Normalization of School Children[1]

Bernadette Baker

Thoughtful students . . . of the *psychology of adolescence* will refuse to believe that the American public intends to have its children sorted before their teens into clerks, watchmakers, lithographers, telegraph operators, masons, teamsters, farm laborers, and so forth, and treated differently in their schools according to the prophecies of their appropriate life careers. Who are to make these prophecies?
(Charles Eliot (1905: 330–331; original emphasis))

There has been, I think, a noticeable increase in the identification of students with disabilities and we're really trying to understand why that is.
(Director of Department of Educational Services, Fairfield School District[2] 2000)

Charles Eliot's 'Fundamental Assumptions in the Report of the Committee of Ten' was published one year after G. Stanley Hall's two volume work on adolescence and had as its implicit target child-study enthusiasts of the new psychology. Part of Eliot's concern was to protect the place of classical curricula content, such as Latin and Greek, in public schools rather than have curricula revolve around judgments of 'child nature.' All children, in his view, should be exposed to the subject matter that prepared the way for university entrance, of which there was more than one kind.[3] In debunking the child-study orientations to curricula, Eliot turned to the available discourse of democracy to sanction what others have described as his patrician preferences (Kliebard 1986). In Eliot's logic, if all public school children are exposed equally to 'high culture' in one of four forms, then it seemingly is not the school that makes a judgment about appropriate life careers. Rather, it is the child's effort in interacting with the subject matter that shapes their future. Under this line of reasoning, the issue of different life careers could be cast back onto students themselves and the singularity of certain kinds of cultural knowledge left unchallenged as the pinnacle of educatedness.

In 2000, the director of the Department of Educational Services in Fairfield school district (a pseudonym) does not have the luxury of masking or encoding schooling's sorting function. Students are labeled, and special and different services are provided. Children are treated differently in their schools, and educators and allied professionals do make the decisions or prophecies. What separates the

138 Bernadette Baker

positions available to Eliot and the director of educational services is not, however, any clear shift from right to left, or from a desire for homogeneity to a celebration of difference, but a reworked discourse of democracy – for Eliot, democracy meant equality-in-sameness, the same access to the same curriculum tracks for all public school children who cannot buy their way out of the system. For the director, it is an unspoken vision of democracy as equality-in-difference – children are different from each other, and therefore a variety of special services are required to educate a variety of children, ironically, in line with the same statewide standards.

This chapter is an attempt to reconsider issues of sameness, difference, equality, and democracy in present public school systems. I focus in particular on the question of (dis)ability and the implications of (dis)ability as an ontological issue before its inscription as an educational one concerning the politics of inclusion. I am especially interested in this analysis in what symbolically links the positions available to Eliot and the director rather than what separates them. That is, I am concerned with understanding and rethinking the everyday dividing, sorting, and classifying practices of schooling through an analysis of old and new discourses of eugenics as 'quality control' of national populations.

The chapter has three sections. First, I examine the vexed question of what the term *eugenics* refers to. Rather than seeing eugenics as a movement that rose in popularity in the late 19th century and fell after the revelations of the Holocaust's horror, I suggest that eugenics was a complicated and heterogeneous series of discourses that have transmogrified into a variety of assumptions and practices, including educational ones in the present. The second section of the chapter examines some of those assumptions and practices, especially the debates that have arisen around the Classificatory systems for identifying disability, both outside and within schooling. In the often well-intended hunt for disability,[4] I will suggest that disability becomes reinscribed as an 'outlaw ontology' (Wrigley 1996), reinvesting eugenic discourse in a new language that maintains an 'ableist normativity' (Campbell 2000).[5] Third, I will consider where such an analysis leaves institutions of formal education, including universities, and the very difficult question of trying to imagine alternatives to sending the posse out[6] in schools.

Eugenics Old . . . Historiographical Debates

Eugenics is a problematic, contentious, and emotive term. To some extent there is disagreement in the historical literature as to how to define or recognize something as eugenicist. It is only to some extent because there are certain things that do seem generally agreed on in regard to eugenics, primarily that it refers at the broadest level to a belief in the necessity of 'racial' or 'national' improvement through the control of population reproduction. This is understood within the historical and sociological literature on eugenics as a code for promoting, through scientific, medical, psychological, educational, and welfare discourses of the late 19th century, a belief in a hierarchy of human races/nations and characteristics, with the pinnacle of racial/national evolution at that time being the presumed qualities of Anglo-Saxon or Teutonic groups primarily of northern and western Europe and

North America. There is general agreement as to the timing of the term's emergence, coined in 1883 by Francis Galton, and also a common recognition of certain practices as eugenic, most notably those associated with the Holocaust and the earlier sterilization campaigns that targeted 'physical and mental defectives,' often broadly conceived to include any minority group thought to be contributing to 'national degeneration.'

Within this general understanding of eugenics as *constructing* and privileging certain kinds of whiteness over certain kinds of color, certain kinds of masculinity over certain kinds of femininity, certain kinds of ability over certain kinds of 'corporeally anomalous' body-minds, and tolerating only narrow versions of heteronormativity and religious devotion, eugenics becomes somewhat swamped. It is difficult to find any discourse circulating in the late 19th century that did *not* draw on such binaries or that did not argue for some kind of racial/national improvement. What, then, was unique to eugenics? Much debate has arisen around this question as to which programs, theories, or moments can be identified as 'truly' eugenicist or not. The debate has emerged in the context of trying to sort out the extent of the legacy of eugenics, that is, how 'it' has effected 'ideas in action and action in ideas' in the present (Garton 2000). The recent historical and sociological literature has pointed to the previous silence on such legacies due to a naïve belief that, after the Holocaust, eugenics simply went away (Kaplan 2000). Such literature also sometimes engages in a forecasting of what may result with continued silence, particularly under the advent of new genetic technologies (Campbell 2000).

The debates arise, then, within an atmosphere that is critical and suspicious of such silence around the effects of eugenics and eugenics as an effect. Despite agreement as to the most easily recognizable aspects of practice, such as sterilization, disagreement can be found in how to approach the study of eugenics in historical perspective. For example, one historian may describe a certain practice as part of eugenic philosophy or see it as a family member, whereas another will label the same practice as a separate philosophical position altogether.

Such debate over labeling and attribution has emerged especially within historical accounts of eugenics in Australia, continental Europe and Scandinavia, the United Kingdom, and the United States. Some histories of eugenics within these contexts, for instance, have portrayed it as a late 19th-century form of scientific racism that eventually gave fascism and Hitler the discursive grounds for propaganda and structured the WWII genocide of persons practicing Judaism, persons defined as having physical or mental disabilities, and persons defined as practicing homosexuality – none of whom Nazi policy saw fully as persons. In Ludmerer's (1972), Pickens's (1968), and Searle's (1971) accounts, for example, eugenics is portrayed as a movement, with its end being attributed to a late 1940s horror at the Holocaust that resulted in a loss of popularity for what had been initially perceived in many quarters as a respectable scientific theory and populist platform.

Other historians contest the portrayal of eugenics as a discrete movement and argue instead that eugenics needs to be understood as a series of discourses (Gould 1981). Some claim that eugenics in the strict sense was a variety of forms of hereditarianism (Garton 2000), whereas others claim that eugenics had intersecting

140   Bernadette Baker

hereditarian and environmentalist elements (Lowe 2000). What is more agreed on in the scholarship that contests eugenics as a discrete movement is that there was a combination of elements and points of view that inhered in the late 19th-century emergence of eugenics as a term and in the formation of eugenic societies and associations. Such histories suggest that a variety of philosophical positions contributed to eugenics' key message – a belief in the necessity of racial or national improvement via quality control of population reproduction – and that these philosophical orientations have mutated into a variety of practices, programs, and policies that have lasted beyond the demise of formal eugenic associations. Michael Roe argues, for instance, that there has been a new surge of interest in genetic technologies and that this interest is fed by dangerously unexamined assumptions that bear vestiges of old-style eugenics. The promotion of genetic technologies, for example, contains an unexamined implicit and explicit belief that such developments 'are for humanity's benefit, even its perfection – physical, psychological, and behavioral. That was the prospect which lured earlier eugenicists, and of course the enchantment remains' (Roe 2000: 6). Writing the history of eugenics in light of the advent of new genetic technologies means to Roe that eugenics does not end in 1945 with the death of Hitler. Gisela Kaplan further reorients how one would write the history of eugenics by putting it into global perspective. She argues that the speed with which ideas travel now means that more so than ever before close scrutiny and vigilance is merited in asking what it is that is being globalized. Kaplan suggests that new versions of eugenics are part of globalization and that this is not surprising given that eugenics was one of the first *globalized* and *globalizing* discourses. She rewrites where eugenics begins, seeing the most significant aspect in the emergence of modern racism, the modern slave trade, transatlantic commerce, and colonialism as being laid by the fall of Constantinople in the 15th century. This incited a search for new trade routes to the East and opened up the voyages that resulted in the invasion of the Americas and the establishment of slave 'trading posts' on the West African coast. It was the experience of slavery in particular that lent eugenics the fears and desires it was to eventually attempt to regulate through social policy centuries later after the drawn-out abolition of slavery post–Civil War in the United States. That is, the idea of mixed blood that the early eugenicists were so concerned about was a direct expression of one of slavery's consequences.

In satirical mode, Kaplan suggests that the spread of eugenic ideas, even in modified or less official forms, was a 'requirement,' for European scholars and bureaucrats had to identify new themes and justify European social and political practice outside Europe. Whereas in the United States, eugenics was applied to the 'problem': the end of slavery. Kaplan argues further that if the idea of 'surprise' that the Holocaust could take place in 'civilized' Europe was expressed, it indicates an underestimation of the effect of more than a century of debates foregrounding explicit attitudes on issues of race as something inclusive of but far more than just 'color.' That these debates happened in the center of 'civilized' Europe required, however, that the practice of eugenics was perceived not as barbaric but as rational, not as criminal but as courageous and progressive. Kaplan asks 'How else could eugenics become palatable?' arguing that there are parallels today that make

The Hunt for Disability 141

eugenic reasonings 'palatable' and seemingly progressive, couched as they are in languages of 'proactive racism' and 'quality citizenship.'

Finally, in his paper 'Writing Eugenics: A History of Classifying Practices,' Stephen Garton has problematized the slide into using the term eugenics as a catchall, as if its meaning has already been settled. Garton's answer to the question 'What do we take as the key signifier of eugenics?' is a long and complicated one. Eugenics, he argues, might refer to a fundamental belief in hereditary deficiency as the basis for many social problems, and arising from this eugenicists might be seen as those committed to policies preventing the breeding of the unfit and promoting that of the 'racially fit.' It might also refer to support for sterilization programs. But Garton argues that there were many who accepted a hereditary basis to 'social inefficiency' and who were more cautious about sterilization, preferring permanent segregation as a means of preventing the propagation of the racially unfit. Many of those, he suggests, were also open to explanations that invoked appeal to the environment as causal of social problems as well. Thus, in Garton's view, if 'both camps' (hereditarian and environmental) are to be accepted, it opens eugenics to the prospect that it was far from a singular ideology or set of policies and practices and that it was imbricated in wider class, race, religion, gender, and ability constructions and worked sometimes in contradictory ways with diverse strands of thought to shape social policies (Garton 2000: 11).

In addition, he cautions against using eugenics to refer simply to any form of population management or intervention. For example, the pronatalism of the early 20th century cannot be conflated with eugenics. Pronatalist stances are fundamentally concerned with an increase in the quantity of population (e.g., populate-or-perish policies), whereas, for eugenics, quantity is a positive danger if it increases 'tainted stock.' What Garton sees as uniquely eugenic in terms of population management is that a concern for the *quality* of population is the key issue.

In Garton's view, then, the orientation to eugenics as a complicated series of hereditarian discourses intersecting with other discourses brings to light how the most favored plans of the early eugenicists both failed and succeeded in terms of their own agenda and influence. The failure that Garton speaks of in regard to eugenics is that the campaign for particular policies that the early eugenicists actively promulgated were not taken up everywhere that they were campaigned for and did not last long when they did. Although this is a controversial position on failure insofar as one might argue that *any* uptake and *any* form of policy implementation, such as sterilization centers, represented a 'success' for eugenics, Garton's point is about seeing the *disagreement* that scientists and policy makers had regarding such recommendations for policy and their underlying rationales. In short, eugenic arguments that linked social problems to heredity and solutions to the control of reproduction were not monolithically supported. Even where such arguments reached the level of policy formation, they were sometimes vetoed, such as in the United Kingdom in the 1930s. Where such policies were implemented, the number of people confined and segregated always fell far short of what their promoters requested.

What this lack of unanimity suggests to Garton is that at a 'practical' level, the most stringent aspect of eugenics platforms and its most favored programs were

142 Bernadette Baker

not necessarily so widespread that there was no contestation arising and were not long-lasting in historical terms, even where they were implemented. This has led Garton to conclude that a eugenics program for racial/national improvement, defined as measures for population control targeted at heredity 'defects,' was on the one hand unsuccessful in spreading the actuality of its most revered recommendations yet highly influential at a different level – the way in which professionals, scientists, educators, and politicians thought about human life and their right to control that of others. What seemed to differ across time was not the belief in that right but the strategies for implementing it. Garton suggests that this has left a difficult legacy for historians, namely to disentangle how eugenics was both far less and far more influential than accounts of it as a discrete movement that rose and fell might suggest.

From Naming the Problem to the Problem of Naming: Reworked Imaginaries

At one level, the historiographical debate summarized above may seem pointless. Whether a practice, judged intention, or policy is called social Darwinistic, eugenic, scientific racism, or population theory it seems that the abiding commonality was what Michel Foucault (1989) has called in a different context 'superiority effects.' The 'top' of the chain of being was inscribed similarly across such nomenclatures and only some were positioned as having the right to modify others. The debates over whether eugenics refers to this or to that phenomenon, period, or program may seem pedantic on that ground, but it is not. Nor are the historiographical debates about trying to minimize the atrocities commonly associated with eugenics. Rather, the nuances that Garton and others have pointed to help explain how on the one hand we might recognize that there has been change without difference in regard to 'superiority effects' across the 20th century – on the surface, a similar image of the ideal citizen still seems to circulate. On the other hand, it helps to explain how some practices have not been sustainable and why others emerge in their place. That is, one can perhaps identify vestiges of the old eugenics as 'quality control directed at hereditary deficiency' in new moments because of the multiple positions spawned around the 'problem' of population governance and the variety of discourses that merge, separate, and transmogrify in responding to new events.

As Lucinda Aberdeen (2000) has noted, though, this does not mean that, all of a sudden, the late 20th century has developed better scholarship to understand eugenics, the past, and its effects. Aberdeen studied how at first phenotypical features, then blood type, then genetic mapping were all strategies used across the 20th century to 'pin' race down and create an 'index' by which peoples could be confirmed as belonging to certain racial categories. New strategies were developed when the old ones failed to deliver the accuracy desired, such as when serological studies of the 1920s and 1930s came to the conclusion that indigenous peoples of Australia by blood type were closer to the 'western European type' than the English. Such blood studies quickly fell out of favor as a scientific tool. Elazar Barkan (1992) has also demonstrated how concepts of race changed in Britain and the

The Hunt for Disability 143

United States between the world wars, reflected in the development of new technical tools for identification in those contexts. Thus, in discussing how racial imaginaries have overridden evidence to the contrary and been reworked around new strategies for identification, Aberdeen (2000: 102) concludes that 'it is not that we are better scholars than the serologists of the 1920s and 1930s but rather that the racialised imaginary in which they worked has been contested and so we can begin to imagine the world otherwise.'

The Impact of the Old Eugenics on Education

Imagining the world otherwise because racial/national imaginaries have been contested is what has opened eugenics and its impact on education to critique. It is also what enables an arbitrary distinction between old and new eugenics. In respect of old and new eugenic discourses in education, the work of Roy Lowe is particularly instructive. Lowe (1997) argues that eugenics discourse has had a massive impact on education and that this has been downplayed by the linkage of eugenics with sterilization policy. He contends that from the outset eugenicists had direct things to say to schools and that this aspect of eugenic thought has proved to be more pervasive and more enduring than the more spectacular arguments around sterilization. Lowe suggests that the impact on schools can be traced even through those historical periods in which one might think social conditions were most inimical to the expression of eugenicist ideas, that is, in the aftermath of the horror of the Holocaust. In England, for instance, eugenicists were called on to give evidence to the Royal Commission on Population in 1949, arguing that 'the different branches of the human race were unequally equipped with the inborn characters that produce and sustain highly organised civilizations.' Despite having to make the expression of ideas more circumspect in the aftermath of the Holocaust, associations such as the Eugenics Society also continued to function. The society found a new focus after WWII, genetics, and in particular the study of 'defective' chromosomes. Further, public pronouncements were made that gave renewed vitality to old ideas about sterilization, couched in new welfare reasonings about the underprivileged. In the United States in the 1950s, Julian Huxley and Frederick Osborne both argued for the use of contraception to limit the fertility of minority groups, particularly African Americans, while in England, Francis Quick advocated a licensing scheme that might limit the number of children borne by 'genetically unfavorable' parents. Other post-WWII approaches tried to preserve the 'best' genes; during the 1970s the Repository for Germinal Choice was established in California to collect and store sperm from Nobel Prize winners.

Thus, Lowe argues that these examples, plus the many more that he documents, provide considerable evidence of the survival and even popularity of eugenic ideas in the closing decades of the 20th century. His historical documentation indicates an arbitrary distinction between old and new eugenic discourses within a variety of institutions. He suggests that in education, specifically, there was no privileged immunity to these wider mutations and recombobulated discourses. Lowe

144 *Bernadette Baker*

identifies five areas of educational policy and practice that were deeply influenced by eugenic ideas for much of the 20th century:

1   Testing – The 'problem' of national degeneration central to eugenics led directly to the search for the means to test the population so as to ascertain its 'ability levels.'
2   Differential Treatment – The explicit and implicit suggestion that at the heart of any understanding of mankind or womankind lay differences and contrasts between races led to the belief that individuals from different ethnic backgrounds had differing educational potential and should be treated differently.
3   Quality of Home Life and Mothering – The concern for national degeneration led to a questioning of both hereditary influences *and* environment. The quality of home life became a focus and separate schooling tracks for girls and boys were established to have girls become more efficient mothers.
4   Transmission of Opinions Through Children's Books and School Texts – To the extent that school books were and remain racialized they have reflected in part the influence of eugenic thinking. Steven Selden's (1999) analysis of American textbooks makes the same point.
5   The Planning of Educational Buildings – Although more oblique, the planning of education buildings was influenced in part by eugenic thinking insofar as there was support for and implementation of the view that the 'future leaders of society' should receive their education both at school and university in institutions whose architecture was a constant reminder of a Greco-Roman and Gothic racial and intellectual heritage of which they considered themselves a part.

Other historians have documented less well-known aspects of eugenics' direct effect on education. Grant Rodwell has indicated how less well-publicized recommendations for 'medical interventions' emerged even in contexts where sterilization may not have been officially sanctioned. Rodwell (2000) demonstrates how the kindergarten movement in Australia became a site for addressing the threat that 'precocious masturbators,' four- and five-year-old children, seemed to represent to national morality. In eugenic terms, precocious masturbators in the kindergarten had to be saved from a tragic future and the country from racial suicide. Accordingly, at a conference on sex hygiene in 1916 at the University of Sydney, Zoë Benjamin, a lecturer at the Sydney Kindergarten Training College, proposed circumcision for boys and clitoridectomy for girls who were identified as precocious masturbators in the kindergarten.

Rodwell and Lowe elaborate how specific sites within education have been indebted to eugenic thinking. Others such as Garton see the most significant effect of eugenics in the uptake of widespread classifying practices that have permeated educational and other institutions. Garton argues that although old-style eugenics might not have achieved a hegemonic status in the full Gramscian sense because it never secured the consent of the dominated and it never secured the full allegiance of the broad middle class, it did become a key moment and a key approach in the development of what Foucault (1979) has called 'dividing practices.' These practices of categorization and classification assumed a divisibility to being and became important to social government between the world wars and well after. Eugenics might not have been the only impetus for dividing practices, but it was, in Garton's (2000: 16) view, 'a central and very significant impetus to the development of a raft of tests, categories and administrative arrangements – IQ tests, psychological tests, personality tests, clinics, visiting medical services, observation wards and the like that emerged in the late nineteenth and early twentieth century to deal with the crisis of problem populations.'

The 'problem populations' were produced through such classifying practices, new ones being created all the time – 'the feeble-minded, the degenerate, the numerous gradations of "mixed race" peoples, the juvenile delinquent, the sexually delinquent girl, the moral imbecile, the psychopath, the sex psychopath, the transsexual, the homosexual, the pervert, the neuropath and so on' (Garton 2000: 16). These were not just new words – they were ways of enforcing others into the subjectivities assumed associated with the words. Garton argues further that each of these new subjectivities had its own unique mix of what was considered heredity, social, racial, psychological, and familial factors in their origins.

It is important to note that in listing such factors of origins (e.g., the heredity, social, racial, psychological, and familial) Garton could just as easily be talking about how children's behavior is analyzed in public schooling today. The production of and hunt for different forms of disability, unreadiness, at-risk-icity, and the explanations for developmental delay that circulate at the turn of the 21st century often pay homage to similar lists of factors. Garton argues of the emergence of eugenics at the turn of the 20th century that it led to a proliferation of problem populations to be analysed and remedied. This is not unique to the early 20th century. To that end, I focus below on the intersection of new eugenics discourse as the hunt for disabilities and the present classifying practices of schooling.

Eugenics New: (Dis)ability and Education

One particularly instructive site in which racial-national imaginaries have been reworked is in regard to notions of (dis)ability. Fiona Campbell (2000) makes a claim for understanding 20th-century discourse on *dis*ability as that which has shifted from the old eugenics to the new. Campbell argues that the pre-1945 old eugenics is characterized as a negative type, often controlled by government bureaucracies and initiated by way of transparent and coercive practices. Crucial to the negative eugenics of the Holocaust's Nazi Aktion T4 program (1939–1941), for instance, where approximately 275,000 people assigned disability labels were murdered, were two particular assumptions: an understanding of the (real) citizen as informed by a contributory or performance ethic and a logic of the strategy of euthanasia as primarily economic, where 'euthanasia was defended as a means of cost cutting, or ridding society, of "useless eaters."' In contrast to the old eugenics,

146   *Bernadette Baker*

yet not in the form of complete rupture, Campbell (2000: 308) argues that the 'eugenic imperative in late modernity' has been transmogrified into a variety of 'positive eugenic'[7] [8] [9] practices 'which seek to eliminate the birthing of bodies marked as "disabled" or, in the event of their/our post-natal "existence" to engage in "perfecting" technologies that morph ableism and enshrine a particular understanding of ableist normativity and (real) human subjectivity.' Put another way, Campbell is arguing that if 'bodies marked as "disabled"' are born at all, 'slipping through the net,' so to speak, then the activity of the posse switches to trying to 'perfect' that 'defective' body-mind to make it more 'normal,' leaving the reference point unquestioned and inscribing as a genuine effect a human subjectivity that defers to this order of things.

In regard to the body-mind marked as 'disabled,' Campbell further suggests that eugenicist practices are presently more covert and insidious and that what they have in common is that at root they concern ontological matters, 'largely unexamined and unspoken preconceptions about who should and should not inherit the world.' In the new eugenics, according to Campbell, the State governs disability more indirectly and the individual has a key role in this governance through a process of responsibilisation, which directs individuals' conduct and relations in a direction that is desired and desirable.

> the State plays a less direct and de-centered role in the governing of 'disability.' Under the mantle of political liberalism boldly proclaiming rampant individualism and freedom of choice, the individual acts as her own overseer, wherein techniques of self-production are not imposed but actively sought. Such technologies of responsibilisation ensure the shaping of conduct (relations of self to self and to others), is mobilised in a desired direction.

Although Campbell's implicit reference here seems to be to adults as their own overseers, in public school systems where (some) students are compelled by law to attend and are subjected to the processes that comprise the institution, the overseeing is initially performed by others. Campbell's further argument is that, under the guise of 'laissez-faire eugenics,' the onus is on personal decision making within an overarching framework of 'risk assessment,' and 'positive eugenics' seems, then, to pertain particularly to the adult-directed activities of schooling where risk assessment is now considered a 'normal' practice and teachers, special educators, psychological and medical experts, and parents are drawn into assessing children's behavior to make decisions about any potential 'problem': 'Disability talk is often conducted in terms of a "problem," a conundrum, or if you like, a headache that simply won't go away' (Campbell 2000: 309).

The conundrum, Campbell suggests, is not a deep fear of the unknown or an apprehensiveness toward the foreign or strange, but rather it is a deep-seated despise of unevenness, asymmetry, or imbalance that places bodies-minds labeled as disabled at the edge of the abyss, pushing the limits of human subjectivity, and creating an outlaw ontology. An outlaw ontology refers to a way of being or existing

The Hunt for Disability   147

that is thought outside the normal and as such to need chasing down, like the unacceptable rogue outlaws of old Western films. Quoting Judith Butler, Campbell points out how it is not enough to say that human subjects are constructed, for the construction of a human is a differential operation that produces the more and the less human, the inhuman, the humanly unthinkable: 'These excluded sites come to bound the "human" as its constitutive outside, and to haunt those boundaries.' Thus Campbell argues that in the new eugenics, ontological matters 'are inextricably bound up with the politics of inclusion' (Campbell 2000: 309).

Christine Crowe (2000) argues for caution, however, in interpreting the shift from eugenics to genetics discourse. The terms of her caution reinforce Campbell's conclusions, though, by illustrating how 'quality control' issues and technologies of responsibilization are still at the heart of 'disability wars,' including those within schools. Crowe sees eugenics as a discrete movement and argues that the terms of genetics discourse, especially those proposals that seek out 'defects' by prenatal screening, turning motherhood into decisions about what kinds of 'bodies' to give birth to, are somewhat different from old-style eugenics. Although both eugenics and genetics are concerned with quality control, the manner of the interventions available is now suggestive of new formulations of 'the problem.' In particular, prenatal screening is a formulation of risk and responsibility that relates to a different kind of 'governmentality' (Foucault 1991) relative to the past:

> Genetics is also oriented towards the quality of offspring, but, unlike the dominant eugenic discourse, conceptualises the relationship between risk and responsibility in significantly different ways. Whilst the eugenics movement may be conceptualized in terms of an attempt at state control of reproductive practices, focused on the prevention of reproduction by the negation of fertility, reproductive technologies are operationalised by appeals to individual responsibility for the health of future offspring. The site of intervention in this case is not the prevention of fertility, but the management of fertility, of conception, such that 'viable' embryos of choice, will be implanted in a woman's body. In other words, one of the significant differences between eugenics and genetic practices . . . is that whereas eugenics aimed at the prevention of fertility of the 'unfit,' genetic practices are oriented toward not the prevention of fertility, but the management of conception.
>
> (Crowe 2000: 176)

Although Crowe's focus is reproductive technologies, one can see a similar shift in debates around inclusive schooling and mainstreaming. Rather than telling a child they simply cannot attend a 'regular' school, the point of prohibition is relocated – the child perceived as 'having' disabilities of a certain kind can now be problematized, marginalized, and 'managed' within the mainstream institution (Slee 1997) – the alterity is brought back to the center to reinforce it. As Campbell notes, the new eugenics, if not effective in preventing certain kinds of conceptions, turns its attention to 'perfecting technologies' that are at base indebted to a perhaps well-intended but nonetheless controlling logic of ableism that hopes to turn

148 *Bernadette Baker*

everyone into the one kind of being at least at some level. The debates over whether mainstreaming is inclusion or assimilation (Slee 1997), whether it genuinely meets the needs of students categorized as disabled more than before (Erevelles 2000), can thus be understood differently as debates that question in one way or another whether the hunt for disability is really about preventing the 'detractors' from limiting the 'progress' of 'the normal.' The use of perfecting technologies, whether it be within mainstreamed classrooms or separate ones, are an instance of what Troy Duster (1990) has called the 'backdoor' to eugenics discourse in the present.

The new eugenics might be provocatively understood, then, as a modified form of the 'quality control' issue that attracted the old eugenicists to lifetime careers of attempting to prove the inferiority of others (Aberdeen 2000). Although not always overtly or directly focused on fertility and reproductive processes, the new eugenics is concerned with perfecting technologies to secure quality citizenship through the homogenization of racial/national populations at some level.

It might be argued, however, that all forms of schooling teleologically seek to govern, discipline, and engineer students' being toward some named ideal. There is no authentic, natural, or romantic state to be returned to in the rearing of humans and in caring for each other. The question then becomes whether one agrees with the ideal(s) so named as the goals of education. New eugenic discourses disallow within their own premises a questioning of those ideals, however. They incite the engineering of students par excellence in the name of seemingly generic terms like citizen, democracy, economic healthiness, and unity. They are linked across sites and frequently establish some people as pollutants or detractors. Even where such classifications are thought to be for the benefit of the recipient, they cannot be disarticulated from population governance strategies that concern image management, especially at a racial/national level. For Campbell, the modifications in discourse that mark the new eugenics have taken three forms: the practices of prenatal screening, disability dispersal policies, and the compulsion towards perfecting and morphing technologies of normalization. It is the latter two strategies in particular, disability dispersal policies and perfecting technologies, that pertain more directly to schooling and that announce the importance of studying the wider implications of the hunt for disability in public education.

Dispersal, Proliferation, and Swarming: The Hunt for Disability

Across the last few decades of the 20th century and into the 21st, there has been a proliferation of categories of educational disability used to mark students as outside norms of child development or as at-risk of school failure. This proliferation has not emerged out of some sinister mean-mindedness but out of the very pragmatic realization that failure at school and the failure of schools have direct consequences for how much one can earn, the quality of life, the garnisheeing of respect from others, or all three, linked as these are. In fact, in their survey of literature on postschooling opportunities for students labeled via special education, titled

The Hunt for Disability 149

'School-to-Work Transition for Youth with Disabilities: A Review of Outcomes and Practices,' Phelps and Hanley-Maxwell (1997: 218) conclude that the

> Studies reported herein reveal the abysmal record of achievement for youth with disabilities. The dropout rate for youth with disabilities exceed those of nondisabled students by nearly a factor of two. The lack of a high school diploma for nearly half of the students with emotional or behavioral difficulties is particularly problematic. For all students with disabilities who do complete school, access to employment and postsecondary education still falls substantially below the levels attained by their nondisabled peers. In general, when students with disabilities do find employment, their earnings tend to be only slightly above the minimum wage in entry-level jobs, and they are faced with limited prospects for promotion and personal growth.

In public schools systems, the labels are usually what qualify a child for special educational services. ADD (attention deficit disorder), ADHD (attention deficit-hyperactivity disorder), BD and SBD (behavior disorder and severe behavior disorder), CD (cognitively delayed), ED (emotionally disturbed), LD (learning disability), and OD (oppositional defiance) are such categories. The proliferation of acronyms is a phenomenon in itself; one could choose almost any letter of the alphabet, add a 'D' to it and find a category defining a school-aged child as a problem or as having a particular problem that is to be recorded in school files. Although Phelps and Hanley-Maxwell's paper is not explicitly devoted to problematizing labeling, they further conclude that

> The evidence suggesting that special education placement and other pull-out or specialized interventions have substantial effects on learning is, at best, limited. . . . [T]hese well-intentioned efforts to create responsive educational tracks have had substantial deleterious effects on learning and achievement for many students. Combined with the evidence that inclusive programs and practices appear to have small to moderate beneficial effects on both academic and social outcomes for children with disabilities . . . the key consideration for educators and researchers becomes determining which educational practices serve all students' learning.
>
> (Phelps and Hanley-Maxwell 1997: 219)

The proliferation of the Ds, the new disability nomenclatures, is not just a new way of speaking about children and adults, teaching and learning, and citizenship and development. It represents what curriculum historian Barry Franklin (1994) has argued is a shift from the moralization of disability to the medicalization of disability during the 20th century. Learning disability, for example, is a newer, medicalizing term that has in effect acted to replace and modify the late-19th-century term *feeblemindedness*. Feebleminded children were initially those deemed unable to make appropriate moral choices because of a perceived lack of mental control

150   *Bernadette Baker*

over volition or will (Longmore and Umansky 2001; Mitchell and Snyder in press). The terminology of learning disability shifts the frame of reference for 'detecting deficit' from theological/moral considerations, however, to secular notions of skill, retention, perception, or literacy, especially under pressure from the latest rhetoric of 'competition in a global economy.' LD was formally rendered an educational category in 1969. In July of that year, the Education Subcommittee of the U.S. House of Representatives Committee on Education and Labor held hearings on the Children with Learning Disabilities Act. Introduced as an amendment to Title VI of the Elementary and Secondary Education Act, the legislation provided federal support for research on the causes and treatments of learning disabilities. Learning disability was thereby bestowed with official recognition, becoming what was called a 'state designated handicapping condition.' There is much dispute over the details of the genesis of the category and its definition (Sleeter 1987). What is more certain is that the availability of a category called learning disability as a 'state designated handicapping condition' saw a consistent growth in the number of children classified as LD since its inception in educational policy. One million children were labeled LD within a year of its inception (Kidder-Ashley, Deni, and Anderton 2000).

In addition, there have been, more recently, noticeable increases in the use of such categories. In the public school district of Fairfield presently, for instance, the topics of learning disability and special education more generally are receiving much attention. On May 19, 2000, a local newspaper focused its educational segment on special education. In an article entitled 'Heading Toward a Crisis? District Grapples with Rising Special Education Costs' reporter Gia Weier noted how the number of students in the district who require special education had risen substantially in recent years, from 3,153 in 1994 to 4,142 as of Dec 1, 1999 (Weier 2000). Children designated LD represent the largest group, at 1,755. Part of the increase has been attributed by local school principals to changes in the identification process. Although in the past a child had to be identified as two years behind his or her peers, the definition has now changed so that it is one year behind. In addition, principals have argued that schools assess students more often, which allows teachers and administrators to assign disability labels at an earlier age than in the past, contributing to the increase. Some principals believed that the increase was circular – once a district is known for providing good services, it draws parents who relocate specifically for those services, increasing the total number of labeled students. The director of the district's Department of Educational Services, quoted in the opening to this chapter, seemed less certain of the mechanisms at play in the increase, however.

The uncertainty as to the mechanisms at play in recent identification increases and the attention paid to special education is not unique to Fairfield, nor is it a trend exclusive to the United States. The question of why a certain kind of educational labeling has become increasingly popular is one that policy analysts, sociologists, and historians have been asking in other nations, including Australia, Canada, England, France, and New Zealand (Albrecht 1981; Birkenbach 1993; Slee 1997; Tomlinson 1984). Henri-Jaques Stiker, in his *A*

The Hunt for Disability 151

History of Disability (1999: 5), for instance, asks what incites the fever for classification and what he calls 'the passion for sameness.'

> Isn't the first question, the one that misfortune itself causes us to forget, this one: why is disability called 'disability'? Why are those who are born or who become different [sic] referred to by all these various names? Why so many categories? Why even such dramatics in the face of what happens. . so often, and which can happen to any of us? . . . [W]here does this huge exercise in naming come from, that labeling that circumscribes one kind of reality . . . and makes us feel it all the more and be afraid of it?

It seems that in education there has been what Foucault (1979) in a different context has referred to as a *swarming* effect. In this case, it is around the hunt for and diagnosis of disability as a negative ontology that schools actively seek to name, and, as the following section discusses, remedy with the best of intentions.

Perfecting Technologies: Morphing Ableism

Several strategies have accompanied the dispersal, proliferation, and swarming around educational disability. These include federal-level policy moralizations, local mainstreaming strategies, reinforcement of public schooling's segregation function, medicalization of students, and cultural conflation and homogenization techniques.

One spin-off from, or perhaps more accurately antecedent, to the swarming around disability identification has been policy proposals and reform. The identification of and hunt for disability has been tied, for instance, to a discourse that privileges international comparison of test scores as signs of quality citizenship and economic prosperity. Feverish problematizations of teachers, teaching, public schools, and students occurred when it was announced through the publication of results from TIMSS, *The Third International Mathematics and Science Survey*, that Japanese and German students had outperformed American ones on some of the standardized exams. The problematizations were reminiscent of those embodied in earlier publications that had catastrophe mentalities, including *A Nation At Risk* and the *National Education Goals 2000*, which stipulated the criteria via which children ought to be judged as 'ready to learn,' thereby producing the category of the deficient, the delayed, the unready, and the broken who were posited as jeopardizing 'the nation,' its reputation, and its economic future, as well as their own personal one.

Besides the federal-level moralizations that have accompanied the naming of 'the detractors' in international comparisons, there have been reformulations of local special educational policies in approximately the last 10 years, a trend known as mainstreaming or inclusive schooling. Mainstreaming generally involves placing students who are perceived as having primarily mild to moderate disabilities in regular or mainstream classrooms, rather than having the students sent to separate

152   *Bernadette Baker*

or special schools for the entirety of their educational program. It is not clear whether the reforms have eventuated from purely economic concerns for downsizing and merging facilities, from trends in educational research, from parental activism, or a combination of these (Skrtic 1995). In the midst of the swarm to figure out why mainstreaming has eventuated and why now, however, the very basis of public schooling's existence is glossed over. Because public schools have historically not been populated by children labeled as severely 'intellectually' disabled, the attention of public school policy has been turned to children who are perceived as 'educable' but outside the norms for child development – students once referred to as 'high grade defectives' (Tomlinson 1984). What lends public schooling its distinctiveness as an institution historically and still now is that it is not and has never been a place for every child.

That is, local mainstreaming policies highlight the previous segregation function of public schooling amid the availability of other institutions.[10] The educational policies of more bureaucratically centralized Western nations, as well as individual states within the United States, have been primarily concerned in the recent past with what is now referred to as mild intellectual or physical disability, and it is on these categories that debates over labeling and special services have most focused. The very existence of schooling as something that is separate from persons who seemingly cannot agentively enter into such debates, such as those classified as 'having' Rett syndrome, is taken for granted as the backdrop to formal public education.[11] Whatever is *perceived* as severe intellectual disability, especially, has historically been placed in the 'too hard' basket and to such an extent that scholars such as Kliewer and Biklen (2001) have had to argue overtly for new lenses for seeing the 'educability' and 'literacy' of students labeled as 'severely mentally retarded,' reminding the reader of the ethics involved: 'The person perceived as defective and the person perceived as competent are both social constructions. People in whom resides the power to define the capacities of other human beings are making moral decisions. On what basis should such decision making proceed?' (Kliewer and Biklen 2001: 11). Like recent Hollywood films that make fun of the Amish under the presumption that the Amish are not likely to be in the audience and to protest their representation as other lobby or interest groups might if they were the targets of comic relief, the belief that agency, resistance, and contestation has to come from the spoken words or actions of an individual or group guarantees that schools are now only places for certain 'kinds' of children. The form of socialization for persons labeled as severely intellectually disabled, for example, has been considered medical rather than educational and brings to light what is often most submerged about public schooling – that is, its segregation function. A mind–body dichotomy seemingly gives the school the purview to somehow work on the intellectual progress of 'the majority.' This in turn is seen as distinct from 'purely' medical kinds of socialization or care associated with perceptions of severe intellectual disabilities. In some locales the distinctions are defended, with parents wanting separate specialized medical services for their children. On other occasions, parents argue for inclusion of their children within public school classrooms because they do not want them segregated from the rest of the school-going

The Hunt for Disability   153

population. One outcome of these debates has been that the distinctiveness between medicine and education has been drawn into question and not just for children labeled as 'having' severe intellectual disabilities. The current medicalization programs for many public school students labeled as behavior disordered or hyperactive undermines the solidity of the distinction between medicine and education as discrete practices for securing social order. In the absence of corporal punishment that might leave a mark on the skin, an array of internally corporal medicalizations have emerged whose marks are more difficult to photograph and therefore to contest.

In addition to federal-level policy pronouncements, mainstreaming, segregation, and medicalization, a further kind of well-intended perfecting technology has been engaged that acts to conflate certain kinds of racial, ethnic, and linguistic heritages with educational disablement. In England and parts of the United States, there is an overrepresentation of children from cultural minorities and working classes in perceived categories of mild disablement relative to population percentages. On the basis of social structures and trends that appear to extend beyond individual nations, the innateness of classifications such as learning disability and emotionally disturbed has been drawn into question. In the United States, for example, many studies across the 1980s noted the overrepresentation of working class children, minority children, or both, in LD classifications (Argulewicz 1983; Brosnan 1983; Carrier 1986; Sleeter 1987; Tucker 1980; Wright and Santa Cruz 1983), while in England Sally Tomlinson's (1984) study of 'educational subnormality' categories similarly documented the overrepresentation of children of immigrants from the Caribbean.

In light of such overrepresentations, a finite number of explanations for this conflation have been proffered, ranging from genetic determinism to historically and sociologically critical accounts of the effects of establishing singular standards. The former seem more well known. Recent arguments, such as the genetic determinism espoused in *The Bell Curve: Intelligence and Class Structure in American Life*, have reinvoked biophysiology as the cause of the overrepresentation. Although such arguments have been debunked many times over, sometimes the critiques still play on the same field as that which is being critiqued, submitting themselves on the same grounds for argument as that which Herrnstein and Murray used (e.g., appealing to further test scores) to disprove Herrnstein and Murray's interpretation of test scores. Such critiques are useful, but they do not destabilize the very faith in the phenomenon of testing on which genetic deterministic arguments regarding intelligence are predicated in the first place.

Therefore, in consonance with other critical approaches to genetically based arguments, another form of 'explanation' for the overrepresentation of 'certain kinds' of children in 'certain categories' of disablement have emerged. In England, Gary Thomas and Georgina Glenny (2000) have argued that emotional and behavioral difficulties are 'bogus needs in a false category,' especially because there is within special education little critical examination of what is being proposed as a 'need': 'There are taken-for-granted assumptions of "help" in the "meeting need" mantra of contemporary special education protocols, and these "needs" have been

154   *Bernadette Baker*

silently transmuted with the assistance of the constructs of academic and professional psychology from the *school's* needs for order, calm, routine and predictability to the *child's* needs for stability, nurture, security, one-to-one help or whatever' (Thomas and Glenny 2000: 286). The authors argue further that in the unspoken assumptions behind special education procedures there is no acknowledgment of the maneuver that has occurred, no recognition of the frailty of the idea 'emotional need,' and 'no willingness to entertain the possibility that emotional needs may be a fiction constructed to escape the school's insecurities about failing to keep order'(Thomas and Glenny 2000: 286). They conclude that in the context of education in England

> In the use of the term 'EBD' there is an indolent espousal of a term that too conveniently packages together difficult, troublesome children [sic] with (the concept of) emotional disturbance. In its use is an insidious blurring of motives and knowledges which imputes problems to children that in reality are rarely theirs. In the dispositional attributions that are therein made, unnecessarily complex judgements about putative need take the place of simple judgements about what is acceptable or unacceptable behaviour for a particular institution. Use of the term 'EBD' enables the substitution of the former for the latter – of the complex for the straightforward – and this in turn perpetuates a mindset about behaviour which distracts attention from what the school can do to make itself a more humane place.
>
> (Thomas and Glenny 2000: 294)

Where minority children, children from working class families, or both, are overrepresented in categories such as LD and EBD, the question arises as to whether such categories are purely a biomedical phenomenon or are rather what Thomas and Glenny (2000: 286) describe as 'the almost explicit conflation of administrative need with quasi-medical category.' This suggests the cogency of considering special education policy as something articulated to broader and enduring social relationships than simply those made manifest in the micropolitics of particular school districts and of interrogating disability as something beyond what is considered 'in' a child or 'had' by a child.

Kathleen McSorley has already developed this line of argument in the United States, questioning the cultural biases inherent in perfecting technologies for helping students develop 'appropriate skills and values.' She notes, for instance, that although the dominant perspective on the placement of students into special programs is to view it as a caring decision and act, the paradigm of deficit and pathology in traditional special education discourse tacitly reinforces 'white privilege' and thus reinforces

> normative references that value, among other things, order and compliance to 'white' rules and dominant codes of power. The perception that readiness for mainstreaming and inclusion is dependent on the learning of appropriate social skills and values is very prevalent among special and regular educators.

The Hunt for Disability 155

However, white educators that I have met fail to acknowledge that these skills are based on a white frame of reference, and fail to question the consequences of this form of gatekeeping.

(McSorley 2000: 30–31)

Like Thomas and Glenny in England, McSorley argues that the cultural bias appears not just in who is slotted into a category or labeled as having special or extra needs, but earlier, in the very formulation and definition of skills, needs, and readiness themselves. Others have pointed to how, even where seemingly stable definitions of an educational disability appear, this is no guarantee of any further kind of coherence in the actions pursued. That is, the formulation and definition of skills, needs, and readiness, even if appearing as consistent across espoused educational policies, does not open onto the use of consistent and agreed on strategies. Thus, the cultural conflation and homogenization techniques that help support the hunt for disability have to be understood for the 'wiggle room' they provide in terms of actual implementation. For example, Kidder-Ashley, Deni, and Anderton (2000) have analyzed the lack of agreement historically and in the present over what LD is and whether it is neurophysiologically based or not. In their paper 'Learning Disabilities Eligibility in the 1990s: An Analysis of State Practices,' Kidder-Ashley et al. surveyed the criteria for identifying and labeling a student as 'having' a learning disability across 40 states. They concluded that

Despite the improved agreement regarding the category label ([now SLD]), there continues to be notable variability from state to state in how SLD eligibility is determined. Although there is nearly unanimous agreement across states that SLD is manifested in a discrepancy between the individual's actual academic achievement and potential for achievement, the states differ dramatically in how this discrepancy is to be documented (Kidder-Ashley et al 2000: 68).

How 'potential for achievement' is ever decided, prophesied, or determined is not discussed, but the authors take hypothetical samples of 'actual achievement,' such as IQ scores, and apply different state definitions to each of the imagined cases. Even with the same 'test scores,' being labeled LD as a student would depend on which state a child lived in. The argument for LD as universally, incontrovertibly, ahistorically, and aculturally 'biomedical' rests on thin ice if it is such that one's address determines the classification. The implementation of perfecting technologies around 'diagnoses' of disability presently requires, then, the possibility for conflating other 'differences,' such as address or perceived forms of cultural embodiment with 'educational disability,' posed in the objectifying language of biomedicine, psychology, and welfare, and submerged as a homogenizing technique.

Tomlinson (1984) found a similar trend regarding such arbitrariness in her empirical study in England, concluding that ESN (educational subnormality, as it was called at that time) was a label resulting more likely from personality clashes between a teacher and a student and that there was no agreement about the one child who was examined, let alone in identifications across schools. The point for

156 *Bernadette Baker*

Tomlinson was thus that the determination of educational or academic disability was culturally biased and not necessarily biomedical or neurophysiological at base. As noted above, children of families who had emigrated from the Caribbean were markedly overrepresented in the labeling process initiated by white teachers, leading Tomlinson to conclude that what was being labeled was not simply a child but a culture.

The disagreements and debates that such studies document suggests that there may be additional and wider historico-cultural forces at play that act to comport the definition of disability and ability in a particular way at a particular time and that underwrite the processes of identification that perpetuate belief in the perspicuity of the categories. Such studies have been important in raising awareness of the value systems that interpenetrate actions within schools and the consequences of disremembering them. But what such studies sometimes neglect to emphasize is how critiques of cultural bias in special education can inadvertently recirculate the forbidden relationship between disability and desire, that is, how disability, whether it is analyzed as 'biomedical' or 'socially constituted through relationships,' *must not be desired*, how it is used as nomenclature for a negative ontology and posed as a way of being that at all cost ought to be avoided. Where a critique of labeling or overrepresentation turns on the view that 'normal' students are really being mislabeled and made closer on a scale to 'genuinely' disabled students, then it does not undermine the presumption that it's better to be dead than disabled. If, as Campbell (2000: 307) has argued, the construction/governing of disability and the compulsion toward an ableist normativity are in fact achieved by the continual reiteration of technologies as 'salvific signifiers' holding out the promise of 'able-bodiedness,' then both the hunt to identify disability, and some versions of its critique, leave unproblematized this promise.

The above analysis has indicated, then, how the persistent figuring of disability as a negative ontology involves the constant rewriting of disability within educational practices of care/welfare and sometimes within the very debates that critique those practices. This rewriting is characteristic of new eugenics discourse, including disability dispersal policies and morphing and perfecting technologies, which appear interwoven through the everyday activities taken for granted as signs of democracy in schooling. In the proliferation and swarming around categories of educational disablement, and in the technologies of policy writing, mainstreaming, segregation, medicalization, and movements between cultural differentiation and homogenization discussed above, *disability* becomes understandable as *the politics of (dis)ability*. A preferred style or way of learning only becomes a learning disability, for example, in light of the impatience and structure of an institution that presents things in a limited number of ways with rigid expectations for what counts as a timely performance. Similarly, to allocate some children and not others as emotionally disturbed really raises the question of what counts as an emotion and what constitutes as a disturbance and to whom. If the degree of surveillance that is directed at children who are so labeled were to be turned on the adults in the school, then perhaps there would emerge many teachers, administrators, and psychologists whose observed behavior might be thought of as disturbing and

The Hunt for Disability   157

emotional. And finally, if these forms of critique or subversion are left to play on a field where distance from 'really' 'disabled' persons is the key to greater inclusion elsewhere,[12] then disability, whether understood as formed through social relations or as biomedical or 'both,' ultimately remains within this logic 'not optimal,' *not* to be desired, even if perceived as temporarily or occasionally 'advantageous.'

Does this recognition of (dis)ability as discursively constituted, and of disability as a form of negative ontology within public schools, thus mean that no efforts at identification, diagnosis, and treatment of children who appear to be 'falling behind' should be engaged with? Does this mean that there are no such things as 'bad behavior' or 'dyslexia'? The following section considers how the resort to service-provision models presumes what perhaps it should explain and examines some of the complexities inherent to disability-positive and disability-negative accounts of ontology.

'Quality Control' and Service-Provision Models

LD, BD, ED, or EBD seem 'easy' examples to draw ambiguity around in discussing the politics of (dis)ability. For example, how you move your body in the classroom may not be how I like to move mine; to call one series of movements a sign of behavior disorder and another self-control is surely imbued with culturally loaded expectations for bodily expressions; and so on – one can imagine this line of argument continuing and take seriously the point that there is 'wiggle room' around the edges as to what constitutes a disorder, disturbance, or delay, and so on.

It may seem that there are 'other conditions,' however, those that require the use of wheelchairs, blindness, or deafness, for instance, that seem more difficult to dispute in terms of labeling. This line of argument would suggest that at the very heart of humanity there are some biological or physiological 'defects' that cannot be denied. The presumed obviousness of such 'conditions' is therefore taken circularly as proof of disability's universal fixity. The question that is then taken to arise under this logic is: Should there not be labeling and the provision of special educational services on the basis of such obvious conditions, which, within the context of schooling, constitute a disadvantage?

The conflation between identification, labeling, and provision is important to note in the above kinds of questions that have been constructed around the provocative issue of (dis)ability and schooling. Important, too, is the presumed nature of that which constitutes the reference point for such 'obvious' questions; labeling does not just lend its effects to the overtly labeled but elevates those who appear outside 'the problem.' As Linda Ware (2000a: 108) asks in problematizing the innateness of an ability–disability binary in educational work, 'What have we done to ourselves by doing these things to them?' If left as an unquestioned technology directed incessantly at children entrapped in compulsory institutions, labeling can itself leave unquestioned the nature of institutions or scenarios in which certain ways of existing are produced and made to 'pop up' as though natural.

Moreover, the line of reasoning which sees some 'conditions' as indisputably biomedical, negative, and 'inside' the person, and others, such as LD or ED, as

158   *Bernadette Baker*

more sociological, kind of fuzzy, and open to abuse, fails to recognize how such distinctions retain at base an empiricist and objectivist medical model that can obscure alternative ways of understanding the multiplicity of effects of labeling something or someone. Within the disability studies literature, for example, the term *disability* is highly contested and is not always seen as a simply negative or repressive term. Disability becomes instead disability-positive, the grounds for the formation of new transnational minority groups (Wrigley 1996), a term that refers to something that can be productive of new alliances, experiences, and subjectivities, a term that can be locally liberating, or open to strategies of reclamation, humor, irony, inversion, subversion, and satire (Linton 1998). Terms such as 'crip culture,' 'gimpy,' and 'Deaf' have thus been reappropriated *and* disputed as to their use, just as the use of genetic technologies and genetic counseling has become a site for disagreement (Sandahl 2001). In some of the literature (e.g., Davis 1997), to presume that disability can only ever be 'read' as disability-negative, or as an outlawed ontology rather than a preferred one, is to reinvoke through a paternalizing sympathy or an impossible form of empathy the very problem being critiqued.

Under the weight of these kinds of debates, the invocation of service-provision models, which are often predicated on the presumption of disability-negative inscriptions of a 'condition,' become both part of the problem and an avenue for refiguring subjectivity. The recognition that the way that things are can generate pain and suffering for students, which are experienced as disabilities, is central to the appearance of service models as sensitive and caring. The logic of provision presently seems to go hand in hand, though, with the logic of assimilation, homogenization, or both. It is steeped in old-world visions of democracy as a right to modify others for citizenship; if those perceived as suffering are to be alleviated, then 'they' need to be identified, categorized, and rescued from themselves through condition-specific programs, while the rest of the group need to be protected from possible 'contaminating' effects. In the process, new discrete groups of 'problem populations' are made available for consumption, and the creativity, ingenuity, and uniqueness that have already emerged as responses to labeling *dis*ability as a negative ontological state remain submerged. Or as Campbell (2000: 309) puts it,

> It is not surprising, then, that people with 'disabilities' become caught up in the vortex of a vertiginous dread of the tragic wishing to emulate and 'normalise' their/our bodies in conformity with the virtues underpinning ableist normativity. Suffering, a perpetual desire for some kind of perfectibility, produces internalized ableism – an attitude of heart that engages in self-hatred, often rendering us incapable of re-seeing our selves simultaneously as the font of containment and creativity/ingenuity.

Given the complexities that seem inherent to acknowledging both the current structure of schooling, and its allied reference points of 'being-able-to' as the incessant rite of passage between grades or stages, then, disability rights activists and scholars in the disability studies field rarely argue against the provision of services or the development of new technologies *in cases where such things can be disarticulated from presumptions of a negative ontology.* As Campbell (2000) notes, though, there is a fine line between 'the provision of services' that minimize pain and suffering and being judged as having an outlaw ontology that is seen negatively for getting 'special' treatment, only to find that the manner of the treatment is often premised on morphing the recipient into accepting uncritically the subjectivities of ableist normativity.

There is, therefore, no agreement in the disability studies field on whether educational labeling and service-provision models in any form are unilaterally 'good' or 'bad.' Rather, the questions and criticisms raised revolve around deeper epistemological and ontological issues that preexist debates about services for all children. The questions raised take the complexity of things as their starting point. They assume that pain, suffering, and creativity are real, that privilege is palpable, and that 'experiences' and so-called conditions or deficiencies are constituted *through* current social relations and institutional structures and are not objectively 'existing in' persons. The questions, and the critique they imply, thus try to consider how the observation of such complexity became possible. Why are norms taken for granted as objective? What restricted image of 'the ideal citizen' do norms for development embody? How might this devalue those excluded from such images? Toward what broader purposes are the construction of norms and deviations directed? And why, in the end, and at the beginning, do others need to be convinced that what I am dealing with is real, without seeing it as being 'in' me or as me 'having' it? As Kenneth Hultqvist (in press) notes in a different context, many present-day questions turn on a familiar quandary: how can issues of multiculturalism and pluralism be considered when operating within a framework of universal norms?

These questions are in a way questions about who or what can be included as fully human in discussions on the 'politics of inclusion' in schools. They are questions about inclusion and 'quality control' before the terms of debates over inclusive schooling are set. They are questions about difference, sameness, and equality that precede the arguments about who can have access to what number of teaching assistants or aides in a school setting and for how long.

This leads to a further series of questions that incite a consideration of the wider orientations underwriting the structure of service-provision models and rhetoric – for example, What power relations inhere the production of categories such as normal and abnormal? Are these relations worthy of perpetuation? And finally, whether intended or not, is labeling a way of morphing 'disability' into the assumptions of an ableist normativity, with all its racial-cultural overtones, rather than questioning certain privileged ontologies and epistemologies to begin with?

It is easy to ask questions and propose no alternatives. It is also easy to be stultified as if caught between a rock and a hard place after reviewing multiple debates that have opened in regard to (dis)ability and education. On the one hand, the pragmatic realization discussed earlier that 'without' certain 'skills' the 'ease' with which one can engage in everyday activities can be compromised, with the experience of suffering and pain produced and exacerbated, overriding any concomitant recognition of ingenuity and creativity, compels something to be done to make

160   *Bernadette Baker*

schools more humane and wider-visioned places.[13] On the other, how can such Utopias come to fruition without reinvoking the very hierarchies that help perpetuate a belief in disability as a negative ontology and a 'conundrum'? How could any 'alternative' avoid recirculating the salvific and redemptive efforts being problematized and not recognize that any 'desire to want to shift social relations, is a kind of nostalgic romance: a conflicted, possibly ruinous place to start?' (Meiners 1999: 350). The final section of this chapter is therefore an admittedly raw attempt to rethink how I am part of the problem rather than its solution and to make an effort at understanding why it is so difficult to imagine genuine alternatives that would not end up being just a better camouflaged posse.

The Question of Special Education and Alternatives: A Headache That Won't Go Away?

One present reality in the United States is that categories of disability are part of policy language, and public schools are compelled to engage in identification and counting if they wish to receive funding. Beyond that bureaucratic imperative, however, to label or not to label a child is currently a provocative and unsettled question in public schools and families, even in school districts that have followed federal and state mandates and guidelines for special education provision (Edgerton 1986). In the case of the Fairfield School District's Department of Public Instruction, the use of educational labeling is described as making free and public education (FAPE) available to all children. Hence being classified as LD, for example, opens up access to extra assistance in activities, such as reading, or gives more time to complete an examination. In the disability rights movement, this is considered recognition and recompense for the way that institutions are structured. That is, if schools are built on the assumption of a model student, then special services are indeed required for children who are pushed outside of that model for such students to interact in and benefit from the institution. It is considered romantic, naïve, and dangerous not to recognize that the school deck is already stacked and therefore, under this view, special provisions for interacting within that stacked system should be provided.

Disability studies literature sometimes contests the liberal lines of reasoning that are often encapsulated in policy documents, however, by suggesting that the persistent identification/labeling of disability as 'in' someone leaves undisturbed the notion of normalcy by failing to challenge professionals' beliefs in 'a legitimate social order' (Brantlinger 1997; Danforth and Rhodes 1997; Skrtic 1995; Tomlinson 1984). Further, such practices are seen as reducing the totality of someone's humanity to a so-called trait (ability/disability), leaving in place an essentializing lens for viewing personhood in the singular (Heshusius 1995), while at the same time negating or submerging how those very practices are implicated in the construction and experience of 'problems' that they seek to address (Allan 1996; Ware 2000b). Danforth and Rhodes (1997) explain the inherent contradiction in much inclusive schooling literature that attempts to honor the reality of 'difficulties at school' and at the same time fails to contest the grounds on which reality is constructed.

> As the national proponents of inclusion have created the foremost progressive edge of disability advocacy, their writings have contributed to the common assumption that specific conditions . . . or deficiency exist 'in' identified students. Assertions that certain students 'have' handicaps or are 'with' disabilities have been stated in the midst of arguments trying to convince educators to accept such students into general education settings. . . . By failing to question and contest the disability construct as universally true and real, inclusion advocates have unintentionally worked against their own integrationist and civil rights purposes, supporting the devaluation and stigmatization of students 'with disabilities' while decrying the same.
>
> (1997: 357)

Such disability studies literature on special education therefore takes its cue from the diversity of interpretations that are now available. The analyses are generally predicated on an historical understanding of shifts in defining normalcy and disability that have moved the locus of reality for those definitions from morality to medicine to culture (Longmore and Umamsky 2001; Stiker 1999). They are also predicated on an anthropological understanding that not every group of humans believes in the existence of such things as a discrete 'mind' or 'body' to which inscriptions of disability-as-objective and 'universal' have been tied in the North (Gabel, Vyas, Patel, and Patel 2001; Ingstad and Reynolds Whyte 1995). In drawing on these historico-anthropological understandings, and the sociological and critical legal scholarship discussed previously, such disability studies analyses reframe the pressure put on parents to consent, or not consent, to the labeling of a child and quite possibly their medicalization, pressures that analyses such as those by Joy-Ruth Mickelson (2000) have documented. It is the difficulties associated with institutional structures, present practices, and the pressures that they bring to bear especially on parents and other educators who are confronted with making decisions about children's welfare that the final section of this paper addresses.

The End of Formal Education as We (Do Not) Know It?

> to complete any study of educational deficiency in special schools, it becomes essential . . . to make a comparative survey of children presumably normal. Only by comparison with 'normals' can we state what characteristics differentiate the backward or deficient.
>
> Cyril Burt (quoted in Lowe 2000: 213)

What is a parent to do? What is a parent to do when they are a public school-teacher and a parent? On the one hand, it seems obvious that parents do not want

162   Bernadette Baker

their children to suffer and are interested in and want 'good things' for their children from schooling. Parents do not want their children to be disadvantaged just because of judgments, interactions, or resources (un)available in an institution that their children are forced to attend. On the other hand, it is presently difficult to determine what constitutes the greater form of suffering. Some parents have been forthright, for example, about the anguish that schooling provokes in making decisions about their children.[14][15] Mickelson (2000) has documented the diversity of parental experiences and orientations to having sons labeled behavior disordered and how the orientations of the same parent shifted over time. Further, one does not have to travel far in most school districts to gain a sense of the complexities of labeling and the politics of inclusion/exclusion. Sometimes a child does not wish to be labeled for special services to save face among peers. At other times, parents actively want a child to be labeled whom teachers do not perceive as having a disability at all because labeling provides access to services that parents could not obtain otherwise. On other occasions, there is parental consent to labeling but not to the recommended medication. In still other instances, teachers wish to have a child labeled, but parents refuse to consent to a description of their child as, for example, emotionally disturbed. Then suspicion arises as to whether that child whose parents 'hold out' is the subject of retribution, oversurveillance, or in contrast being ignored or left out, with the charges flying back and forth.

Moreover, teachers can feel (and are) forced to confront, handle, or respond to situations perceived as violent, difficult, and dangerous in the immediacy of the school grounds, while other times parents are forced to educate teachers about the *positive* things their child brings to the room, redirecting vision and thereby attempting to undo the inscription of disability-as-conundrum, problem, or extra work. These are not minute events in the lives of any of those involved in schooling and the determination of disability, nor are they easily, if ever, resolved. The positions taken up sway between the poles that Danforth and Rhodes (1997) note, moving from the assumption that disability is objectively 'in' a child to the view that what is labeled as and experienced as disability is socially constituted and produced *between* bodies-minds in human relationships. The intense personal feelings such tensions and interactions generate in public schools should not just be dismissed as bad form or 'tsk-ed, tsk-ed' by those removed from such daily situations. How classifications came to be and continue to be such a focal point of what brings parents and other educational professionals together is not a natural or inevitable event, however.

Classifying and dividing practices are, though, difficult to address because they are caught in the loop that enables them – the very loop that Cyril Burt articulated in 1920; it is only possible to develop a differentiating typology based on an a priori species-typical functioning baseline. This baseline asserts the 'essential' normative body-mind. The species-typical benchmark body-mind in turn produces the figuring of disease and disability (Campbell 2000). These figurings, though well-intended, evidence the new 'eugenics of normalcy' (Fox Keller 1992) and the effort to normalize school children toward an ableist normativity that fails to question its privilege and results in the kinds of anguish that parents, teachers, and

The Hunt for Disability   163

children often experience and express. As Campbell (2000) has already noted, the illusion of choice in the present, whether to label or not, whether to submit to more perfecting technologies or not, is used to mask the eugenic specter and when combined with the juridogenic authority of law, expressions and decisions about (dis)ability become much more than simply someone's opinion, much more than 'she said, he said' at the local school. They have real effects and real consequences for real children's human subjectivity and for those adult subjectivities that assert who or what a (better) human is.

It is, therefore, remarkably ironic that an Oxbridge/Ivy League curricula argument of Charles Eliot at the turn of 20th century can now challenge in a romantic and indirect way the practices of sorting, discipline, and punishment that all formal education engages in. Who are to make the prophecies and what kind of quality control toward proper citizenship are such prophecies engaged in? What is the whole range of effects that the hunt for disability produces and perpetuates?

I have found a common argument put forth within schools and in conversations with psychological or medical experts is that it is the examination results broadly conceived that determine prophecies and decisions, but this merely begs the question. Results refer back to further results that refer back to further results that prevents any questioning of the very institution of examinations as a source of objectification, discipline, and punishment. As noted above, IQ tests are in many states the baseline for determining LD (Kidder-Ashley, Deni, and Anderson 2000). The results seem to tell of a gap between 'actual' and 'expected' achievement, although where the standards for expected achievement comes from is often not articulable, especially in regard to the classroom observations that precede entrance into further rounds of formal testing, such as IQ. What constitutes a 'third-grade reading level' as opposed to a 'fourth-grade reading level,' for instance, can usually be defined by educational professionals at the elementary level, but where such standards have emerged from is rarely part of professional wisdom. At most the standards for determining third-grade and fourth-grade reading levels are guesstimated to be from 'the research' or 'experience' or to be set by the publishers of the reader series being used, verified earlier somewhere in some survey of data that no one can name. Yet such implicit standards are incredibly powerful organizers of perception that make some students appear as problems and confer on others a star status.

This historical forgetting is not surprising, nor should teachers be blamed for conveying it. Schooling and the selective filtering toward tertiary study to which it is articulated fundamentally rely for existence on that which is seemingly impossible to question – the propensity to classify, divide, withhold, and promote on the basis of various forms of evaluation that mask their indebtedness to matters ontological. Argues Foucault (1979) on this point:

> the marks that once indicated status, privilege and affiliation were increasingly replaced – or at least supplemented – by a whole range of degrees of normality indicating membership of a homogenous social body ([e.g. citizenship]), but also playing a part in classification, hierarchization and the distribution

164   *Bernadette Baker*

of rank. In a sense, the power of normalization imposes homogeneity; but it individualizes by making it possible to measure gaps, to determine levels, to fit specialities and to render the differences useful by fitting them one to another. It is easy to understand how the power of the norm functions within a system of formal equality, since within a homogeneity that is the rule, the norm introduces, as a useful imperative and as a result of measurement, all the shading of individual differences.

(184)

Perhaps a cynical way of understanding the hunt for disability, then, is that it has become so convenient in a system of 'formal ([theoretical]) equality,' so proliferating, so amenable to swarming because institutions can make judgments about further categories such as race, class, sexuality, and gender by calling them 'individual differences' or something else ('intelligence') and refer for security's sake to the exam results. Yet, as Stephen Jay Gould argued 20 years ago, test results do not represent a solid anything. In foreshadowing the arguments to come in *The Mismeasure of Man*, Gould (1981: 24) argued that the abstraction of intelligence as a single entity, the presumption of 'its' location within the brain, its quantification as one number for each individual, and the use of these numbers to rank people in a single series of worthiness invariably led to the assertion 'that oppressed and disadvantaged groups – races, classes, and sexes – are innately inferior and deserve their status.' Gould's historical excavation of reification (how the concept of intelligence became converted into an entity) and of ranking challenges such forms of justification and practices on which the hunt for disability is predicated.

If the previous reading of the hunt is to be labeled as cynical, though, then there is another way of looking at things. Gould's historical analysis of intelligence as a reified concept opens to view how the new eugenics operates through examinations and observations in more insidious if unintentional ways. The analyses of exam results that point to which population groups fail or succeed at what do not simply tell us of the existence of racism or sexism or classism or ableism. Exams are already the vectors of such -isms, sites for the recirculation of power, a form of discipline and punishment that assume ontologies can be segregated, graded, and differentially valued before any body-mind even enters the examination room. Rather than a direct confrontation in which the teacher, administrator, medical personnel, or researcher stands at the door and says, 'No. You cannot go there because I said so,' there is an indirect mechanism at work – the difficult interpersonal confrontation that gatekeeping makes inevitable is supposedly bypassed by the authorizing function of the examination.

The examination combines the techniques of an observing hierarchy and those of a normalizing judgment. It is a normalizing gaze, a surveillance that makes its possible to qualify, to classify and to punish. It establishes over individuals a visibility through which one differentiates them and judges them. That is why, in all the mechanisms of discipline, the examination is highly

The Hunt for Disability   165

ritualized. . . . At the heart of the procedures of discipline, it manifests the subjection of those who are perceived as objects and the objectification of those who are subjected.

(Foucault 1979: 184–185)

This authorizing function is of course prevalent throughout formal education. Teachers/professors in all institutional tiers use tests, grade papers, give permission, establish or participate in gatekeeping structures by conferring credentials, and so on. It is not as if any educator is immune from the filtering implications of these activities and can claim a pure or non-contradictory position on the matter. Is formal education therefore doomed to nonexistence under the weight of critiques such as Campbell's? Should schools just admit openly at the point of enrollment that only some of the children will be 'suited' to what goes on in them? The vanishing point toward which such questions are headed appear mired in a binary of alternatives, one based on disappearance (i.e., 'Just get rid of the whole system'), the other on greater transparency (i.e., 'Just admit from the outset that the current system is an irresolvable and ongoing problem that maintains ontological hierarchies.').

The difficulty of imagining society without schools as they currently are with their baby-sitting and sorting functions or of drawing Utopian pictures of how they might be without presumptions of an ableist normativity is the difficulty of having been normalized as a schoolchild, of having a subjectivity colonized by a concern to 'be able to' do something, of having been constantly examined to 'prove' that one can get the point, make the point, or draw the picture of 'the alternative.' The fact that I cannot answer my own wish for an alternative, that I cannot draw that picture, that I 'fail' to conceptualize within my 'perceptual processes' a solid vision of 'something better' after laying out a range of problems and debates, may tell me something after all – the 'inability' in an apparently satisfying way of proposing something 'better' is itself an entrapment in the very limits of discourse on ability and betterness that is being rethought.

But this seemingly stultifying embeddedness in the very thing being critiqued is nothing new to note. In the 1930s and long before Foucault, Carter G. Woodson's Afrocentric critique *The Mis-education of the Negro* so incisively noted that you do not need to slam the door in someone's face if you get him to slam it in his own. Forty years later in *Discipline and Punish*, we can see the rewording, where Foucault described at length the shift from overt torture to 'the gentle way in punishment,' the production of 'docile bodies,' and the ramifications of panopticon-style surveillance, where technologies of self-monitoring are internalized under the presumption that someone is always watching and recording anyway.

This watching is not always innocuous or positive. It is not akin to making sure that your child doesn't drown while playing near water. In schools and universities, this is a systematized watching and form of classification that tells people who they are and ought to be based on a narrow range of cultural values. There is no form of observation outside power relations, no assertion of knowledge without power effects, and no exercise of power without knowledge effects. The mutually

166   *Bernadette Baker*

constitutive dynamics of power-knowledge and their subjectivity and internalization effects inhere in the well-intended evaluation efforts and classifactory practices of major social institutions, including schools and universities, *and* in the very efforts to rethink and reshape them.

Thus, if my alternative was to assert that it is normal for there to be a 'range' of human body-minds, this assertion does not do away with the concept of normativity but reinvokes it in different form. As an alternative slotted into the current format of schooling, it would come dangerously close to a Spencerian social Darwinism of 'leave as you find' – the top of the tree would remain undisturbed and the real difficulties of actually getting around, through, and by in schools for many of the people forced to attend them could be glossed over as 'fate.' Similarly, if another alternative was to argue that disability is a reality, a fact of life, of every life, and ought not be taken as a negative ontology that must be made to disappear paradoxically by hunting it down to assimilate it, then this too does not break the circle of normalization that allows whatever is thought of as an ability to fly by uncontested. Whatever an institution seems not set up to 'handle' and throws back onto the recipient as a disability would remain unquestioned.

In both alternatives, the perfecting technologies that sought to morph the 'patient' into an image of the norm through a passion for sameness could be resecured through an ironic commitment to an undefined 'democracy.' Or as Roe (2000) puts it, the 'enchantment' for corporeal perfection would continue, obscured in this case by the nomenclature of 'free and public education' and 'the provision of services.' In the effort toward democratic education in the form of inclusive schooling, nationwide institutions simply have not, will not, do not want to, or know how to give up the act of classifying, sorting, and hierarchizing human beings, reduced in the end to ability levels or test scores. The theories of child development that undergird the postulation of abilities by age or stage remain wedded to the structures of schooling.[16] The challenge as I see it then is not how to tinker with the school, the university, examinations, or substituted portfolios but whether it is even possible to imagine the world otherwise. Is the situation such that, as Derrida argues, there is no philosophy, but everything is normative?[17] If so, then, is it simply a matter of which norms you happen to agree with? Or is there a genuine possibility for not requiring such things as examinations in negative ways as indicators of 'social order'? And if social order is merely a euphemism for what might more accurately be called the colonization of privilege, then it becomes clear how I am part of the problem rather than the solution, for the very employment of someone within a school or university is dependent on the assertion of (dis)abilities that such institutions both produce and govern.

Is the big picture so desperate, though? Can nothing at all be done without merely camouflaging the posse in more intricate form? If, as Foucault (1979) further asserts, disciplinary practices organize analytical space, then the question that those who organize education are left with, after the diversionary function of the examination and the normalizing function of schooling is exposed, is whether it is ever OK to think of some humans as normal and some humans as not, some humans as positively able and some as disabled in a negative way. Reversals are

The Hunt for Disability   167

again instructive. If those who set the minimum wage, for example, were compelled to live on it for the rest of their lives, no escape possible, then what might that wage be? In a similar vein, if the answer to the above question is yes, that it is OK to assert some humans as normal and some as not, some as on target and some as delayed, some as able to organize their 'perceptual processes' and some not, then what orientation to human life might result if those who answered yes were forced to bear the repressive brunt of policies asserting negative ontologies? Although disability-positive such as that argued for by persons who self-identify as Deaf Culturalists is one thing,[18] disability-negative, the construction of disability as a headache that won't go away and that is the object of the hunt within the specific site of schooling, is quite another. What would happen if, before inflicting them on others thought less human, less valuable, less educable, less everything that matters within a school, the whole range of effects of educational policies regarding disability had to hit home through *everyone's* sense of self as an outlawed ontology? Perhaps if the negative othering effects were applied to forms of corporeality that were initially thought of as positive, clear, stable, and nonproblematic, there would be time and space for reconsidering a wider range of the implications of the new eugenics, ableist normativity, and disciplining technologies before sending the posse out in schools.

In a final series of reversals, then, it seems important to consider just what skills are actually thought necessary or as 'needs' that define who the educationally problematic are and what 'quality citizenship' is. In a reversal of a medical logic that tests for disease by a presence of something, the 'disease' of the schoolchild who is labeled as disabled in one form or another is identified by an absence – the thing, the knowledge-as-commodity, skill-as-commodity, or self-control-as-commodity that is supposed to be carried inside as one might carry lunch in a backpack is considered missing or not timely enough. In the end, this means that the appropriate speed or action is considered absent as well, and that in a submerged eugenic reasoning this 'defect' is presumed to infect and create problems for more 'normal' others in the vicinity if left undiagnosed or addressed. But let's pretend that public schooling is not concerned purely with literacy, math, and that nebulous thing called academic achievement and that its arbitrary focus is in fact physical education. Let's extend the reversal and imagine that PE is *the* thing, the knowledge-performance that matters to how I judge you, who you can be, and what you can have. How fast *can* you run, move, slide, or roll? If I beat you, does that make you a problem? Or is the problem the notion of beating, of winning and losing, of faster and slower, of normal and abnormal in the face of rhetoric claiming respect for human diversity?

Notes

1 I have drawn this title from a subtitle in Fiona Campbell's (2000) paper on disability and eugenics that plays on the analogy of the hunt and the posse. Although Campbell's paper lies within the realm of critical legal theory and does not reflect on education, it has been an important source of inspiration in thinking through the issues I discuss here. Her work appears in a volume on the history and sociology of eugenics in

168   *Bernadette Baker*

Australia. Campbell's chapter is almost entirely about eugenic discourse in the United States, however.

2 Fairfield is a pseudonym.

3 Eliot, via the Committee of Ten of which he was a member, suggested that there were four routes or four kinds of subject matter that could lead to meeting university entrance requirements. I see this 'opening out' as an accommodation to prevent the complete eradication of the classical content such as Latin and Greek, the presence of which had been seriously questioned by other educators. The upshot was that classical content was still given a place on the curriculum by the Committee of Ten. Eliot was also one of the executive committee members of the first international symposium on eugenics, making his characterization by Kliebard (1986) as patrician seem an understatement.

4 The shift between '(dis)ability' and 'disability' or with emphasis, '*dis*ability,' in this sentence (and throughout the chapter) is significant and deliberate. The latter two terms refer to perceptions of *unable to* as a negative, outlaw, or problem ontology. The former term highlights the obvious binary and the inherent relationality – there is rarely an assertion of what counts as *dis*abled or unable to without a simultaneous assertion of what *able to* means and why. I use the terms disability, *dis*ability, or disabilities, therefore when referring to psycho-medical frameworks that assume certain things as 'defects.' These terms are thus used when I am summarizing dominant educational literature or processes that presume the objectivity of a pathologizing model. I use (dis)ability when overtly pointing to and emphasizing the politics of ability.

5 By ableist normativity, Campbell is not in my view referring to a static or simplistic structural binary between the 'have's' of ability and the 'have-nots' of disability. The terms *ableism* and *ableist normativity*, if at all commensurate, are not indebted, in her chapter, to sovereign notions of power but rather to circulatory notions of Foucaultian power-as-effects. This means that the term *ableist normativity* refers to how discourses – including technologies, programs, prescriptions, policies, and lines of reasoning – and everyday activities constitute as normal: certain ways of appearing, of accomplishing something, and of being seen as fully human. The normativity that this whole process constitutes is not permanent or static – new technologies can, for instance, destabilize what was previously thought of as natural. But at any given moment, or in a specific scenario, what is instantiated is a particular view of ability as *the* view of how a human should look or appear or perform – hence ableist normativity is an effect of the discourses that are brought to bear on reasonings about ontology and through activities of caring.

6 Sending the posse out in schools is a reference to both Wrigley's (1996) and Campbell's (2000) use of the metaphor of hunting, posses, and tracking down activities in the 'diagnosis' and 'remedy' of disabilities. Wrigley argues that sometimes it appears that disabilities are assumed purely medical artifacts to be weeded out, found out about, or 'hunted' in order to make the persons assigned the label 'disabled' back into a 'normal' person. Campbell extends the metaphor, referring to the techniques for identification and the obsession with technologies for 'rectification' as aspects of a posse employed to engage in the hunt of so-called corporeally anomalous persons. In both cases, the authors are not arguing that those involved in such activities are either literal hunters of human flesh, or are members of eugenics societies, etc. Rather, they note the complexities and the complicities involved in discourses that constitute (dis)ability and the politics entailed in the well-intended activities of caring. In this chapter, I will not be focusing on the topic of teachers who are labeled as 'having' disabilities, but rather on the posse in relation to children who have little choice but to go to school and be subjected to its practices. For an account of student teachers' reflections on the 'having' of disabilities, see Gabel (2001).

7 See Henri-Jaques Stiker's *A History of Disability*, though, for an account of practices that preceded the emergence of the term but might also be understood as eugenic.

The Hunt for Disability 169

8 Kaplan explains the extent of eugenic campaigning's 'success' by highlighting the cultural context in which eugenics emerged and took hold. Racism, imperialism, and eugenics are not necessarily the same in her view, indicating how the preexisting imperialism of European nations and the preexisting slavery and racism of Canada and the United States differentially underwrote the local reception of eugenics in such places. Overall, however, she argues that eugenic associations emerged within the most economically influential and industrializing western European countries and gained footholds in those countries that had colonized other parts of the world, spreading rapidly to other places that had direct experiences of slavery or reservation systems at home, such as New Zealand and Australia. It became a globalizing discourse in that it attempted to redefine how everyone was to see themselves as part of a hierarchical world system that eugenic discourse now proffered as 'scientific.' Not surprisingly, then, in Kaplan's view, the campaigns for sterilization were translated into surgery in a variety of contexts including many U.S. states (Pernick, 1996), Scandinavia (Broberg and Roll-Hansen, 1996), and Australia (McGregor, 2000).

9 The terminology that is now deployed in the historical and sociological critiques of eugenics attempts to capture the complexities of 20th-century shifts: 'negative' or 'hard' genetics and 'positive' or 'soft' eugenics, as well as old and new eugenics. The use of quotation marks in some of the couplets is key in that such descriptors suggest the difficulty of studying eugenic programs in the past and indicate further the political site that the interpretation of their effects on the present have become. Negative or hard genetics refers to events such as the Holocaust and sterilization programs. Positive or soft eugenics are seen as having the same values that lie at the back of negative or hard genetics but to some extent masking them through modified strategies. This has become controversial because it has problematized methods such as Maria Montessori's, which were previously seen as child-centered and now seen as eugenicist because the pedagogical methods were directed toward controlling racial/national improvement by problematizing some humans as 'lower races' while leaving untouched the false sense of superiority attributed to others. To that end, the difference between negative and positive or hard and soft eugenics has been made in terms of the methods promulgated rather than as a distinction in philosophical orientation – both are about 'quality control.'

10 Public schools were preceded in North America, for instance, by the equivalent of asylums, private schools, and orphanages. The fact that in the later 1800s and throughout the 1900s, not all children were forced, or allowed, to go to a public school indicates how the availability of other institutions limited public education's domain. Public schools were never designed for every child, especially those designated 'insane' or 'feebleminded,' and they are still not attended by every child.

11 Ingunn Moser and John Law (2001) argue that what needs to be rethought are terms such as agency, voice, and resistance: to talk of giving 'voices' is to take the risk of limiting articulation to that which is verbal, textual, or linguistic. But this, at least in the context of disability is to prejudice the result. Indeed it is to take the risk that 'voices' that happen to be non-verbal are simply not recognized, or disqualified. Which is yet another reason why we prefer to talk of articulation.

12 Douglas Baynton (2001) has documented this line of argument historically in the United States, for example, in campaigns for the right to vote by white women and by men and women of specific racial minorities. The right to vote was predicated in part on distancing one's 'group' from inscriptions of disability as a negative ontology.

13 Begging of further historicization is any conflation between 'quality control' dis- course in the old eugenics and 'quality of life' discourse in newer espoused goals of schooling.

14 Although intrinsically related, I am not discussing here the forms of pedagogy in special or 'exceptional' education that target concepts of giftedness and talent.

15 It is stating the obvious to note that most parents are not employed as public school teachers and therefore interact with teachers as though they are a distinct and sometimes foreign group.

170 Bernadette Baker

16 For an historicization of how the idea of stages of child development became wedded to the structures of public schooling, see Baker (2001).

17 Francois Ewald: Is there a philosophy of Jacques Derrida?
Jacques Derrida: No.

FE: Therefore there is no message? JD: No message.
FE: Is there anything normative?
JD: Of course there is, there is nothing but. For full text of interview see G. Biesta and D. Egea-Kuehne (2001), pp. 55–76. This quote is from p. 71.

18 There is actually no agreement in Deaf literature as to whether deafness is a disability or whether there is a discrete 'Deaf Culture.' I use the term disability-positive here, then, to refer to the idea that what has historically been called a *disability* in mainstream literature and medicine (i.e., deafness) is now being listened to as a positive state of being. For an account of the social movement called Deaf Awareness and the politics of deafness as an epistemological rather than auditory question, see Owen Wrigley (1996). For further analysis of (de)constructions of deafness as a linguistic, not disability, minority see Brenda Brueggeman (1999) and Harlan Lane (1997).

References

Aberdeen, L. (2000). Australian scientific research, 'Aboriginal blood,' and the racial imaginary. In M. Crotty, J. Germoc and G. Rodwell (eds.), '*A race for place': Eugenics, Darwinism, and social thought and practice in Australia* (pp. 111–112). Newcastle, AU: University of Newcastle Press.

Albrecht, G.L. (ed.). (1981). *Cross national rehabilitation policies: A sociological perspective*, vol. 25. London: Sage.

Allan, J. (1996). Foucault and special educational needs: A 'box of tools' for analysing children's experiences of mainstreaming. *Disability and Society*, 11(2), 219–233.

Argulewicz, E.N. (1983). Effects of ethnic membership, socio-economic status, and home language on LD, EMR, and EH Placements. *Learning Disabilities Quarterly*, 6(Spring), 195–200.

Baker, B. (2001). *In perpetual motion: Theories of power, educational history, and the child.* New York: Peter Lang.

Barkan, E. (1992). *Retreat of scientific racism: Changing concepts of race in Britain and the United States between the world wars.* Cambridge, UK: Cambridge University Press.

Baynton, D. (2001). Disability and the justification of inequality in American history. In P. Longmore and L. Umansky (eds.), *The new disability history: American perspectives* (pp. 33–57). New York: New York University Press.

Biesta, G., and Egea-Kuehne, D. (eds.) (2001). *Derrida and education.* New York: Routledge.

Brantlinger, E. (1997). Using ideology: Cases of nonrecognition of the politics of research and practice in special education. *RER*, 67(4), 425–460.

Broberg, G., and Roll-Hansen, N. (1996). *Eugenics and the welfare state: Sterilization policy in Denmark, Sweden, Norway, and Finland.* East Lansing: Michigan State University Press.

Brosnan, F. L. (1983). Overrepresentation of low socioeconomic minority students in special education programs in California. *Learning Disabilities Quarterly*, 6(Fall), 517–525.

Brueggeman, B.J. (1999). *Lend me your ear: The rhetorical construction of deafness.* Washington, DC: Gallaudet University Press.

Campbell, F. (2000). Eugenics in a different key? New technologies and the 'conundrum' of 'disability.' In M. Crotty, J. Germov, and G. Rodwell (eds.), '*A race for a place': Eugenics, Darwinism, and social thought and practice in Australia* (pp. 307–318). Newcastle, AU: The University of Newcastle Press.

The Hunt for Disability 171

Carrier, J.G. (1986). *Learning disability: Social class and the construction of inequality in American education*, vol. 18. New York: Greenwood Press.

Crowe, C. (2000). Inheriting eugenics? Genetics, reproduction and eugenic legacies. In M. Crotty, J. Germov and G. Rodwell (eds.), *'A Race for a place': Eugenics, Darwinism, and social thought and practice in Australia* (pp. 173–180). Newcastle, AU: The University of Newcastle Press.

Danforth, S., and Rhodes, W. (1997). Deconstructing disability: A philosophy for inclusion. *Remedial and Special Education*, 18(6), 357–366.

Davis, L.J. (1997). Constructing normalcy: The bell curve, the novel, and the invention of the disabled body in the nineteenth century. In L. J. Davis (ed.), *The Disability Studies Reader* (pp. 9–20). New York: Routledge.

Duster, T. (1990). *Backdoor to eugenics*. London: Routledge.

Edgerton, R. (1986). A case of delabeling: Some practical and theoretical implications. In L.L. Langness and H.G. Levine (eds.), *Culture and retardation* (pp. 101–126). Denver, CO: D. Reidel Publishing Company.

Eliot, C.W. (1905). The fundamental assumptions in the report of the Committee of Ten, 1893. *Educational Review*, 30, 325–343.

Erevelles, N. (2000). Educating unruly bodies: Critical pedagogy, disability studies, and the politics of schooling. *Educational Theory*, 30(2), 25–48.

Foucault, M. (1979). *Discipline and punish: The birth of the prison*. New York: Vintage Books.

Foucault, M. (1989). *Foucault live: Interviews 1966–84*. New York: Semiotext(e).

Foucault, M. (1991). Governmentality. In G. Burchell, C. Gordon, and P. Miller (eds.), *The Foucault effect* (pp. 87–104). Chicago: University of Chicago Press.

Fox Keller, E. (1992). Nature, nurture, and the human genome project. In D. Kevles and L. Hood (eds.), *The code of codes*(pp. 281–299). Cambridge, MA: Harvard University Press.

Franklin, B. (1994). *From 'backwardness' to 'at-risk': Childhood learning difficulties and the contra- dictions of school reform*. Albany: State University of New York Press.

Gabel, S. (2001). 'I wash my face with dirty water': Narratives of disability and pedagogy. *Journal of Teacher Education*, 52(1), 31–47.

Gabel, S., Vyas, S., Patel, H., and Patel, S. (2001). Problems of methodology in cross-cultural disability studies: An Indian immigrant example. In B. Altman and S. Barnhart (eds.), *Research in social science and disability*, vol. 2 (pp. 209–228). Thousand Oaks, CA: Sage.

Garton, S. (2000). Writing eugenics: A history of classifying practices. In M. Crotty, J. Germov and G. Rodwell (eds.), *'A Race for a Place': Eugenics, Darwinism, and social thought and practice in Australia* (pp. 9–18). Newcastle, AU: The University of Newcastle Press.

Gould, S. (1981). *The mismeasure of man*. New York: W. W. Norton.

Herrnstein, R., and Murray, C. (1994). *The bell curve: Intelligence and class structure in American life*. New York: Free Press.

Heshusius, L. (1995). Holism and special education: There is no substitute for real life purposes and processes. In T. Skrtic (ed.), *Disability and democracy: Reconstructing (special) education for postmodernity* (pp. 166–189). New York: Teachers College Press.

Hultqvist, K. (in press). The traveling state, the nation, and the subject of education. In B. Baker and K. Heyning (eds.), *Dangerous coagulations? The uses of Foucault in the study of education*. New York: Peter Lang.

Ingstad, B., and Reynolds Whyte, S. (eds). (1995). *Disability and culture*. Berkeley: University of California Press.

Kaplan, G. (2000). European respectability, eugenics, and globalisation. In M. Crotty, J. Germov and G. Rodwell (eds.), *'A Race for a Place': Eugenics, Darwinism, and social thought and practice in Australia* (pp. 19–28). Newcastle, AU: The University of Newcastle Press.

172 Bernadette Baker

Kidder-Ashley, P., Deni, J., and Anderton, J. (2000). Learning disabilities eligibility in the 1990s: An analysis of state practices. *Education*, 121(1), 65–72.

Kliebard, H. (1986). *The struggle for the American curriculum*. Boston: Routledge and Kegan Paul.

Kliewer, C., and Biklen, D. (2001). 'School's not really a place for reading': A research synthesis of the literate lives of students with severe disabilities. *The Journal of the Association for Persons with Severe Handicaps*, 26(1), 1–12.

Lane, H. (1997). Constructions of deafness. In L. Davis (ed.), *The disability studies reader* (pp. 153–171). New York: Routledge.

Linton, S. (1998). *Claiming disability: Knowledge and identity*. New York: New York University Press.

Longmore, P., and Umansky, L. (eds.). (2001). *The new disability history: American perspectives*. New York: New York University Press.

Lowe, R. (1997). *Schooling and social change, 1964–1990*. London: Routledge.

Lowe, R. (2000). Eugenics, scientific racism and education: Has anything changed in one hundred years? In M. Crotty, J. Germov, and G. Rodwell (eds.), *'A Race for a Place': Eugenics, Darwinism, and social thought and practice in Australia* (pp. 207–220). Newcastle, AU: The University of Newcastle Press.

Ludmerer, K.M. (1972). *Genetics in American society*. Baltimore: Johns Hopkins University Press.

McGregor, R. (2000). 'Breed out the colour': Reproductive management for White Australia. In M. Crotty, J. Germov and G. Rodwell (eds.), *'A Race for a place': Eugenics, Darwinism, and social thought and practice in Australia* (pp. 61–70). Newcastle, AU: The University of Newcastle Press.

McSorley, K. (2000). Moving from oppression to democracy: Reframing the preparation of special education teachers. *Educators for Urban Minorities*, 1(2), 2738.

Meiners, E.R. (1999). Writing (on) fragments. *Qualitative Studies in Education*, 12, 347–362.

Mickelson, J.-R. (2000). *Our sons were labeled behavior disordered: Here are the stories of our lives*. Troy, NY: Educator's International Press.

Mitchell, D., and Snyder, S. (eds). (in press). *Eugenics in America, 1890–1935: A disability studies sourcebook*. Ann Arbor: University of Michigan Press.

Moser, I., and Law, J. (2001). 'Making voices': New media technologies, disabilities, and articulation. *Centre for Science Studies and the Department of Sociology*. Lancaster University. Retrieved on 17 January 2001 from: http:00www.comp.lancs.ac.uk0sociology0soc060jl.html

Pernick, M. (1996). *The black stork: Eugenics and the death of 'defective' babies in American medicine and motion pictures since 1915*. New York: Oxford University Press.

Phelps, A., and Hanley-Maxwell, C. (1997). School-to-work transitions for youth with disabilities: A review of outcomes and practices. *Review of Educational Research*, 67, 197–226.

Pickens, D. (1968). *Eugenics and the progressives*. Nashville: Tennessee University Press.

Rodwell, G. (2000). The unkindest cut of all: Eugenics, masturbation and circumcision. In M. Crotty, J. Germov and G. Rodwell (eds.), *'A Race for a place': Eugenics, Darwinism, and social thought and practice in Australia* (pp. 235–247). Newcastle, AU: The University of Newcastle Press.

Roe, M. (2000). Eugenics' challenge to liberal humanism: A personal traverse. In M. Crotty, J. Germov and G. Rodwell (eds.), *'A Race for a place': Eugenics, Darwinism, and social thought and practice in Australia* (pp. 3–8). Newcastle, AU: The University of Newcastle Press.

The Hunt for Disability   173

Sandahl, C. (2001, April). Queering the crip and cripping the queer: Solo autobiographical performance art. In *The Body in Real Time*. Symposium conducted at the meeting of the Disability Studies in the Humanities Symposium, Madison, WI.

Searle, G. R. (1971). *The quest for national efficiency*. Oxford, UK: Blackwell.

Selden, S. (1999). *Inheriting shame: The story of eugenics and racism in America*. New York: Teachers College Press.

Skrtic, T. (ed.). (1995). *Disability and democracy: Reconstructing (special) education for post-modernity*. New York: Teachers College Press.

Slee, R. (1997). Inclusion or assimilation? Sociological explorations of the foundations of theories of special education. *Educational Foundations*, Winter, 55–71.

Sleeter, C. (1987). Why is there learning disabilities? A critical analysis of the birth of the field in its social context. In T. Popkewitz (ed.), *The formation of school subjects: The struggle for creating an American institution* (pp. 224–232). New York: Falmer Press.

Stiker, H.-J. (1999). *A history of disability*, trans. William Sayers. Ann Arbor: University of Michigan Press.

Thomas, G., and Glenny, G. (2000). Emotional and behavioural difficulties: Bogus needs in a false category. *Discourse*, 21(3), 283–298.

Tomlinson, S. (1984). *Educational subnormality: A study in decision-making*. London: Routledge and Kegan Paul.

Tucker, J. (1980). Ethnic proportions in classes for the learning disabled: Issues in non-biased assessment. *Journal of Special Education*, 14 (Spring), 93–105.

Ware, L. (2000a). Writing, identity, and the other: Dare we do disability studies? *Journal of Teacher Education*, 52(2), 107–123.

Ware, L. (2000b). Inclusive education. In D.A. Gabbard (ed.), *Education in the global economy: Politics and the rhetoric of school reform* (pp. 111–120). Hillsdale, NJ: Lawrence Erlbaum.

Weier, G. (2000). Heading toward a crisis? District grapples with rising special education costs. *Isthmus*, 5. http://isthmus.com/

Woodson, C.G. (1993). *The mis-education of the Negro*. Trenton, NJ: Africa World Press. (Original work published 1933).

Wright, P., and Santa Cruz, R. (1983). Ethnic composition of special education programs in California. *Learning Disabilities Quarterly*, 6 (Fall), 387–394.

Wrigley, O. (1996). *The politics of deafness*. Washington, DC: Gallaudet University Press.

Part III

The Consequences of Assessment and the Possibility of Fairer and More Equitable Alternatives

10 Untangling the Racialization of Disabilities

An Intersectionality Critique across Disability Models[1]

Alfredo J. Artiles

Introduction: Disrupting Orthodoxies in the Racialization of Disabilities

The quest for educational equity has been elusive and fraught with paradoxes through-out the history of American education, particularly for racial minorities and disabled learners. These two groups have complicated and politically charged histories linked to assumptions of deficit often used to justify inequities. Both have endured significant barriers and injustices ranging from limited access to educational resources to overrepresentation in poorly funded schools and negative post-school outcomes (Anyon 2005). Although massive political and technical resources have been deployed in efforts to secure educational equity, remedies for one group can have deleterious consequences for the other, thus muddling the effects of well-intentioned justice projects. For instance, under the Individuals with Disabilities Education Act (IDEA), students with disability diagnoses are extended rights and entitlements intended to ensure educational equity on the assumption that disability diagnosis is beneficial to covered students. However, this guiding assumption has been critiqued by racial minority groups who have argued that disproportional diagnoses of disability in students of color creates a "double bind" that further compounds the structural disadvantages that each group has historically endured (Artiles 2011).

The racialization of disability is of concern because disability diagnoses for racial minorities often have concomitant negative consequences, such as educational segregation, limited access to the general education curriculum, and a host of negative long-term outcomes (Artiles 2003). This problem is connected to poverty, geographical location, cultural practices, and ideologies of difference (Albrecht et al. 2012; Artiles 1998). Moreover, it is visible across a range of disabilities – including high-incidence categories such as learning disabilities, intellectual disabilities, emotional/behavioral disorders, and speech/language impairments – accounting for approximately four million students (i.e., two thirds of the special education population; U.S. Department of Education 2009).

The evidence has consistently shown that African American learners have substantially higher probabilities than their counterparts to be diagnosed with high incidence disabilities. At the national level, these students are three times more likely to be diagnosed as intellectually disabled and over 200% more likely to be diagnosed with emotional/behavioral disorders. American Indian/Alaska Native students have a 50% greater chance than their peers to be identified as learning disabled (U.S. Department of Education 2006). Latino/a students are overrepresented in some categories in certain regions, states, and school districts, though not at the national level (Artiles et al. 2011).

These statistics defy easy explanation. For instance, despite the disproportionate poverty rate among these groups (e.g., Latinos/as), racial inequities are *not* observed in disability categories generally associated with biological causes linked to poverty, such as sensory and orthopedic impairments and multiple disabilities (Losen and Orfield, 2002). Moreover, after controlling for poverty, race still makes a significant contribution to predicting a disability diagnosis (Skiba et al. 2008).

While the problem is longstanding, the racialization of disability has received more attention in the last decade (Waitoller et al. 2010). Federal government actions have intensified: there is an increase in the number of published studies acknowledging federal funding support, technical assistance centers have been created to address the problem, and there have been key changes in IDEA (i.e., requirements for reporting, monitoring, and eliminating racial inequities in placement patterns). Despite progress, unsettling questions remain unanswered: how do legal protections for one marginalized group – e.g., people with disabilities – become sources of inequities for another marginalized group, such as racial minority students? What types of evidence would be needed to document the ways in which the equity agenda of the IDEA collides with racial groups' search for justice? Why have research and policy communities given so much attention to this longstanding problem in the last 10 years? Perhaps more importantly, why have the historical and cultural sedimentations of race and disability, and their complex intersections, not been theorized and analyzed in this scholarship?

The racialization of disability has not occurred in a vacuum. Scholars have documented how "disability has always been racialised and how race has been conceived as disability" (Bolaki 2011: 48). Since at least the 19th century, race and disability have been intertwined and linked to ideologies of evolutionary hierarchy – "nonwhite races were routinely connected to people with disabilities, both of whom were depicted as evolutionary laggards or throwbacks" (Baynton 2001: 36). Moreover, attributions of disability were often used to justify the institution of slavery and deny basic rights to African Americans (Baynton 2001).

Douglas Baynton argued that "not only has it been considered justifiable to treat disabled people unequally, but the *concept* of disability has been used to justify dis- crimination against other groups by attributing disability to them" (2001: 33, emphasis in original). The racialization of disabilities reminds us that racial minorities have been consistently subjected to such "double bind" discrimination (Artiles 2011). Unfortunately, the racialization of disability scholarship has been dominated by the notion of "damage imagery" – the idea that African Americans and other racial minorities "are and historically have been psychologically damaged" (Scott 2007: 1). It is typically assumed that damage imagery is the byproduct of innate inferiority and/or the sequela of poverty or inferior cultural practices;

The Racialization of Disabilities   179

the result is deficit-driven narratives about racial minorities in which mental and cognitive pathology are paramount (Scott 2007; Valencia 2010).

Despite recurrent historical convergences, scholars in psychology, education, and medicine artificially maintain a divide between race and disability, enforcing troubling silences and invisibilities. Key dimensions of marginalized groups are simultaneously visible and invisible. How and for what purposes do scholarly communities manage to maintain what Ned Mitchell (2011) described as the "absent presences" of raced and disabled bodies? What work is accomplished when race and disability are kept in separate spheres? (Bell 2011).

Most scholarship on the racialization of disability has been grounded in the so-called medical model in which the unit of analysis is the individual, completely devoid of social or historical influences. My colleagues and I have found a profound silence about race in research based on this model (Artiles et al. 1997). The medical model fragments the individual, focusing either on race or on disability, rarely examining the interplay of race and disability with other key dimensions such as social class and gender.

Social and cultural models of disability have also been used, though to a lesser extent, in analyses of racial inequities in special education. The social model locates disability in a societal plane, "conceptualized as a discourse of opposition, directed primarily against societal oppression" (Schillmeier 2010: 4), particularly against barriers imposed by an ableist society, prejudices and biases against disability, and deficit models that dismiss the lived experiences, viewpoints, potential, and contributions of disabled people. The cultural model, in turn, raises the question of the social construction of disability, though it has been less concerned with the perspective of disabled people as a minority group, and more with the inequities endured by racial minorities as they are disproportionately placed in special education (Patton 1998).

We know little about how scholarship based on these models has paid attention to the historical intersections of race and disability, how it has framed justice questions, and the similarities and differences among the analyses conducted from the vantage points of medical, social, and cultural models. Given these substantial gaps, an alternative interdisciplinary analytical project is needed. Two theoretical aspects are central to this project.

First, we need to use the lens of intersectionality to analyze these bodies of research for "race and disability are always imbricated with gender, sex, sexuality, and class" (Dolmage 2011: 27). The notion of intersectionality emerged in critical race theory, and has been subsequently developed in the social sciences and humanities, precisely as a resource to understand the complexity of people's identities and experiences in stratified institutions and societies (Collins 2003; Crenshaw 1991). Intersectionality is a useful theoretical framework to understand the tensions between the lived experiences of people with multiple intersecting identities and communities' needs for identity politics: racial minorities and disabled people need group identities for material and symbolic purposes, but this does not mean group categories are essentializing artifacts as community members embody complex intersectional identities (Crenshaw 1991). Intersectionality attends to identity

180　*Alfredo J. Artiles*

categories – such as race and disability – because they have meaning, social gravity, and consequences; indeed, "power has clustered around certain categories and is exercised against others" (Crenshaw 1991: 375). Thus, intersectionality affords crucial insights about the racialization of disability, compelling us to focus on both the power of assigning categories to individuals and on the authority of those categories "to have social and material consequences" (Crenshaw 1991: 376).

Second, we can benefit from a *contrapuntal* reading of intersectionality in the scholarship produced from the medical, social, and cultural models. *Contrapuntalism* links ideas and practices that are regarded as being opposites or in contradiction, thereby revealing points of contact across these bodies of work that are not readily apparent. "A contrapuntal reading is to emphasize and highlight the disjunctions, not to overlook or play them down" (Said 1993: 146). From a contrapuntal standpoint, we are compelled to cross the liminal spaces between different disability lenses. As Said explained in the context of discussing exile, "because the exile sees things both in terms of what has been left behind and what is actual here and now, there is a *double perspective* that never sees things in isolation" (p. 60, emphasis added). Thus a crucial implication of a contrapuntal analysis is an unceasing concern with *what* to read (i.e., disproportionality research grounded in seemingly contradictory models of disability) attached to an unremitting mindfulness about *how* to read – i.e., being reminded of the "intertwined and overlapping histories" (Said 1993: 18) of race and disability as they intersect with gender, social class, and language. Through a contrapuntal analysis, we can "be able to think through and interpret together experiences that are discrepant, each with its particular agenda and pace of development, its own internal formations, its internal coherence and system of external relationships, all of them coexisting and interacting with others" (Said 1993: 32).

What can we gain from using the double vision of a contrapuntal analysis of intersectionality to read disproportionality research across medical, cultural, and social models of disability? First we can gain insights about blind spots in these literatures to understand how various categories and domains of experience have been disaggregated; such analysis will allow us to read these categories and realms of experience in an integrated fashion and as mediated by institutional processes (Ribet 2010). Moreover, a contrapuntal reading of intersectionality in this research literature will enable us to claim that

> "disability and race do more than intersect in order to reinforce or intensify ideological stereotypes . . . it is not simply that the inherent, acquired or attributed characteristics possessed by members of racial groups are interpreted based on a white supremacist construct of ability. Literally physical or psychological disablement (as well as social and political subordination) can also be a process that results in disability imposed through racial power relations"
> (Ribet 2010: 217).

Thinking through critical interdisciplinary questions can help us approach the racialization of disabilities from a more complex perspective. These questions

The Racialization of Disabilities   181

include the following: how has research on the racialization of disabilities examined the historical entanglements of race and disability? How has it examined intersections in categories of difference (e.g., race, disability, social class, gender)? What insights about racial inequities in special education result from the analysis of research based on purportedly opposing models of disability? I argue that a contrapuntal analysis of the racialization of disabilities using an intersectional prism promises important insights into these questions and illuminate generative and enduring questions about educational justice. Following Chris Bell (2011), this analytical project enables us to keep alternative disability models in conversation with one another; it will ultimately assist us to re-interpret the cultural dynamics of *difference* that mediate representations of marginalized groups.

I first provide an overview of research on disproportionate representation, various disability models, and intersectionality. I then present a contrapuntal critical reading of intersectionality in the scholarship on the racialization of disabilities across disability models, and conclude with reflections on future inquiries into this topic.

SETTING THE CONTEXT: RACIALIZATION OF DISABILITY RESEARCH, DISABILITY MODELS, AND INTERSECTIONALITY

Why Are There so Many Minority Students in Special Education? A Historical Outline

The research on why there are so many minority students in special education (see Harry and Klingner 2006) paints a complex picture in which individual factors, institutional practices, organizational forces, and fiscal and bureaucratic pressures contribute to the racialization of disability (Skiba et al. 2008). There is little consensus on a theoretical explanation of the problem; some studies do not even specify the theoretical frameworks that guide their analyses. Research has tended to examine the role of individual *or* structural factors, mostly from a quantitative perspective (Waitoller et al. 2010). This literature commonly concludes that a disproportionate number of racial minorities live in poverty, which in turn can mediate the onset of certain disabilities, particularly those conditions with biological etiologies. For instance, American Indians/Alaska Natives are overrepresented in the category of deaf-blindness, and, along with African Americans, are disproportionately diagnosed with developmental delays. However, developmental delays are not consistently diagnosed with clear biological roots. Indeed, this diagnosis tends to be grounded in a view of human development that largely ignores its cultural roots (Rogoff 2003). There is evidence of systemic forces at play – e.g., student race makes a significant contribution to risk of being identified as disabled, even after statistically controlling for poverty level; students who are racial minorities tend to be placed in segregated programs more often than their White counterparts *with the same disability diagnosis* (Skiba et al., 2008).

182   *Alfredo J. Artiles*

Nonetheless, some commentators still question whether the racialization of disabilities is a problem, claiming that concerns are likely grounded in an opposition to special education. *They overlook the significance of the problem.* First, disproportionality raises the question of misidentification in the case of overrepresentation, and exclusion from services in the case of under-identification. Second, overrepresentation adds another layer of marginalization and disadvantage for racial minority students – particularly since disability identification is closely associated with long-term negative consequences that include persistent lower academic achievement, higher risk of placement in the juvenile justice system, higher school dropout rate, and lower access to higher education (Artiles et al. 2010). Third, these commentators overlook the specific arguments involved: critics of the racialization of disabilities remind us of the histories of using disability to justify inequities for disabled people as well as for racial minorities and women, of the material and symbolic negative consequences of the entanglement of race with disability and its relation to the concept of the "normal."

Changes to federal law in 2004 require states to track and address racial disproportionality. This legal change was welcomed by most commentators as a step forward. But confusion about the new legal requirements and manipulations of racial disproportionality definitions and metrics, along with converging pressures stemming from educational accountability reforms, are shaping a perverse policy climate and landscape (Artiles 2011). For instance, disproportionality may be deepening in some states and districts, but it is not acted upon because of placement threshold requirements. Daryl Scott (2007) documented similar problems in examining the persistent association between race and mental health pathology: "the threshold for what experts considered a mental health problem continuously shifted" (p. xiv). This difficulty is exacerbated because federal law now requires that states determine whether disproportionality is present; if so, they must decide if such patterns are the result of inappropriate practices that must be redressed through specific actions and extra resources. Unfortunately, a sizable number of states are concluding that high disproportionality levels are *not* the result of inappropriate identification practices (Artiles 2011).

Discussions about the disability models underlying this research are virtually nonexistent. The de facto lens has been the medical model, though some analyses have been grounded in social and cultural models. I outline these paradigms in the next section as a means to inform the contrapuntal reading of intersectionality in this research across disability models.

Ways with Theories: Professional Visions of Disability

I outline key ideas of the three disability models, though there are not impermeable lines demarcating the models (Shakespeare 2006) and there are points of tension among them (Ribet 2010, personal communication).[2]

Medical Model

The medical model's defining characteristic is the assumption that disability is located in biological impairments within the individual, "neglecting the reality of discrimination" (Watermeyer 2013: 14); policies and services consequently aim to fix the disabled person (Crossley 1999).[3] Implicit in the "damaged body" trope of the medical model are uninterrogated assumptions about a normal body. Thus, this model is driven by a "moral imperative to 'healthy normalcy'" (Watermeyer 2013: 29) that will cure or rehabilitate impairments; it regards disabled people as different and inferior, a premise that justifies their exclusion and creates barriers for rights and entitlements (Crossley 1999), or as Tobin Siebers (2008) described it, for the "right to have rights" (p. 176). Given the biological roots of disability, it is assumed that "the social disadvantages and exclusion that accompany the disability can be explained as natural and not ascribable to any social cause. Because disability is not socially caused, the disabled individual has no claim of right to social remediation, and any benefits or assistance that society chooses to bestow on persons with disabilities can be viewed as a charitable response" (Crossley 1999: 651–652). The medical model views disabled people as dependent upon professionals, not only to validate their condition via a diagnosis, but also to determine and provide the best treatment or prosthetics needed to be cured or rehabilitated, to decide on relevant social benefits, and to certify any entitlement to exemptions (e.g., work), as long as individuals agree to receive the prescribed treatment (Crossley 1999). The perspective of the disabled is irrelevant, and hence, no efforts are made to gather or use such information (Linton 1998).

Despite the strong critiques raised against the medical model, it pervades the legal, policy, and professional domains. It has been the primary lens to examine the racialization of disability. Because the medical model foregrounds the individual as the unit of analysis, it disaggregates race from disability and other markers of difference (e.g., gender, social class, and language), resulting in a fragmented individual. In this model, racial and cultural differences can be construed as comparable and indexed as demographic markers (Artiles et al. 2010).

Social Model

The social model of disability offers "new and *political* understandings of disability . . . which is seen as interacting with social, cultural, historical, legal, and medical dis- courses, as well as further complicating factors such as race, ethnicity, gender, age, and class" (Connor and Ferri 2005: 110). The social model sees the idea of disability as the product of oppression and structural exclusion that should be eliminated (Shakespeare 2006). This vision has significant implications for policy; instead of fixing disabled bodies, it encourages policies informed by an "accommodation imperative" that change the social and physical structures of society (Crossley 1999: 658). Disabled scholars and activists have led the way in developing the social model of disability.[4] This model regards disability as a social construction, thereby locating disability in society (not the body), and drawing distinctions

184   *Alfredo J. Artiles*

between disability and impairment. In this view, the presence of an impairment does not necessarily constitute a disability. Disability arises out of society's ableist assumptions and practices about what is considered normal. Thus, it is a social environment that "disables" a person in a wheelchair if stairs are the only means to reach different building floors. The "wheelchair user is disadvantaged not by her inability to walk, but by the way in which buildings are designed and constructed" (Crossley 1999: 654).

The concept of the impairment-disability binary has been criticized. Indeed, disabled authors have called attention to the messy and ambiguous overlaps between bodily aspects of their experiences and societal dimensions of both impairments and disabilities. Experiencing impairments rests on cultural meanings, emphasizing the "interpenetration of impairment and disability" (Shakespeare 2006: 37). More- over, the social model can elaborate its attention to the psychological realm and the body (i.e., impairment) (Watermeyer 2013).

This model also encourages attention to the cultural construction of disability as reflected in the images and perceptions of people with disabilities in popular culture, policies, media stereotypes, and the like. These constructions contribute to the *othering* of disabled individuals and mediate processes of exclusion that this community endures over time (Crossley 1999). Embedded in these constructions are assumptions about "normal" that structure cultural and material worlds that cater to the needs of nondisabled individuals (Watermeyer 2013). The social model is critical of the notion of "normalization" because it rests on ideologies of homogeneity and control that date back to the 19th century when statistical reasoning and technologies were produced (Crossley 1999; Watermeyer 2013). However, just as the social model has criticized the essentialist logic embedded in the idea of normal, the emergence of the social model has required the adoption of a kind of "strategic essentialism" (Garland-Thomson 1997: 283). Moreover, criticisms have been raised about the social model's attention to the experiences of Western white middle class males with physical disabilities (particularly in its early work) (Watermeyer 2013).[5]

Cultural Model

The third perspective is reflected in a body of scholarship concerned with racial disproportionality. This corpus of scholarship shares some traits that I label "the cultural model." For instance, this work critiques the racialization of disability with an utmost concern for the oppression endured by racial minorities (Patton 1998). This work also relies, to some degree, on a social construction view of disability. Finally, some analyses based on the cultural model tend to be informed by a dynamic and historically based notion of culture that opens analytical spaces to examine the agency and cultural assets of communities (Artiles et al. 2010). It is not clear, however, how issues of intersectionality are addressed in this scholarship.

To summarize, the racialization of disabilities has been studied primarily through the lens of a medical model, with some attention by those using social and

The Racialization of Disabilities 185

cultural models. But do the differences among models result in disparate framings of the problem, alternative insights across analyses conducted from different models, and distinct ways of engaging with the intersections of race and disability? Before I address these queries through a contrapuntal reading, I provide an introduction to the concept of intersectionality.

Complexity in Analysis of Unjust Practices: The Promise of Intersectionality

Intersectionality examines the influence of power to provide limited frames for people's multidimensional experiences, particularly those of women of color, as a response to "the tendency to treat race and gender as mutually exclusive categories of experience and analysis" (Crenshaw 1989: 139). Intersectionality acknowledges that "systems of race, social class, gender, sexuality, ethnicity, nation, and age form mutually constructing features of social organization" (Collins 2000: 299). Intersectionality thus rejects the "separability of analytical and identity categories" and captures "the relationships among multiple dimensions and modalities of social relations and subject formations" (McCall 2005: 1771). Intersectionality challenges essentialist views of groups, single-axis analyses, and additive models of identity (Crenshaw 1991). Intersectionality's sensitivity to within-group diversity challenges the logic of "group unity equals group uniformity" (Hancock 2007: 65). Intersectional analysis aims to document the convergence of multiple forms of oppression in people's lives as shaped by distinct markers of difference. An implication of this analytic perspective includes policy responses that are sensitive to the convergence of multiple forms of oppression (Crenshaw 1991; Hancock 2007).

There are a number of types of intersectionality. I discuss structural and political intersectionality here and other types when critiquing the racialization of disability in the next section. Crenshaw (1991) describes structural and political intersectionality. Structural intersectionality refers to how intersectional locations make the experiences of groups qualitatively different. In this analysis, structural intersectionality suggests that boys of color from low-income backgrounds, particularly African Americans and American Indians, at the intersection of race, gender, and class experience their identification as disabled and efforts to address it in ways qualitatively different from that of White middle-class boys. In turn, political intersectionality emphasizes that intersectional identities may be situated "within at least two subordinated groups that frequently pursue conflicting political agendas. The need to split one's political energies between two sometimes-opposing groups is an additional dimension of intersectional disempowerment" (Crenshaw 1991: 360). Thinking in terms of political intersectionality suggests that low-income boys of color with disabilities or with a heightened probability of disability identification are situated within multiple subordinated groups that frequently pursue conflicting political agendas. This liminal position creates a sort of intersectional disempowerment that middle-class boys with disabilities, low-income boys of color without disabilities, and White girls and girls of color rarely experience. Intersectional analysis has the potential to address this problem. The

186 *Alfredo J. Artiles*

bulk of the evidence on racial inequities is based on quantitative analyses, mostly based on a medical model. A few quantitative studies have been informed by cultural perspectives. There are fewer qualitative studies designed with cultural processes in mind.

This section discusses trends in this research with regards to intersectionality across the three disability models, with specific focus on the use of the unitary approach and hybrid narratives. I used the scholarship of a few established authors working in the medical, social, and cultural models of disability to exemplify distinctive inquiry features of each model. I selected articles that broadly addressed at least two vectors of discrimination, even though some of these authors did not originally set out to conduct intersectional analyses.

Written on the Body: The Unitary Approach

Many disproportionality studies rest on a "unitary approach" to identity. As described by Ange-Marie Hancock (2007) this approach endorses a universalistic perspective in which one "variable" or marker of difference, such as race or class, is assumed to be both more important than the others and stable. Thus, researchers set to identify the one variable that has the greatest explanatory power in predicting special education placement. Inquiries are generally constrained by adherence to the medical model of disability, as outlined above. Typically, secondary datasets at the school district, state, or (less frequently) national levels are used to gauge the factor that best explains/predicts placement. Structural conditions in the special education field offer incentives for a unitary approach in disproportionality research. For example, federal law defines learning disabilities diagnosis as unrelated to socioeconomic and cultural differences. Thus, the law indirectly prevents intersectional analyses of disabilities with other markers of difference.

The search for *the* variable with the greatest explanatory power is sometimes imposed through methodological means, such as use of covariates. One such example is the work of Jacob Hibel and his colleagues in which they investigated "how student and school characteristics relate to the student's placement into special education" (2010: 313). These authors explained that "disproportionate representation may be especially likely to occur for those types of disabilities that rely more on a teacher's judgment and contextual factors (e.g., LD, EBD) than those types that rely on relatively more objective criteria (e.g., MR, visual impairment)" (314). Building on the force of a unitary logic, individual judgments, such as teacher referral decisions, were examined as mediated by a single factor – e.g., teacher's race or school/classroom demographics.[6] This led them to conclude that teacher judgments of acceptable student achievement or behavior are necessarily based on the performance of the teacher's particular referent group, which naturally consists of the other students in the school. Thus, the student's peers within his or her school provide the normative standard for identifying whether the student is disabled and so is eligible for special education (315).

For this approach, not only is disability an objective condition that is written on the body (Watermeyer 2013), but it is also the result of linear and unidirectional causal influences (even though the links between these factors are often correlational) that move from membership in a racial or ethnic group, to living in poverty, and end up in disability status. Donald MacMillan and Daniel Reschly, for instance, concluded that "social class, and not ethnicity, would explain more variance in the rates of detection for these high-incidence disabilities, particularly MMR" (1998: 20). Hibel and his colleagues offered a comparable theory by explaining that class and race effects for lower income African American and Hispanic children are compounded by greater exposure to factors "that themselves contribute to disability identification," including biological trauma (e.g., low birth weight, poor nutrition, and child health) and increased exposure to environmental toxins; "social trauma" such as being raised in poverty or by a single or teenage parent; and having parents who are high school dropouts or second-language learners, depressed, disorganized, unemployed, or incarcerated and who reside in high-risk neighborhoods. These factors may result in the lower cognitive and behavioral performance displayed by low-income minority students when they begin kindergarten (2010: 316). Other studies have applied similar intersectional reasoning (Hosp and Reschly 2003; Oswald et al. 1999; Skiba et al. 2005).

Four themes stand out in the unitary work: (a) essentializing sociocultural groups; (b) stripping historical and structural influences from the study of people's actions and decisions or framing them as static factors with linear relations; (c) neglecting the problematic historical intertwining of race and dis/ability; and (d) assuming that disabilities are objective features located in the individual. In this sense, the unitary approach naturalizes the racialization of disabilities, marshalling evidence that conceivably legitimizes racial disproportionality.

Hybrid Circular Narratives: Between Intra-Categorical and Unitary Intersectionalities

Let us now review what I call "hybrid circular narratives" of intersectionality. One form of intersectional analysis is concerned with examining intra-categorical complexity. This perspective "interrogates the boundary-making and boundary-defining process of categorization. . . . It acknowledges the stable and even durable relationships that social categories represent at any given point in time, though it also maintains a critical stance toward categories. . . . It also tends to focus on particular social groups at neglected points of intersection" (McCall 2005: 1773–1774).

Work by disability studies scholars that relies on premises from this perspective includes Erevelles and Minear (2010), who linked Critical Race Feminist Theory with Disability Studies Theory in their assessment of the historical nexus between race and disability (see also McCall and Skrtic 2010). They situated the connections between race and disability in historic and postcolonial contexts, arguing for an intersectional analysis that avoids limiting the scope of inquiry to a single marker of difference. Taking the history of the eugenics movement and its concomitant conflation of race with disability, they argued that "the continued association of race and disability in debilitating ways necessitates that we examine

188 *Alfredo J. Artiles*

how eugenic practices continue to reconstitute social hierarchies in contemporary contexts via the deployment of a hegemonic ideology of disability that have real material effects on people located at the intersections of difference" (133–134). Similarly, in a recent paper (Artiles 2011), I situated the racialization of disability in historical context by exploring conflation of the two in laws covering "ugly" and impaired bodies. I went on to stress the complicity of research communities in this conflation by revealing associations drawn between racial minority status and deviance, illness, and depressed abilities.

Bringing together frameworks deployed in both Cultural and Disability Studies affords a number of opportunities for nuanced analysis of intersectional identities because the theoretical apparatuses in these scholarly communities engage with complexity in contextualized and systematic ways. These frameworks afford powerful tools to examine disability as it is constituted discursively, culturally, and institutionally across multiple contexts, ultimately revealing that disability is a protean notion that requires situated scrutiny with sociocultural and historical imaginations.

Other intriguing patterns emerge in work based on the social and cultural models. Works grounded in a social model start with a compelling critique of disability as historically and bureaucratically situated, showing how definitions evolve over time, ultimately reminding us of the ways in which race, class, gender, and disability have had entangled histories. In this sense, these works are rooted in an intra-categorical intersectional frame, though the focus is on disability. That is, disability is at the center, with all of the other difference markers linked to it. This is apparent in the fact that these inquiries do not include comparable in-depth critiques of race, social class, and gender – in other words, critiques of other difference markers are proffered only to the extent they inform disability. These works provide a more balanced theorizing of other markers when they acknowledge, for instance, that special education placement was used to maintain the racial segregation of schools in the post-*Brown* era (Baker 2002; Connor and Ferri 2005). Thus, on the one hand, disability is socially constructed and is a tool of exclusion for racial minority students, but on the other hand, oppression is stressed only in discussions of race. While such analyses reveal how disability is constituted and used with specific purposes – i.e., through the concerted efforts of cultural, historical, and ideological processes – some scholarship on the racialization of disabilities grounded in social or cultural models only foregrounds oppression as it relates to race in its analysis. In other words, while these works pay attention to processes and instrumentality in the analysis of disability, they stress the end result when dealing with race.

When the tropes of disability and race converge and the analysis focuses on the racialization of disability, complications crystalize. One such example arises when researchers premise their work with the caveat that "*certain* disability categories may be considered more problematic than others" (Connor and Ferri 2005: 111; emphasis in original), an assumption which stands in tension with understandings of disability as social construction. A quasi-unitary framework emerges since the bulk of the analysis relies on studies framed from a unitary vantage point. For example, evidence on student placement by student race is discussed to support the argument about the racialization of disability, but certain structures and blind spots are left intact. Scholarship committed to a cultural model (Artiles et al. 2005), has made the same move in some studies, serving as reminder of the protean nature of disability as analyses morph from a critique of disability as a social construct to a medically based category (as embodied in the databases used in these studies) *within the same investigation*. Such studies may theorize disabilities as socially constructed, but call some categories "subjective" or "soft," with a structural argument leveled against special education, namely that the bureaucratic and middle-class nature of this system oppresses families of color (Blanchett 2006). Agency and within-group diversity in low-income racial minority communities tend to be invisible in this work, which may reflect an essentialized view of these groups.

In all fairness, scholars using social and cultural models are aware and do recognize more complex views of culture and give analytical space to agency when working with marginalized communities. My point is that a contrapuntal analytic stance shows that competing views of race, disability, and intersectionality coexist in this work, in part, because we use some of the analytical tools of the medical model (e.g., analysis of placement patterns by race and disability category) that we strive to contest.

A contrapuntal reading of the research literature makes visible the coexistence of tools and premises from opposing paradigms within and across work based on distinct disability models. Researchers using a medical perspective have occasionally drawn tools from social and cultural models. For instance, MacMillan and Reschly (1998) drew on arguments based in social construction to argue for strengthening measurement precision. They argued that race and ethnicity are ambiguous constructs measured in disparate ways and "should not be interpreted as scientific and anthropological in nature . . . yet, that is exactly how they are treated in the OCR overrepresentation dataset" (18–19). They highlighted the inaccuracies and inadequacies of racial categories for capturing information about within-group diversity and mixed race groups and noted that schools collect such data idiosyncratically. Their arguments are used to justify the need to control for ethnicity, particularly as it is often a proxy for social class, which seems to be their preferred explanation for the disproportionality problem.

These authors acknowledge the ambiguous and unstable nature of ethnicity for identity purposes while also arguing that it is necessary to take within-group diversity in racial and ethnic minority groups into consideration when analyzing the overrepresentation of students of color. *The implication is that we do not know who these learners really are.* Yet *within the same analysis*, these authors summoned an essentialist model of White students and a medical frame of disability to support a poverty hypothesis. They cite a study that found the prevalence of mild intellectual disabilities to vary as a function of social class: the lower the social class, the higher the prevalence of disability, with no occurrences in the highest status. The authors' reliance upon essentialist models and a medical frame are illuminated by

190 *Alfredo J. Artiles*

the following disclosure: the "study was conducted in Aberdeen, Scotland involving only White subjects, thereby avoiding the confound of ethnicity and social class" (MacMillan and Reschly 1998: 19). This comment then implies that, in some cases, the measurement of ethnicity and disability is no longer problematic. The authors assumed there is no within-group diversity in White communities, ignoring the cultural history of Europe, and the United Kingdom in particular. This is a longstanding trope in the "othering" of non-White communities that keeps White folks at the center of defining consequential categories like ability and dis/ability. Following a longstanding tradition in the history of the United States and the social sciences, these authors made two problematic conceptual moves within the same article. First, they equated race with ethnicity, which deflects discussion of race: "the origins of . . . ethnicity lie in an attempt to find another way of talking about race" (Harris 2001: 1773). Second, the authors relied on a recognition/de-recognition dynamic to "see race" (i.e., the racial identities of particular bodies) in order to de-recognize or not see race (i.e., a structural system of group-based privileges and disadvantages produced by sociohistorical forces) (1758).

To conclude, a contrapuntal reading of the disproportionality literature enables us to discern hybrid patterns in intersectional analysis and warns us about the need for strengthening theoretical clarity and its concomitant methodological implications. A contrapuntal perspective enables us to challenge our assumptions about coherence and purity within conceptual models. A "contrapuntal analysis should be modeled not . . . on a symphony but rather on an atonal ensemble; we must take into account all sorts of spatial or geographical and rhetorical practices . . . all of them tending to elucidate a complex and uneven topography" (Said 1993: 318). A contrapuntal analysis of the racialization of disability could stimulate conversation between seemingly opposite or contradictory disability models, and between their respective ontological assumptions about disability and race. A contrapuntal analysis asks: what can we learn about the nature of disability and race in bodies of academic work that are deemed to be distinct and even mutually exclusive?

This initial critique suggests the potential of an intersectional analysis grounded in a contrapuntal perspective for studying the racialization of disability. This analysis illustrated the ambivalent status of categories and illuminated the shifting topographies between the discursive and material dimensions of these categories (McCall 2005). Indeed, race and disability have mimetic properties across and within the various models of disability. While the study of race and disability intersections often relied on a unitary approach, a contrapuntal reading of the disproportionality literature based on alternative disability models also revealed complex hybrid patterns in intersectional analysis, and suggested the need to strengthen theoretical clarity and its concomitant methodological implications. Social and cultural approaches to disability used medically based tools and analytic strategies to address race-disability intersections. While we possess sophisticated toolkits to theorize and study race and ability discrimination, we routinely fail to deploy them when studying the racialization of disability. What cultural dynamics are at play to produce this state of affairs? To what extent does the history of the racialization

The Racialization of Disabilities   191

of disability – and the ways in which intersectionality has been addressed in the research across the medical, social, and cultural paradigms – constitute what Fischer called "involutionary change," where the construction, treatment, and consequences of race and disability intersections become "more elaborately the same"? (cited in Danforth et al. 2006: 19).

This preliminary analysis identified connections not readily perceived, connections between notions such as race and disability that are often dichotomized. To some extent, this emerging contrapuntal analysis suggested a blurring of boundaries between paradigms. An intersectional prism, in turn, revealed the protean nature of disability and race not perceptible through single-axis analysis. The potentially negative consequences of hybrid circular narratives require us to forge a new language about the complex intersections between race and disability. This contrapuntal analysis suggests that we undertake what Lennard Davis described as the Chris "'Bell imperative' to think more clearly, more politically, about disability" (Davis 2011: xi) and its entanglements with race.

In closing, I offer several reflections to consider for further developments in this line of work:

1   *Prepare the next generation of scholars with an intersectional imagination.* We need more scholars using intersectional analysis to study racial inequities in special education. In the United States, few doctoral programs in special education – and even in Disability Studies! – include training in intersectional analysis. Theoretical and methodological attention to intersectionality will stimulate the growth of communities of scholars that can benefit from each other's engagement with this perspective.

2   *Take advantage of the potential of intersectionality: Probe the depths within categories.* Intersectionality provides tools for complex "intergroup" analyses, going beyond examining a single dimension of a category (e.g., race, gender, and class), at the expense of dimensions *within* categories (McCall 2005). McCall, for example, has produced quantitative intersectional analyses in which "different contexts reveal different configurations of inequality in a particular social formation" (1791). This is the direction that Erevelles and Minear are taking, examining the lived experiences of individuals as located in "structural conditions within which . . . social categories are constructed by, and intermeshed with each other in specific historical contexts" (2010: 131). Studies could also address a variety of other intra-categorical issues, such as what Cathy Cohen (1999) described as the "politics of secondary marginalization" through which marginalized individuals with privilege – in our case male students of color – police those without privilege (i.e., disabled male students of color). To my knowledge, studies examining secondary marginalization processes in the racialization of disabilities have not been conducted.

3   *Add detail and texture to analysis of categories.* An implication of the previous point is the need to look at neglected categories or subdimensions of

192 *Alfredo J. Artiles*

categories. Although racial inequity in special education research has made visible the historical intersections of race and disability, "visibility in and of itself does not erase a history of silence, nor does it challenge the structure of power and domination, symbolic and material, that determines what can and cannot be seen" (Hammonds 1994: 141). For instance, certain racial groups (e.g., Latinos/as and American Indians), and language minorities have been largely invisible in special education research. Other dimensions such as gender require more complex analysis: a great deal of attention has been given to boys in special education, particularly from racial minority backgrounds (the majority in a number of disability categories), without drawing on important scholarship on gender and sexuality from other fields. Such scholarship can provide more insight about gender differences in school disengagement, violence, and crime. A nuanced analysis of categories and their intersections also requires attention to students' agency. The research to date has primarily used static demographic markers to identify students, overlooking their active, innovative, and improvisational lives.

4   *Build coalitions to advance equity agendas.* While there are always complications in building coalitions (see Engel and Munger 2003), this project can advance equity agendas in politically profound ways, creating possibilities for coalitions not previously considered (see Crenshaw 1991). Although coalitions between inclusion advocates and individuals addressing the racialization of disability, for instance, could have been formed in the early years of the inclusive education movement, such work could be pursued in the future.

5   *Nurture disciplinary reflexivity through contrapuntal critiques.* Using contrapuntal critiques in examining intersectionality offers opportunities for dialogue across communities of scholars within and between disciplines. They can explore the benefits and consequences of "strategic borrowing" of analytical tools across disability models. For instance, statistics about race and disability deployed in the medical model have already been used for research grounded in the social and cultural models. Previous uses of racial statistics in this literature compel analysts to fragment and purify identities by extracting the potential intersections with other markers of oppression. But, as Kenneth Prewitt (2012) challenged us, "can there be a policy that misuses race statistics" (1)? There is already evidence about gaming strategies being used in states and districts to avoid sanctions from federal policy requirements to monitor racial disproportionality. The point is not that racial statistics are useless; indeed, complex statistical analyses of intersectionality are possible due to methodological advances. Here, the contrapuntal reading of this research allowed us to unveil how analytical tools are used across disparate disability standpoints that do not necessarily subscribe to the tools' core assumptions. An unintended consequence is that the scholarship on racialization of disability (independent of its theoretical commitments) continues to use tools that maintain the focus on traits typically located in the individual. This prevents us from broadening the analytic spotlight to account for influences such as the nature of the categories involved, the role of ideological influences in the

design of curricula and assessment, and the mediating force of institutional racism in the racialization of disability. In turn, these contrapuntal readings of disparate research traditions can inform disciplinary reflexivity to raise questions about the postulates and toolkits deployed to understand the complex predicament described as the racialization of disability.

Ultimately, this line of analysis promises to answer Bell's "invitation to keep race and disability in conversation with one another. It is an invitation to rethink embodiment and representation" (2011: 4). A critique of the research on the racialization of disability affords us opportunities to examine "particular social groups at neglected points of intersection of multiple master categories" (McCall 2005: 1780). It enables us to prevent shifting views of *difference* from reifying enduring educational injustices in the contemporary policy, research, and practice landscapes of U.S. education.

Corresponding author: Professor Alfredo J. Artiles, Mary Lou Fulton Teachers College, Arizona State University, Interdisciplinary B, Room B353, 1120 S. Cady Mall, Tempe, AZ 85287–1811. Email: aartiles@asu.edu.

Notes

1 I acknowledge the support of the Equity Alliance and I am grateful to the Center for Advanced Study in the Behavioral Sciences at Stanford University for the residential fellowship that allowed me to research and articulate the theoretical foundations of this analysis. Endorsement by these organizations of the ideas expressed in this manuscript should not be inferred. Earlier versions of this article were presented as keynote lectures/plenary talks at the Emerging Scholars Conference, Chapman University (September 2011), the 2011 annual meeting of the National Association of Multicultural Education, and the Race and Disability Lecture Series at the University of Illinois-Chicago (February 2013). I am grateful to Phil Ferguson, Kris Gutierrez, Elizabeth Kozleski, Tom Skrtic, Stan Trent, and the Sociocultural Research Group for their encouragement and substantive feedback and suggestions. I also acknowledge the feedback of three anonymous reviewers; their critiques and suggestions improved the quality of this article. I remain responsible, however, for the shortcomings of this work.

2 I use the term "model" in the broadest sense to make visible the premises and constructs used by communities of individuals. This perspective is aligned with Goodwin's notion of "professional vision": the "socially organized ways of seeing and understanding events that are answerable to the distinctive interests of a particular social group" (1994: 606). Thus, I summarize three alternative professional visions or models of disability.

3 The term "medical model" is commonly used in disability theory. Oliver (1996) uses instead the term "individual model" to pinpoint the model's primary emphasis on an individual unit of analysis, with medicalization constituting but one key element. Watermeyer explained that the problem does not necessarily reside in the medical sciences field, but in a "mode of performing medicine" (2013: 30–31). Moreover, Shakespeare has questioned the presumed clear differences between the medical model and a "family" of social contextual approaches (one of which is the social model); in fact, he concluded that the term medical model "is not a coherent or useful concept" (2006: 18).

194 *Alfredo J. Artiles*

4 There are important distinctions in scholarship using the social model of disability according to geographical location. The United Kingdom and the United States differ in the origins and evolution of the model, the disciplines and actors participating in each community, and the versions of the model they deploy. The UK perspective has been largely informed by a Marxist critique in which the oppressive weight of disability is foregrounded; this way, "society itself is situated as the 'patient' to be investigated" (Watermeyer, 2013, p. 31). Disabled scholars and activists have played a central role in this movement, though nondisabled people have also participated. In the United States, work has also included disabled and nondisabled scholars and activists; however, cultural dimensions of disability are made prominent, particularly in relation to a minority group perspective applied to disabled people. Work produced in the humanities, liberal arts, and to a lesser extent the social sciences has increased substantially in the United States, and more recently, a Disability Studies in Education group has emerged to carry out this project as applied specifically to education matters.

5 See Schillmeier (2010), Shakespeare (2006), and Watermeyer (2013) for critiques of the social model of disability.

6 In some instances, these decisions are studied with an *additive* intersectionality perspective in which interactions among several factors are analyzed—e.g., teacher's race, social class, and gender. Unlike the unitary approach, these analyses examine the simultaneous influence of race, social class, and gender in disability identification. The end result, however, can be a ranking of these factors depending on the predictive value or the size of the statistical effect. Hancock (2007) reminds us this approach presumes static groups and predetermined generalizations about the influence of these factors. Equally important, this perspective assumes the various analytic categories—e.g., race, gender, class, and disability—had independent political developments from one another (Hancock 2007). The result is to analyze disability as completely separate from the history of racial groups, as if these histories have never intersected.

References

Albrecht, S. F., Skiba, R. J., Losen, D. J., Chung, C.-G., and Middelberg, L. (2012). Federal policy on disproportionality in special education: Is it moving us forward? *Journal of Disability Policy Studies*, 23(1), 14–25.

Anyon, J. (2005). *Radical possibilities: Public policy, urban education, and a new social movement.* New York: Routledge.

Artiles, A. J. (1998). The dilemma of difference: Enriching the disproportionality discourse with theory and context. *Journal of Special Education*, 32, 32–36.

Artiles, A. J. (2003). Special education's changing identity: Paradoxes and dilemmas in views of culture and space. *Harvard Educational Review*, 73, 164–202.

Artiles, A. J. (2011). Toward an interdisciplinary understanding of educational equity and difference: The case of the racialization of ability. *Educational Researcher*, 40, 431–445.

Artiles, A. J., Kozleski, E., Trent, S., Osher, D., and Ortiz, A. (2010). Justifying and explaining disproportionality, 1968–2008: A critique of underlying views of culture. *Exceptional Children*, 76, 279–299.

Artiles, A. J., Rueda, R., Salazar, J., and Higareda, I. (2005). Within-group diversity in minority disproportionate representation: English language learners in urban school districts. *Exceptional Children*, 71, 283–300.

The Racialization of Disabilities   195

Artiles, A. J., Trent, S. C., and Kuan, L.-A. (1997). Learning disabilities research on ethnic minority students: An analysis of 22 years of studies published in selected refereed journals. *Learning Disabilities Research & Practice*, 12, 82–91.

Artiles, A. J., Waitoller, F., and Neal, R. (2011). Grappling with the intersection of language and ability differences: Equity issues for chicano0latino students in special education. In Richard Valencia (ed.), *Chicano school failure and success: Past, present, and future*, 3rd edn (pp. 213–234). London: Routledge/Falmer.

Baker, B. (2002). The hunt for disability: The new eugenics and the normalization of school children. *Teachers College Record*, 104, 663–703.

Baynton, D. C. (2001). Disability and the justification of inequality in American history. In Paul K. Longmore and Lauri Umansky (eds.), *The new disability history: American perspectives* (pp. 33–57). New York: New York University Press.

Bell, C. (ed.). (2011). *Blackness and disability: Critical examinations and cultural interventions*. East Lansing, MI: Michigan State University Press.

Blanchett, W. (2006). Disproportionate representation of African American Students in special education: Acknowledging the role of white privilege and racism. *Educational Researcher*, 35(6), 24–28.

Bolaki, S. (2011). Challenging invisibility, making connections: Illness, survival, and black struggles in Audre Lorde's work. In Chris Bell (ed.), *Blackness and disability: Critical examinations and cultural interventions* (pp. 47–74). East Lansing, MI: Michigan State University Press.

Cohen, C. (1999). *The boundaries of blackness: AIDS and the breakdown of black politics*. Chicago, IL: University of Chicago Press.

Collins, P. H. (2000). *Black feminist thought: Knowledge, consciousness, and the politics of empowerment*, 2nd edn. New York: Routledge.

Collins, P. H. (2003). Some group matters: Intersectionality, situated standpoints, and black feminist thought. In T. L. Lott and J. P. Pittman (eds.), *A companion to African-American philosophy* (pp. 205–229). Oxford, UK: Blackwell.

Connor, D. and Ferri, B. (2005). Integration and inclusion – A troubling nexus: Race, disability, and special education. *The Journal of African American History*, 90(102), 107–127.

Crenshaw, K. (1989). Demarginalizing the intersection of race and sex: A black feminist critique of antidiscrimination doctrine, Feminist Theory, and Antiracist Politics. *University of Chicago Legal Forum*, 140, 139–167.

Crenshaw, K. (1991). Mapping the margins: Intersectionality, identity politics, & violence against women of color. *Stanford Law Review*, 43(6), 1241–1299.

Crossley, M. (1999). The disability kaleidoscope. *Notre Dame Law Review*, 74(3). 621–716.

Danforth, S., Taff, S., and Phil Ferguson, P. (2006). Place, profession, and program. In Ellen Brantlinger (ed.), *Who benefits from special education? Remediating (fixing) other people's children* (pp. 1–26). Mahweh, NJ: Erlbaum.

Davis, L. (2011). Foreword. In Chris Bell (ed.), *Blackness and disability: Critical examinations and cultural interventions* (pp. viii–xi). East Lansing, MI: Michigan State University Press.

Dolmage, J. (2011). Disabled upon arrival: The rhetorical construction of disability and race at Ellis island. *Cultural Critique*, 77, 24–69.

Engel, D. M., and Munger, F. W. (2003). *Rights of inclusion: Law and identity in the life stories of Americans with disabilities*. Chicago, IL: University of Chicago Press.

Erevelles, N., and Minear, A. (2010). Unspeakable offenses: Untangling race and disability in discourses of intersectionality. *Journal of Literary & Cultural Disability Studies*, 4, 127–146.

196 Alfredo J. Artiles

Garland-Thomson, R. (1997). Feminist theory, the body, and the disabled figure. In Lennard Davis (ed.), *The disability studies reader* (pp. 279–292). New York: Routledge.

Goodwin, C. (1994). Professional vision. *American Anthropologist*, 96(3), 606–633.

Hammonds, E. (1994). Black (W)holes and the geometry of black female sexuality. *differences*, 6(2–3), 126–145.

Hancock, A.-M. (2007). When multiplication doesn't equal quick addition: Examining intersectionality as a research paradigm. *Perspectives on Politics*, 5, 63–79.

Harris, C. (2001). Equal treatment and the reproduction of inequality. *Fordham Law Review*, 69, 1753–1783.

Harry, B., and Klingner, J. (2006). *Why are so many minority students in special education? Understanding race and disability in schools*. New York: Teachers College Press.

Hibel, J., Farkas, G., and Morgan, P. (2010). Who is placed into special education? *Sociology of Education*, 83, 312–332.

Hosp, J. L., and Reschly, D. J. (2003). Referral rates for intervention or assessment: A meta-analysis of racial differences. *Journal of Special Education*, 37, 67–80.

Linton, S. (1998), *Claiming disability*. New York: New York University Press.

Losen, D. J., and Orfield, G. (2002). *Racial inequities in special education*. Cambridge, MA: Harvard Education Press.

MacMillan, D. and Reschly, D. J. (1998). Overrepresentation of minority students: The case for greater specificity or reconsideration of the variables examined. *Journal of Special Education*, 32, 15–24.

McCall, L. (2005). The complexity of intersectionality. *Signs*, 30(3), 1771–1800.

McCall, Z., and Skrtic, T. M. (2010). Intersectional needs politics: A policy frame for the wicked problem of disproportionality. *Multiple Voices*, 11(2), 3–23.

Mitchell, N. (2011). Sexual, ethnic, disabled, and national identities in the "Borderlands" of lation0a America and African America. In Chris Bell (ed.), *Blackness and disability: Critical examinations and cultural interventions* (pp. 113–126). East Lansing, MI: Michigan State University Press.

Oliver, M. (1996). *Understanding disability: From theory to practice*. New York: St. Martin's Press.

Oswald, D. P., Coutinho, M. J., Best, A. M., and Singh, N. N. (1999). Ethnic representation in special education: The influence of school-related economic and demographic variables. *Journal of Special Education*, 32, 194–206.

Patton, J. M. (1998). The disproportionate representation of African Americans in special education: Looking behind the curtain for understanding and solutions. *Journal of Special Education*, 32(1), 25–31.

Prewitt, K. (2012). When you have a hammer . . . . The misuse of statistical races. *Du Bois Review*, 9, 281–301.

Ribet, B. (2010). Surfacing disability through a critical Race Theoretical Paradigm. *Georgetown Law*, 2(2), 209–252.

Rogoff, B. (2003). *The cultural nature of human development*. New York: Oxford University Press.

Said, E. (1993). *Culture and imperialism*. New York: Vintage Books.

Schillmeier, M. (2010). *Rethinking disability: Bodies, senses, and things*. New York: Routledge.

Scott, D. M. (2007). *Contempt & pity: Social policy and the image of the damaged black psyche, 1889–1996*. Chapel Hill, NC: University of North Carolina Press.

Shakespeare, T. (2006). *Disability rights and wrongs*. New York: Routledge.

Siebers, T. (2008). *Disability theory*. Ann Arbor, MI: The University of Michigan Press.

Skiba, R. J., Poloni-Staudinger, L., Simmons, A.B., Feggins, L.R., and Chung, C.G. (2005). Unproven links: Can poverty explain ethnic disproportionality in special education? *Journal of Special Education*, 39, 130–144.

Skiba, R. J., Simmons, A.B., Ritter, S., Gibb, A.C., Rausch, M.K., and Cuadrado, J. (2008). Achieving equity in special education: History, status, and current challenges. *Exceptional Children*, 74, 264–288.

U.S. Department of Education (2006). *26th annual report to congress on the Implementation of the individuals with disabilities education act, 2004.* Washington, DC: Westat.

U.S. Department of Education (2009). *Children with disabilities receiving special education under Part B of the individuals with disabilities education act* (Office of Special Education Programs, Data Analysis Systems, OMB No. 1820–0043). Washington, DC: Author.

Valencia, R. (2010). *Dismantling contemporary deficit thinking: Educational thought and practice.* New York: Routledge.

Waitoller, F., Artiles, A. J., and Cheney, D. (2010). The miner's canary: A review of overrepresentation research and explanations. *Journal of Special Education*, 44, 29–49.

Watermeyer, B. (2013). *Towards a contextual psychology of disablism.* New York: Routledge.

11 Examining Assessment for Students with Special Education Needs in Aotearoa New Zealand

Creating New Possibilities for Learning and Teaching for All

Missy Morton and Annie Guerin

In this chapter we explore how sociocultural approaches to curriculum, pedagogy and assessment can support educators to recognize all students as the learners they are and can be. We focus specifically on students often marginalized on the basis of labels like 'special educational needs.' A brief overview of Aotearoa[1] New Zealand's education policy context is presented. Traditional Western epistemologies and beliefs that underpin many assumptions and classroom practices for these students are examined. We then describe some of the implications and outcomes of these views for these learners, their families and their educators.

An alternative culturally responsive model for supporting the construction of all students as learners is introduced and discussed with a focus on students' access to both learning opportunities and learner roles within Aotearoa New Zealand school contexts. We understand assessment processes as being one of the key drivers for curriculum and pedagogy. We stress the importance of all teachers being able to make use of assessment for learning to support their decisions about pedagogy and curriculum for all students.

Our work has focused on developing inclusive pedagogies that identify and resist deficit discourses, recognize, celebrate and build on learner competence and value collaborative learning (Guerin 2015; Morton 2015). We understand inclusive education to mean that students are present, participating and belonging in their local schools. To support inclusive pedagogies, we have adopted an approach to assessment that stresses the importance of assessment for learning – even in a context that might put more emphasis on summative assessment, in particular for accountability purposes. We have used narrative assessment to notice, recognize, report and build on students' learning and to support their roles as assessment partners. We briefly describe the significant features of *narrative assessment*. Narrative assessment is an approach grounded in sociocultural understandings of learning: learning is always in interaction (with people, places and/or things). Given that most learning happens outside of the classroom, narrative assessment is an approach that supports gathering and interpreting information about learning that is noticed in a variety of contexts by a variety of people. Narrative assessment is ipsative comparing and contrasting a student's current learning with that same student's previous learning or learning in different contexts. This approach to assessment can be used for summative purposes to report on a student's learning over a particular period of time; we've usually called these collections of stories a 'string' to indicate that 'progress' is not necessarily linear. The collections of stories can be recorded and shared in multiple formats across multiple media. It's important that students are also able to access their own stories of learning. Narrative assessment is a very powerful formative assessment tool, supporting teachers' own learning about their teaching. Narrative assessment is also used to describe the learning of groups of students.

In this chapter, we focus on Tom's learning as documented through narrative assessment. Tom was a 12-year-old student in primary (elementary) school. We chose Tom's learning and assessment to illustrate the processes we describe here because these stories provide a particularly rich example of documenting and sharing learning across many contexts and across time. Students like Tom are often described as some of the most difficult to include in classrooms, to see as participating and achieving in a national curriculum. Finally, we draw on a culturally responsive model of pedagogy to conclude with a detailed description of what has changed for Tom, his family, his peers and his teachers and their colleagues. As we examine the consequences of these approaches for Tom, we revisit their alignment to key educational policy goals in an Aotearoa New Zealand context.

Aotearoa New Zealand's Education Policy Context

Since 1989, disabled students in Aotearoa New Zealand have been legally entitled to access the same quality of education as their peers. A number of policies, initiatives and resources have supported this right. Although many students do well within the education system significant rates of disparity are still observed between those students recognized as low and high achievers in New Zealand schools (OECD 2014).

Of concern are the experiences and access to learning opportunities for students who are recognized as having special education needs (Education Review Office 2014; Human Rights Commission 2014; Macfarlane 2012). Access to learning opportunities and achievement are recognized as having direct links to life opportunities such as employment and wellbeing (Ministry of Education 2014a). Access in this context is more than just physical presence. In describing what an inclusive school looks like, the Ministry of Education also emphasizes participation, belonging, learning and recognizing and celebrating achievement (Ministry of Education 2014b). Access to learning opportunities can be determined by assessment practices that inform teaching, yet Aotearoa New Zealand students with special needs are often excluded from assessment processes (ERO 2012a, 2012b, 2012c; Guerin 2015). Schools are challenged to address this inequity, with government agencies recognizing that improvements in educational outcomes for students with special education needs are unachievable if the students are not being assessed. Within this scenario opportunities to plan focused, personalized programs of learning from authentic assessment are lost (Guerin 2015).

In line with other western nations over the last 30 years, Aotearoa New Zealand's educational policies and practices have been influenced by neoliberal reforms. These reforms have signaled a change in focus from direct state administration and governance of schools to one of self-management by local school communities. The notion of choice has been promoted throughout educational decision making, e.g., schools choosing their own professional development arrangements and families choosing where to enroll their children. The reality of authentic choice making is questioned (Morton and Gordon 2006).

Student progress and achievement in Aotearoa New Zealand is now identified and recognized through standards-based measures for all students from Year 1 (5 years) to Year 8 (up to 14 years). This current focus on standardized assessment in the school system aligns with an approach to learning that assumes development is predictable, sequential and measurable. Unlike other countries no national exams are administered within standards-based assessments in primary (elementary) schools. Teachers are expected to make professional judgments about the achievements of all of their students based on their observations, notes and assessments. Teachers grade students as being above, at, below or well below the national standards of their peers.

The construction of students with special education needs as learners is challenged through their ongoing positioning of being well below peers in achievement over their schooling years (Guerin 2015; McIlroy and Guerin 2014). This positioning can reinforce the notion of curriculum as irrelevant and of teachers requiring specialist knowledge to be able to teach this group of students (Kearney 2011; Macartney and Morton 2013; Rutherford 2012). The importance and impact of community context, culture or relationships on learning can be ignored within the narrower constraints of these constructions of assessment (McIlroy and Guerin 2014).

The *New Zealand Curriculum* (NZC)

Education in New Zealand is supported by three mandated curricula – The *New Zealand Curriculum* (Ministry of Education 2007), The *Māori Curriculum Te Marautanga o Aotearoa* (Ministry of Education 2008) and the early childhood curriculum, *Te Whāriki* (Ministry of Education 1996). The work discussed in this chapter utilizes the *New Zealand Curriculum* as it is situated within English medium education.

Since 2007, Aotearoa New Zealand schools have worked within the *New Zealand Curriculum* (*NZC*). This is a framework curriculum that supports schools to investigate and develop responsive curriculums that meet their community's needs rather than simply prescribing step-by-step progressions (Hipkins, Bolstad, Boyd and McDowall 2014). The *New Zealand Curriculum* includes both traditional individualistic and sociocultural understandings of curriculum and pedagogy (Morton 2015). It is constructed as a document based on human rights and inclusive discourses. It values a sociocultural approach that recognizes learning in many contexts, emphasizing a transformational model of learning that values the

Assessment in Aotearoa New Zealand 201

co-construction of knowledge (McIlroy and Guerin 2014). Teachers and students are recognized as learning together and from each other.

Within the curriculum document all students are recognized as learners and educators are encouraged to recognize and value the many unique ways that students can demonstrate knowledge. Historically special education discourses have identified some students as 'not ready' for learning, reinforcing the need for specialist or alternative curriculum. The *New Zealand Curriculum* challenges this discourse. All students are capable of learning at level one, that is, all students are recognized as learners within the curriculum. Educators are also encouraged to value the knowledges of students and their whānau (family). Learning is recognized as occurring within a range of contexts, and is not limited to classrooms in schools.

The *NZC* also frames learning within subject or learning areas that are outlined in an assumed hierarchical matrix of levels. These levels can be interpreted as guides for individual achievement and progress. Each curriculum area is described as a separate subject. Although the learning areas have stated achievement objectives by level the curriculum document asserts that learning is not always linear, and that learning can be supported across the various areas, rather than confined by them (Ministry of Education 2007).

The *NZC* introduces the key competencies – 'capabilities for living and lifelong learning' (Ministry of Education 2007: 12). The five key competencies are thinking, managing self, using languages, symbols and text, participating and contributing and relating to others. The key competencies draw on knowledge, attitudes and values. Hipkins et al. (2014: 38) suggest that they can provide a space to help students to 'engage with diverse others and ideas by focusing on what goes on in the spaces between ideas and between people rather than on the ideas or on the people themselves.' These five key competencies need to be woven into every learning area of the curriculum, thus challenging educators to think about connections within learning and the wider purposes of learning. These considerations also force educators to rethink traditional constructions of assessment and to reconsider the purposes of assessments within their work (Hipkins et al. 2014).

Hipkins (2007: 5) noted that new dimensions of learning are highlighted by the inclusion of the key competencies at the heart of the curriculum. These dimensions challenge some assumptions that are deeply embedded in traditional assessment practices:

- The knowledge, skill, or attitude being assessed is in a fixed state, what the test shows now is true forever.
- If the learning sampled in this one assessment is valid then the result is indicative of overall learning and ability in this area.
- Competency resides in individuals separately from the contexts in which they demonstrate it.
- Variations in an individual's assessment results that occur on different but related occasions are caused by measurement errors or poorly designed tasks.

Traditional Views of Assessment, Learning and Learners Described as Having Special Education Needs

Practices in education in general, and special education in particular, have historically focused on the individual, and in particular on individual differences, deficits and remediations (Valle and Connor 2011). Smith and Barr (2008: 405, emphasis added) have described the '*ideology of the individual* [that] refers to the finding that educators . . . typically interpret the task of dealing with difference in terms of knowledge derived from *individual models* of human development.'

A number of researchers in assessment have critiqued the history of traditional approaches to assessment. Brantlinger (2000), Broadfoot (2007) and James (2006), for example, have described the ways these traditional approaches emphasize identifying (indeed proving the existence of) immutable characteristics – both abilities and disabilities. Once such an assessment has determined that a particular individual is ineducable, these individuals are then denied access to curriculum and to teaching, or at best are given access to a very narrow range of 'learning goals' taught in a very prescriptive manner. This has resulted in unequal access to curriculum and learning opportunities for some students (Macartney and Morton 2013; Macfarlane, Blampied and Macfarlane 2011).

Macartney and Morton (2013) further argue that focusing on an individual, and in particular their perceived deficits without consideration of context, raises a number of issues. When approaches to assessment focus on individual deficit, contexts are potentially ignored. In sociocultural perspectives on teaching and learning, contexts are understood as an integral part of children's learning. These contexts are multi-faceted and include teachers' expectations and frameworks for interpreting children's actions. Teachers' expectations and frameworks both shape, and are shaped by, the opportunities teachers provide for students to show their understanding and their competence.

James (2006) has also challenged the focus on the individual as learner. Writing about the close connections between assessment, theories of learning and teaching, James argued that learning is a social activity dependent on interactions between people and mediating tools such as language. Assessing learning outcomes needs to recognize the impact of social as well as individual processes through which learning takes place. James argues that 'this requires expansion of perspectives on learning and assessment that take more account of insights from the disciplines of social-psychology, sociology and anthropology' (48).

In summary, curriculum, pedagogy and assessment form an intricate and dense web of connections. Researchers in assessment understand the power of assessment to drive both curriculum and pedagogy (Broadfoot 2007; Hatherly and Richardson 2007). Smith and Barr (2008) have described how views of curriculum intersect with understandings of teaching and learning. Whereas teaching is concerned with imparting a prescribed syllabus, to ensure content is 'covered,' assessment is as much about surveillance of teacher performance than it is about student understanding. Teachers become pressured to 'explain away' student failure to learn as an inherent characteristic, a fixed (lack of) ability that in turn predicts future failures to learn. When teachers, and teacher educators, hold these more traditional understandings of curriculum, pedagogy and assessment, which result in a focus on student deficit, it is really not surprising that they doubt their own abilities to teach certain students. They wonder how the curriculum they are supposed to teach can be relevant to certain students. Danforth, Taff and Ferguson (2006: 1) summarize this as 'Curriculum comes into play only when teaching is attempted, and teaching is attempted only when learning is thought possible.'

Teachers may question how some children and young people can possibly participate in a curriculum that sets out a sequence of levels of learning objectives – a sequence that makes it look as if it is only possible to participate in the 'upper levels' having demonstrated competence in previous levels. Teachers may doubt their ability to be teachers in relation to children and young people who are not recognized as learners (Guerin 2015; Morton and McMenamin 2011). Families feel that their voices are not recognized, their perspectives not valued. Many families describe how they feel marginalized; when they describe how their children have done something that should be celebrated, their stories are dismissed as not really presenting evidence of learning or accomplishment, as this evidence was not gathered by a professional, or did not take place in a classroom (Macartney and Morton 2013; Morton, McMenamin, Moore and Molloy 2012). In these circumstances, children and their families, while present in a school setting, are less likely to feel a sense of belonging.

Work by Russell Bishop and colleagues has documented how Māori students and their whānau have been framed as deficient (see for example Berryman and Woller 2013; Bishop, Berryman, Tiakiwai and Richardson 2003) and blamed for their perceived failure within the education system. These authors argue for a reconnection of culture, identity, values and beliefs to our educational practices (Berryman and Woller 2013; Bishop, Berryman, Tiakiwai and Richardson 2003; Macfarlane, Macfarlane and Glynn 2012). They recognize relationships as central to all students being able to participate and flourish in classrooms and schools. Relationships between teachers, students and students' whānau and families are only possible when teachers work at knowing their students.

Sociocultural Views of Assessment, Learning and Learners

In New Zealand, sociocultural understandings of curriculum, pedagogy and assessment have been a feature of *Te Whāriki*, the early childhood education curriculum, since 1996 (Ministry of Education 1996). *Te Whāriki* states that 'Children learn through responsive and reciprocal relationships with people, places, and things' (14). Margaret Carr has led this work in New Zealand (see, for example, Carr 2001). The *New Zealand Curriculum* further promotes these ideas, as schools are required to think about assessment, teaching and learning that is responsive to the unique strengths and needs of their students.

In 2007, we began work on a project to develop the *New Zealand Curriculum Exemplars for Learners with Special Education Needs* (Ministry of Education 2009a, 2009b; Morton et al 2012). The work of Carr and colleagues supported our investigations into an approach to assessment that could focus on looking for and reporting on the learning that students were able to show when given sufficient opportunities to demonstrate their competence. We sought an alternative to traditional forms of assessment that privileged age and predetermined markers to construct 'children's learning and development as universal and children as passive recipients of knowledge' (Macartney and Morton 2013).

We decided to explore narrative assessment because it focuses on actions and relationships in learning. This approach enables the teacher to see the child and his or her learning in a wider context. Students are neither compared to others, nor to standards. In this way, narrative assessment values and fosters the students' progress and achievement, and at the same time recognizes that this progress is socially mediated and co-constructed. It links learning stories (or narratives) to the key competencies, learning areas and effective pedagogy of the *New Zealand Curriculum*. Unlike traditional school assessment, the narratives of the students themselves, family and others are valued as contributions within the assessment process. Learning is recognized across the many contexts within which the child lives and works. This includes recognizing the impact of family pedagogy on ways that children and adults interact and learn from and with each other across a number of contexts (Fleer 2003; Li and Fleer 2015). Working with families can support greater understandings of the ways children learn to engage with and make sense of learning.

Thinking about sociocultural theory and its impact across a range of education contexts, Macfarlane, Macfarlane and Webber (2015) identify three themes that are pivotal to realizing educational outcomes that are responsive to learner strengths and needs. They are 'the importance of *people working in partnership*, the worthiness of *protecting diversity and uniqueness*, and the significance of *participation as an enabler of success* in learning contexts' (16). Within the example discussed in this chapter, narrative assessment is recognized as an assessment approach that values these three themes, honoring them through collaboration and a recognition of all people as learners. Teacher understandings of curriculum and pedagogy are identified as pivotal to providing spaces for teaching and learning to be recognized in its many forms.

Culturally Responsive Ways of Working

Recent research focused on outcomes for Māori learners (Berryman and Woller 2013; Bevan-Brown 2006; Bishop & Berryman 2006; Bishop, O'Sullivan & Berryman 2010; Macfarlane 2000, 2007; Macfarlane 2012; Wearmouth, Berryman, & Glynn 2009) has identified approaches that support educators to make sense of culturally responsive ways of working. Bishop, O'Sullivan, & Berryman, (2010) suggest that programs that have focused on Māori students have also realized benefits for other minoritized and non-minority students. The research and literature on culturally responsive ways of working provides educators with opportunities to reflect and reimagine reciprocity and responsiveness in their practice (McIlroy and

Guerin 2014). The narrative described in this chapter utilizes one such approach, the Educultural Wheel (Macfarlane 2004).

The *Educultural Wheel*

Within our work the *Educultural Wheel* is recognized in Aotearoa New Zealand as a framework for inclusive practice. Five core values in terms of understanding a Māori worldview are identified. These values are expressed as key cultural concept bases for effective classroom strategies (Macfarlane et al. 2012). The first four core values develop and support the realization of the fifth core value, pumawanatanga. The concepts are relational and entwined. Although they are described individually here, none occur without the other, and they strengthen each other. They are

- whanaungatanga (building relationships)
- rangatiratanga (teacher effectiveness)
- manaakitanga (ethic of caring)
- kotahitanga (ethic of bonding)
- pumanawatanga (morale, tone, pulse – breathing life into the other four values).

(Macfarlane et al. 2012)

The *Educultural Wheel* (Macfarlane 2004) provides a useful lens for the critical examination of some ways we worked with Tom to participate in learning and assessment. The values draw on the principles of New Zealand's founding document – the Treaty of Waitangi. They support effective pedagogy and the principles of the *New Zealand Curriculum* (Ministry of Education 2007). In the rest of this chapter, the five values of the *Educultural Wheel* are described separately along with the successful strategies we developed and the positive outcomes that arose from working with and within these values.

Introducing Tom

Tom loves animals and being on his family's farm. He loves horse riding and swimming. From a very young age, Tom has loved reading books. He attends his local school in a rural community in Aotearoa New Zealand. Tom lives with his mum, dad and older sister. He is labeled as nonverbal, communicating through symbols, gesture and utterances. Tom has no specific diagnosis. In the education and health system, he is recognized as having very high needs. This means he is recognized as requiring the highest level of support to access learning opportunities.

The term 'we' in the following discussion refers to the team of key people who worked with Tom during his time at his local primary school. The term applies to Tom's mother and father, Annie working as a specialist teacher and a paraprofessional who worked within Tom's classrooms in every year of his primary schooling. As classroom teachers and some paraprofessionals changed most years, these

206   *Missy Morton and Annie Guerin*

people were part of the collective 'we' for periods ranging from one to two years. The school principal was not a direct member of the team, but oversaw the work done by this group of people.

Using Narrative Assessment to Support Tom's Participation in His Learning

Figure 11.1 uses the *Educultural Wheel* to summarize many of the ways that Tom's emerging role as a learner was supported and developed through his school and family's use of narrative assessment.

Whanaungatanga

Whanaungatanga is about building respectful working relationships (Ministry of Education 2011). For the team of people supporting Tom's learning, three key issues were identified in our work together. How best could we could create and develop learning communities for and with our students? How could we support family and student participation and engagement? How could we share information together, respecting and valuing each other's knowledge and practices?

Working relationships were recognized in many forms, with family being recognized as pivotal in all decision making. Building many positive relationships including those with the students and between the students was recognized as a professional responsibility. Part of this process was recognizing Tom and his peers as participants in many learning communities in a range of contexts within and outside of school. For example Tom was in a class with same age peers. He participated in horse riding lessons with children of various ages. He took part in swimming lessons at the local aquatic center. This reminded adults that Tom's learning was not confined to classroom – stories of his learning could be found across contexts and people.

The adults supporting Tom's learning through the Individual Education Plan (IEP) process formed a stable learning community throughout his time at primary school. This community focused on Tom's learning, but also on their learning goals as they worked together. Classroom teachers changed over time, but were able to transition to working within the group as information was shared and Tom made visits to future classrooms prior to entering them on a full time.

Supporting student and family participation took time. Time spent building Tom's trust and our trust of each other was highly valued. Tom hated change and our appreciation of the impact of change made us consider the consequences of any change on his ability to cope. At times, this meant recognizing when we had pushed things too far and he had a meltdown. As part of building trust with Tom's family and others supporting him, we often acknowledged our mistakes and planned differently for future events. Rather than being annoyed with us and our errors, Tom's family frequently commented that our experiences were reflective of their own and that what worked one day may not the next. This reciprocal trust was pivotal to developing respectful relationships where we shared the responsibilities

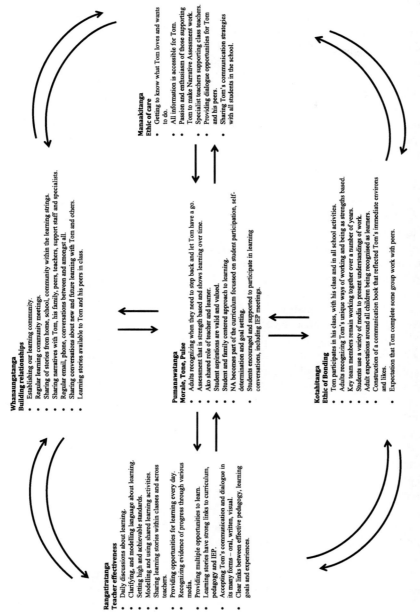

Figure 11.1 How we used narrative assessment to support Tom's participation in his learning

for supporting Tom to become the learner we saw he was and could be. This trust was developed in many small ways on a day-to-day basis. We shared Tom's learning stories (narratives about Tom's observed learning at school, home and in the community) with him, his family, specialists and others supporting him. Tom's grandparents (who lived outside of his town) commented on his progress and the stories they had read with pride. Students were critical participants in discussions about learning – their own and Tom's.

When other students passed comments about Tom's learning, we stopped and listened to them. We repeated those comments within classes so that the students would know we valued their input. Tom's work was on the wall with the work of his peers. It may have been in a different format to that of his peers, but it was visible with a clear message that Tom was a learner who had the same responsibility as his peers to complete tasks. The availability of his learning stories within the classroom offered opportunities for his peers to comment on learning, and their aspirations for their own learning. We recognized the impact of cooperative and shared learning activities for Tom to be recognized as someone who could contribute to a group or a class.

One of our key messages was that everyone has a voice; that all students belong. Learning stories also recognized this voice in contexts outside of the classroom. Family members, peers and educators contributed stories about Tom's skills. Fleer's (2010) and Li and Fleer's (2015) work on family pedagogy resonates with our experiences of family informing our understandings of Tom and the ways he chose to interact and make sense of his world. This was particularly important as Tom's learning stories began to demonstrate a gap of at least six months between his demonstration of communication skills at home and at school. We learned very quickly that if we wished to teach Tom a new skill, his sister was the person who had the biggest impact on his engagement with a task. We also began to teach skills in home that we wished him to learn at school, knowing that it may be six months before we observed this knowledge within the school. The impact of sharing ways of working was not limited to school and home. One of the specialists working with Tom changed her reporting from a traditional speech language diagnostic format to a narrative format. These narratives were included in the learning story strings developed each year.

Key adults working with a focus on Tom's learning met regularly. New ideas were shared at these meetings. We developed learning story frameworks that could work for us and for Tom. We made sense of the *New Zealand Curriculum* and how it could recognize Tom's and our learning efforts. We discussed problems in our work, and identified better ways of working. An example is our decision to introduce the use of visual symbols across all school environments and to teach them to all students so they could understand how to use them to communicate. In this way, not only did Tom have more opportunities to communicate with his peers and for them to understand him, but other students who may have struggled with communication or text were also able to access communication easily. We used email, phone and everyday conversations to stay in touch with a focus on making learning better for all of us.

Assessment in Aotearoa New Zealand 209

The team supporting Tom involved a large number of adults. It was important to share information with everybody. Prior to Tom's IEP meetings, participants received narrative assessment strings that detailed observations of learning from many people in home and school settings. The narratives gave us the chance to provide outside specialists with strengths-based information that revealed skills that may not have been visible to them during one-off visits to assess Tom. In this way, we hoped the information would also strengthen their assessment work. The narratives also gave us a strengths based platform to support our IEP meetings.

A significant consideration in our work was that Tom's narratives would be shared with wider family members, and that they would get the chance to participate in and read the many narratives about their treasured son, nephew and grandson. We also recognized this as supporting manaakitanga – the caring, nurturing relationships that families and communities develop as they watch their children grow and learn.

Manaakitanga

Manaakitanga is about an ethic of caring (Macfarlane 2004). It is about relationships of sincerity, integrity and respect (Ministry of Education 2011). The concept of manaakitanga challenged us to consider how we could develop shared understandings of assessment that could be valid and valued. We worked hard to make sense of how these shared understandings could shape the ways we carried out assessment and used the data from our assessments. An important focus for us was to know and understand Tom's skills and aspirations – a challenging task as we struggled at times to make sense of Tom's behaviors and communications. Central to the concept of care is taking the time to get to know the student and their whānau/family (Guerin 2015; Macfarlane 2012). We used everyday opportunities to watch, talk, sing, play and learn with Tom. We watched how Tom and his peers played and worked. We asked his family questions again and again. Over time, we developed our knowledge of the things Tom loved to do and we developed learning around his interests. We took the time to understand the ways he communicated. We recognized the need to personalize his learning, to use as many modes as possible to build on his interests and to support his curious mind. At times, the knowledge of specialists helped us to move forward. At other times, we developed creative solutions through shared brainstorming. For example, we noticed that Tom would often look towards certain students when they were talking. We had great difficulty getting Tom to return to class following lunch break. He refused to walk back with an adult, often dropping to the ground, screaming. When we asked one of the identified students to walk back to class with Tom, verbally reminding him 'Back to class,' we observed Tom returning to class within a couple of minutes.

Tom was labeled as nonverbal. For us, this meant he communicated in sounds, and at times gestures, but not in easily understandable (to us) words. A challenge for us was to think about how we could recognize dialogue within our relationships with him. We began to think about the many ways we could record observations with Tom. We used photos, video and PowerPoint that could be played

210   *Missy Morton and Annie Guerin*

back on his computer. We photographed his attempts at writing, drawing, playing, communicating and participating with this peers. We labeled what he was doing and the roles he was performing. For example, when Tom and his class went on a ski trip, we videoed him and provided a copy of the video on his laptop. When he watched the video, we told him we recognized him as a skier, a risk taker (flying down the learner slope) and, like his peers, a learner trying something new, scary and fun. We gave Tom many opportunities to return to view videos, photos and PowerPoints as he wished. We observed his choices as it helped us to understand what was engaging and interesting to him. This information helped us plan future teaching and learning opportunities.

The concept of manaakitanga was not restricted to thinking about Tom. Teacher confidence and capability had a huge impact on Tom's learning. Some teachers felt more confident and capable to teach all their students than others. We had to think about how to use the resources we had for the best outcomes. This included specialist teacher support for planning, co-teaching and assessment with classroom teachers. The specialist and classroom teachers may have worked on ways of recognizing new learning for Tom. This may have been as simple as understanding Tom copying the actions of a peer as new learning. When learning was reframed in this way, teachers began to make sense of how they could work with Tom rather than put themselves under pressure to try and make him 'fit' the predetermined cognitive domains of his peers. In this way, the ethic of caring extended beyond Tom to include educators and others that supported him.

Manaakitanga challenges us to think about the consequences of assessment, especially for the students being assessed. Narrative assessment recognized Tom's strengths. Historically, assessments placed him within a deficit position. His family stated that they were already well aware of his challenges, but that they wanted to know what he could do. They recognized him as learning, but education and health assessments had not valued or validated this view.

Narrative assessment provided opportunities to think about and observe learning that had purpose for Tom and his family. For example, the school had received guidance to suggest it undertook an adult-guided play program based on activities similar to those toddlers may engage in. Tom's family had photos of him playing soccer at home with his dad. At school, we had observed Tom moving around the playground and picking up some equipment, but then dropping it and moving on. He often stood near children playing, but did not appear to know what to do next. If he wanted something, he moved towards adults, not students. We thought about what Tom was already understanding in play and what could support him to make further choices in play. We agreed as a team to teach Tom how to communicate to his peers that he wanted to play. We also taught the students what Tom was communicating through gesture so they could make a decision about whether they wanted to play with him. We dedicated some time in his regular classroom to teach the whole class some rules of play. We played some games using the equipment Tom favored most (a rope and a ball). Every time Tom approached an adult, a student stepped in front of the adult and accepted the equipment Tom offered. Over the years, our narratives showed that Tom was able to play with his peers in a

Assessment in Aotearoa New Zealand 211

range of playground activities. At times he chose to be on his own. At other times he was capable of playing with others, using his unique communication strategies that the children understood. This learning and assessment had both validity and value. Stories recorded progress over time, informed new teaching and learning, and provided opportunities for adults to reflect on pedagogy. Tom learned skills that were relevant and useful in his interactions with his playmates. He could participate in games, as part of his life in and outside of schools.

We believed that Tom was a capable learner. We made sure we told him so. We would tell Tom on a daily basis what goal we were working on and what progress we had observed. His peers did the same. We worked in the belief that this could support Tom to trust us and to understand that we recognized him as capable. This developed trust between us and supported the reciprocity that manaakitanga demands.

Rangatiratanga

Ranagtiratanga is related to teacher effectiveness and commitment. As Tom entered a variety of classrooms over his time at primary school, support staff and specialist teachers worked to help classroom teachers get to know him and to make sense of his strengths and needs. Narrative assessment strings were shared with classroom teachers before and during his time in their classes so they would have some understanding of Tom's skills and challenges. We hoped this would strengthen teacher understandings of Tom's growing communication, play and literacy skills and provide a shared platform for our work together.

Many teachers had not taught a student who was working at level one of the curriculum (traditionally children aged five to six years) over a long period of time. Sometimes teachers felt unsure of what to do. Sometimes we all did. Some teachers were relaxed about teaching Tom. These teachers were observed to apply the same pedagogical approaches to all of their students, rather than focusing on what was different about Tom. This included setting high but achievable standards, providing many opportunities to learn, making connections between prior and new learning and encouraging reflective thought and action. What became clear in classroom observations was that the teacher's knowledge of pedagogy and effectiveness appeared to influence the learning opportunities for Tom far more than his impairments. For example, when planning a Science unit on sound, Tom's Year 7 teacher chose to identify the sounds he loved and hated as a source for making connections between the learning and his world. Students within the classroom completed research projects that were shared at the end of the unit. Tom's presentation included pictures of sounds that he enjoyed and despised. Tom was able to push the button on the computer so the narrated slideshow could play. The teacher modeled an expectation that Tom would be undertaking learning on sound, as were his peers. He was expected to make a presentation that would be shared with others and his peers had an opportunity to provide feedback. Tom was able to complete his Science work, with goals and assessment reflecting his current learning needs and strengths along with the other students.

An important consideration for classroom teachers and support staff (paraprofessionals) was the power of collaborative learning communities which offered the opportunity to develop shared understandings of professional responsibilities and setting expectations that were both high and achievable. We worked with best intentions for Tom, but each year we had to negotiate ways of working with a focus on his learning and developing our capabilities in response to what we observed. Part of this process was identifying learning goals for ourselves rather than solely for Tom. When we set goals for ourselves we were able to see that we also were learners and did not need to be the 'experts' educationalists are often perceived to be. This shared responsibility made it much easier to cope with the many challenges we faced as we made sense of pedagogy, curriculum and assessment that recognized all students as learners. Part of this responsibility was a school-wide understanding that we were all responsible for all the students in our care. This recognition led to a decision amongst the staff to have the visual symbols that supported Tom's communication put across all school environments. At one of the weekly assemblies the students were introduced to the symbols and copies of the charts that would be used throughout the school. This act validated symbols as an authentic means of communication for everyone in the school community.

Recognizing Tom as a learner meant recognizing and valuing his unique means of communication. He often used gesture, symbols, a small set of sounds and physical actions to express his joy, anger, frustration, humor and expectations. After a couple of years, his classmates were well aware of these strategies, but other children at school did not understand their purpose. As we focused on preparing all students as lifelong learners, we recognized an opportunity for all students to learn about the many ways we can communicate. Tom's family worked with school staff to design a gesture dictionary that had a photo showing an action and an explanation of what the action may be communicating, e.g., Tom touching a peer's arm. The photo was accompanied by text: 'When I touch your arm . . . I am asking you for something/I want to play.' The dictionaries were placed in every classroom and the specialist teacher introduced all students to the dictionaries, discussing them with the students prior to them being placed in the rooms. In this way, teachers became advocates for all students to be able to communicate their needs and wants. It also supported a school-wide valuing of the diverse strengths and needs we all bring to our communities.

The use of learning stories supported this validation and valuing of Tom's learning as we labeled many of the skills that Tom was demonstrating within these narratives. These books were shared across classes and teachers. They contained language we had discussed with Tom and his peers in their class – language that described them all as learners. Tom revisited these stories on his laptop and by walking around the classroom looking at work on the walls constantly. We were teaching Tom the labels of learning through the books and our everyday conversations about them. We were also demonstrating the high expectations we had for Tom to our peers, other teachers and support staff in the school. Over time, we began to observe Tom's peers using the same labels of learning with each other.

Narrative assessment made clear links between the curriculum's key competencies, learning areas and effective pedagogy and the day-to-day learning Tom was undertaking. Learning stories shared expectations of Tom as a learner, a participant in his own schooling and someone who could demonstrate skills and needs to help us plan future learning.

Central to teacher effectiveness was the ability to provide a responsive curriculum, with work that stimulated Tom and connected with his world. It was important to accept his attempts at writing, drawing, building, participating, dancing, playing and communicating as valued. The learning stories gave us a platform to showcase these unique ways of being for Tom. Traditional assessments did not recognize any of these skills or accept a 'non-literate' student as a learner. When teachers thought about multiple ways of knowing and being, Tom's skills became more evident. An example is when we provided Tom with models of his name, using playdough, sand, rice, glitter, raised text and bolded versions of his name. After five years, he seemingly did not recognize his name. One day, when working on a voice-assisted story for his Science work Tom independently typed his name on the computer. We were unsure how long he had possessed this knowledge, but we did learn that when he wished us to know, he would show us his skills.

Kotahitanga

Kotahitanga is related to the ethic of bonding. Being valued as a participant, as someone who belongs is central to inclusive communities (Macfarlane 2012). As a learning community, we believed it was our collaborative responsibility to enable Tom's sense of belonging. How would we recognize his unique potential and strengths? We had to work out the best ways we could work together for Tom's needs to be met. Narrative assessment forced us to pay attention to the language that was being used in assessments and its impact on Tom, his peers and wider family/whānau.

Each year Tom moved class with his peers, but a core group of adults remained focused on his learning throughout his time at primary school. The stability of this group proved to be invaluable as information was not constantly repeated and time wasted on constantly informing people unfamiliar with Tom about his learning.

The learning story strings that were shared and developed over time became tools to support investigations into our constructions of ourselves and Tom as learners and teachers. We used these opportunities to rethink how we wrote school reports, who was contributing to the comments on them and how they could identify progress within a *New Zealand Curriculum* framework. At the end of the year, Tom's family was also presented with a book of photographs and learning stories that reflected the many activities undertaken within the academic year. The book was strengths based, focusing on learned skills and future learning. It was ipsative, recognizing Tom's progress against previous achievements, rather than on comparing his work alongside age peers. The books also valued the key competencies and the many opportunities Tom had to participate and contribute

214 *Missy Morton and Annie Guerin*

with his peers, both disabled and non-disabled, his problem-solving abilities and self-management skills across a range of learning areas.

Tom's learning stories demonstrated that, across classes, there were opportunities for him to work alongside peers who were supportive and who also recognized him as a partner in their learning together. When teachers used shared learning approaches Tom was more likely to demonstrate competence. The team designed and developed a communication book for Tom. Through his use of this book, he demonstrated a clear preference for certain peers. On one occasion he was observed taking a peer's hand, walking her over to his desk, turning the pages, finding her photo and placing her hand on the photo. We interpreted this as Tom's way of communicating to this girl that she was his friend. One way that teachers supported Tom's sense of belonging was to accept the many ways work was presented as a valid contribution. When students had to complete a research project, Tom was supported to do this using photos, video and simple text in an electronic format. In this way, Tom could show his peers that he too was learning with them.

Every day in small ways, Tom's sense of belonging was supported through adults and peers who stopped and talked to him, used visual symbols and waited for him to initiate or respond to communicate with them. Tom's impairments could at time make it difficult for him to join in, but there was a school-wide expectation that he would participate in activities such as the end-of-year Christmas concert with his peers and school camps. The onus was on those adults supporting Tom to make sense of how learning and participation could look within these contexts.

Pumanawatanga

Pumanawatnga relates to the morale, the tone or the pulse of the school environments and relationships with its community (Macfarlane 2004). It is about a school being responsive to its community's unique needs and strengths. For students and teachers, this means teaching, learning and assessment can be seen as reciprocal processes that recognize each person as belonging, as having a say in their own learning (Ministry of Education 2011). Within this process, teachers and students share their roles together. Māori recognize this within the concept of ako.

As educators, it was our responsibility to provide Tom with multiple opportunities to show us what he knew and could do across contexts. Narrative assessment provided a platform for sharing this information from home, school, specialist and community contexts. When we shared information, we had the opportunity to think about how we could provide Tom with further opportunities for learning. This is not to say all teachers felt confident to plan for and teach Tom in these outside environments. Tom's access to and participation in learning opportunities was often determined by a teacher's belief in whether he could participate rather than by his impairments.

Clear links between the personal world of Tom and the curriculum were essential in honoring his uniqueness. Narrative assessment and our continuing use of a collaborative learning community supported all of us to make sense of his strengths and potential. It also provided us with opportunities to reflect on our

Assessment in Aotearoa New Zealand 215

pedagogical decision making. The actions described in the previous four themes supported the school in recognizing Tom as a valuable community member who could share learning and teaching responsibilities with other members.

Summary

In this chapter, we have sought to challenge historical approaches to assessment that have not recognized all students as the learners they are and can be. We have argued that sociocultural understandings of learning and teaching can inform assessment approaches that recognize capability in its many diverse forms. We argue that the use of narrative assessment can enhance access to learning opportunities for all students, but especially those students who are not recognized as participants in learning in traditional assessment landscapes. We have provided examples from our work with students, their families and educators to suggest culturally responsive ways of working as informing more democratic ways of working.

Note

1 Aotearoa is the name given to New Zealand by Māori, the indigenous people of Aotearoa New Zealand. Throughout this document we use the expression Aotearoa New Zealand.

References

Berryman, M., and Woller, P. (2013). Learning about inclusion by listening to Māori. *International Journal of Inclusive Education*, 17(7–8), 827–838.

Bevan-Brown, J. (2006). Teaching Maori students with special education needs: Getting rid of the too hard basket. *Kairaranga*, 7(Special edition), 14–23.

Bishop, R., and Berryman, M. (2006). *Culture speaks: Cultural relationships and classroom learning.* Wellington, NZ: Huia Press.

Bishop, R., Berryman, M., Tiakiwai, S., and Richardson, C. (2003). *Te Kotahitanga: Experiences of year 9 and 10 Māori students in mainstream classrooms, Final report to the Ministry of Education.* Wellington: Ministry of Education.

Bishop, R., O'Sullivan, D., and Berryman, M. (2010). *Scaling up education reform: Addressing the politics of disparity.* Wellington, NZ: NZCER Press.

Brantlinger, E. (2000). Using ideology: Cases of the nonrecognition of the politics of research and practice in special education. In S. J. Ball (ed.), *Sociology of education: Major themes* (pp. 1066–1106). London: RoutledgeFalmer.

Broadfoot, P. (2007). *An introduction to assessment.* New York: Continuum.

Carr, M. (2001). *Assessment in early childhood settings: Learning stories.* London, UK: Paul Chapman.

Danforth, S., Taff, S., and Ferguson, P.M. (2006). Place, profession and program in the history of special education. In E.A. Brantlinger (ed.), *Who benefits from special education? Remediating (fixing) other people's children* (pp. 1–25). Mahwah, NJ: Lawrence Erlbaum Associates.

Education Review Office. (2014). *Towards equitable outcomes in secondary schools: Good practice*. Wellington, NZ: Author.

Fleer, M. (2003). Early childhood education as an evolving 'community of practice' or as lived 'social reproduction': Researching the 'taken for granted'. *Contemporary Issues in Early Childhood*, 4(1), 64–79.

Guerin, A. (2015). *'The inside view' Investigating the use of narrative assessment to support student identity, wellbeing and participation in learning in a New Zealand secondary school*. Unpublished PhD thesis. University of Canterbury, Christchurch.

Hatherly, A., and Richardson, C. (eds.) (2007). *Building connections: Assessment and evaluation revisited*. Castle Hill, NSW, Australia: Pademelon Press.

Hipkins, R. (2007). *Assessing the key competencies: Why would we? How could we?* Wellington, NZ: Learning Media Ltd.

Hipkins, R., Bolstad, R., Boyd, S., and McDowall, S. (2014). *Key competencies for the future*. Wellington, NZ: NZCER Press.

Human Rights Commission. (2014). *Making disability rights real: Whakatūturu ngā Tika Hauātanga*. 2nd report of the independent monitoring mechanism of the convention on the rights of persons with disabilities. Auckland, NZ: Author.

James, M. (2006). Assessment, teaching and theories of learning. In J. Gardner (ed.), *Assessment and Learning* (pp. 47–60). London, UK: Sage.

Kearney, A. (2011). *Exclusion from and within school: Issues and solutions*. Rotterdam: Sense.

Li, L., and Fleer, M. (2015). Family pedagogy: Parent-child interaction in shared book reading. *Early Child Development and Care*, 185(11–12), 1944–1960.

Macartney, B., and Morton, M. (2013). Kinds of participation: Teacher and special education perceptions and practices of 'inclusion' in early childhood and primary school settings. *International Journal of Inclusive Education*, 17(8), 776–792.

Macfarlane, A. (2000). The value of Māori ecologies in special education. In D. Fraser, R. Moltzen, and K. Ryba (eds.), *Learners with special needs in Aotearoa New Zealand*, 2nd edn (pp. 77–98). Palmerston North, NZ: Dunmore Press.

Macfarlane, A. (2004). *Kia hiwa ra! Listen to culture: Maori students' plea to educators*. Wellington, NZ: NZCER.

Macfarlane, A. (2007). *Discipline, democracy, and diversity: Working with students with behavior difficulties*. Wellington, NZ: NZCER Press.

Macfarlane, A., Blampied, N., and Macfarlane, S. (2011). Blending the clinical and the cultural: A framework for conducting formal psychological assessment in bicultural settings. *New Zealand Journal of Psychology*, 40(2), 5–15.

Macfarlane, A., Macfarlane, S., and Glynn, T. (2012). In S. Carrington and J. MacArthur (ed s.), *Teaching in Inclusive School Communities* (pp. 163–188). Brisbane: John Wiley & Sons.

Macfarlane, A., Macfarlane, S., and Webber, M. (eds). (2015). *Sociocultural realities: Exploring new directions*. Christchurch: University of Canterbury Press.

Macfarlane, S. (2012). *In pursuit of culturally responsive evidence based special education pathways in Aoteraroa New Zealand: Whaia kit e ara tika* (Unpublished doctoral dissertation) University of Canterbury, Christchurch, NZ.

McIlroy, A.M., and Guerin, A. (2014). Flying under the radar: Democratic approaches to teaching in neo-liberal times. In R. Wills, M. Morton, M. McLean, M. Stephenson and R. Slee (eds.), *Tales from school: Learning disability and state education after administrative reform* (pp. 213–226). Rotterdam, The Netherlands: Sense.

Ministry of Education. (1996). *Te Whàriki. He Whàriki Màtauranga mò ngà Mokopuna o Aotearoa: Early childhood curriculum*. Wellington, NZ: Learning Media.

Ministry of Education. (2007). *The New Zealand curriculum*. Wellington, NZ: Learning Media.

Ministry of Education. (2008). *Te Marautanga o Aotearoa*. Wellington, NZ: Learning Media.

Ministry of Education. (2009a). *Narrative assessment: A guide for teachers*. Wellington, NZ: Learning Media.

Ministry of Education. (2009b). *Through different eyes*. http://www.throughdifferenteyes.org.nz/home2

Ministry of Education. (2011). *Tātaiako: Cultural competencies for teachers of Māori learners*. Wellington, NZ: Author.

Ministry of Education. (2014a). *Focus on priority learners*. http://www.minedu.govt.nz/theMinistry/EducationInitiatives/InvestingInEducationalSuccess/Report/Part2/FoundationElements/Focus.aspx

Ministry of Education (2014b). *What an inclusive school looks like*. http://inclusive.tki.org.nz/about-inclusive-education/

Morton, M. (2015). Using DSE to recognize, resist, and reshape policy and practices in Aotearoa New Zealand. In D. Connor, J. Valle and C. Hale (eds.), *Practicing Disability Studies in Education: Acting Toward Social Change* (pp. 197–216). New York: Peter Lang.

Morton, M., and Gordon, L. (2006). *In the public good? Preparing teachers to be inclusive educators. Report of a New Zealand research project*. Paper presented to the American Educational Research Association Conference, 7–11 April 2006, San Francisco.

Morton, M., and McMenamin, T. (2011). Learning together: Collaboration to develop curriculum assessment that promotes belonging. *Support for Learning*, 26(3), 109–114.

Morton, M., McMenamin, T., Moore, G., and Molloy, S. (2012). Assessment that matters: The transformative potential of narrative assessment for students with special education needs. *Assessment Matters*, 4, 110–128.

OECD (2014). *Education at a glance 2014: New Zealand*. http://www.oecd.org/edu/New%20Zealand-EAG2014-Country-Note.pdf

Rutherford, G. (2012). In, out, or somewhere in between? Disabled students' and teacher aides' experiences of school. *International Journal of Inclusive Education*, 16(8), 757–774.

Smith, R., and Barr, S. (2008). Towards educational inclusion in a contested society: From critical analysis to creative action. *International Journal of Inclusive Education*, 12(4), 401–422.

Valle, J., and Connor, D. (2011). *Rethinking disability; A disability studies approach to inclusive practices*. New York, NY: McGraw Hill.

Wearmouth, J., and Berryman, J., with Glynn, T. (2009). *Inclusion through participation in communities of practice in schools*. Wellington, NZ: Dunmore Press.

12 The Refinement of the Idea of Consequential Validity within an Alternative Framework for Responsible Test Design

Albert Weideman

Introduction

Where school exit examinations are arranged as public, government-initiated tests, they are almost inevitably high-stakes assessments. Their results are likely to be employed either as evidence of potential employability in the world of work, or for admission to further or higher education. The fact that they are usually organized on a national scale further significantly increases their impact. As a consequence, their quality should be beyond question, both in respect of public opinion and as regards expert judgment. In many national contexts, however, the actual assessment practices and outcomes of such high-stakes tests are below the desirable quality, and may fall short of even rudimentary criteria for fairness.

How do education authorities tasked by national governments to design and administer these tests go about ensuring a fair measurement of ability? How do they deal with contextual challenges that arise both from legal and constitutional requirements for the instruction and assessment that need to be provided in schools? What do, or can, they learn from current ideas about responsible test design, and specifically the notion of being sensitive to the impact of assessments (initially called consequential validity) on especially the social, economic and political dimensions of the lives of those who take high-stakes assessments? Are there ways of ensuring that the design of these assessments can be such that the interpretations of their results will enhance rather than constrain their appropriateness, and contribute to their fairness?

This contribution will deal with the challenges of one specific set of high-stakes tests in a national environment: the measurement of language ability in what are known in South Africa as "home languages" at the exit level (Grade 12) of secondary school. It will briefly describe, first, the constitutional, legal and administrative framework within which these assessments of language ability are to be conducted. Second, it will make a number of observations as regards the challenges of offering instruction in (and by implication assessment of) "home languages" in an urbanizing environment, problematizing the very notion of "home language". Third, it will identify the current variation in the high-stakes assessment of a diversity of languages, which is not only unacceptable but unfair, mainly because of the differential subsequent impact it has on different groups of learners. Having thus identified the problem, the argument will turn to how a possible solution may be informed by a refinement of the idea of consequential validity (Davies 2011; Davies and Elder 2005; McNamara and Roever 2006; Messick 1988, 1989; Weideman 2011, 2012), if placed within a larger framework of principles for responsibly designing language tests. It will conclude with a consideration of the appropriateness of the current public provision of language instruction at school, which refers to its contextual or ecological validity (Arzubiaga, Artiles, King and Harris-Murri 2008). That brief consideration of a broader view of the contextual nature of language interventions and assessments means that one should also be mindful of what the present discussion will not do: it is only obliquely related to current concerns with accountability and of how assessment contributes or fails to contribute to ensure that in public education (Sahlberg 2007, 2010). Accountability, as one of the principles within a framework for responsible assessment design, will nonetheless be considered, since assessment principles are interrelated: the adequacy or validity of a measure of ability is affected, for example, by its consistency, its theoretical defensibility, its appropriateness, its usefulness and its fairness, in fact by a whole range of considerations, including accountability.

A First Challenge: The Recognition of Diversity

In the South African constitution (Republic of South Africa 1996a), 11 languages are recognized as official languages, equal in legal and public status. In order to provide for instruction in all these languages at school (Department of Education 1997; Republic of South Africa 1996b), education authorities have identified these as "home languages", and the specific policy frame in which instruction (and assessment) in them has been planned to take place is known as the *Curriculum and Assessment Policy Statement* (*CAPS*) (Department of Basic Education 2011). *CAPS* is therefore a condition for both the goals and content of instruction (curriculum), and for the testing or assessment of whether its goals have been met. As regards law and policy, then, the languages are equal, and should be offered and provided for equally. The ability to use a "home language" competently is finally assessed in a high-stakes exit examination taken by secondary school learners at the end of Grade 12, together with a range of assessments in their other subjects (Department of Education, 2008a; 2008b; Department of Basic Education 2010, 2012a, 2012b). That examination is nationally coordinated, and the combination of marks for continuous assessment (awarded by teachers at the schools pupils have attended), and for those obtained in the final examination, is a huge administrative effort. The biggest component of that is the marking of examination scripts, usually by teachers specifically recruited for this additional task. The collated results then have to be certified as being fair by a semi-independent statutory body for quality assurance in school education, Umalusi (the Council for Quality Assurance in General and Further Education and Training) (cf. Umalusi 2012b, 2012c, 2012d). The main point is that, in the case of the examination of the 11 home languages, there is a legally binding condition that they be treated equally, as required by law and policy. What is more: language diversity is not only constitutionally

220 *Albert Weideman*

required at the outset, but also subsequently recognized and accepted as essential parts of public school provision (Du Plessis and Du Plessis 2015).

Such recognition of diversity is, however, understandably difficult to translate into fair and equal education provision, or into equitable assessment, a point to which I shall be returning later.

A Second Challenge: Identifying and Managing Variation

The combination of having a high-stakes examination and a requirement of equality among a diversity of assessments makes even slight variations in these assessments problematic. Just how high the stakes are in the case of the exit-level assessments for what are known as the National Senior Certificate (NSC) examinations is demonstrated by the fact that, in a modernizing and developing economy such as South Africa's, educational qualifications increasingly determine employability. This is fully recognized also in the home language examinations that are part of the exit-level assessments: according to *CAPS*, the overarching purpose of the instruction in a "home language", which by implication must also determine the character of the assessment, is that the ability to use such a language gives learners access to the world of work.

What is more, access to the world of higher education is largely determined by tertiary institutions' use of a weighted index of performance in the Grade 12 exit examinations, called the Admission Points Score or APS. It is well known that university education adds significantly to one's earning capacity, and that it therefore has an enduring effect that lasts for all of one's working life. In order to gain access to university or tertiary study, university administrators use the APS as the single most significant contributor to the access decisions that they make (Nel and Kistner 2009). In this index, home language accounts for a proportionately larger percentage of points (some 16%) than other subjects (Steyn 2014). That explains the concerns of Umalusi that the results for home language assessments should be equivalent (Kane 2010) across both the various languages and over the three sets of papers (and one continuous assessment mark) in each of them. If there is any variation among them, such lack of equivalence would indicate an unfair outcome (Kunnan 2000, 2004), since some groups of learners would have an unfair advantage over others in the same testing population (Kane 2010) merely because they wrote the examinations for a different home language.

Umalusi's fears are founded when one considers the variation evident, as Steyn (2014) observes, even at the most basic level when the average performances of groups of learners are compared across languages, both for "home language", and for "first additional language" (see Table 12.1, below).

The almost 12% variation in average marks for home language, not to speak of the unacceptably wide range of 28% in first additional language marks, already indicates that learners are being treated unequally. Press reports highlighting this (e.g., Rademeyer 2012) have a further social impact: that of undermining the credibility of the national examinations. When one adds to this patent shortcoming the

Responsible Test Design 221

Table 12.1 Results of the Grade 12 NSC examination of 2011 (Rademeyer 2012: 7)

Subject: Home language	Average mark	Subject: First additional language	Average mark
English	55.7%	English	47.2%
Afrikaans	59.3%	Afrikaans	52.6%
Pedi	59.8%	Xhosa	65.0%
Sotho	60.3%	Zulu	75.2%
Xhosa	63.7%		
Zulu	67.2%		

claims being made in academic analyses that exit-level school results for language are not good predictors of academic performance at university (Van Rooy and Coetzee-Van Rooy 2015; but cf. Myburgh 2015 for a potentially different view), the integrity of these examinations is clearly under threat. In a system where a weighted index such as the APS is employed to determine access to higher education, the most substantial proportion of the index cannot be allowed to be under suspicion. In the public mind, and in the view of many university administrators, additional access criteria therefore need to supplement or even supersede the information provided by the results of these examinations. Such additional criteria are to be found, in this case, in the results of privately administered so-called benchmark tests, including tests of academic literacy, that measure the ability of candidates to use language for academic purposes (for examples, see ICELDA 2015). While the authors of these tests would probably prefer them to be used solely as placement tests, i.e., for identifying those who, after gaining access to further study, need academic literacy support, the lack of integrity of their public counterparts makes it tempting for administrators to use the results also for eligibility screening, i.e., for access purposes. That elevates these tests to high-stakes assessments.

The credibility of language examinations at school is further undermined by comparisons of results across a longer time period, which have been compiled by the quality assurance body, Umalusi, itself. As Table 12.2 below indicates, the average marks for home languages for the period 2008–2011 again show variations of about 12% among lowest (just less than 53%) and highest (just over 64%).

There are actually two further issues associated with these comparisons. First, a Tshivenda candidate would have a one out of 500 chance to fail, while candidates in other languages would have to face an up to 60 times greater possibility. Second, when the home languages results are compared to those of other subjects, there is no doubt that their averages are exceptionally high (Department of Basic Education 2012c; Umalusi 2012d): for the years 2009 to 2012, mathematics, for example, had a 48.4% pass rate, with history (at 77.5%) and mathematical literacy the closest to the almost 100% pass rate of home and some additional languages, but still a good way off. Once again, the variation is an indication of a potentially unfair and untrustworthy set of results.

222   *Albert Weideman*

Table 12.2 Four-year average learner performance in the HL examinations across provinces, and their pass rates: 2008–2011 (Umalusi 2012a: 9; Du Plessis 2014a)

	Average 2008–2011	*Average pass rate*
Sesotho	52.9	98.8
English	53.0	94.0
Afrikaans	55.5	96.5
Setswana	55.7	99.2
Sepedi	57.4	99.0
IsiXhosa	59.5	99.6
IsiZulu	60.0	99.0
SiSwati	61.7	99.1
Xitsonga	62.7	99.0
Tshivenda	63.4	99.8
IsiNdebele	64.4	99.4

A Third Challenge: The Scale of the Impact

A further challenge has to do with the scale of the impact of the language examinations. While other subjects (such as mathematics, mathematical literacy or history) are chosen from amongst a wide range of alternatives, and therefore affect only a portion of the candidates, language examinations are taken by everyone sitting for the NSC examination. So the numbers of pupils in the latter case are large: close to half a million learners on average wrote the examinations in the different home languages (HLs) every year between 2008 and 2011, as the following table (see Table 12.3) from the Umalusi Certification Database (Umalusi 2012a) illustrates.

With the exception of Ndebele, all of these examinations are written by tens of thousands of learners. What is more, as Du Plessis (2014a) points out in her discussion of these figures, more than 80% of the pupils write an examination in a home language other than English. Yet the latest census figures show that less than 10% of the South African population are first language speakers of English (Figure 12.1).

Moreover, the scale of the impact of inequality and unfairness that is demonstrated in further observations and more detailed analyses, apart from those already mentioned, is beyond argument. Du Plessis and Du Plessis (2015) observe that their content analyses of the various papers across three of the languages (for Afrikaans, English and Sesotho) have revealed a lack of construct equivalence (i.e., differences in what is assessed), as well as a lack of scalar (measurement unit) equivalence. There are differences, within supposedly similar sections, both in the number of questions asked, in the marks being awarded per question, and in their level of cognitive demand (Du Plessis 2014b). The scoring is also problematic: in Afrikaans, for example, there are, in one 30-mark section in the first paper, only three questions that are subjectively scored, in comparison with more than five times as many (16) in the Sesotho paper and more than nine times as many (28) in the English one. The lack of item, task type, and marking specifications

Table 12.3 Average number of students writing each HL examination annually by province (2008–2011)

Home languages examined	Numbers of examinees
Afrikaans	49,432
English	87,785
Sepedi	55,151
Sesotho	25,205
Setswana	34,986
IsiNdebele	3,325
SiSwati	13,804
Tshivenda	14,341
IsiXhosa	57,479
Xitsonga	20,740
IsiZulu	110,100
TOTAL	**472,348**

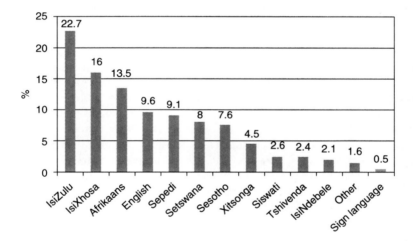

Figure 12.1 Distribution of the Population According to Percentage of First-Language Speakers (Statistics South Africa 2012: 24).

undermines the validity of the papers (Du Plessis 2014b). The conclusion reached by these researchers is that the "language papers analysed . . . provide (mostly subjective, but certainly unreliable) evidence of basic language ability" (Du Plessis and Du Plessis 2015).

A Possible Explanation for and Response to the Dilemma

How can the variation that is evident be understood, and, having been understood, how can it be managed and corrected? Were one to cast around for an explanation, one would have to start with the ambiguity of the notion of "home language" in

South Africa. As has been observed, official languages, of which there are 11, are treated as "home languages" in education. As is evident from the figures above, that does not mean that those who take "home languages" at school necessarily have these languages as their first or mother tongue. Home language is not equivalent to first language, and there are several reasons for that.

First, pressures of urbanization made it impossible, even during the time of apartheid, to provide education in schools for all prospective learners on the basis of a first language. In cities, people from many different language backgrounds gather to take up the opportunities offered by urbanization. So one might have a Sesotho language background, but the nearest school may be one that offers instruction in Xhosa. Second, such resource constraints are not the only complication. The language variety may be even more difficult to handle for other reasons, too. With ethnic intermarrying being normal in urban settings, one may in fact have two "home languages": the Zulu that your father speaks, or the Sepedi of your mother (or yet another language: that of your grandmother, or of another relative or main caregiver who looks after you before you reach school age, while your mother and father are at work). Third, after the demise of apartheid, the upward class mobility of your parents may even (as is indeed especially prevalent in lower middle and middle class urban households) cause a learner to end up in either an English medium of instruction school, or an Afrikaans language of learning environment quite early on in his or her school career, since these schools have a tradition of quality, not to speak of better qualified teachers. Such a choice may even be influenced by parents wishing to steer away from township schools, since their teachers are less qualified. Also, these schools are more likely to be affected by strikes and disruptions because their members belong to a union whose power supports the governing alliance, and are thus largely immune to official sanction. So language choice is therefore available, but constrained, and may not necessarily coincide with the most prominent language used at home.

This explanation for the variation in marks noted above may raise questions about the appropriateness of the constitutionally enshrined and the current institutionally sanctioned organizational arrangements that attempt to accommodate multilingualism at school (for a discussion, see Du Plessis and Du Plessis 2015). I shall return to this point later, but already note here that no immediate, legally possible solution presents itself to the dilemma of variation.

The response of the education department that is embodied in their official curriculum, *CAPS*, is to emphasize that *level* of command of a language, and not native speaker fluency, is the norm for home languages. It therefore stresses a principle of "*high* knowledge and *high* skills", and the criteria to be employed in assessing these as "*high* . . . standards" (Department of Basic Education 2011). It is clear that they have acknowledged the dilemma (that home language cannot be equated with first language), and have introduced a distinction between the high level of command of a language required for all home languages and that required for another level, that of "First Additional Language". Quite possibly this distinction is a carry-over from a previous curriculum dispensation, where languages were taught at Higher Grade and Standard Grade levels (Du Plessis and Du Plessis 2015), a distinction

Responsible Test Design   225

that was later abandoned, but the solution it provides still requires equal assessment across languages.

A Multiplicity of Responses to Unfair Assessment

Where there are officially recognized quality assurance bodies for high-stakes national examinations, such as Umalusi in the current case, it is understandable that there would be concern about patent unequal and unfair assessment. From the descriptions and analyses aforementioned, it is clear that their concern is justified. Hence Umalusi's commissioning of several reports to gain a better understanding of the problem. These are summarized in Du Plessis (2014a), and also referred to in a later report (Du Plessis, Steyn and Weideman 2015) compiled for Umalusi by experts from the Inter-Institutional Centre for Language Development and Assessment (ICELDA; see ICELDA 2015).

Briefly, what the aforementioned reports had identified was that the home language assessments in question lacked comparability, not only because examiners had not adhered to assessment guidelines, but also because the manner in which questions in some papers had been set made too low a cognitive demand on learners. The suspicions raised in earlier reports about lack of comparability within every one of the three papers, and across the various languages, have all been confirmed in the subsequent and fourth report (Du Plessis, Steyn and Weideman 2015), as well as in more detailed analyses of subsets of papers (Du Plessis 2014a, 2014b; Du Plessis and Du Plessis 2015; Du Plessis and Weideman 2014; Steyn 2014).

Most of the three early reports made to Umalusi propose partial solutions to the problem. Of all of the reports commissioned the solution proposed by the ICELDA team appears to be the most comprehensive, and will be referred to in more detail below. Despite the multiplicity of solutions suggested in all of the reports already commissioned, however, no action has yet been taken.

A Solution That Goes Back to the Origin of the Problem

In their initial briefing of the team of applied linguists commissioned by Umalusi to tackle the problem, it was mutually agreed that the most productive way of dealing with the unequal assessment outcome was to consider the alignment (or lack of it) of the various language papers with the curriculum. The same curriculum is in force for all home languages, and since *CAPS* provides the only policy formulation of the standard expected, it was not only the sensible starting point, but perhaps the most important one.

In examining the curriculum, the team concluded that its approach – communicative and "text-based" (Department of Basic Education 2011: section 2.5) – clearly has its roots in communicative language teaching, an approach to language instruction that is often theoretically justified with reference to the work of Hymes (1972), Habermas (1970) and Halliday (1978). The specific aims of the curriculum therefore predictably refer to the mastery of language for a variety of purposes,

226   Albert Weideman

and in a multiplicity of spheres of discourse (cf. Patterson and Weideman 2013): academic, aesthetic, ethical, political, economic and social. The aims also refer to general, functional uses of language that occur across these various discourse types, functions that for example include those of greeting, asking for information, gathering information in other ways, and analyzing it, arguing, expressing opinions, and so on (Department of Basic Education 2011). These distinctions without doubt go back the functional view of language encountered in the work of Searle (1969), Wilkins (1976) and others.

The identification of the essence of the goal of achieving communicative competence in *CAPS* allowed the investigators to articulate more clearly the construct that needed to be assessed, which they did as follows (Du Plessis, Steyn and Weideman 2015):

> The assessment of a differentiated language ability in a number of discourse types involving typically different texts, and a generic ability incorporating task-based functional and formal aspects of language.

The purpose of this formulation of what should be assessed was to provide a basis for equivalent and ultimately equal assessment. Not only was construct articulation in fact suggested as a starting point by Umalusi, but it was also identified as the potential source of a productive reconceptualization of the problem. A formulation of the construct of what should be measured provides a new yardstick for validating the interpretation of the curriculum. It applies both to the language instruction that precedes the assessment, and to the assessment itself. It thus has the potential of showing where both instruction and assessment fall short, or misinterpret the policy that is supposed to guide them. Simultaneously, the problem of washback is addressed: that of current and past examples of assessment, having over time drifted further and further away from the intentions of the curriculum, acquiring a life of their own, in influencing instruction through assessment practices, rather than both instruction and assessment remaining subject to policy. Furthermore, this formulation of the construct provides a conceptualization of what should be taught and assessed that could potentially be productively employed in designing a solution, a point to which we shall return in considering below what necessary and sufficient conditions apply to the design of language assessments.

Validity, Validation and the Responsible Design of Assessments

The consideration of the impact of assessment, in the current case in respect of the social and economic consequences of assessment, was given some prominence in Messick's notion of consequential validity (Messick 1988, 1989; Weideman 2012). As an idea that guides and conditions assessment design, it therefore constitutes a component of the currently orthodox view of validity (Davies and Elder 2005), an umbrella term for the process of validation that an assessment has to be subjected to in order to qualify as a responsibly designed measurement instrument. While

Responsible Test Design 227

there can be no denying that validity remains to some the most important and overriding design principle for language tests – in Messick's formulation (1980: 1019) it is the "complex and holistic concept [of] . . . test validity" – its employment as an umbrella concept has been challenged in recent times (Du Plessis 2016; Myburgh 2015; Rambiritch 2012; Van Dyk 2010; Weideman 2012).

The "unifying" concept of validity, and especially the currently orthodox view that validity cannot be a quality of a test, has been undermined by two eventualities. First, its conceptualization as not being a quality or characteristic of a test has been questioned (Borsboom, Mellenbergh and Van Heerden 2004; Popham 1997). Second, in order to promote it, several reinterpretations have been made. Kane, ostensibly following Messick's (1980; 1981) definition of validity as "an overall evaluative judgment of the adequacy and appropriateness of inferences drawn from test scores", has strongly associated validity with interpretations attached to test scores (Kane 1992), not with the test itself, proposing an interpretive, argument-based approach to validation (Kane 2001, 2010, 2011). Bachman and Palmer (1996: 17 *et passim*), on the other hand, have attempted to shift the emphasis by proposing usefulness as the "most important quality" of a test, while Kunnan (2000: 1) has asserted the "primacy of fairness". In Bachman and Palmer's view, usefulness encompasses the construct validity of a language test. Such reinterpretations of the "unitary" view of validity are conceptually useful in proposing further potentially important dimensions of assessments, but at the same time unintentionally serve to introduce a measure of disunity. Instead of clarifying validity, such reinterpretation potentially introduces a conceptual confusion. Xi (2010), for example, still frames fairness in terms of validity, calling for the "integration of fairness into validity", whereas Kane (2010) sees them as different, though related ('intertwined') emphases. Such modification of an original concept may explain why the operationalization of validity as formulated by Messick (1980, 1981, 1988, 1989) has been considered as being neither feasible (Davies and Elder 2005; Xi 2008) nor adequate to address social concerns in language test design and administration (McNamara and Roever 2006; Rambiritch 2012).

The main problem with the current orthodoxy is that it makes validity dependent on interpretation. No amount of interpretation of an assessment result (the score obtained) can, however, make the result produced by an inadequate test, such as the home language examinations under scrutiny here, a dependable, trustworthy or valid score. That is why those who hold to the orthodox view (that validity is not a quality of a test) employ all manner of circumlocutions and synonymous concepts to replace it: adequacy (Messick), effectiveness (Lee 2005: 2) or "measuring only the skill or the ability under investigation" (McNamara and Roever 2006: 81). In the emerging alternative view that will be attempted here, there is thus recognition that that the subjective process of the validation of a test is intertwined with or remains dependent, among other things, on the objective quality of the measurement, that includes its technical force (objective validity) or adequacy, as well as on the subjective process of theoretically defending the idea of the ability being measured (conventionally regarded as its construct validity), the appropriateness of the interpretations of its scores and so on. Making validity dependent on

228   *Albert Weideman*

interpretation is merely "confusing the meaningful, legitimate technical interpretation of the effects of measurement with those effects (the test scores) themselves" (Weideman 2012: 4). Instead, interpretation and scores (the technical effects of the test) are, respectively, subjective and objective components of the process of validation (Weideman 2009).

The component of validity that is most relevant for this contribution, however, is that of the consequential validity or impact of an assessment, a consideration that, as has already become evident in the previous discussion, has become strongly associated with notions of fairness. How all of the conventional concepts, such as test reliability, test validity and clarity of construct, cohere with disclosed ideas of interpretability, usefulness, fairness and the like now needs further exploration.

A Framework of Design Principles for Language Assessment

The idea of assessment principles being technically stamped conditions for the design of language assessments contributes to the articulation of a coherent set of requirements for responsible test design. I specifically employ the notion of responsible assessment design in order to indicate that it is an idea that can encompass all of the interrelated conditions, such as reliability, validity, fairness and beneficence, that are conventionally identified as contributing to the validation of a language test or other educational assessment. By "responsible design", I therefore mean that we respond to conditions for design in order to plan, shape, form and achieve the actual assessment instrument or (set of) language tests. Norms and factual assessments are therefore two sides of the same design coin: conditions are the norms for the design, and the factual assessment its norm-dependent, implementable form. If these conditions are, furthermore, design conditions, one may argue (Weideman 2012, 2014, 2017) that their characteristic of planning, giving shape to and forming designed solutions to large-scale language problems makes their technical design function the leading or characterizing dimension of such an undertaking. The technical aspect of experience coheres with other cultural dimensions, such as the analytical, the social, the economic, the aesthetic, the juridical and the ethical, as well as with natural dimensions of experience, like the physical, organic, emotional and so on. Consequentially, each analogically connects with the technical to yield, in such an analogical concept or idea, a condition or requirement for the design of an assessment. How these are further worked out and may be interpreted by the designers of language tests as either constitutive (necessary) or regulative (sufficient) conditions for test design (Weideman 2009) has been discussed extensively elsewhere (Weideman 2014, 2016). I shall, therefore, focus mainly on the connections of the technical design of language assessments with its juridical, ethical and related aspects.

In particular, in the case of the home language examinations under scrutiny here, the design condition that relates to the regulative conditions associated with the juridical and political dimensions of assessment should be considered: the examinations should be free from bias, both on an individual and group basis (Kane 2010), transparent in their purpose, defensible in public, legitimate in the

Responsible Test Design 229

employment of their results and fair to all in their assessment of ability. Since this is a design principle, how it is interpreted and employed will differ across different cases, but the home language examinations described in this study clearly fail on all these criteria. Because they are unreliable and unfair, they also do not have what Green (2014: 58) calls "beneficial consequences" for those whose language abilities they measure.

In the emerging framework of constitutive and regulative principles for test design that is being employed here, it is indeed clear that the design conditions are interrelated, a connection that shows also in their application: for a test to have positive impact or beneficial consequences, in other words to demonstrate care, consideration and compassion for those who take it, one needs fairness in the senses defined above. The juridical and political dimensions of the assessment, and its ability to treat test takers fairly, lay the foundation for the ethical considerations that will follow and its positive consequences.

The framework proposes a set of just more than a dozen conditions which responsibly designed assessments must satisfy (Weideman 2012: 8f.), though each, of course, needs further interpretation to make its realization contextually relevant:

- Systematically integrate multiple sets of evidence in arguing for the validity of a test.
- Specify clearly and to the public the appropriately limited scope of the test, and exercise humility in doing so.
- Ensure that the measurements obtained are adequately consistent, also across time.
- Ensure effective measurement by using a defensibly adequate instrument.
- Have an appropriately and adequately differentiated test.
- Make the test intuitively appealing and acceptable.
- Mount a theoretical defense of what is tested in the most current terms.
- Make sure that the test yields interpretable and meaningful results.
- Make not only the test, but information about it, accessible to everyone.
- Obtain the test results efficiently and ensure that they are useful.
- Align the test with the instruction that will either follow or precede it, and as closely as possible with the learning.
- Be prepared to give account to the public of how the test has been used.
- Value the integrity of the test; make no compromises of quality that will undermine its status as an instrument that is fair to everyone.
- Spare no effort to make the test appropriately trustworthy.

It should be noted that many of these conditions are traditional criteria for assessment design, the first relating to the validation argument for tests, and another (consistency) to their reliability, yet another (adequacy) to validity, to face validity (intuitive appeal), construct validity (or theoretical defensibility), usefulness and so on, and have been extensively discussed in the language testing literature. How these criteria can be employed in order to achieve a responsibly designed solution to the dilemma under discussion will be the focus of the next section.

230   Albert Weideman

Applying Requirements for Responsible Design to the Home Language Examinations

The analyses of the examinations under discussion that have been referred to in this contribution indicate that they have failed to satisfy the conditions of, respectively, being systematically validated, being consistent, adequate, theoretically defensible, meaningful, useful, aligned with the language instruction that precedes them, accountable, possessing integrity and trustworthy. All of these requirements, and more, need to be addressed in any proposed redesign.

The core report to Umalusi (Du Plessis, Steyn and Weideman 2015) on the home language examinations already indicates how the criterion of systematicity may be approached and applied in such a case: it provides a validation argument for the curriculum (*CAPS*) that may be the basis eventually for a validation procedure for the assessment as well. Moreover, the report locates the starting point for a redesign of the examinations in articulating the construct that should, according to the policy (curriculum), be assessed: a differentiated and general functional ability of high-level language ability. That formulation of the construct offers "a theoretical defence of what should be tested in the most current terms" (Weideman 2012: 9), satisfying yet another crucially important criterion relating to construct validity. At the same time, it also provides a delimitation of the scope and range – admittedly ambitious – of the assessment. It furthermore has the potential of making possible a closer alignment of the assessment and the language instruction that precedes it.

In order to make the home language examinations more reliable and consistent, the team's proposal is that 60 of the 300 marks allocated to the examinations should be in the form of a general Test of Advanced Language Ability (TALA) (Steyn 2014). The further proposal is that this test be piloted, in both construct equivalent and translated versions, in several other languages in order to achieve a comparable or equivalent set of assessments across languages. To this end, the base test, TALA, has been piloted and refined, Afrikaans versions (the Toets van Gevorderde Taalvaardigheid or TOGTAV) have already been piloted and a Sesotho version is in preparation. To these should obviously be added, as the research continues, tests for the other languages, but the initial indications are that a compromise between the best elements of the translated and construct equivalent versions yields promising results, especially in respect of reliability (see Table_12.4, below, from Weideman, Du Plessis and Steyn 2015).

Table 12.4   Reliability indices (Cronbach's alpha) of various TALA/TOGTAV pilots

Version of test	Reliability (alpha)
TALA first pilot (187 items; n = 1244)	0.958
TOGTAV 1 first pilot (196 items; n = 368)	0.955
TOGTAV 2 first pilot (187 items; n = 357)	0.944
TALA (reduced 60-item version; n = 1244)	0.900
TOGTAV 2 (reduced 60-item version; n = 357)	0.831

How the conditions cohere is evident when we consider, furthermore, that an introduction of a multiple choice component into an otherwise subjectively scored set of assessments not only potentially increases test consistency, but also contributes to the tests measuring more adequately or effectively, and to their being more differentiated, and in an appropriate manner. The newly designed tasks are, in terms of the construct, highly relevant and appropriate as well. What is more, such effectiveness or validity is achieved at the same time that another requirement is more fully satisfied – efficiency and utility – and this is in an examination that is currently a huge logistical challenge. The multiple choice format is simply much easier to have efficiently machine-scored than employing markers.

As has been noted, the proposal for the redesign also entails a more specific formulation of the construct that satisfies yet another condition: that of the theoretical defensibility of what is assessed. Consequently, the theoretical rationale for the test can be found in socially disclosed perspectives on language that are still widely used, and therefore current. By distinguishing between a differentiated and general functional ability in high-level language use, the proposed construct further allows a more differentiated specification of papers and subtests. If the three-paper arrangement stands, one could therefore think of designing them in such a way that the first two cover, in two sets, the differentiated abilities mentioned in the curriculum (*CAPS*): for example, academic, political and economic discourse ability in the one, and aesthetic, ethical and social in the other. If such a division is acceptable, it would also be possible to specify the kind, type and format of question much more precisely across papers in the different languages. The Test of Advanced Language

Table 12.5 Subtests, components and allocation of marks

Subtest and task type	Construct component(s) measured	Marks
Scrambled text	Cohesion and grammar; understanding relations between different parts of a text; sequence and order	5
Vocabulary knowledge	Vocabulary comprehension	10
Interpreting graphs and visual information	Understanding text type (genre); interpreting graphic and visual information; making distinctions; basic numerical computation	8
Text comprehension	Understanding metaphor and idiom; distinguishing between essential and non-essential information; classifying, categorizing and handling data that make comparisons; extrapolating; synthesizing	25
Grammar and text relations	Vocabulary comprehension; textuality (cohesion and grammar); understanding text type (genre); communicative function	12

232   *Albert Weideman*

Ability (TALA) and its equivalents in other languages, which can then be administered as a third paper, would have an even more tightly prescribed set of specifications, perhaps as in the current design, as set out in Table_12.5, above.

Moreover, the 60-mark allocation to TALA and its equivalents would in this plan constitute 20% of the total of 300 marks, creating a degree of overlap and equivalence of a reliable component of the assessment, which makes it possible to make statistical adjustments across the totals that would further aid comparability and possible mark adjustment, in order to ensure fairness.

Three other criteria will potentially be easier to satisfy, should these proposals be acceptable. The first is that the results would become more interpretable and therefore meaningful; the second is that information about the assessment would potentially become more accessible to those concerned (educators, pupils, administrators, employers); and the third is that giving a public account of what the purpose, goals, and outcomes of the assessments are, will become so much easier.

The likelihood of the proposed changes enhancing the quality of the assessment in several ways simultaneously makes it a feasible proposal for the equal treatment of test takers, and for achieving fairness in assessment. That in turn would make the impact, the social and economic consequences of the examination a great deal more beneficial to those who have to submit to this assessment.

One should note that this proposal for a refinement of assessment practices to achieve fairness is neither exclusively quantitative in nature nor solely based on argument. In the literature on achieving fairness in testing, it is often left unsaid that the desire to have a solely empirical approach harks back to a previous, modernist style of assessment; often the implied impossibility of achieving fairness relates to a lack of a quantitative or empirical basis. The contextually appropriate design proposed for assessing ability in home languages made in this chapter thus strives to achieve fairness through a mix of techniques and plans.

The solution proposed is a provisional one and comprises a plan and assessment design that is given in and for a highly specific case. It should therefore also be evaluated in that context before any judgment can be made of its wider applicability. In the next section, a brief discussion of that context is given in order to determine the feasibility of the design.

Context, Feasibility and Political Will

How likely is it that the designs to achieve the greater fairness discussed earlier will be acceptable and accepted in the national political context in which they have been made? It is known that education policy and practice, especially as regards language instruction (Weideman, Tesfamariam and Shaalukeni 2003), are highly resistant to change. What is more, in the South African context, a number of developments have undermined the credibility of its nominally independent or semi-independent statutory bodies. That might make a body such as Umalusi hesitant to adopt and promote changes that might run into political headwinds. Though it still too early to say, it is therefore more than likely that the best outcome to be hoped for currently is that the proposals may stimulate debate, and may eventually

Responsible Test Design 233

indirectly influence assessment practices, by having raised public awareness of how national high-stakes assessments can be refined and modified for the better.

The debate that has already arisen, and that is likely to intensify, is one that may also yield further and other solutions that are contextually appropriate. They may not, however, all be legally possible. As the constitutional and bureaucratic arrangements for languages now stand, there is not much leeway. Promoting English as additional language examinations to the most important component of the NSC, instead of home languages, has been informally suggested (by native users of English, predictably), but that would undermine the constitution and the equal treatment of languages. So, although there are other possibilities, the best alternatives would have to seek and achieve fairness while recognizing diversity and equality among a range of languages. The requirements that the solution be implementable and practical (Green 2014) and have ecological validity (Arzubiaga et al. 2008) may require a highly imaginative redesign of these assessments. In exploring that, one may encounter trade-offs and accommodations in designs that are conceptually encapsulated in the analogical link between the leading technical function of assessment designs and the economic dimension of experience. The format and shape of such design accommodations would, however, still need to fulfill the other conditions for the responsible test design outlined earlier.

The argument of this contribution has been that any alternative design could be responsibly achieved with reference to a set of coherent conditions for language assessment. Any alternative requires, finally, that its designs to ensure greater fairness be led by a technical ethics, an intention to design an assessment that is deliberately undertaken and characterized by care, considerateness and compassion for those affected.

References

Arzubiaga, A. E, Artiles, A. J., King, K.A., and Harris-Murri, N. (2008). Beyond research on cultural minorities: Challenges and implications of research as situated cultural practice. *Exceptional Children*, 74(3), 309–332.

Bachman L.F. & Palmer, A.S. 1996. *Language testing in practice: Designing and developing useful language tests.* Oxford: Oxford University Press.

Borsboom, D., Mellenbergh, G. J., and Van Heerden J. (2004). The concept of validity. *Psychological Review*, 111(4), 1061–1071.

Davies, A. (2011). Kane, validity and soundness. *Language Testing*, 29(1), 37–42.

Davies, A., and Elder, C. (2005). Validity and validation in language testing. In Hinkel, E. (ed.), *Handbook of research in second language teaching and learning* (pp. 795–813). Mahwah, NJ: Lawrence Erlbaum Associates.

Department of Basic Education (2011). *Curriculum and assessment policy statement: Grades 10–12 English Home Language.* Pretoria: Department of Basic Education.

Department of Basic Education (2012a). *Report on the national senior certificate examination results.* Pretoria: Department of Basic Education.

Department of Basic Education. (2012b). *National senior certificate examination schools subject report 2012.* Pretoria: Department of Basic Education. Pretoria.

234   Albert Weideman

Department of Education (1997). *Language-in-education policy 14 July 1997*. Published in terms of section 3(4) (m) of the National Education Policy Act, 1996 (Act 27 of 1996). *Government Gazette*, 18546: 19 December 1997.

Department of Education (2008a). *National curriculum statement grades 10–12 (General). Subject assessment guidelines. Languages: Home language, first additional language, second additional language.* Pretoria: Department of Basic Education.

Department of Education (2008b). *National senior certificate report.* Pretoria: Department of Education.

Du Plessis, C. (2014a). *A historical and contextual discussion of Umalusi's involvement in improving the standards and quality of the examination of Home Languages in Grade 12. Interim report to Umalusi.* Bloemfontein: Inter-Institutional Centre for Language Development and Assessment (ICELDA).

Du Plessis, C. (2014b). Issues of validity and generalisibility in the Grade 12 English Home Language examination. *Per linguam*, 30(2), 1–19. Retrieved on 23 October 2015 from: http://dx.doi.org/10.5785/30-2-602

Du Plessis, C. (2016). *Developing a theoretical rationale for the attainment of greater equivalence of standard in the Grade 12 Home Language exit-level examinations.* PhD thesis, University of the Free State, Bloemfontein.

Du Plessis, C., and Du Plessis, T. (2015). Dealing with disparities: the teaching and assessment of official languages at first language level in the grade 12 school-leaving phase in South Africa. *Language, culture and curriculum.* Retrieved on 23 October 2015 from: DOI: 10.1080/07908318.2015.1083999

Du Plessis, C., Steyn, S., and Weideman, A. (2015). Towards a construct for assessing high level language ability in Grade 12. Report to Umalusi. Retrieved on 26 October 2015 from: http://www.umalusi.org.za/docs/research/2013/psw.pdf

Du Plessis, C., and Weideman, A. (2014). Writing as construct in the Grade 12 Home Language curriculum and examination. *Journal for Language Teaching*, 48(2), 121–141. http://dx.doi.org/10.4314/jlt.v48i42.6

Green, A. (2014). *Exploring language assessment and testing.* New York: Routledge.

Habermas, J. (1970). Toward a theory of communicative competence. In H. P. Dreitzel (ed.), *Recent sociology 2* (pp. 115–148). London: Collier-Macmillan.

Halliday, M.A.K. (1978). *Language as social semiotic: The social interpretation of language and meaning.* London: Edward Arnold.

Hymes, D. (1972). On communicative competence. In J.B. Pride and J. Holmes (eds.), *Sociolinguistics: Selected readings* (pp. 269–293). Harmondsworth: Penguin.

ICELDA (2015). Inter-institutional centre for language development and assessment. Retrieved on 12 November 2015 from: http://icelda.sun.ac.za

Kane, M. T. (1992). An argument-based approach to validity. *Psychological Bulletin*, 112(3), 527–535.

Kane, M. T. (2001). Current concerns in validity theory. *Journal of Educational Measurement*, 38(4), 319–342.

Kane, M. T. (2010). Validity and fairness. *Language Testing*, 27(2), 177–182. DOI: 10.1177/0265532209349467

Kane, M.T. (2011). Validity score interpretations and uses: Messick lecture, language testing research colloquium, Cambridge, April 2010. *Language Testing*, 29(1), 3–17.

Kunnan, A.J. (2000). Fairness and justice for all. In A.J. Kunnan (ed.), *Fairness and validation in language assessment: Selected papers from the 19th Language Testing Research Colloquium, Orlando, Florida* (pp. 1–14). Cambridge: University of Cambridge Local Examinations Syndicate.

Kunnan, A J. (2004). Test fairness. In M. Milanovic and C. Weir (eds.), *Studies in Language Testing*, 18, 27–45. Cambridge: Cambridge University Press.

Lee, Y-J. (2005). Demystifying validity issues in language assessment. Applied Linguistics Association of Korea Newsletter. October. http://www.alak.or.kr/2_public/2005-oct/article3.asp

McNamara, T., and Roever, C. (2006). *Language testing: The social dimension*. Oxford: Blackwell.

Messick, S. (1980). Test validity and the ethics of assessment. *American Psychologist*, 35(11), 1012–1027.

Messick, S. (1981). Evidence and ethics in the evaluation of tests. *Educational Researcher*, 10(9), 9–20.

Messick, S. (1988). The once and future issues of validity: Assessing the meaning and consequences of measurement. In H. Wainer and I. H. Braun (eds.), *Test validity* (pp. 33–45). Hillsdale, New Jersey: Lawrence Erlbaum Associates.

Messick, S. (1989). Validity. In R. L. Linn (ed.), *Educational measurement*. 3rd edn (pp. 13–103). New York: American Council on Education/Collier Macmillan.

Myburgh, J. (2015). *The assessment of academic literacy at pre-university level: A comparison of the utility of academic literacy tests and Grade 10 Home Language results*. Unpublished MA dissertation. Bloemfontein: University of the Free State.

Nel, C., and Kistner, L. (2009). The national senior certificate: Implications for access to higher education. *South African Journal for Higher Education*, 23(5), 953–973.

Patterson, R., and Weideman, A. (2013). The typicality of academic discourse and its relevance for constructs of academic literacy. *Journal for Language Teaching*, 47(1), 107–123. DOI: http://dx.doi.org/10.4314/jlt.v47i1.5

Popham, W. J. (1997). Consequential validity: Right concern – wrong concept. *Educational measurement: Issues and practice* (Summer), 16(2), 9–13.

Rademeyer, A. (2012). Gr. 12's + syfers = uiters swak. *Volksblad*, 16 February, p. 7.

Rambiritch, A. (2012). *Accessibility, transparency and accountability as regulative conditions for a post-graduate test of academic literacy*. Unpublished doctoral thesis. Bloemfontein: University of the Free State.

Republic of South Africa. (1996a). *Constitution of the Republic of South Africa*. Act No. 108 of 1996. Pretoria: Government Printers.

Republic of South Africa. (1996b). *South African Schools Act No. 84 of 1996, as amended*. Government Gazette: Pretoria.

Sahlberg, P. (2007). Education policies for raising student learning: The Finnish approach, *Journal of education policy*, 22(2), 147–171.

Sahlberg, P. (2010). Rethinking accountability in a knowledge society. *Journal of educational change*, 11, 45–61.

Searle, J.R. (1969). *Speech acts: An essay in the philosophy of language*. London: Cambridge University Press.

Statistics South Africa. (2012). *Census 2011 Census in brief*. Pretoria: Statistics South Africa.

Steyn, S. (2014). Towards the development of equal and fair Home Language assessments: Outline of a pilot study. MS. Interim report to Umalusi.

Umalusi (Council for Quality Assurance in General and Further Education and Training). (2012a). *The standards of the National Senior Certificate Home Language examinations: A comparison of South African official languages*. Pretoria: Umalusi.

236 Albert Weideman

Umalusi (Council for Quality Assurance in General and Further Education and Training). (2012b). *Developing a Framework for assessing and comparing the cognitive challenge of Home Language examinations*. Pretoria: Umalusi.

Umalusi (Council for Quality Assurance in General and Further Education and Training). (2012c). Retrieved on 6 June 2012 from: http://umalusi.org.za.html 2012.

Umalusi (Council for Quality Assurance in General and Further Education and Training). (2012d) *Technical report on the quality assurance of the examinations and assessment of the National Senior Certificate (NSC) 2012*. Pretoria: Umalusi.

Van Dyk, T. (2010). *Konstitutiewe voorwaardes vir die ontwerp en ontwikkeling van 'n toets vir akademiese geletterdheid*. Unpublished Ph.D. thesis. Bloemfontein: University of the Free State.

Van Rooy, B., and Coetzee-Van Rooy, S. (2015). The language issue and academic performance at a South African university. *Southern African Linguistics and Applied Language Studies*, 33(1): 31-46.

Weideman, A. (2009). Constitutive and regulative conditions for the assessment of academic literacy. *Southern African Linguistics and Applied Language Studies Special Issue: Assessing and Developing Academic Literacy* (ed. J. Geldenhuys), 27(3), 235–251.

Weideman, A. (2011). Academic literacy tests: Design, development, piloting and refinement. SAALT *Journal for Language Teaching*, 45(2), 100–113.

Weideman, A. (2012). Validation and validity beyond Messick. *Per Linguam*, 28(2), 1–14.

Weideman, A. (2014). Innovation and reciprocity in applied linguistics. *Literator*, 35(1), Art. #1074, 10 pages. http://dx.doi.org/10.4102/lit.v35i1.1074

Weideman, A. (2017). *Responsible design and applied linguistics: theory and practice*. Cham: Springer Publishing International. DOI 10.1007/978-3-319-41731-8.

Weideman, A., Du Plessis, C., and Steyn, S. (2015). Diversity, variation and fairness: Equivalence in national level language assessments. Paper prepared for presentation at Language, Education & Diversity conference, Auckland, November 2015.

Weideman, A., Tesfamariam, H., and Shaalukeni, L. (2003). Resistance to change in language teaching: Some African case studies. *Southern African Linguistics and Applied Language Studies*, 21(1 & 2), 67–76.

Wilkins, D. (1976). *Notional syllabuses: A taxonomy and its relevance to foreign language curriculum development*. London: Oxford University Press.

Xi, X. (2008). Methods of test validation. In E. Shohamy and N. Hornberger (eds.), Language testing and assessment. *Encyclopedia of language and education* 7 (pp. 177–196). New York: Springer Science + Business Media.

Xi, X. (2010). How do we go about investigating test fairness? *Language Testing*, 27(2), 147–170. DOI: 10.1177/0265532209349465

13 Culturally Responsive Experimental Intervention Studies

The Development of a Rubric for Paradigm Expansion

Aydin Bal and Audrey A. Trainor

The purpose of this chapter is to present a culturally responsive research (CRR) rubric for experimental intervention studies, its underlying theoretical framework, and the methodology of its development. We aim to operationalize culturally responsive experimental intervention research and to expand the conceptualization of methodological rigor to include the role of culture in special education research. Recently, special education scholars have called for increased attention to the cultural aspects of intervention studies, analyzing results, and disseminating implications that address enduring disparities in educational opportunities and outcomes that youth from nondominant cultural and linguistic backgrounds experience in schools (Arzubiaga et al. 2008; Klingner et al. 2005; Ortiz and Yates 2010; Sugai, O'Keeffe and Fallon 2012). Moreover, special education scholars explored the cultural responsiveness and ecological validity of special education interventions in diverse contexts of local education systems and for students from nondominant communities (Bal 2011b; García and Ortiz 2008; Klingner, Sorrells and Barrera 2007).

We examined experimental special education intervention research as a cultural activity system with its naturalized, taken-for-granted practices, artifacts, and assumptions. Our aim is for the CRR rubric to be used as a methodological tool for developing culturally responsive intervention research to augment the field's understanding and ability to address the increasingly diverse strengths, needs, and goals of youth with ability differences as situated in the complex ecologies of education systems. Our intention was not to set indelible margins for culturally responsive intervention research. We see this rubric as a living artifact providing a set of principles in systematic and accessible ways, enhancing researchers' reflexivity, and expanding experimental intervention research that is the most privileged methodology of knowledge production.

Experimental research must develop tools and methods that adequately and critically develop an empirical understanding of social realities such as structural reproduction of ideologies of race, ability, and class in the United States and how they matter in the lives of dominant and nondominant students to effectively address contemporary research questions (Apple 2013; Giroux 1983; Leonardo

238 *Aydin Bal and Audrey A. Trainor*

2010). We see this as a necessary step in addressing the enduring disparities in education opportunities and outcomes via ecologically valid and sustainable interventions.

Increasingly disparate outcomes by race, class, and ability in U.S. schools coexist with legislative directives for educators to use *evidence-based practices* in standardization-oriented, schoolwide intervention models, such as responses to intervention and positive behavioral interventions and supports. The development of criteria for CRR addresses an identified gap in knowledge and practice: a dearth of studies designed to elicit such evidence that also include nondominant participants using CRR methods (Haager, Klingner and Vaughn 2007; Sugai et al. 2012; Vincent et al. 2011). To illustrate, Lane, Kalberg, and Shepcaro (2009) conducted a comprehensive review of evidence in support of interventions aimed at changing challenging behaviors for youth identified with behavioral disorders (BDs). The authors used Horner et al.'s (2005) quality indicators and criteria that operationalized a study's description of participants sufficient for replicability and generalizability as meeting two conditions: (a) identification of a specific disability and (b) a description of the method used to identify or diagnose the disability. In doing so, Lane and colleagues did not address participants' sociodemographic factors outside of official disability labels. Furthermore, neither Horner et al.'s (2005) rubric nor Lane et al.'s (2009) application of these criteria for quality of evidence addresses multiple interpretations of the function of behaviors, a central tenet in intervention for behavioral modification and one that potentially varies according to socially constructed notions of aberrant behaviors and explanations of their functions in different contexts.

Philosophical and empirical analyses of the regimes of truth and social movements such as the recent, evidence-based practices movement in social sciences have been introduced (Sandler and Apple 2010). The present work is informed by that extant critical literature on the culture of evidence in education and social science research. But its purpose is different: The CRR rubric joins the current discourse on epistemology in special education literature and extends earlier efforts to identify rigor or quality indicators of experimental research in special education (Gersten et al. 2005; Horner et al. 2005; Odom et al. 2005). Informed by an interdisciplinary literature from psychology, science studies, and special/education, we aimed to curate the rubric as a methodological tool to remediate the discourse on rigor in experimental interventions.

This work is timely. Special education literature has manifested an epistemological tension since the 1990s as the field expands its unit of analysis from an individual subject to the whole school context via schoolwide interventions, such as response to intervention and positive behavioral interventions and supports (Bal 2011b). Additionally, the CRR rubric fills a gap in special education scholarship regarding the cultural practices of research, including drawing conclusions from results and identifying implications (Arzubiaga et al. 2008). Neither the original rubrics detailing quality indicators for special education experiments nor subsequent applications of these earlier rubrics address this issue (Chard et al. 2009; Lane et al. 2009). Finally, the CRR rubric emphasizes the critical role of *situated*

A Rubric for Paradigm Expansion   239

knowledge in experimental research. Mainstream positivist and postpositivist conceptualizations of experimental studies in education and special education in the United States have privileged the so-called objective and culture-free knowledge over situated knowledge (Brantlinger 1997; Milner 2007). That is, the field engages in "the privileging of knowledge *about* poor people and racial and ethnically marginalized people over knowledge produced *within and by* these communities" (Sandler and Apple 2010: 328). This rubric positions the situated knowledge, diverse cultural and linguistic practices, and experiences that nondominant students bring to schools as a value-added construct within experimental design.

In the following sections, we first discuss the rationale for developing the present rubric in more detail. Next, we identify the theoretical foundations of the rubric that employ a dialectical, process-oriented view of culture. These theoretical perspectives frame knowledge production in education research as a socially, historically, and spatially constructed and a culturally mediated process. We then review our method for development of the rubric, using existing quality indicators for special education research (Gersten et al. 2005; Horner et al. 2005) and principles of CRR in education and psychology (e.g., American Psychological Association [APA] 2003, 2005; Engeström 2011; Klingner et al. 2007; Ladson- Billings and Tate 2006; Rogoff 2003; Sue 1999) as models. Finally, we discuss specific rubric items and related implications.

Rationale for CRR

Researchers have recorded long-lasting disparities in academic, social, and economic opportunities and outcomes between nondominant youth from historically marginalized communities and their peers from dominant groups (e.g., Anyon 2005; Darling-Hammond 2010; Ferri and Connor 2005; Losen and Orfield 2002; Wagner et al. 2006). The U.S. Department of Education and Office for Civil Rights (2012) issued a report detailing how quality of educational opportunities were diminished based on race, gender, language, and disability status, thus contributing to the marginalization of nondominant communities. The findings of this report highlight several key affronts to equal access to education, including the ongoing obstacles to desegregate U.S. schools: limited access to college preparatory and advanced placement secondary courses, limited resources to instructional technology, and racial disproportionality in school disciplinary actions involving suspensions and expulsions (U.S. Department of Education and Office for Civil Rights 2012).

For students who receive special education, these disparities are pronounced and complicated by disproportionate identification of disability and service delivery in restrictive settings. In what has been identified as a historical pattern, the most recent report to Congress on the implementation of the Individuals With Disabilities Education Improvement Act of 2004 documented an elevated risk of disability identification in what are considered judgmental disabilities such as learning disabilities (LDs) and BDs for Native American and African American students as compared to all other race/ethnicities combined. Furthermore, the risk of disability identification was 1.63 and 2.28 times higher, respectively, in the category of BD, a disability category with some of the lowest indicators of academic and postschool success, such as 56% rate of high school completion (U.S. Department of Education and Office of Special Education and Rehabilitation Services 2011).

Additionally, minority students with disabilities have diminished access to inclusive education settings that are generally associated with positive outcomes, such as enrollment in postsecondary education (U.S. Department of Education and Office of Special Education and Rehabilitation Services 2011). This problem is compounded by the overrepresentation of Native Americans and African Americans when the disability category is the focus of analysis because they are both overrepresented in BD. Only 35% of youth identified with BD are served in the most inclusive settings (i.e., spending 80% or more of the school day in a general education classroom). Fully 17% of youth identified with BD are in separate settings such as residential and treatment settings, the third highest percentage of students served in separate settings by disability category after students who are deaf and blind (30%) and those who have multiple disabilities (25%; U.S. Department of Education and Office of Special Education and Rehabilitation Services 2011).

When students experience similar behavioral difficulties – with or without a disability label – those from nondominant backgrounds more often face exclusionary disciplinary actions. These outcomes also have a historically racialized presence in schools. Nearly 40 years ago, researchers found that African American students were up to 3 times more likely than their White peers to be suspended (Children's Defense Fund 1975). These disparities hold today, with African American, Latino, and Native American youth significantly more likely to experience exclusionary school discipline correlated with academic failure and involvement in juvenile justice system (Krezmien, Leone and Achilles 2006). Recent national data show that nondominant students are punished more often and more severely, for example, being subjected to mechanical restraints for less serious incidents, such as disrespectful behavior and dress code violations (for more detailed results, see Office for Civil Rights 2012).

Demographic projections show that students from nondominant backgrounds will make up more than half the student population nationwide in the near future. Each year, millions of U.S.-born cultural and linguistic minority students, as well as newly arrived immigrant and refugee youth, enter school with diverse strengths, needs, interests, and experiences. These youth attend predominantly urban schools that significantly lack adequate academic, linguistic, and social supports and fall short of providing positive social climates (Anyon 2005; Suárez-Orozco and Suárez-Orozco 2001). There is a critical need to generate valid knowledge to understand these challenges to educational equity and to design culturally relevant, academically rich, and sustainable education systems that disrupt and transform the inherent conditions reproducing inequalities in the United States (Ladson-Billings and Tate 2006; Paris 2012).

The increasing diversity in schools, the ever-widening outcome and opportunity gaps, and the historical marginalization of nondominant communities constitute

A Rubric for Paradigm Expansion 241

a systemic tension and requires a paradigm expansion for developing new theoretical models and intervention methodologies considering dynamic contexts of education systems and goals, practices, histories, and political interests of participants and researchers (Artiles 2011; Darling-Hammond 2010; Klingner et al. 2005; Ladson-Billings 2006).

Marginalization of Nondominant Communities and the Role of Research

For too long, nondominant communities have been excluded from educational and psychology research (Graham 1992). In a meta-analysis of the 180 intervention studies of students identified with LDs, Swanson and Hoskyn (1998) found that the majority of the intervention studies did not report participants' race or ethnicity. In addition, the results are rarely disaggregated by race/ethnicity (Artiles, Trent and Kuan 1997; National Research Council 2002a; Trainor and Bal 2014). Students identified as English language learners, in particular, are often excluded from experimental studies to establish internal validity (Solano-Flores 2008). Although this limits external validity or generalizability of the findings, the outcomes of intervention studies are often presented as objective or culture- or race-free and their results as evidence supporting practices for all students, including those from nondominant communities who were excluded from participation in research (Klingner et al. 2007).

When researchers focus on youth and families from nondominant backgrounds, representation of those participants is deficit in orientation. Deficit-oriented representations are associated with the study of participants' sociodemographic background based on contextualized, static individual characteristics (e.g., individuals' social skills) or overly generalized categories and loosely identified group traits such as learning styles (e.g., racial learning style; Gutiérrez and Rogoff 2003). In education research, nondominant youth and families have long been positioned as being at risk for academic failure and behavioral problems via theories such as the culture of poverty or eugenics (Baker 2002; Erickson 2009; Gieryn 1995; Snyder and Mitchell 2010). Furthermore, research methodologies and training are culturally responsive to dominant cultural group practices (e.g., White males with able bodies) and have inherited biases and prejudice toward nondominant groups including racial minorities, people with disabilities, people living in poverty, and immigrants (Scheurich and Young 1997).

In psychology and education research, complex constructs such as race, disability, and class are treated as independent variables and innate characteristics of individuals – often via problematic proxy indicators such as free or reduced-price meals for socioeconomic status. The historical misuse of race to study the effect of race, for example, has been promulgated as an explanation and justification of the racial hierarchy via culturally biased tools (e.g., IQ tests or behavioral checklists) and often-inadequate statistical analyses (e.g., using single-level models that did not allow to examine the nested structure of student-level and school-level determinants; Bonilla-Silva and Zuberi 2008).

242   Aydin Bal and Audrey A. Trainor

The privileged use of culturally biased research tools as objective and culture-free is exemplified by the founding figures of psychology in the West. Francis Galton, G. Stanley Hall, and others who developed personal trait measures such as intelligence and personality tests established psychology as a field of individual difference. These influential figures offered self-governing, isolated individuals whose abilities and disabilities were mainly determined by hereditary characteristics (e.g., race) as the unit of analysis. They were also strong supporters of White supremacy and the eugenics movement, which sought to improve genetic quality and purity of a society (i.e., dominant group) through the practices of selective breeding and sterilization (Baker 2002). These ideologies and interests were embedded in the foundational constructs (e.g., intelligence, self-esteem, self-determination, motivation, and personality traits), measurements, and knowledge hierarchies (e.g., statistical analyses of individual differences) and became the dominant paradigm of psychology and education in the United States. And eventually, these ideologies and tools created a well-oiled machine in formal schooling and in education research that identify and "fix" deficits within individual children (Erickson 2009).

To additionally complicate those issues, academies of higher education, responsible for research and its dissemination for the purpose of solving education's greatest challenges, reflect their own history of marginalization of scholars from nondominant groups (Acker, Webber and Smyth 2012; Barclay 2012; Diggs et al. 2009; Lather 2004). First, research-intensive universities continue to struggle to support and retain scholars from historically marginalized groups (e.g., scholars of color and disabled scholars), thus contributing to marginalization of the work of nondominant scholars (Alex-Assensoh 2003). Second, nondominant scholars are likely to have heavy service loads and function as resources for their peers and students from similarly marginalized backgrounds, thus facing obstacles to tenure and promotion in institutions that value productivity over collegiality (Jayakumar et al. 2009). Third, nondominant scholars who choose to pursue lines of research that investigate culture, race, or racial inequalities are often viewed negatively in academic settings where dominant-group scholars perceive such scholarly pursuits as racially motivated, biased, and unscientific (Barclay 2012; Fenelon 2003). In particular, methods used to critique and research questions that focus on power/privilege may be infrequently employed by researchers from dominant groups and lead to questions about, or defense of, rigor during the implementation and dissemination of research (DeCuir and Dixson 2004; Milner 2007; Stanley 2007). In short, the marginalization of students, families, and researchers from nondominant groups contributes to the systemic tension in special education research and its inadequacy for addressing complex issues and inequalities, calling for paradigmatic expansion regarding the culture of knowledge production. Systemic tensions are a key to understand the sources of problems as well as the innovative and generative potential for systemic transformation in a scientific field (Engeström 2008). The purpose of the CRR rubric is to expand current paradigms of knowledge production and

A Rubric for Paradigm Expansion   243

develop CRR, with a focus on experimental interventions because experimental design is privileged and touted as the most effective methodology of knowledge production in special education.

Paradigmatic Expansion

Kuhn (1962) noted, "Paradigms prove to be constitutive of science . . . [they] provide scientists not only with a map but also with some of the directions" (22). According to Kuhn, progress in a scientific field takes place as dialectical episodes. The conceptualization of scientific truth is not universal but bounded by time and space. Scientific truth cannot be established solely by objective criteria; it is defined by a collective conceptual agreement of a given field as situated in specific social, historical, and spatial contexts (e.g., political interests; Gieryn 1995). The relative continuity of foundational conceptual agreements in all scientific fields can be interrupted and challenged by fundamental changes in the content of its study, thus potentially creating systemic tensions (Kuhn 1962). Each scientific discipline solves systemic tensions via paradigm expansion to establish a consensus about a more encompassing paradigm for understanding and addressing those tensions (Kuhn 1962). For example, in the field of physics, moving from Newtonian mechanics to relativistic mechanics is an example of paradigm expansion. Such paradigm expansions require a discovery period and a revolutionary reconfiguration that lead to the expanded paradigm with an updated conceptual map directing new methodologies. Gieryn (1995) asserted that expanded paradigms change the culture of scientific fields directing new inquiries and asking novel questions of existing data.

Experimental psychology, most specifically its behaviorist conceptualization, has been the main influence in the mainstream special education research paradigm in the United States (Kauffman and Landrum 2006). This view takes the individual as the unit of analysis and looks for universal laws of human behaviors. Culture is often regarded as an extraneous variable associated with homogenous, static group characteristics (e.g., values, customs, or behaviors). Theories highlighting the complex nature of human learning and development and the role of culture in, for example, Bourdieu's social reproduction theory (e.g., concept of habitus), Erikson's developmental theory of identity, or Bronfenbrenner's ecological systems theory have been adapted by social scientists in accordance with the unit of analysis: self-governing, morally directed, rational selves in a universal time and stable spaces (Popkewitz 1997).

Criticism of narrowly focused epistemologies and ontologies in psychology and education research is not new. Some have argued the current experimental studies employing highly controlled laboratory-based experimental methodology (stimulus-response) are overly deterministic and not well suited to understanding higher psychological processes that involve reasoning, language, and goal-oriented actions (Cole 1996). Although highly controlled laboratory-based research contributes to the knowledge base of elementary (physiological) psychological

244 *Aydin Bal and Audrey A. Trainor*

functions, a developmental-historical methodology such as ethnological analyses of cultural group practices is necessary for understanding the higher psychological functions. Wilhelm Wundt, widely recognized as the founding figure of experimental psychology, acknowledged this limitation on the field's knowledge production, asserting, "Only through a synthesis of their respective insights could a full psychology be achieved" (Cole 1996: 29). Against Wundt's explicit warnings, however, proponents of experimental methodology complemented a narrow view of epistemology with behaviorism, inferential statistics, and standardized aptitude and achievement tests to study both elementary and higher psychological functions.

Alternative conceptualizations of experimental methodology focusing on cultural mediation and dynamic interactions of human and context include Vygotsky and his followers, who developed sociocultural theory, a historical materialist theory of learning, and experimental methodology aligned with Wundt's earlier work and encompassed both the study of elementary and higher psychological functions. Vygotsky (1976) called this experimental methodology "the functional method of double stimulation" (74). In double stimulation experiments, "The subject is put in a structured situation where a problem exists . . . and the subject is provided with active guidance towards the construction of a new means to the end of a solution to the problem" (van der Veer and Valsiner 1991: 169). Sociocultural conceptualization of experimental psychology and its intervention methodology are increasingly used in education research, organizational studies, and learning sciences for designing expansive learning contexts inside and outside of schools (Sannino, Daniels and Gutiérrez 2009; for the use of the functional method of double stimulation in special education, see Bal et al. 2014).

An intended contribution of the CRR rubric as a research tool is to facilitate a paradigmatic expansion in special education interventions that involves examining the critical and generative role of culture and contexts to provide fuller and dynamic understanding of human learning, development, and ability. The focus on intervention experiments is deliberate because these designs are privileged and have a defined and peer-reviewed initial set of quality indicators. We use the term *culturally responsive research* to refer to scholarship that applies the tenets of cultural responsiveness in inquiry, communication, and interaction in education. Addressing persistent problems of equity requires critical attention to the cultural notion of knowledge production in the field of special education (Artiles et al. 2010; McDermott and Varenne 1995; National Research Council 2002b).

The Cultural Practice of Knowledge Production

All stages of intervention research, from question inception to dissemination, are "culturally and socially mediated and negotiated" (Arzubiaga et al. 2008: 310). Research tools mediate scientific processes of knowledge production. As cultural artifacts, those tools are heavily instantiated with constantly shifting cultural practices, ideologies, identities, and interests that evolve over time and are negotiated and orchestrated in local sociopolitical contexts (Scheurich 1997). To illustrate,

A Rubric for Paradigm Expansion   245

with its dominant conceptualization, intervention itself has been used as a linear, ableist tool to fix differences constructed as deficits within an individual or a cultural group such as newly arrived immigrant families or deaf people (Snyder and Mitchell 2010). Grounded in sociocultural theory, CRR takes intervention as a cultural practice that is open for negotiation and adaptation:

> An ongoing transformational process that is constantly re-shaped by its own internal organizational and political dynamic and by the specific conditions it encounters or itself creates, including the responses and strategies of local and regional groups who may struggle to define and defend their own social spaces, cultural boundaries and positions within the wider power field.
> (Long 2001, as cited in Engeström 2011: 603)

In our view, universalist, culture-free perspectives that do not critically consider disabled, racialized, gendered, or classed experiences and enduring structural inequalities are products of culture and history through local performances of researchers, participants, and consumers of research. The significance and implications of research results can be fully understood if and when the specific contexts of the researchers, the participants, and scientific fields frame the work. Conceptualizing research as situated cultural practice acknowledges the regimes of power/knowledge as central players in the reproduction of disparities in access, influence, and thus, predictable variance in outcomes (Leonardo 2009; Soja 2010; Young 1990).

Research requires a constellation of analytic tools as cultural artifacts – both ideal and material – for examining the individual and social processes of learning and development, including the examination of disparate education opportunities and outcomes. Researchers risk contributing to the reproduction and obfuscation of structural inequalities when only certain methodological tools are promoted as the most effective way to answer all research questions, or when the quality indicators of any given methodology fail to acknowledge research as a situated practice, and both may also lead to routinized implementation and dissemination decisions (Trainor and Bal 2014). The establishment of experimental designs as a "gold standard" and the development and application of quality indicator rubrics in special education without attention to diversity and equity have overlooked, and continue to overlook, complicated research questions and contributed to the persistence of inequalities.

Gutiérrez (2006) used the term *White innocence* to explain how researchers, including those from nondominant communities, may reproduce dominant models of racial hierarchy. White innocence is not a simplistic reference to the racial identification of researchers; rather, it refers to "the dominant subject position that preserves racial subordination and the differential benefits for the *innocent* who retains her own dominant position vis-à-vis the 'objects' of study" (Gutiérrez 2006: 4). From this perspective, researchers are "all implicated in some way in maintaining *White innocence*" (4). Bonilla-Silva and Zuberi (2008) expanded the conceptualization of White innocence to *White logic* and examined the taken-for-granted reasoning and methodologies about empirical reality: "White logic assumes a historical posture that grants eternal objectivity to the views of elite Whites and condemns the views of non-Whites to perpetual subjectivity" (17). Gutiérrez (2006) and Bonilla-Silva and Zuberi (2008) used a dialectic view toward knowledge production and emphasized the role of structure (institutions), ideologies, individual factors, and race-based interests in scientific knowledge production.

Working with nondominant communities and the associated conceptualizing of culture and cultural difference play critical roles in understanding salient education problems and their solutions. Culturally responsive researchers should be reflexive toward mundane research activities and develop a critical understanding of research as a cultural practice that is loaded with deep struggles over power/privilege. Similar to practitioners who often struggle to identify how culture may shape their views and daily practices of teaching/learning (Craig et al. 2000), education researchers must interrogate the normalized, culturally situated practices and perspectives purported to be objective and culture-free.

Following Latour (1993), we posit that researchers using experimental design must examine what they are actually producing, that is, the amalgams of nature and culture instead of what has been conceptualized as "working within a purified realm of knowledge" (48). As such, we include factors related to researchers (e.g., training, prior experiences, and positionality) and to research processes (e.g., negotiation of sites, methods of recruitment, and data collection) in the CRR rubric (see, e.g., the CRR Rubric Item 6 in the section "Design and Logic"). Attention to these details is critical to making visible the taken-for-granted processes of knowledge production, at times resulting in continued marginalization of nondominant people.

For the development of the rubric, we eschewed static and overly deterministic conceptualizations of culture such as those often associated with the inheritance of values, beliefs, traditions, norms, and interactional styles (e.g., making eye contact). Instead, we take culture as a dynamic, multifaceted, and generative process that cannot be reduced into a set of overgeneralized traits and outcomes that are frozen in time and space (Bal 2011a). We employed sociocultural theory of culture, examining the dynamic interactions of individual, institutional, and interpersonal factors (Rogoff 2003). The guiding principle of this view is that culture mediates all human activities: "Humans develop through their changing participation in the socio-cultural activities of their communities, which also change" (Rogoff 2003: 11). A process-oriented model of culture can

> [1] inform future research priorities and policy making in general and special education; [2] document how special education practice, research, and policy [are] enacted in racially and economically stratified schools and communities; and [3] lead to significantly improved educational outcomes for students from historically underserved groups.
>
> (Artiles et al. 2010: 296)

Conceptualizing Culture as a Dynamic Process

M. Cole (1996) aptly stated, "Culture is very difficult for humans to think about. Like fish in water, we fail to 'see' culture because it is the medium within which we exist" (8). Because the study of culture is interdisciplinary, we focused the operationalization of CRR on recent and comprehensive scholarship relevant to learning, development, and collective knowledge production activities, drawing from work in education, psychology, and science studies (e.g., APA 1990, 2003; Banks et al. 2007; Bonilla-Silva and Zuberi 2008; M. Cole 1996; Latour 1993; Rogoff 2003; Tillman 2002). For the purposes of the CRR rubric, we operationalized culture as the residue of collective problem-solving activities and collections of cultural artifacts perfected over generations and through history that reflects a social group's efforts to adapt, survive, and thrive in ever-changing local and global circumstances (Bal 2011a; Gallego, Cole and the Laboratory of Comparative Human Cognition 2001). Four key considerations in our operationalization are *mediation through artifacts, cultural activity as a unit of analysis, intersectionality*, and *ecological validity*.

Mediation through Artifacts

Culture can be seen as a link between larger social and institutional factors to individual behaviors and thoughts. Culture is a mediator of everyday human activities via artifacts. "An artifact is an aspect of the material world that has been modified over the history in its incorporation into the goal-directed human action" (Cole 1996: 117). Artifacts both enable and constrain individuals' actions. As active social agents, people do not solely resist or passively internalize the culture; people do use and make cultures (Varenne and McDermott 1998). Two interconnected processes regarding the reproduction and transformation of culture are internalization and externalization. In cyclical relationships, internalization processes are about membership and reproduction of a cultural system (e.g., family, academia, or a scientific field). Externalization is about production of new or revised artifacts assisting the transformation of systems such as the dissemination of standards by a state's department of education or the development of a privacy policy articulated by medical organizations. New or revised artifacts are then internalized by group members and remediate collective activities.

All cultural artifacts – regardless of simplicity or complexity – are simultaneously ideal and material (e.g., a pen or a language): "Being manufactured for a *reason* and put into *use* – the neutral object acquires a significance. This significance is the ideal form of the object" (Bakhurst 1990, as cited in Cole 1996 : 118). In this sense, tools that mediate knowledge production activities in experimental research, such as the *Diagnostic and Statistical Manual of Mental Health Disorders* (American Psychiatric Association 2013), IQ tests, behavioral questionnaires, and the APA style manual, have ideal and material components.

Culture and cultural mediation of scientific knowledge production via artifacts should be understood with their material and ideal underpinnings in the

248 *Aydin Bal and Audrey A. Trainor*

context of group interests such that "culture is not so much a product of sharing as a product of people hammering each other into shape with well-structured tools already available" (McDermott and Varenne 1995: 326). To illustrate, Leonardo (2010) examined the concept of race as an artifact invented by White Europeans for achieving their economic and political interests, mediating human actions, perceptions, and institutions with its ideal (e.g., how individuals conceive race in their daily lives) and material (e.g., racialized relationships and institutions organized around race) foundations.

Cultural Activity as a Unit of Analysis

The process-oriented conceptualization of culture offers a new unit of analysis for researchers. This unit is the artifact-mediated, goal-oriented collective activities in which individual, institutional, and interpersonal factors dynamically amalgamate in specific social, historical, and spatial contexts. This new unit of analysis requires developmental research perspectives that focus on the dynamic interactions and historical configurations of artifacts and on the unequal distribution of social strata, positions, and opportunities. The power/privilege differentiations are reproduced, mapping to social categories based on disability, race, class, and gender identities, as well as goals and institutional rules, roles, and division of labor (Engeström and Miettinen 1999).

The CRR rubric requires researchers to go beyond cultural determinism as well as cultural neutralism that have dominated education research (Gallego et al. 2001). The rubric employs a robust theory of culture that takes into account complex interactions of individual, institutional, and interpersonal factors in a given context, such as conducting an experimental study of a direct instruction-based reading intervention for racial minority youth in a juvenile correctional facility in Arizona in 2014. From the CRR perspective, researchers' tasks are to understand "the dynamic patterns of individuals' participation in building on historical constellations of community practices, continuing and transforming across generations" (Gutiérrez and Rogoff 2003: 23) and to specify the complexities of real life in which particular interventions are applied (Cole, Hood and McDermott 1997).

To conduct CRR, researchers must take into consideration "how people *assume*, but are also *given*, and *co-construct* multiple positions (e.g., insider, competent or engaged) across contexts, depending on a host of forces that include local communities' practices and history, as well as a person's biographical trajectory" (Arzubiaga et al. 2008: 319). To do this, education researchers must not only focus on cultural group categories and outcomes such as disproportionately higher special education identification and dropout rates among African American, Latino, and Native American students. Researchers must also include an examination of processes (e.g., the racialization of disability, the individualization of success and failure, special education referral, and the institutionalized acts of exclusion based on ability differences) and institutions (e.g., universities, local education agencies, testing services, publishers, grant funders, and clearinghouses such as the Institute of Education Sciences or the National Science Foundation) that reproduce, regardless of intentionality, disparities.

This all-encompassing approach is necessary because culture is composed of processes that are deeply embedded in a cultural community, such as the field of special education as modus operandi; thus, they are highly naturalized and strategically invisible. For example, examining the social-historical reproduction of disabilities, McDermott, Goldman, and Varenne (2006) stated that, in the U.S. education system, the cultural notion of LD is embedded not in individual children with academic difficulties but in the concerted activities of professionals such as psychologists, teachers, and policymakers, among others, whose responsibilities include producing definitional evidence of LD. In such a well-organized system of disabling, it is not accidental that challenges nondominant students experience are largely explained by examining inherited qualities or assumed cultural group traits (e.g., collectivism or the culture of poverty).

Intersectionality

The third key consideration is intersectionality, a concept from critical legal theory and feminist studies (Crenshaw 1989), recently operationalized in the context of research methodologies in psychology and education (Cole 2009; García, Ortiz and Sorrells 2012; Museus and Griffin 2011). Simply put, intersectionality is a critical analytic framework that affords the simultaneous examination of multiple indicators of experiences and identities, some of which afford privilege whereas others act as signifiers of marginalization (Crenshaw 1989). Intersectionality is complex and not only includes personal experiences, but also allows for a focus on sociohistorical and structural context and activity systems. Intersectionality demonstrates how multiple political agendas interact and influence human experiences of privilege and marginalization in dynamic ways (Museus and Griffin 2011). For example, special education labels can be considered both as conduits for receiving individualized education, largely by dominant-group parents, and as stigmatizing license for schools to blame identified youth for classroom disruptions, largely by parents from nondominant groups (Trainor 2010).

Across epistemologies, the construct of intersectionality has been employed for the purpose of understanding the dynamic notion of culture and its role in education. Shaw, Chan and McMahon (2012) conducted a secondary analysis of the large-scale database to examine instances of harassment of people with disabilities, analyzing variables of disability, race, and gender. Shaw et al. thereby acknowledge that any one of these variables has variable potential and contributes to a collective indicator of disability harassment; still, their work centers on individual characteristics and diversity across groups rather than examining their contexts and activities. By contrast, Covarrubias (2011) examined the academic attainment, citizenship, and income of people of Mexican descent who participated in the U.S. census in 2009, and focused his analysis on access to educational opportunities and intragroup diversity.

The inclusion of intersectionality herein is used to complexify the treatment of what have traditionally been considered variables associated with culture (i.e., participants' race). Attempts to qualify and quantify intersectionality could be considered as efforts to "discipline" research in ways that are overly simplistic and do not allow for dealing with what Lather (2013) called the "messy conceptual labor, difference, otherness and disparity, and incompleteness of the positive norm" (642). Although this warning may be important to heed, our current conceptualization of culture and evidence without any nod to intersectionality is a high-priority concern here.

Ecological Validity

The last and most encompassing consideration in the CRR rubric is ecological validity, a foundational concept to experimental research (Cole et al. 1997). We see cultural responsiveness in experimental intervention research as an ongoing, negotiated, and contextually situated process in which ecological validity must be considered across multiple phases of an experimental study. Under the umbrella of ecological validity fall the familiar components of construct validity, interpretation validity, and population validity. Experimental psychologists entertained discussions of ecological validity in the early 20th century to expand the constricted locus of experiments "not representative of the larger patterns of life" (Brunswik 1943, as cited in Cole et al. 1997: 50). Bronfenbrenner (1979, 2005) further elaborated the roles of psychological and social contexts, or participants' ecologies, that comprise research settings, bridging real-life tasks, events, objects, and experimental conditions.

Ecological validity has been found to increase applications of neurological and cognitive assessments, interventions, and importantly, the design and implementation of culturally responsive experimental research (Bernal, Bonilla and Bellido 1995). In the development of the CRR rubric, we followed three criteria for ecological validity: (a) congruency with participants' real-life situations; (b) authenticity representative of participants' larger social, economic, and political contexts; and (c) analytic and interpretive consistency between the data and participants' goals, histories, activities, and understandings of the experimental conditions (Cole et al. 1997).

The Culture of Evidence

The relationship between evidence and education research has generally been one of legitimization. From Dewey and his contemporaries to present-day theorists, the need to strengthen the claims made about teaching and learning belies concerns about what counts as knowledge and what accurately depicts education (Lagemann 2000). Special education scholars have invested in definitions of "science" and "evidence," legitimizing and aligning with general education views about evidence-based practices. Evidence-based practices are a key component of federal legislations and reform efforts, including the Individuals With Disabilities

A *Rubric for Paradigm Expansion* 251

Education Improvement Act of 2004, No Child Left Behind, and Race to the Top (Turnbull 2005). The framing of evidence-based claims as a primary tool to increase standardization and accountability is a lever in shifting funding and research foci toward a narrow conceptualization of evidence. Borrowing from medical sciences, Bowker and Star (2000) called this process a *convergence principle* explaining the selective attention that takes place by changing the world, such that the system's description of reality becomes true:

> For example, consider the case where all diseases are classified purely physiologically. Systems of medical observation and treatment are set up such that physical manifestations are the only manifestations recorded. Physical treatments are the only treatments available. Under these conditions, then, logically schizophrenia may only result purely and simply from a chemical imbalance in the brain. It will be impossible to think or act otherwise.
>
> (p. 49)

Leading special education scholars (Chard et al. 2009; Gersten et al. 2005; Odom et al. 2005) who outlined the quality indicators in special education research clearly suggested that evidence-based practices are defined through the implementation of experimental research. The establishment of evidence from experimental research, presumed by many to be rigorous, culture-free, objective, and effective (i.e., what works), is posited as a method for addressing persistent challenges to educating youth with disabilities through the design of intensive special education interventions. Nevertheless, at least two major problems emerge from the narrowing of education research. First, "what works" is not really working: Negative academic and postschool outcomes for youth with disabilities placed in the special education system have persisted over decades (National Research Council 2002a; Wagner et al. 2006). Second, evidence based on the conceptualization of randomization reduces the roles of culture, context, and researcher–participant interactions into static categories, disregarding the institutionalized practices of exclusion and marginalization and participants' personal and collective histories such as experiences with racism, ableism, and sexism.

As a result, other relevant and perhaps more salient factors contributing to exclusion and marginalization are obscured. Scholarly work that offers critique of the dominant framework has been positioned outside of the evidence base. Because evidence established through randomized experiments is considered culture-free and generalizable across a variety of groups and contexts, its application is too restricted to encompass ontological and epistemological approaches used to address a multitude of research questions. This is problematic because paradigmatic expansion has been instrumental in solving complex questions in other scientific fields (Kuhn 1962). In the development of this rubric, our intention was to curate an artifact to remediate experimental intervention research toward a paradigmatic expansion in special education.

We are aware that in social sciences the rubric format has been used as a tool of control for demarcation of constructed binaries (i.e., science/nonscience). By noting the limitation of the rubric format, and given its cultural–historical supposition, we acknowledge that the CRR rubric cannot and should not set the margins of research activities. Additionally, some of the principles that guided the development of the CRR rubric overlap with quality rubrics for single-subject design (Horner et al. 2005) and qualitative research methodologies (Brantlinger et al. 2005). Although the CRR rubric can inform researchers conducting descriptive, single-subject, or qualitative studies to engage in CRR, its focus is on experimental research, as reflected in the review of theoretical and empirical work on experimental methodology and cultural responsiveness. We see this rubric as a cultural artifact that provides set of principles and considerations for cultural responsiveness in a systematic and practical format. In what follows, we discuss the development and application of the CRR rubric.

CRR Rubric Development and Application

We aim to expand – not to replace – commonly accepted standards and quality indicators in special education experiential research. Although areas of overlap between the CRR rubric and existing quality indicator rubrics of experimental research (Chard et al. 2009; Gersten et al. 2005) exist, such as presenting sociodemographic information and prior training about interventionists, we have expanded issues in design and implementation, such as sampling, that have implications for generating evidence in addressing strengths, needs, interests, and experiences of youth identified with disabilities. Basing our argument and rubric items on the principle that research is itself a cultural practice, our ultimate goal is to provide a conceptual tool to enhance researchers' reflexivity and responsivity during the conceptualization, design, implementation, and dissemination of research.

Review of the Literature

For developing the CRR rubric, we reviewed education and social science literatures to identify guidelines, rubrics, conceptual papers, empirical research articles, and research syntheses on cultural responsiveness in research and education interventions. We searched three electronic databases: ERIC, PsycINFO, and Google Scholar. The following combinations of keywords were used: *culturally responsive* or *culturally competent* or *culturally adequate* or *cultural competency* or *cultural adequacy* or *cultural responsiveness* and *research*. The searches included dates ranging from 2000 to 2010. We also manually searched reference lists from selected publications and contacted experts on equity and diversity in education and psychology, seeking information on existing rubrics and related sources. Our search revealed no published rubric or checklist for use in evaluating CRR. Next, we synthesized the resulting relevant conceptual papers, guidelines, and empirical studies that detailed the related tenets of cultural responsiveness in teaching, assessment, interventions, and research and highlighted strategies for conducting rigorous CRR.

Rubric Development

We created rubric items by reviewing the literature base, examining tenets associated with CRR, and identifying criteria from extant theoretical and empirical scholarship. Findings from the literature review were organized into domains for rubric-item development following the American Education Research Association (AERA) standards for reporting on empirical research (AERA 2006). These domains are (a) problem formulation, (b) design and logic, (c) sources of evidence, (d) measurement/assessment process, (e) analysis and interpretation, and (f) dissemination. We created ratings for the levels of rigor for each criterion (Chard et al. 2009).

We used a 3-point Likert-type scale (0–2) to represent the variance in cultural responsiveness ratings for each criterion. Ratings of 0 are indicative of an absence of documentation of the role of culture, employing a culturally neutral approach. Ratings of 1 are indicative of documentation that culture was viewed merely as a categorical, static variable via proxy indicators (e.g., race) determining participants' perceptions and behaviors. Ratings of 2 are indicative of documentation that an approach focusing on the affordances and constraints of the contexts in which individual, institutional, and interpersonal factors intersect. Following an iterative process, we sent the original rubric to two experts in the area of measurement and evaluation and four experts in the areas of special education, culturally relevant pedagogy, and education research. We revised rubric items based on those experts' feedback. The final 15-item rubric is included in Table 13.1. We then applied the rubric to a set of experimental studies identified by Test et al. (2009) as rigorous of evidence-based practices in special education transition (see Trainor and Bal 2014, for a detailed account of this application). We made minor modifications in this final version of the CRR rubric.

Later, we provide a discussion of each rubric item and rating to illustrate the relationship between extant literature, rubric criteria, and rating schema in six domains of the AERA (2006) standards for reporting on research: problem formulation, design and logic, sources of evidence, measurement/assessment process, analysis and interpretation, and dissemination.

Problem Formulation

Cultural artifacts and contextual factors such as the dominant individualistic behaviorist paradigms of learning and experiential intervention studies in the era of accountability and standardization shape researchers' thinking and planning as they develop investigations. Social, historical, and spatial contexts (e.g., location, demographics, ideologies, languages, and a groups' history with discrimination and power/privilege) at both group and individual levels, relative to both researchers and participants, all play some role in the way we conceptualize problems and design research questions (Ashing-Giwa 2005; Goodley and Runswick-Cole 2010). In the development of this rubric, we used disability studies, specifically

Table 13.1 Rubric for Culturally Responsive Experimental Intervention Research

	0	1	2
1. Foundational construct(s) of the study	The construct under examination (e.g., LD, social skills, intelligence, self-determination and at risk behaviors) is implied but it is not explicitly discussed.	The construct under examination is explicitly discussed as universal. It is based on a norm-referenced sample representative of people from dominant backgrounds. Evidence of alternative conceptualizations of the construct is not presented based on the studies with nondominant groups.	The construct under examination is addressed comprehensively and critically; multiple perspectives and/or competing ideas are discussed with evidence of alternative conceptualizations.
2. Relevancy of the research problem	The relevancy of the research problem to the interests and needs of participants and local communities or to the researchers and the research field is not explicitly discussed.	The relevancy of the research problem is discussed, as it relates to the research field and/or the researcher's interests or line of inquiry.	The relevancy of the research problem addresses the research field and/or the researcher's interests or line of inquiry and the participants' and local communities' strengths, needs and interests.
3. Critical and comprehensive review of the relevant literature	The review of extant literature results in a narrow rationale for the study that does not address what is known with multiple and/or conflicting views about the concept(s) under investigation and research problem.	The review of extant literature includes scholarship as it relates only to the concept(s) under investigation and research problem.	The review of extant literature is critical and creates a dialogue with studies employing alternative methodologies and perspectives on the concept(s) under investigation and research problem.
4. Justification of the theoretical framework	The theoretical framework of the study (e.g., behaviorism, *cognitivism*, or social constructivism) is not discussed explicitly. It is taken for granted.	The theoretical framework of the study is discussed abstractly, only as it relates to the construct under examination.	The theoretical framework is discussed comprehensively and critically as it relates to material, social and historical contexts of the study and participants' lives, experiences and preferences. The framework is justified with its limitations and strengths to study the topic, participants and the specific context of the study.

5. Description of the participants	Description of participants' demographic characteristics includes two or fewer characteristics (e.g., gender, race, income level, education, gender, and disability).	Description of participants includes more than two individual characteristics (e.g., gender, race, income level, formal education, and disability).	Description of participants includes both individual characteristics and the institutional and social dimensions (e.g., institutional and cultural group histories, rules and power differentiations) as related to the context of the intervention for both the control and intervention groups.
6. Description of the researchers and interventionists	Description of researchers and interventionists (e.g., teacher, translator) includes two or fewer individual characteristics (e.g., gender, race and language).	Description of researchers and interventionists includes more than two individual characteristics (e.g., race, economic background, gender, and disability); however, the description is limited to the dimension of the individual.	Description of researchers and interventionists includes individual characteristics and the contextualized institutional dimensions and relational positions among and between the participants and interventionists (e.g., status and insider/outsider positions).
7. Description of the sampling procedures	Recruitment and sampling methods are not discussed.	Recruitment and sampling methods are discussed but lack detail about the rationale for the inclusionary criteria (e.g., exclusion of English Language Learners) and the congruency between recruitment methods and participants' experiences and preferences (e.g., language preference or method of contact).	Recruitment and sampling methods include differentiation based on participants' living conditions, experiences and preferences, maximizing the potential to include nondominant communities (e.g., people with disabilities or ELLs) into intervention studies as participants and/or researchers.
8. Description of the research setting	Description of the research setting is not discussed.	Description of the research setting includes the school and community characteristics relevant to the construct under examination.	Description of the setting includes political, material, social, and historical factors and their interaction within the context of the intervention process.

(*Continued*)

Table 13.1 (Continued)

	0	1	2
9. Description of data collection strategies	A rationale for the data collection strategies is not discussed.	A rationale for the data collection strategies is provided; however, it is limited to a technical discussion of the methodology.	A rationale for the data collection strategies includes consideration of participants' preferences, needs, strengths and interests. Multiple methods of data collection are used and maximize accessibility (e.g., providing interviews and measurement tools in participants' language, using participant-selected locales). Description of evidence includes interactions between the researchers, interventionists and participants.
10. Ecology of the intervention	The intervention includes a contrived context, task, and control for variables to the extent that its application in outside of the research contexts (i.e., real life) is unlikely.	The intervention includes controlled variables and experimental conditions and that generally represent participants' experiences and preferences in non-research contexts, yet the properties of the intervention align more closely with those of the interventionists.	The intervention is aligned with participants' experiences and preferences in non-research contexts (i.e., real life). The integrity of the participants' experiences and contexts is balanced with the intervention.
11. Intervention design	*Culture-free approach:* The intervention does not consider fundamental aspects of cultural and linguistic diversity that participants, interventionists and researchers bring to the study. The diversity of the material, social and historical contexts is not discussed.	*Culturally sensitive approach:* The intervention incorporates methods and procedures to integrate individual and within-group diversity. These include a combination of the following: researchers' and interventionists' training for working with historically marginalized groups; including participants' interests, perspectives and practices, and inviting community representation; ensuring availability and accuracy of translation of intervention materials and procedures; considering the implications of legal issues (e.g., citizenship status); and/or examining the applicability of interventions to participants' lives.	*Culturally responsive approach:* The intervention study incorporates methods and procedures to address diversity but also meets all three fundamental criteria for culturally responsive interventions: to improve academic achievement, skills, and knowledge, and social outcomes; to affirm participants' cultural group and personal identities; and to facilitate the development of participants' critical perspectives both to develop an awareness of and capacity to challenge inequities that they experience.

12. Assessment of intervention efficacy	The validity, reliability and language of the measurement(s) are not discussed.	The validity, reliability and language of the measurement(s) are discussed, but the measurements are standardized and norm-referenced for a population other than the sample.	The validity, reliability and language of the measurement(s) are inclusive of the range of populations representative of participants – OR – the limitations of the measurement(s) and the lack of availability of normed-referenced tools for use with the sample is explicitly discussed.
13. Presentation of findings	The results are not disaggregated according to the participant sociodemographic characteristics.	The results are disaggregated according to participant characteristics between and within the intervention and control groups, but are limited to gender, race, income level, or language or disability.	The results are disaggregated according to participant between and within the intervention and control groups and include intersections of participants' sociodemographic characteristics (e.g., race, class, and disability identification).
14. Analysis and interpretation	*Culture-free approach*: Participant's cultural, linguistic, and economic backgrounds and contextual factors are not included in data analysis and interpretation.	*Cultural deterministic approach*: Participant's backgrounds and contextual factors are analyzed as categorical and static variables. Differences among the participants are interpreted based on the dis/advantages associated with living conditions, demographic characteristics, or participants' lack of competencies in mainstream skills and knowledge.	*Cultural instrumentalist approach*: Participant's backgrounds and contextual factors are analyzed as dynamic, complex, and dialogical. Differences within the participants are interpreted as situated in affordances and constraints of the physical, social, and historical relations of the context. Factors under consideration include organizational structures, power distribution, and participants' identities and preferences.
15. Discussion of dissemination	Dissemination strategies are limited to the presentation of data in the article.	Dissemination strategies extending beyond the article are discussed.	Dissemination strategies are strategically selected to maximize sharing of knowledge (e.g., the data were shared with practitioners, policymakers and nondominant families) with clear practical benefits to participants' communities writ large.

258   Aydin Bal and Audrey A. Trainor

with relation to the problem formulation phase. Research in the field of disability studies in education emerged in the past two decades and has opened the door to the understanding of factors regarding education and dis/ability. Scholars in disability studies have provided critical examinations of social and historical constructions of dis/ability through the analyses of historicity and positionality (Connor and Ferri 2013; for an extensive review of disability studies in education, see Danforth and Gabel 2007). Disability studies scholars suggest that disability is a social and political construct that becomes meaningful and consequential in the specific cultural contexts. They reject the idea that disability is a problem within the person that must be fixed (Ferri and Connor 2005). Therefore, special education intervention research has remained distinct from this perspective. Ontological and epistemological differences have continued to act as a gulf between the mainstream special education and disability studies (Barnes and Sheldon 2007).

People with disabilities are experts in their experiences and should be instrumental in research and practice (Connor 2009). As will become clear in the ensuing discussion of the rubric, insider perspectives are central to CRR. Insiders in this conceptualization go beyond a single identity of either participants or researchers, speak to intersectionality, and are further differentiated from disability studies' conceptualizations by sharing importance with the key considerations in the CRR rubric, sociocultural theorists' formulation of the cultural activity as the unit of analysis.

Theorizing inquiry requires researchers to formulate questions and hypotheses and to design experimental studies, inseparable from their views and values about inquiry, dominant practices in their fields, and available funding opportunities and priorities (Arzubiaga et al. 2008). If experimental designs are considered a gold standard and among policymakers and funding agencies, scholars may be inclined to formulate research questions prior to preliminarily examining the complexity of the problem from multiple perspectives as experienced by local stakeholders that include surveying gaps in knowledge (Sandler and Apple 2010). This sequence violates the tenet that scientific inquiry and its design be question driven (Phillips 2006).

Theorizing content is embedded with the privileged ideologies and practices from the researchers' fields. Therefore, constructs under examination may reflect a limited, researcher-centric operationalization of a process that lacks ecological validity (Bernal et al. 1995). To avoid these potential pitfalls at the stage of conceptualization of constructs, research methodologies, and their underlying theories, CRR positions rigorous research as that which attends to the experiences, cultural practices, and ideologies of researchers and participants as members of cultural communities and institutions (Ashing-Giwa 2005).

Item 1: Foundational Constructs of the Study

Although literature reviews typically discuss the constructs of interest, a score of 2 on this rubric item requires researchers to include in this discussion multiple perspectives of and competing ideas about the construct under investigation

A Rubric for Paradigm Expansion 259

(e.g., LD, literacy, social skills, or at-risk behaviors). Lesser scores reflect a lack of such discussion or treatment of the constructs of interest as universal and ahistorical. Such discussion is an acknowledgement that researchers' conceptualizations are themselves the result of specific contexts that include the rules and traditions of academia (Bernal et al. 1995). To illustrate, the identification of LD is historically based on social constructs of intellectual capacity and achievement measured by artifacts such as aptitude and achievement tests and, more recently, on the conceptualization of how students respond to academic instruction and tiered interventions available in their local schools (Trainor 2010). Although all research about LD does not need to restate the trajectory of the label, acknowledgement of the lack of consensus and ongoing issues of epidemiology and identification accuracy is pertinent to LD research, especially in studies that include samples of youth from nondominant backgrounds (National Research Council 2002a). Research warranting a score of 2 on this item would include studies that both acknowledge that a disability label is marked by disagreements and also provide an operationalized definition contextualized by the original research being presented.

Item 2: Relevancy of the Research Problem

Here, relevancy of the research problem extends beyond researchers' interests to include relevancy to participants' lives and interests. This item is parallel to culturally responsive practices that require both the validation of a diversity of life experiences and goals and the understanding of prejudice, institutionalized ableism, racism, and the historical marginalization of nondominant communities that affect researchers' and participants' actions in abstruse ways (Gopaul-McNicol 1998; Scheurich and Young 1997; Tyson 1998). An optimal score of 2, therefore, exceeds merely situating the description of the problem in the context of a scientific field through the presentation of extant findings. A score of 2 is an indication that the relevancy of the research problem addresses both the researcher's line of inquiry and the participants' and local communities' interests, strengths, and needs. Culturally responsive researchers ascertain the ways in which experimental study and the results are potentially of benefit to a research field and to participating communities.

Item 3: Critical and Comprehensive Review of the Relevant Literature

Such a review includes extant literature documenting the researchers' complex understandings of the constructs of interest, including multiple and competing perspectives representative of the literature. Researchers should use a critical lens and pose questions that expose what is not known relevant to nondominant communities, as well as the theories and methodologies developed in those communities (Graham 1992; Scheurich 1997; Tillman 2002). Critical examination of a body of inquiry is recognized as an essential process for effective education researchers using experimental design and quantitative analysis (Floden 2009) and as an

260　*Aydin Bal and Audrey A. Trainor*

essential skill in the study of problems with diversity and equity foci (Castagno and Brayboy 2008).

A score of 2 on Item 3, therefore, is reserved for those reviews that not only include sufficient depth on the construct of interest but also include the scope of research that addresses points of controversy and dissent framed by the review. For example, if a review of postsecondary transition research framing an experimental study on parent involvement characterizes parents of nondominant youth with disabilities as having low expectations, an effective critical review would also include a synthesis of literature that addresses the historical exclusion of nondominant parents in postsecondary transition decision-making processes and how those parents have been represented over decades of research through a deficit-oriented lens asserting that parents' lack of resources limits their children's success (Trainor and Bal 2014). Moreover, a comprehensive review scoring a 2 on this rubric is illustrated by exhaustive and critical literature reviews that include trends and outlier results, particularly when the construct of interest is linked with learning and development of nondominant youth (Castagno and Brayboy 2008; Ladson-Billings and Tate 2006).

Item 4: Justification of the Theoretical Framework

Results of an experimental intervention study confirm the quantitative relationships between a set of variables in a given study. Theoretical frameworks guide researchers' interpretations of the connection and meaning of the findings in the real world (Bonilla-Silva and Zuberi 2008). The explicit identification of underlying theories in the mainstream special education (e.g., behaviorism or cognitive-behaviorism), medical-based definition of disability, and discussions of the possibilities and constraints of those theoretical frameworks have been neglected (Brantlinger 1997). In the absence of such reflexivity, certain theoretical assumptions and constructs are treated as objective: The naturalized theoretical positions such as ableism, individualism, and universalism undergird many studies examining disproportionate representation of nondominant students in special education (Harry and Klingner 2006). To illustrate, in the disproportionality literature, race has been used as a proxy indicator of culture that determines individuals' actions, perceptions, and performances. The conceptualization of race and disability as objective, unchangeable individual attributes is a theoretical assumption. As such, researchers commonly present their findings on the effect of race, such as a disproportionate representation of African American students in office discipline referrals, and interpret the findings causally.

The biological conceptualization of race is informed by ableism and eugenics and has been challenged by critical special education scholars, largely from nondominant communities, as it legitimized racial stratification and the racialization of deviance (Artiles 2011; Harry and Klingner 2006). Similarly, disability studies scholars have challenged singular, biological conceptualizations of disability and forwarded the culturally mediated and socially constructed notion of disability (Ferri and Connor 2005; Florian 2007; Snyder and Mitchell 2010).

A Rubric for Paradigm Expansion   261

In education research, critical theorists conceptualize race as an ever-evolving relational construct that has a central role in the formation of individual selves and national identity in the United States: Race relationships should be "articulated in the specificities of their historical conditions. Race may shift and morph in its relative significance to racialized groups, but its centrality in U.S. society is absolute insofar it represents a central axis of self and social understanding" (Leonardo 2009: 129). Thus, discussion and justification of the theoretical framework, as it relates to material and ideological contexts of the study, the unit of analysis, and the constructs under examination, are warranted. A score of 2 indicates that the underlying theoretical framework is revealed and comprehensively discussed regarding its affordances and constraints.

Design and Logic

Although the unit of analysis is centrally important to decisions made at each stage of research, it is an overarching consideration during study design. Researchers use the unit of analysis as the point of reference when selecting who will be included as participants and identifying appropriate methods for answering the research questions. Contextual factors such as those that influence relationships among and between researchers and participants (Fine et al. 2003; Merriam et al.2001) have the potential to shape the research landscape and the logic used in research design. Ashing-Giwa (2005) cited the maltreatment of African American men in the Tuskegee syphilis experiment, a sociohistorical factor that not only damaged the lives of individual participants but also eroded trust between researchers and the African American community in difficult-to-measure ways. Legislation regulating research may address humane treatment and begin to restore working relationships; however, the distal effects of prior discriminatory practices are difficult to gauge. Members of some groups may have greater reservations about participating in research. Similarly, researchers may anticipate mistrust and avoid attempts to include nondominant communities.

From inception and design, the CRR rubric attempts to minimize and address contradictions associated with contextual factors by expanding the purpose of research and thus the research questions themselves, beyond the concerns of the researchers, their field, and the private and governmental agencies they often serve. Researchers employing CRR promote both the interests of members of the investigatory community and members of the participating communities. To attain this goal, a culturally responsive intervention study ideally includes members of participant communities at all stages of research (e.g., people with dis- abilities; Arzubiaga et al. 2008; Tillman 2002). When this is not possible, engaging in CRR requires formal and informal efforts to gain understanding of the range of participant perspectives and to acknowledge existing gaps (Wells, Merritt and Briggs 2009). The items in this section are framed as *descriptions* to accommodate flexibility in evaluation. We are aware that researchers often make pragmatic decisions during the study. Therefore, the rubric items in this section highlight the importance of providing details about the logic of the design so that

262   *Aydin Bal and Audrey A. Trainor*

consumers of research can evaluate the extent to which the work represents cultural responsiveness.

Item 5: Description of the Participants

Experimental methodology demands that researchers define their sample, thoroughly providing information about participants' sociodemographic backgrounds such as disability identification, race, gender, age, immigration status, education, and income as minimally required for publication (AERA 2006; APA 1990, 2005). However, in the special education literature, experimental studies include limited information about the participants, reporting only gender and/or disability identification of the participants (Swanson and Hoskyn 1998; Trainor and Bal 2014). In this rubric, we ask intervention researchers to provide a detailed account of participants' sociodemographic characteristics and histories. We also ask researchers to go beyond this surface, providing the institutional and social contexts within which the participants learn and work. For instance, living in a Southwestern border state with institutionalized racism and anti-immigrant attitudes is an important factor for refugee students of color whose performances are the foci of an intervention (Bal and Arzubiaga 2014).

Sociodemographic descriptors such as race and disability status, however, have multiple uses. Some researchers intend to use demographic information as fixed individual traits that can function as a control variable when comparing data across groups (James 2008). An important distinction is that studies of race and disability as constructed variables indicative of dynamic and situated processes help explain social phenomena. Language used in experimental studies describing sociodemographic characteristics also constitutes frames of reference related to the study of the construct of interest. Racial terminology, for example, is instantiated with power vis-à-vis historical and spatial variation, muddling their meanings at best, or, at worst, are inaccurate (Fisher et al. 2002; James 2008).

Description of participants reveals researchers' sampling methods. In relation to experimental research designs, in particular, either the samples have not been described in such a way that facilitates replication, or the samples themselves are not representative of the cultural and linguistic diversity of U.S. classrooms (Padilla 2004). Calls for the inclusion of diverse groups of participants abound (Fisher et al. 2002; Graham 1992; Whiting et al. 2008). Furthermore, researchers' conceptualizations of cultural diversity and homogeneity are critical to both the description of participants and to the study's sampling design. Including diverse groups, such as not only people who share a common experience (e.g., having been identified with an LD) but also those who hail from a range of backgrounds (e.g., being at various points on a continuum of bilingualism), is possible. Another conceptualization of *diversity*, albeit common but less straightforward in our view, is that the term means people not included in the dominant group. We align Item 5 to definitions of diversity allowing for consideration of within-group diversity that is centrally important to CRR practices (Gelman 2004). Identifying sociodemographic characteristics in relation to the constructs of interest is necessary but deceptively simplistic. A score of 2 is meant to reflect the complexities inherent in discussions of participant characteristics such as the intersection of two variables (e.g., disability identification and race) and the institutional dimensions that contribute to the context of the research setting (McDermott et al. 2006).

Item 6: Description of the Researchers and Interventionists

This rubric item acknowledges that participants are not alone in enacting identities relative to experiencing learning, development, and research. The same issues that surface in the description of participants are apparent in the description of researchers and interventionists. Researchers and interventionists also embody and are embodied by professional and other historical and interpersonal factors, including prejudices or selective attention. Extant work in the field of psychology has demonstrated the importance of interventionists' background and efficacy of psychotherapy (Fisher et al. 2002; Pope-Davis et al. 2001). Additionally, prior rubrics for quality indicators of special education experimental research include an item for the provision of information about the interventionists and the researchers themselves (e.g., training in the intervention and experience with participating communities) as a key quality indictor (Chard et al. 2009). This has a critical importance for intervention studies in terms of replication and fidelity of implementation. Hence, on Item 6, scoring a 2 requires that the same components present in Item 5 be discussed in similar depth with the researchers as the key referents.

Item 7: Description of the Sampling Procedures

Intervention researchers should include nondominant youth as participants if the intervention may be used with that population. When participants from nondominant backgrounds, such as students identified as English language learners, are omitted or included in insufficient numbers, narrow findings may be interpreted too broadly and generalized inadequately (Graham 1992; Klingner et al. 2007). Furthermore, replication, one affordance of randomized experiments, cannot be widely implemented to test hypotheses with specific subgroups (Padilla 2004). Additionally, sampling diverse populations in sufficient numbers for generalization has been posited as one way to augment the implementation experimental designs to align with cultural responsiveness (Calamaro 2008).

In CRR, sampling necessarily includes the establishment of personal relationships within the communities where the participants learn, live, and go to school (APA 2003; Banks et al. 2007; Whiting et al. 2008). Initial efforts to build trust by increasing presence in research settings and including members of diverse communities on the research team are two strategies (Ashing-Giwa 2005). The intervention researchers should specifically attempt to include people with disabilities into the project as researchers, consultants, and advisory board members. This will challenge the exclusionary practices in research and maintain participatory social justice (Bal 2012). The participatory social justice perspective requires all

264   Aydin Bal and Audrey A. Trainor

local stakeholders (e.g., family members and students), specifically those who are historically marginalized, to be included in decision-making activities (Bal 2012). A score of 2 incorporates researchers' documentation of congruency between recruitment methods, participants' experiences, and study design. Researchers need to increase their ability and tolerance for spending adequate time in the field among the participating communities prior to intervention and transparently documenting limitations that lacking such contact may impose on the design.

Item 8: Description of the Research Setting

A fundamental premise of CRR is that activities related to the construct of interest are, as is the research itself, an object of inquiry. The description of setting (e.g., social and institutional contexts of the experiments), therefore, must be sufficiently comprehensive, providing information about the activity setting and the extent to which the research mediated that setting. To illustrate, there are several studies that have shown that lack of material and financial resources in schools is a better predictor of students' academic achievement problems than student-level factors such as family income or early phonemic awareness (Klingner et al. 2007). A score of 2 incorporates in-depth descriptions of contextual factors, their interactions, and the ways in which the research setting is representative of participants' everyday contexts (Pope-Davis et al. 2001).

Sources of Evidence

Building participants' trust and responsiveness through researchers' consideration of the strengths, needs, interests, and experiences of a diverse population requires transparency not only in sampling but also in intervention design and data collection (Wells et al. 2009). Of particular concern is the design of instruments and other intervention components that yield "reliable, valid, and culturally consonant" scores (Ashing-Giwa 2005: 134). This outcome entails paying careful attention to intervention components' relevancy, measurement techniques, and language (Bernal et al. 1995; Padilla 2004). Intervention research is implicitly and explicitly connected to the researchers' aim to understand outcomes. In CRR, researchers consider the community-level outcomes, in addition to individual-level outcomes, expanding the unit of analysis (Chouinard and Cousins 2007). These considerations may be conceptualized as contextual – that is, they include the analysis of the locale in which the intervention is likely to be implemented, beyond the implementation of research as well as the larger societal factors (Pope- Davis et al. 2001).

Item 9: Description of the Data Collection Activities

Measurement and observational tools and practices mediate data collection. Such tools and activities are typically planned for uses that meet the interests, strengths, and experiences of researchers. Generating data in alignment with CRR requires researchers to use diverse methods of data collection that reflect participants' real-life experiences and contexts (APA 2003; Chouinard and Cousins 2007; Whiting et al. 2008). In CRR, data collection should be informed by the research literature on culturally relevant pedagogies. This body of evidence, over time, demonstrated that improved classroom performance follows lessons and tasks that reflect multiple ways of learning, knowing, and performing (García and Guerra 2004; Lee and Slaughter-Defoe 2004). A score of 2 on the CRR rubric is reserved for studies employing data collection activities and instruments that are transparent about efforts to meet participants' everyday practices and discuss the interactions between researchers, interventionists, and participants.

Item 10: Ecology of the Intervention

We developed this rubric item following current conceptualizations of ecological validity in experimental research studies, specifically in developmental psychology and neuropsychology (Bronfenbrenner 1979; Spooner and Pachana 2006). Experimental conditions should be congruent with participants' perceptions and real-life situations outside of the experimental conditions. Furthermore, interpretive consistency between the data and participants' understandings of conditions should be maintained. Studies receiving a score of 2 reflect alignment between the intervention and participants' experiences and/or preferences in non-research contexts (i.e., real life). The integrity of the participants' real life and perspectives is balanced with the experimental design (Cole et al. 1997).

Item 11: Intervention Design

Consideration for honing procedures, measurements, and interventions that are specific to the shared goals and needs of a community is prioritized (Banks et al. 2007; Coard, Wallace, Stevenson, and Brotman 2004; Ladson-Billings 1995). As the rubric score of 2 indicates, optimal intervention design accounts for diversity within groups, ensuring that the design is not based on stereotypes or static conceptualizations of participants' identities and experiences. Furthermore, a score of 2 encompasses tools for critique so that researchers and participants are in positions to interrogate and challenge inequity conceptualized as culturally relevant pedagogy by Ladson-Billings (1995). These aspects of the highest evaluation mark are parallel to extant research in culturally responsive practices in health sciences, sometimes referred to as elements of empowerment among people with medical problems (e.g., Garrett, Dickson, Young, Whelan, and Forero 2008; Jackson 2009).

Measurement Process

Measurement tools and process are culturally mediated: "Culture-free tests cannot be constructed because tests are inevitably cultural devices" (Solano-Flores and Trumbull 2003: 7). Despite tacit agreement among researchers and practitioners that measurements must be congruent with students' preferences and individual and group experiences (e.g., racial discrimination), appropriate use of culturally

266   *Aydin Bal and Audrey A. Trainor*

responsive tools continues to be problematic in the identification of disability, preferences, strengths, and needs for youth from historically marginalized groups as situated in specific local context (Figueroa and Newsome 2006; Solano-Flores 2008). Thus, the selection of culturally responsive measurement tools and methods continues to be an explicitly stated tenet and criterion for CRR (AERA 2006; APA 2003, 2005; Frierson et al. 2010).

Item 12: Assessment of Intervention Efficacy

Experimental research often employs instruments that purport to measure changes in participants' aptitude and performance, and yet these data collection instruments are perhaps among the most fervently critiqued tools. In psychology, the use of norm-referenced instruments illustrative of specific aspects of reliability and validity has been prioritized in research (APA 2003; Fisher et al. 2002). Yet the underrepresentation of some samples of participants continues to set the stage for legal challenges to the identification of linguistic and racial minority youth as disabled. In both research and practice, the use of inappropriate instruments continues to be documented (Figueroa and Newsome 2006; Wilkinson et al. 2006).

The significance of this criterion has long been acknowledged in experimental research. Assessment tools are cultural artifacts whose constructs, concepts, and language inherently exemplify material and ideal components of these artifacts (Frierson et al. 2010; Solano-Flores 2008). The ratings indicate the extent to which the detailed description of assessments and measurements explicated validity, reliability, and cultural congruence with participants. When documentation of the validity and reliability of the tools includes the range of populations in the study's sample, or when the lack of such instrumentation constitutes an acknowledged limitation, a score of 2 is warranted.

Analysis and Interpretation

Making sense of data and drawing conclusions about the implications of the findings, congruent with the tenets of CRR, entails avoiding the reification of broad generalizations of people from historically marginalized groups and deficit-oriented conclusions that fail to expand the possibility for social change (APA 2003; Fisher et al. 2002). Several scholars have argued that education research, even when claiming to take aim at inequity, has failed to address enduring affronts to equal opportunities and outcomes (Apple 2013; Ladson-Billings 2006). The related conceptualizations of socially just research, science for the sake of the public good, and inquiry that aims for emancipation and transformation are embedded in, as well as embed, CRR. As such, analysis and interpretation must be contextually situated and must include multiple perspectives with their historical materiality (Justice for whom? What public? Whose interest?) and acknowledge and entertain issues of power in knowledge production (Leonardo 2009).

Item 13: Presentation of Findings

Klingner et al. (2007) stated, "Unfortunately, the results from control-group, randomized or quasi-experimental designs tend to be overgeneralized . . . without a close-enough look at variance and possible treatment X attribute interactions or school or teacher effects" (227). Combined with the inherited belief about universality of scientific truth, this tendency, Klingner et al. suggest, may result in misidentification of students from nondominant racial and linguistic backgrounds as "nonresponders" to evidence-based practices. The presentation of results in CRR adheres to both the tenets of experimental designs by avoiding generalizations where they are not warranted based on the failure to meet design criteria expressed in the CRR rubric (e.g., acknowledgement that insufficient participation by linguistic minority students makes the results not generalizable to this group). A score of 2 indicates that intersecting sociodemographic variables and the contextual variables are presented in close proximity to one another, so that they can be considered in tandem and so that results can be disaggregated based on sociodemographic characteristics of the participants in both experiment and control groups.

Item 14: Analysis and Interpretation

In CRR, the conceptualization of culture throughout the analysis and interpretation of data must be transparent and explicit. We anchored this criterion to arguments for the expansion and importance of culture as pertains to teaching and learning (Erickson 2009; Ford, Grantham and Whiting 2008; Gutiérrez and Rogoff 2003) and professional guidelines for research (AERA 2006; APA 2003). Therefore, the role of culture as contextual and activity oriented is interrogated as a method of identifying the relevant individual, institutional, and interpersonal factors. A score of 2 on this criterion indicates that the researchers anchor culture to an instrumental theoretical frame that expands the potential for this analysis, tackling the intersectionality of sociodemographic factors (e.g., the interactions of race, class, and disability among Latino immigrant communities) and the interpersonal contexts of research and practice Arzubiaga et al 2008. To the greatest extent possible, then, analysis and interpretation are situated in their specific social, historical, and spatial contexts (Gutiérrez and Rogoff 2003; Soja 2010).

Dissemination

Dissemination of research should translate into its local uses and practical applications (National Center for the Dissemination of Disability Research 1999). For researchers, one typical use is to augment or sharpen the precision and reach of policy and to support organizational change. Attention to use in CRR requires that researchers understand the contexts in which people live, work, and learn so that research implications for the broader society address local issues (APA

268   *Aydin Bal and Audrey A. Trainor*

2003; Banks et al. 2007). As schools are becoming more diverse, dissemination of research findings must include consideration of this issue.

Item 15: Discussion of Dissemination

In CRR, dissemination of implications for practice and further research should be contextually framed and any limitations in generalizability need to be acknowledged. In addition to publishing results in scholarly journals, presenting results to participants' communities via multiple media, using accessible language (e.g., in braille or in participating community's language), and focusing on the practical implications are essential (APA 2003; Ashing-Giwa 2005). A score of 2 is assigned to studies when dissemination strategies are strategically selected to maximize knowledge sharing with clear, practical benefits to participants' immediate communities writ large.

Discussion

In the present chapter, we explore the cultural responsiveness of experimental intervention research and its significant implications, specifically for working with nondominant youth experiencing academic and behavioral difficulties in schools. Conducting intervention research employing methodologies that are culturally responsive is a priority posited by scholars concerned with the enduring problems of inequity in special education identification and service delivery such as disproportionate representation of nondominant students (e.g., Artiles et al. 2010; Haager et al. 2007; Vincent et al. 2011). At the same time, special education scholars have published several seminal works operationalizing rigor in research methodologies, tethering ongoing problems to a lack of a strong empirical knowledge base (Brantlinger et al. 2005; Chard et al. 2009; Gersten et al. 2005; Lane et al. 2009; Odom et al. 2005). Operationalizing CRR, however, has received less attention than the operationalization of rigor in experimental research, often conceptualized as culture free or largely absent consideration of race, class, and gender.

The development of this rubric addresses the knowledge gap resulting from definitions of rigor operationalized without attention to cultural practices embedded in and resulting from scientific inquiry. The application of this rubric for the purposes of ascertaining the extent to which evidence is culturally responsive can be found in other publications (Trainor and Bal 2014). Our review of the literature did not evidence a rubric for the consideration of CRR. However, criteria for the concept of cultural responsiveness in research did surface. Our work was to identify these criteria and to bring them together in the form of a rubric, a commonly used format in our field, special education, for the purpose of examining rigor as pertains to operationalizing CRR.

We recognize some of our rubric items may challenge the dominant applications of positivistic and postpositivistic methodologies. We value experimental designs and have conducted intervention research. Hence, our aim is to contribute to the development of culture-conscious experimental research by paying closer

A *Rubric for Paradigm Expansion* 269

attention to contextual factors and interaction effects producing ecologically valid and sustainable interventions that address complex issues. We support CRR, even if doing so necessitates decisions in design, implementation, and dissemination that may not strictly adhere to historically privileged approaches to experimental research. Our work essentially blends notions of responsivity and reflexivity, a construct typically associated with qualitative methods, into experimental research. This may require researchers to be open and critical and to report limitations more transparently than is currently common practice. This rubric may make an important contribution through the expansion of identified criteria for rigor and broader notions of what counts as evidence.

We also acknowledge that the dominant conceptual framework of special education intervention research may presuppose a deficit in need of fixing, and that this position is ableist (Campbell 2008; Ferri and Connor 2005). The tension between intervening and efforts to normalize people with disabilities illustrates yet another dialogue about oppression and equity. Viewing disability through a scope focused on measurement and intervention is foundational to special education rarely interrogating and challenging the underpinnings of ableism as addressed by disability studies and critical special education scholars who examine historical and structural manifestations of dominant views of normalcy and dis/ability. Dialogue about how interventions may be beneficial for all has an important role in CRR, and we acknowledge that our rubric only opens the door to such a discussion for a paradigm expansion. Working within experimental design, this rubric highlights the importance of people with disabilities as decision makers and their situated knowledge in design, implementation, and dissemination. We invite intervention researchers and disability studies scholars to further this dialogue.

In agreement with Bonilla-Silva and Zuberi (2008), we think a research field is at its best when it is reflexive via a continuous critical examination of its tools and methods. Without such examination, perspectives, experiences, and goals of dominant social groups are accepted as natural, logical, and normal. The rubric is our continuing effort in responding to the call for strengthening rigor, applicability, and effectiveness of experimental intervention research in special education (Chard et al. 2009; Odom et al. 2005; Ortiz and Yates 2010) and for creating race-conscious, culturally responsive practices in education research in general (Erickson and Gutiérrez 2002; Ladson-Billings 2006; Leonardo 2009).

Science "is not about certainty, but about uncertainty" (Erickson and Gutiérrez 2002: 22). Our hope is that the rubric as a living artifact will be negotiated and adapted by practitioners in and through the cultural activity of education research that is complex, ever-shifting, and ambiguous in nature. One goal of the CRR rubric is to increase our potential as researchers to address the disparities in access, outcome, and opportunity. Another goal is to address dialectical tensions within education research because the dominant research paradigm for knowledge production has not been able to adequately address and perhaps even reproduce the status quo, inadvertently increasing the disparities.

The use of the CRR rubric can facilitate praxis, a continuous critical reflection and action, to challenge naturalized and thus taken-for-granted practices

270 *Aydin Bal and Audrey A. Trainor*

and ideologies of knowledge production and to design culturally responsive intervention studies. Our hope is that this rubric will be instrumental in the necessary paradigm expansion in special education to understand the cultural nature of learning and development and constructs such as race, class, gender, and disability. Doing so will provide additional ways to explore and address the historical exclusion and marginalization of nondominant communities in knowledge production activities and the widening and deepening inequalities.

Note

The authors thank Alfredo J. Artiles, Alba A. Ortiz, Sylvia Linan-Thompson, Jim Wollack, and Sonya Sedivy for their feedback on the initial design of the rubric: *Culturally Responsive Research Rubric.*

References

Acker, S., Webber, M., and Smyth, E. (2012). Tenure troubles and equity matters in Canadian academe. *British Journal of Sociology of Education*, 33, 743–761. DOI: 10.1080/01425692.2012.674784

Alex-Assensoh, Y. (2003). Race in the academy. *Journal of Black Studies*, 34, 5–11. DOI: 10.1177/0021934703256058

American Educational Research Association (2006). Standards for reporting on empirical social science research in AERA publications. *Educational Researcher*, 35(6), 33–40. DOI: 10.3102/0013189X035006033

American Psychiatric Association (2013). *Diagnostic and statistical manual of mental disorders*, 5th edn. Washington, DC: Author.

American Psychological Association (1990). *Guidelines for providers of psychological services to ethnic, linguistic, and culturally diverse populations.* Washington, DC: Author.

American Psychological Association (2003). Guidelines on multicultural education, training, research, practice, and organizational change for psychologists. *American Psychologist*, 58, 377–402. DOI: 10.1037/0003-066X.58.5.377

American Psychological Association (2005). *APA guidelines for providers of psychological services to ethnic, linguistic, and culturally diverse populations.* Washington, DC: Author.

Anyon, J. (2005). *Radical possibilities: Public policy, urban education, and a new social movement.* New York, NY: Routledge.

Apple, M.W. (2013). *Can education change society?* New York, NY: Routledge.

Artiles, A.J. (2011). Toward an interdisciplinary understanding of educational equity and difference. *Educational Researcher*, 40, 431–445. DOI: 10.3102/0013189X11429391

Artiles, A.J., Kozleski, E., Trent, S., Osher, D., and Ortiz, A. (2010). Justifying and explaining disproportionality, 1968–2008. *Exceptional Children*, 76, 279–299. DOI: 10.1177/001440291007600303

Artiles, A.J., Trent, S., and Kuan, L.-A. (1997). Learning disabilities empirical research on ethnic minority students. *Learning Disabilities Research & Practice*, 12, 82–91.

Arzubiaga, A.E., Artiles, A.J., King, K., and Harris-Murri, N. (2008). Beyond research on cultural minorities. *Exceptional Children*, 74, 309–327. DOI: 10.1177/0731948711417552

Ashing-Giwa, K. T. (2005). Can a culturally responsive model for research design bring us closer to addressing participation disparities? *Ethnicity & Disease*, 15, 130–137.

A Rubric for Paradigm Expansion 271

Baker, B. (2002). The hunt for disability. *Teacher College Records*, 104, 663–703. DOI: 10.1111/1467-9620.00175

Bal, A. (2011a, July). *Cultural psychology: Understanding mind in culture in a diverse world.* Pre-congress workshop conducted at the annual meeting of European Congress of Psychology, Istanbul, Turkey.

Bal, A. (2011b). *Culturally responsive school-wide positive behavioral interventions and supports framework.* Madison: Wisconsin Department of Public Instruction.

Bal, A. (2012). Participatory social justice for all. In L. G. Denti and P. A. Whang (eds.), *Rattling chains: Exploring social justice in education* (pp. 99–110). Boston, MA: Sense.

Bal, A., and Arzubiaga, A. (2014). Ahıska refugee students' configuration of resettlement and academic success in U.S. schools. *Urban Education*, 49, 635–665. DOI:10.1177/0042085913481363

Bal, A., Kozleski, E.B., Schrader, E.M., Rodriguez, E.M., and Pelton, S. (2014). Systemic transformation in school: Using Learning Lab to design culturally responsive school-wide positive behavioral supports. *Remedial and Special Education*, 35, 327–339. DOI: 10.1177/0741932514536995

Banks, J.A., Au, K.H., Ball, A.F., Bell, P., Gordon, E.W., Gutiérrez, K.D., Zhou, M. (2007). *Learning in and out of school in diverse environments.* Seattle, WA: LIFE Center and SRI International.

Barclay, L. (2012). Natural deficiency or social oppression? The capabilities approach to justice for people with disabilities. *Journal of Moral Philosophy*, 9, 500–520. DOI: 10.1163/174552412X628823

Barnes, C., and Sheldon, A. (2007). "Emancipatory" disability research and special educational needs. In L. Florian (ed.), *The Sage handbook of special education* (pp. 231–245). London: Sage.

Bernal, G., Bonilla, J., and Bellido, C. (1995). Ecological validity and cultural sensitivity for outcome research. *Journal of Abnormal Child Psychology*, 23, 67–82. DOI: 10.1007/BF01447045

Bonilla-Silva, E., and Zuberi, T. (2008). *White logic, White methods: Race and methodology.* New York, NY: Rowman & Littlefield.

Bowker, G.C., and Star, S.L. (2000). *Sorting things out: Classification and its consequences.* Cambridge: MIT Press.

Brantlinger, E. (1997). Using ideology: Cases of nonrecognition of the politics of research and practice in special education. *Review of Educational Research*, 67, 425–460. DOI: 10.3102/00346543067004425

Brantlinger, E., Jimenez, R., Klingner, J., Pugach, M., and Richardson, V. (2005). Qualitative studies in special education. *Exceptional Children*, 71, 195–207. DOI: 10.1177/00144029 0507100205

Bronfenbrenner, U. (1979). *The ecology of human development.* Cambridge, MA: Harvard University Press.

Bronfenbrenner, U. (2005). *Making human beings human.* Thousand Oaks, CA: Sage.

Calamaro, C.J. (2008). Culture competence in research. *Journal of Pediatric Health Care*, 22, 329–332. DOI: 10.1016/j.pedhc.2008.05.007

Campbell, F.A.K. (2008). Exploring internalized ableism using critical race theory. *Disability & Society*, 23, 151–162. DOI: 10.1080/09687590701841190

Castagno, A.E., and Brayboy, B.M.J. (2008). Culturally responsive schooling for indigenous youth. *Review of Educational Research*, 78, 941–993. DOI: 10.3102/0034654308323036

Chard, D.J., Ketterlin-Geller, L.R., Baker, S.K., Doabler, C., and Apichatabutra, C. (2009). Repeated reading interventions for students with learning disabilities: Status of the evidence. *Exceptional Children*, 75, 263–281. DOI: 10.1177/001440290907500301

272 *Aydin Bal and Audrey A. Trainor*

Children's Defense Fund (1975). *School suspensions: Are they helping children?* Cambridge, MA: Washington Research Project.

Chouinard, J.A., and Cousins, J.B. (2007). Culturally competent evaluation for aboriginal communities. *Journal of Multidisciplinary Evaluation*, 4, 40–57.

Coard, S.I., Wallace, S.A., Stevenson, H.C., and Brotman, L.M. (2004). Towards culturally relevant preventive interventions. *Journal of Child and Family Studies*, 13, 277–293. DOI: 10.1023/B:JCFS.0000022035.07171.f8

Cole, E.R. (2009). Intersectionality and research in psychology. *American Psychologist*, 64, 170–180. DOI: 10.1037/a0014564

Cole, M. (1996). *Cultural psychology: A once and future discipline.* Cambridge, MA: Harvard University Press.

Cole, M., Hood, L., and McDermott, R.P. (1997). Concepts of ecological validity. In M. Cole, Y. Engeström and O. Vasquez (eds.), *Mind, culture, and activity* (pp. 49–56). New York, NY: Cambridge University Press.

Connor, D.J. (2009). *Urban narratives: Life at the intersections of learning disability, race, and social class.* New York, NY: Peter Lang.

Connor, D.J., and Ferri, B.A. (2013). Histrocizing dis/ability. In M. Wappett and K. Arndt (eds.), *Foundations of disability studies* (pp. 29–67). New York, NY: Palgrave Macmillan.

Covarrubias, A. (2011). Quantitative intersectionality: A critical race analysis of the Chicana/o educational pipeline. *Journal of Latinos and Education*, 10, 86–105. DOI: 10.1080/15348431.2011.556519

Craig, S., Hull, K., Haggart, A.G., and Perez-Selles, M. (2000). Promoting cultural competence. *TEACHING Exceptional Children*, 32, 6–12. DOI: 10.1177/004005990003200302

Crenshaw, K. (1989). Demarginalizing the intersection of race and sex. *University of Chicago Legal Forum*, 139–167.

Danforth, S., and Gabel, S. (2007). *Vital questions facing disability studies in education.* New York, NY: Peter Lang.

Darling-Hammond, L. (2010). *The flat world and education: How America's commitment to equity will determine our future.* New York, NY: Teachers College Press.

DeCuir, J.T., and Dixson, A.D. (2004). So when it comes out, they aren't that surprised that it is there. *Educational Researcher*, 33(5), 26–31. DOI: 10.3102/00131 89X033005026

Diggs, G.A., Garrison-Wade, D.F., Estrada, D., and Galindo, R. (2009). Smiling faces and colored spaces: The experiences of faculty of color pursuing tenure in the academy. *Urban Review*, 41, 312–333. DOI: 10.1007/s11256–008–0113-y

Engeström, Y. (2008). *From teams to knots: Activity-theoretical studies of collaboration and learning at work.* New York, NY: Cambridge University Press.

Engeström, Y. (2011). From design experiments to formative interventions. *Theory & Psychology*, 21, 598–628. DOI: 10.1177/0959354311419252

Engeström, Y., and Miettinen, R. (1999). Introduction. In Y. Engeström, R. Miettinen and R.-L. Punamäki (eds.), *Perspectives on activity theory* (pp. 1–16). New York, NY: Cambridge University Press.

Erickson, F. (2009). Culture in society and in educational practices. In J. Banks and C. A.M. Banks (eds.), *Multicultural education*, 7th edn (pp. 33–58). Hoboken, NJ: Wiley.

Erickson, F., and Gutiérrez, K. (2002). Comment: Culture, rigor, and science in educational research. *Educational Researcher*, 31(8), 21–24. DOI: 10.3102/00131 89X031008021

Fenelon, J. (2003). Race, research, and tenure. *Journal of Black Studies*, 34, 87–100. DOI: 10.1177/0021934703253661

Ferri, B.A., and Connor, D.J. (2005). Tools of exclusion: Race, disability, and (re) segregated education. *Teachers College Record*, 107, 453–474. DOI: 10.1111/j.1467–9620.2005.00483.x

A Rubric for Paradigm Expansion   273

Figueroa, R.A., and Newsome, P. (2006). The diagnosis of LD in English learners. *Journal of Learning Disabilities*, 39, 206–214. DOI:10.1177/00222194060390030201

Fine, M., Weis, L., Weseen, S., and Wong, L. (2003). For whom? Qualitative research, representations, and social responsibilities. In N. Denzin and Y. Lincoln (eds.), *Handbook of qualitative research* (pp. 107–131). Thousand Oaks, CA: Sage.

Fisher, C.B., Hoagwood, K., Boyce, C., Duster, T., Frank, D. A., Grisso, T., . . . Zayas, L.H. (2002). Research ethics for mental health science involving ethnic minority children and youths. *American Psychologist*, 57, 1024–1040. DOI: 10.1037/0003-066X.57.12.1024

Floden, R.E. (2009). Empirical research without certainty. *Educational Theory*, 59, 485–498. DOI: 10.1111/j.1741-5446.2009.00332.x

Florian, L. (2007). *The Sage handbook of special education*. London, England: Sage.

Ford, D.Y., Grantham, T.C., and Whiting, G.W. (2008). Culturally and linguistically diverse students in gifted education. *Exceptional Children*, 74, 289–306. DOI: 10.1177/0014402 90807400302

Frierson, H., Hood, S., Hughes, G., and Thomas, V. (2010). A guide to conducting culturally responsive evaluation. In J. Frechtling (ed.), *The 2010 user-friendly handbook for project evaluation* (pp. 75–96). Arlington, VA: National Science Foundation.

Gallego, M., Cole, M., and the Laboratory of Comparative Human Cognition. (2001). Classroom cultures and cultures in the classroom. In V. Richardson (ed.), *The handbook of research on teaching*, 4th edn (pp. 951–997). Washington, DC: AERA.

García, S.B., and Guerra, P.L. (2004). Deconstructing deficit thinking. *Education and Urban Society*, 36, 150–168. DOI: 10.1177/0013124503261322

García, S.B., and Ortiz, A.A. (2008). A framework for culturally and linguistically responsive design of response-to-intervention models. *Multiple Voices for Ethnically Diverse Exceptional Learners*, 11, 24–41.

García, S.B., Ortiz, A.A., and Sorrells, A.M. (2012). Intersectionality as a framework for research and practice in special education. *Multiple Voices*, 13, 1–3.

Garrett, P., Dickson, H., Young, L., Whelan, A., and Forero, R. (2008). What do non-English-speaking patients value in acute care? *Ethnicity & Health*, 13, 479–496. DOI: 10.1080/13557850802035236

Gelman, C. (2004). Empirically-based principles for culturally competent practice with Latinos. *Journal of Ethnic & Cultural Diversity in Social Work*, 13, 83–108. DOI: 10.1300/J051v13n01_05

Gersten, R., Fuchs, L.S., Compton, D., Coyne, M., Greenwood, C., and Innocenti, M.S. (2005). Quality indicators for group experimental and quasi-experimental research in special education. *Exceptional Children*, 71, 149–164. DOI: 10.1177/001440290507100202

Gieryn, T.F. (1995). Boundaries of science. In S. Jasanoff, G.E. Makle, J.C. Petersen, and T. Pinch (eds.), *Handbook of science and technology studies* (pp. 393–443). Thousand Oaks, CA: Sage.

Giroux, H.A. (1983). Theories of reproduction and resistance in the new sociology of education: A critical analysis. *Harvard Educational Review*, 53, 257–293.

Goodley, D., and Runswick-Cole, K. (2010). Emancipating play: Dis/abled children, development and deconstruction. *Disability & Society*, 25, 499–512. DOI: 10.1080/0968759 1003755914

Gopaul-McNicol, S.A. (1998). A theoretical framework for training monolingual school psychologists to work with multilingual/multicultural children: An exploration of the major competencies. *Psychology in the Schools*, 34, 17–29. DOI: 10.1002/(SICI)1520-6807

Graham, S. (1992). Most of the subjects were White and middle class: Trends in published research on African Americans in selected APA journals, 1970–1989. *American Psychologist*, 47, 629–639. DOI: 10.1037/0003-066X.47.5.629

274   *Aydin Bal and Audrey A. Trainor*

Gutiérrez, K.D. (2006). White innocence: A framework and methodology for rethinking educational discourse. *International Journal of Learning*, 12, 1–11.

Gutiérrez, K.D., and Rogoff, B. (2003). Cultural ways of learning: Individual traits of repertoires of practice. *Educational Researcher*, 32(5), 19–25. DOI: 10.3102/0013189X032005019

Haager, D., Klingner, J.K., and Vaughn, S. (2007). *Evidence-based reading practices for response to intervention*. Baltimore, MD: Brookes.

Harry, B., and Klingner, J.K. (2006). *Why are so many minority students in special education?* New York, NY: Teachers College Press.

Horner, R.H., Carr, E.G., Halle, J., McGee, G., Odom, S., and Wolery, M. (2005). The use of single-subject research to identify evidence-based practice in special education. *Exceptional Children*, 71, 165–179. DOI: 10.1177/001440290507100203

Jackson, K.F. (2009). Building cultural competence. *Children and Youth Services Review*, 31, 1192–1198. DOI: 10.1016/j.childyouth.2009.08.001

James, A. (2008). Making sense of race and racial classification. In T. Zuberi and E. Bonilla-Silva (eds.), *White logic, White methods: Racism and methodology* (pp. 31–45). Lanham, MD: Rowman & Littlefield.

Jayakumar, U., Howard, T.C., Allen, W.R., and Han, J.C. (2009). Racial privilege in the professoriate. *Journal of Higher Education*, 80, 538–563. DOI: 10.1353/jhe.0.0063

Kauffman, J.M., and Landrum, T.J. (2006). *Children and youth with emotional and behavioral disorders: A history of their education*. Austin, TX: ProEd.

Klingner, J.K., Artiles, A.J., Kozleski, E., Harry, B., Zion, S., Tate, W., . . . Riley, D. (2005). Addressing the disproportionate representation of culturally and linguistically diverse student in special education through culturally responsive educational systems. *Education Policy Analysis Archives*, 13(38). http://epaa.asu.edu/ojs/article/view/143

Klingner, J.K., Sorrells, A.M., and Barrera, M. (2007). Three-tiered models with culturally and linguistically diverse students. In D. Haager, J. Klingner, and S. Vaughn (eds.), *Evidence-based practices for response to intervention* (pp. 223–244). Baltimore, MD: Brookes.

Krezmien, M.P., Leone, P.E., and Achilles, G.M. (2006). Suspension, race, and disability. *Journal of Emotional and Behavioral Disorders*, 14, 217–226. DOI: 10.1177/10634266060 140040501

Kuhn, T.S. (1962). *The structure of scientific revolutions*. Chicago, IL: University of Chicago.

Ladson-Billings, G. (1995). Toward a theory of culturally relevant pedagogy. *American Educational Research Journal*, 32, 465–491. DOI: 10.3102/00028312032003465

Ladson-Billings, G. (2006). From the achievement gap to the education debt. *Educational Researcher*, 35(7), 3–12. DOI: 10.3102/0013189X035007003

Ladson-Billings, G., and Tate, W.F. (2006). *Education research in the public interest*. New York, NY: Teachers College Press.

Lagemann, E.C. (2000). *An elusive science: The troubling history of education research*. Chicago, IL: University of Chicago Press.

Lane, K., Kalberg, J., and Shepcaro, J. (2009). An examination of the evidence base for function-based interventions for students with emotional and/or behavioral disorders attending middle and high schools. *Exceptional Children*, 75, 321–340. DOI: 10.1177/001440290907500304

Lather, P. (2004). Scientific research in education: A critical perspective. *British Education Research Journal*, 30, 760–773. DOI: 10.1080/0141192042000279486

Lather, P. (2013). Methodology-21: What do we do in the afterward? *International Journal of Qualitative Studies in Education*, 26, 634–645. DOI: 10.1080/09518398.2013.788753

Latour, B. (1993). *We have never been modern*. Cambridge, MA: Harvard University Press.

Lee, C., and Slaughter-Defoe, D. (2004). Historical and sociocultural influences on African-American education. In J. Bank and C.A.M. Banks (eds.), *Handbook of research on multicultural education* (pp. 462–490). San Francisco, CA: Jossey-Bass.

Leonardo, Z. (2009). *Race, whiteness, and education.* New York, NY: Routledge.

Leonardo, Z. (2010). Ideology and its modes of existence: Toward an Althusserian theory of race and racism. In Z. Leonardo (ed.), *Handbook of cultural politics and education* (pp. 195–217). Rotterdam, Netherlands: Sense.

Losen, D.J., and Orfield, G. (2002). *Racial inequity in special education.* Cambridge, MA: Harvard Education Press.

McDermott, R., Goldman, S., and Varenne, H. (2006). The cultural work of learning disabilities. *Educational Researcher,* 35(6), 12–17. DOI: 10.3102/00131 89X035006012

McDermott, R., and Varenne, H. (1995). Culture as disability. *Anthropology & Education Quarterly,* 26, 324–348. DOI: 10.1525/aeq.1995.26.3.05x0936z

Merriam, S.B., Johnson-Bailey, J., Lee, M.-Y., Kee, Y., Ntseane, G., and Muhamad, M. (2001). Power and positionality. *International Journal of Lifelong Education,* 20, 405–416. DOI: 10.1080/02601370120490

Milner, H.R. (2007). Race, culture, and researcher positionality. *Educational Researcher,* 36, 388–400. DOI: 10.3102/0013189X07309471

Museus, S.D., and Griffin, K.A. (2011). Mapping the margins in higher education. *New Directions for Institutional Research,* 151, 5–13. DOI: 10.1002/ir.395

National Center for the Dissemination of Disability Research (1999). *Disability, diversity, and dissemination.* Austin, TX: Southwest Education Development Laboratory.

National Research Council (2002a). *Minority students in special and gifted education.* Washington, DC: National Academies Press.

National Research Council (2002b). *Scientific research in education.* Washington, DC: National Academies Press.

Odom, S.L., Brantlinger, E., Gersten, R., Horner, R.H., Thompson, B., and Harris, K. (2005). Research in special education: Scientific methods and evidence-based practices. *Exceptional Children,* 71, 137–148. DOI: 10.1177/001440290507100201

Office for Civil Rights. (2012). *A snapshot of opportunity gap data.* Retrieved from https://www2.ed.gov/about/offices/list/ocr/docs/crdc-2012-data-summary.pdf

Ortiz, A.A., and Yates, J.R. (2010). Enhancing scientifically-based research for culturally and linguistically diverse learners. *Multiple Voices,* 11, 13–23.

Padilla, A.M. (2004). Quantitative methods in multicultural education research. In J. A. Banks and C.A.M. Banks (eds.), *Handbook of research on multicultural education,* 2nd edn (pp. 127–145). Hoboken, NJ: Wiley.

Paris, D. (2012). Culturally sustaining pedagogy. *Educational Researcher,* 41, 93–97. DOI: 10.3102/0013189X12441244

Phillips, D.C. (2006). Muddying the waters: The many purposes of educational inquiry. In C.F. Conrad and R.C. Serlin (eds.), *The Sage handbook for research in education* (pp. 7–21). Thousand Oaks, CA: Sage.

Pope-Davis, D.B., Liu, W.M., Toporek, R.L., and Brittan-Powell, C.S. (2001). What's missing from multicultural competency research. *Cultural Diversity & Ethnic Minority Psychology,* 7, 121–138. DOI: 10.1037/1099–9809.7.2.121

Popkewitz, T.S. (1997). A changing terrain of knowledge and power: A social epistemology of educational research. *Educational Researcher,* 26, 18–29.

Rogoff, B. (2003). *The cultural nature of human development.* New York, NY: Oxford University Press.

Sandler, J., & Apple, M.W. (2010). A culture of evidence, a politics of objectivity. In Z. Leonardo (ed.), *Handbook of cultural politics and education* (pp. 325–340). Rotterdam, Netherlands: Sense.

Sannino, A., Daniels, H., and Gutiérrez, K. (2009). *Learning and expanding with activity theory*. New York, NY: Cambridge University Press.

Scheurich, J.J. (1997). *Research method in the postmodern*. London, UK: Falmer.

Scheurich, J.J., and Young, M.D. (1997). Coloring epistemologies: Are our research epistemologies racially biased? *Educational Researcher*, 22(4), 5–10. DOI: 10.3102/0013189 X026004004

Shaw, L.R., Chan, F., and McMahon, B.T. (2012). Intersectionality and disability harassment. *Rehabilitation Counseling Bulletin*, 55, 82–91. DOI: 10.1177/0034355211431167

Snyder, S.L., and Mitchell, D.T. (2010). *Cultural locations of disability*. Chicago, IL: University of Chicago Press.

Soja, E.W. (2010). *Seeking spatial justice*. Minneapolis: University of Minnesota Press.

Solano-Flores, G. (2008). Who is given tests in what language by whom, when, and where? *Educational Researcher*, 37, 189–199. DOI: 10.3102/0013189X08319569

Solano-Flores, G., & Trumbull, E. (2003). Examining language in context. *Educational Researcher*, 32(2), 3–13. DOI: 10.3102/0013189X032002003

Spooner, D.M., and Pachana, N.A. (2006). Ecological validity in neuropsychological assessment. *Archives of Clinical Neuropsychology*, 21, 327–337. DOI: 10.1016/j.acn.2006.04.004

Stanley, C.A. (2007). When counter narratives meet master narratives in the journal editorial review process. *Educational Researcher*, 36, 14–24. DOI: 10.3102/00131 89X06298008

Suárez-Orozco, C.E., and Suárez-Orozco, M.M. (2001). *Children of immigration*. Cambridge, MA: Harvard University Press.

Sue, S. (1999). Science, ethnicity, and bias. *American Psychologist*, 54, 1070–1077. DOI: 10.1037/0003-066X.54.12.1070

Sugai, G., O'Keeffe, B.V., and Fallon, L.M. (2012). A contextual consideration of culture and school-wide positive behavior support. *Journal of Positive Behavior Interventions*, 14, 197–208. DOI: 10.1177/1098300711426334

Swanson, H.L., and Hoskyn, M. (1998). Experimental intervention research on students with learning disabilities. *Review of Educational Research*, 68, 277–321. DOI: 10.3102/00346543068003277

Test, D.W., Fowler, C.H., Richter, S.M., White, J., Mazzotti, V., Walker, A.R., Kortering, L. (2009). Evidence-based practices in secondary transition. *Career Development for Exceptional Individuals*, 32, 115–128. DOI: 10.1177/ 0885728809336859

Tillman, L.C. (2002). Culturally sensitive research approaches: An African-American perspective. *Educational Researcher*, 31(9), 3–12. DOI: 10.3102/00131 89X031009003

Trainor, A.A. (2010). Reexamining the promise of parent participation in special education: An analysis of cultural and social capital. *Anthropology & Education Quarterly*, 41, 245–263. DOI: 10.1111/j.1548–1492.2010.01086.x

Trainor, A.A., and Bal, A. (2014). Development and preliminary analysis of a rubric for culturally responsive research. *Journal of Special Education*, 47, 203–216. DOI: 10.1177/0022466912436397

Turnbull, H.R. (2005). Individuals with disabilities education act reauthorization. *Remedial and Special Education*, 26, 320–326. DOI: 10.1177/07419325050260060201

Tyson, C.A. (1998). A response to "Coloring Epistemologies: Are Our Qualitative Research Epistemologies Racially Biased?" *Educational Researcher*, 27(9), 21–22. DOI: 10.3102/0013189X027009021

U.S. Department of Education and Office for Civil Rights. (2012). *Helping to ensure equal access to education*. Washington, DC: Author.

U.S. Department of Education and U.S. Office of Special Education and Rehabilitation Services (2011). *Thirtieth annual report to Congress on the implementation of the IDEA, 2008.* Washington, DC: Author.

van der Veer, R., and Valsiner, J. (1991). *Understanding Vygotsky.* Oxford, England: Blackwell.

Varenne, H., and McDermott, R. (1998). *Successful failure: The school America builds.* Boulder, CO: Westview.

Vincent, C., Randall, C., Cartledge, G., Tobin, T., and Swain-Bradway, J. (2011). Towards a conceptual integration of cultural responsiveness and school-wide positive behavior support. *Journal of Positive Behavior Interventions,* 13, 219–229. DOI:10.1177/1098300711399765

Vygotsky, L.S. (1976). *Mind in society: The development of higher psychological process.* Cambridge, MA: Harvard University Press.

Wagner, M., Newman, L., Cameto, R., and Levine, P. (2006). *The academic achievement and functional performance of youth with disabilities.* Menlo Park, CA: SRI International.

Wells, S.J., Merritt, L.M., and Briggs, H.E. (2009). Bias, racism and evidence-based practice: The case for more focused development of the child welfare evidence base. *Children and Youth Services Review,* 31, 1160–1171. DOI: 10.1016/j.childy-outh.2009.09.002

Whiting, G.W., Ford, D.Y., Grantham, T.C., and Moore, III, J.L. (2008). Multicultural issues: Considerations for conducting culturally responsive research in gifted education. *Gifted Child Today,* 31, 26–30. DOI: 10.4219/gct-2009–840

Wilkinson, C., Ortiz, A., Robertson, P., and Kushner, M. (2006). English language learners with reading-related LD. *Journal of Learning Disabilities,* 39, 129–141. DOI: 10.1177/00222194060390020201

Young, I.M. (1990). *Justice and the politics of difference.* Princeton, NJ: Princeton University Press.

Afterword

Beth Harry

My mother was white and my father was black. In the U.S., I would be considered 'bi-racial'. However, since my son's father was black, my son, Mark, is not 'bi-racial', but 'black'. When Mark was 14, the love of his life was Angie, a girl whose skin color and facial features were so much like his that she could have been his sister. One day, Mark presented me with the conundrum of racial identification in this way: 'Ma, Angie's mom is white and her dad is black so she's bi-racial. But she looks just like me. How come she gets to be bi-racial and I get to be black?'

So – what's a mother to say?

As I tried to explain to Mark that the binary view of 'race' was an attempt to ensure that there was such a thing as 100% pure whiteness, and that any deviation from that reference point would be termed black, I also had to explain that the opposite was not true; that is, to be less than 100% black would not entitle one to a white identity. Further, I succeeded in totally confusing my son by pointing out that if the Africans who had been brought to the West had overthrown their captors and grasped the reins of power, they may well have determined blackness to be the reference point, whereby to be less than fully black would have been to be white, hence a white Barak Obama, Colin Powell, and a white (dare I say?) Bob Marley! To complicate matters further, these designations would have carried the stigma of whiteness; to be white would be to be ugly, threatening, in a word – inferior.

What's Disability Got to Do with It?

The eugenics movement provided the context for the conflation of race and disability. Eugenecists, concerned with sorting people by intelligence as well as by 'race', designed elaborate and fraudulent classification systems for both constructs. These arguments were widely disseminated and insidiously supported by the conditions of poverty and abuse in which people of color and people with disabilities were forced to exist. Further, the holocaust of the slave trade and the colonizing of half the world by major European powers created deeply embedded beliefs about the inferiority of dominated peoples of color across the globe. As a result of the eugenics movement's persuasion that there was a biological basis for racial and intellectual classification, numerous societies institutionalized this racism through laws that ensured the exclusion and oppression of dominated groups.

In an ironic twist, these two streams of thought converged even further in the mid-20th century. Sharing a logic of equality, the civil rights and disability rights movements of the 1950s and 1960s resulted in legal and social pressures that had tremendous positive results for all children's access to schooling, but also produced unintended negative consequences that have continued to challenge U.S. society to this day. With the slow but inevitable enactment of the 1954 *Brown* decision, children of color finally gained the right to attend schools with their white peers; with the enactment of the Education for All Handicapped Children Act of 1975 (EHA), children designated disabled gained the right to attend public schools. Yet the history of separation and exclusion, the vision of inferiority and superiority, and the assumption of 'white property rights' continued to be reflected in the intense sorting and classifying paradigm that dominates the education system and in particular, special education.

Certainly, special education in the U.S. has come a long way since the passage of the EHA. The 1990 revision of the law and its re-titling as the *Individuals with Disabilities Education Act* (IDEA) represented a shift away from a view of 'the disabled' as a monolithic group, to an understanding of the individuality inherent in each and every person with a disability. Nevertheless, one perspective that remained constant was the application of a medical model to the interpretation of 'disability'. Based on this model, the law and the services it provides rely on a classification system that is categorical in nature, and which assumes a biological basis for differential or non-normative functioning. From this belief flows a multiplicity of dilemmas related to definitions, identification, assessment, and placement of children whose social, cognitive, or academic development does not fit prescribed norms.

Science has long repudiated the fallacy of race as a biological construct, and socio-cultural theorists and researchers have emphasized the intertwined nature of innate ability and social context. Nevertheless, these understandings cannot erase the socially constructed beliefs that continue to require individuals to represent themselves as racially identifiable beings, with biologically based affiliations to one group or another. Similarly, individuals with developmental or learning differences must be determined to fit a classification in order to receive services. In both groups, those whose identifiable differences cross two or more categories will be named 'bi-racial' or as having 'co-morbid' conditions. Bolstered by modern societies' unquestioning belief in the power of science to sort and classify humanity, the constructs of race and disability have nothing and yet everything in common, fueled, as they are, not only by the drive to classify and separate, but also by a shared history of exclusion and discrimination. They are fueled by the belief that difference is equivalent to deviance.

This book highlights the dilemmas resulting from the ongoing commitment to classifying human beings according to perceived physical and developmental features and capabilities. The widely ranging chapters provide key concepts that assist us in challenging the legacy of the colonial and eugenics histories. For example, instead of seeing individuals as 'bi-racial' or their conditions as 'co-morbid', an intersectional understanding allows us to see the wholeness that includes details of geography, language, social status, or personal history. The use of narrative assessment allows us to challenge the 'power of numbers' and to refute the bureaucratic and political imperatives of a medicalizing hunt for innate disability. A concern for qual(equ)ity refocuses our gaze from counting and measuring to assessing the consequences that our decisions impose on children's identities. Perhaps most important to those of us who would claim the role of researcher, a contrapuntal analysis of the logic of our assumptions can lead us to develop modes of inquiry that are truly responsive to the contradictions in our own thinking and to the vast array of cultures and individualities that constitute the world of the 21st century. These perspectives present a vision that suggests that perhaps my son's children will not have to choose which part of themselves should represent their true identities. Rather, they may be schooled in educational systems that will encourage the full expression of their wholeness and the full range of their authentic selves.

Index

Note: Page numbers in italics indicate figures and tables

Aberdeen, L. 142, 143
accountability, national testing regimes and 17–19
accountability-based reform: arguments against 36; concerns with 35–6; disproportionate representation and 47–8; growth in 1; students with SEND and 34–6; *see also* Programme for International Student Assessment (PISA)
accountability systems, growth in 1
Adar, S. 127
Admission Points Score (APS) 220
African American students, intellectual disability/emotional disturbance categories and 47
Ambrose, A. 75
American Education Research Association (AERA) 253
Anderton, J. 155
Annual Yearly Progress (AYP) 5
antiblackness, defined 134
Aotearoa New Zealand, assessment in 198–215; culturally responsive ways of working and 204–5; education policy context 199–200; *Educultural Wheel* and 205–15; *New Zealand Curriculum* (NZC) 200–1; overview of 198–9; sociocultural views of 203–4; special education needs and 202–3; *see also Educultural Wheel*
artifacts, mediation through 247–8
Artiles, A. 3, 94, 129
Ashing-Giwa, K. T. 261
Ashley, M. 98
'Assessment for Learning: From Theory to Practice' (Beller) 21
assessment industry: growth of 1; international perspective of 32–43

(*see also* special educational needs and disability (SEND)); in Israel, standardised tests in 15–28; national testing 68–84; Response to Intervention (RTI) 47–64; Sweden, national testing in 72–84; *see also* individual headings
assessments: high-stake 4–5; new eugenics of 3
assessment systems: criticisms of 1–4; cultural competence and 4; economic trends/constraints and 3; introduction to 1–9; negative developments in 2–3; Response To Intervention and 2–3; school curricula and 2; socio-historical contexts of 4–5
Attention Deficit Disorder Information and Support Service (ADDISS) 99
Attention Deficit Hyperactivity Disorder (ADHD) 91, 121; American Indian cultures and 93; Australia draft guidelines for 93; Brazilian diagnosis of 93; diagnosis of, among minority ethnic groups 92; gender and 98–9; National Collaborating Centre for Mental Health and 93
Atweh, B. 71, 82–3
Australia, high-stakes tests in 18–19
Australian Curriculum, Assessment and Reporting Authority (ACARA) 18–19

Bachman L. F. 227
Baker, E. 5
Ball, S. J. 19, 28, 108
Banhatti, R. G. 93
Barkan, E. 142–3
Barr, S. 202
Baynton, D. 178
Bean, P. T. 91

Index

behavioural disorders, psychopathologization of 91–100; class and 95–8; gender and 98–9; introduction to 91; race and 91–5; risks of 99–100
Bell, C. 181, 193
Bell Curve: Intelligence and Class Structure in American Life, The (Herrnstein and Murray) 153
Beller, Michal 21–2
Bender, W. 50
beneficial consequences 229
Benjamin, Z. 144
Bergh, A. 73
Berkeley, S. 56
Berryman, M. 204
Biklen, D. 152
Bingley, I. 91
Bishop, R. 203, 204
Björklund, J. 73
Black middle class parents, educational experiences/strategies of 108–15; labels and 109–10; overview of study project 108–9; SEN assessments and 113–15; special needs and, assessing 110–13
Black Panthers 125
Blanchett, W. 47
Boaler, J. 71, 83
Bonilla-Silva, E. 245–6, 269
Booher-Jennings, J. 25–6
Bowker, G.C. 251
Brantlinger, E. 202
Broadfoot, P. 202
Bronfenbrenner, U. 250
Brown v. Board of Education 121
Bunar, N. 75
Burt, C. 161, 162
Butler, J. 147
Butterfly Brigade 125
Bynoe, A. 91

Calhoon, M. 43
Campbell, F. 145–7, 156, 158–9, 163
Cantwell, D. 98
Carnoy, M. 1
Carr, M. 203–4
Cartledge, G. 49
cartography 94
categories, differential usage of 3
Chan, F. 249
Chapman, P.D. 17
Children with Learning Disabilities Act 150
Civil Rights Project 42

class: chaos of lives and 97; lack of self-control/material items and 97; territorializing home and 97–8
Classificatory systems for identifying disability 145–8
Clausen-May, T. 72
CLD learners *see* culturally and linguistically diverse (CLD) learners
Cohen, C. 191
Cole, C. 35
Cole, M. 247
colour-evasive approach 129
commensuration 17, 22
Condliffe, B.F. 83
Confederation of Swedish Enterprises 74
consequential validity 4
contrapuntalism: defined 180; of disproportionality literature 189–91; intersectionality analysis using 180–1
convergence principle 251
Council for Exceptional Children (CEC) 120
Covarrubias, A. 249
Crenshaw, K. 185
CRI *see* culturally responsive instruction (CRI)
Critical Race Feminist Theory 187
Critical Race Theory (CRT) 91, 104–5; *see also* disability
Cross, C. 48
Crowe, C. 147
CRR rubric *see* culturally responsive research (CRR) rubric for experimental intervention studies
cultural activity as unit of analysis 248–9
culturally and linguistically diverse (CLD) learners 49; case studies of 58–62; components related to provisions for 53, 54–5, 56; state guidance on 57
culturally responsive instruction (CRI), Response to Intervention models and 49–50, 58
culturally responsive research (CRR) rubric for experimental intervention studies 237–70, 254–7; analysis/interpretation 266–7; artifacts, mediation through 247–8; cultural activity as unit of analysis 248–9; culture as dynamic process and 247–50; defined 244; design and logic 261–4; development/ application of 252–3; dissemination of research 267–8; ecological validity and 250; evidence and, culture of 250–2;

evidence sources 264–6; intersectionality and 249–50; knowledge production and 244–6; literature review for 252; measurement tools/process 265–6; nondominant communities and role of 241–3; overview of 237–9; paradigm expansion and 243–4; problem formulation 253, 258–61; rationale for 239–41

culturally responsive ways of working 204–5

cultural model, racialization of disability 179, 184–5

culture: artifacts and, mediation through 247–8; of evidence 250–2; externalization processes and 247; internalization processes and 247; process-oriented model of 246

culture as dynamic process 247–50; artifacts and 247–8; cultural activity as unit of analysis 248–9; ecological validity and 250; intersectionality and 249–50

Curriculum and Assessment Policy Statement (CAPS) 219

Dahan, Y. 20
Danforth, S. 160–1, 162, 203
Daniels, H. 99
Darling-Hammond, L. 5
Davis, L. 191
Delancey Street 125
Delgado, R. 115
Deni, J. 155
Diagnostic and Statistical Manual of Mental Health Disorders (APA) 247
Diana v. Board of Education 124–5
disability 104–17; as ableist normativity 151–7; Black middle class parents, educational experiences/strategies of 108–15; Campbell and 145–7; Classificatory systems for identifying 145–8; construction of, story about 105–8; context/outline of 104–5; hunt for 148–51; introduction to 104; labels and 109–10; moralization to medicalization shift of 149–50; new eugenics and 145–8; othering of individuals with 184; as outlaw ontology 146–7; racialization of (*see* racialization of disabilities); service-provision models and 157–60; as White property right 115–16

disability-negative 158–9
disability-positive 158–9
Dis/ability Studies and Critical Race Theory (Dis/Crit) 104, 129; disproportionality and 129–33
Disability Studies Theory 187
Discipline and Punish (Foucault) 165
discourse theory 68–9
disproportionality in racial representation research 181–2; contrapuntal analysis of 189–91; unitary approach to 186–7
disproportionality issues: Dis/Crit and 129–33; IDEA and 47–8; RTI use to address 51, *52–3*, 53, 56; Section 504 of Rehabilitation Act and 127–9
diversity recognition, South Africa 219–20
dividing practices 145
Donovan, M. 48
double stimulation 244
Dovrat Committee 19–21
Drasgow, E. 36
Dred Scott v. Sandford 120–2
Du Bois, W.E.B. 127
Dulfer, N. 19
Dumas, M.J. 133–4
Du Plessis, C. 222, 225
Du Plessis, T. 222
Duster, T. 148
Dwivedi, K. 93

ecological validity 250
Economic and Social Research Council (ESRC) 108, 116
education: impact of new eugenics on 145–8; impact of old eugenics on 143–5; special education provision and 160–7
educational achievement, international comparisons of 1–2
educational disability: cultural bias and 153–5; labels and 149; overrepresentations and 153; policy reforms and 151–7; proliferation of categories of 148–50; special education provision and 160–7; swarming effect and 151–2
educational red-lining 134
educational subnormality categories 153
Educational Testing Service (ETS) 21
educational triage 25–6
Education for All Handicapped Children Act 279
Education Reform Act of 1988 18
Education Week 123

284 *Index*

Educultural Wheel 205–15, *207*; described 205; kotahitanga value 205, *207*, 213–14; manaakitanga value 205, *207*, 209–11; pumanawatnga value 205, *207*, 214–15; ranagtiratanga value 205, *207*, 211–13; Tom learning/assessment use of 205–6; whanaungatanga value 206, *207*, 208–9
Edwards, P. 50, 58
Eliot, C. 137, 163
ELLs *see* English language learners (ELLs)
Emerson, E. 120–1
Emotional Disabilities (ED) 121
emotional disturbance 47
England, high-stakes tests in 18
English language learners (ELLs) 58–60
English Speakers of Other Languages (ESOL) 60–2
equity in mathematics testing 70–1
Erevelles, N. 187, 191
ERIC database 252
ESOL *see* English Speakers of Other Languages (ESOL)
Espeland, W. N. 17, 28
eugenics 137–57; Crowe and 147; defining 138–9; educational disability and new 148–51; educational policy/practice influenced by old 143–5; Garton and 141–2; Kaplan and 140–1; key message 140; legacy of 139; mainstreaming policies and 151–7; new, disability and 145–8; old, historiographical debates of 138–42; overview of 137–8; racial imaginaries and 142–3; as scientific racism 139
Every Child Matters 34
Every Student Succeeds 34
evidence, culture of 250–2
evidence-based practices 238
exclusion and testing 72
exclusion categories, student-based 39
experimental intervention studies, culturally responsive research for *see* culturally responsive research (CRR) rubric for experimental intervention studies

Fancher, M. P. 132
Farmer, S. 133
Faulkner, A. 91
feeblemindedness 149–50
Feniger, Y. 20
Ferguson, P. M. 203
Ferri, B. 2–3
Figlio, D. 34
Fleer, M. 208

Foucault, M. 68–9, 81, 142, 145, 151, 163–4, 166
Fox, N. J. 97
Franklin, B. 149
free and public education 160
Free Appropriate Public Education (FAPE) 125
freedom by residence rule 120–1
'Fundamental Assumptions' in the Report of the Committee of Ten' (Eliot) 137
Furlow, C. 43

Gadler, U. 72–3
Galton, F. 139, 242
Gap Talk 95
Garton, S. 141–2, 145
gender, psychopathologically related diagnosis and 98–9
ghetto 94
Gieryn, T. F. 243
Gillborn, D. 95
Gillies, V. 96
Glenny, G. 153–4
Glide Church 125
globalisation, standardised tests and 16, 17
Goldman, S. 249
Google Scholar 252
Gorard, S. 96
Gordon, E. 5
Gordon Commission 5
Gould, S. 164
Green, A. 229
Gregg, L. 50
Gutiérrez, K. D. 245, 246

Habermas, J. 225
Hacking, I. 3–4
Hall, G. S. 137, 242
Halliday, M. A. K. 225
Hancock, A.-M. 186
Hanley-Maxwell, C. 149
Hanushek, E. A. 34
Harris, C. 115
Harry, B. 3, 47, 114
'Heading Toward a Crisis? District Grapples with Rising Special Education Costs' (Weier) 150
Hibel, J. 186, 187
high grade defectives 152
high-stakes tests 4–5; in Australia 18–19; in England 18; *vs.* low-stakes tests 16; negative consequences of 18, 22, 33–4; teaching to the tests and 25; in United States 17–18

Hipkins, R. 201
History of Disability, A (Stiker) 150–1
Hoeg, P. 70–1
home languages assessment, South Africa
218–33; design principles for 228–9;
diversity and, recognition of 219–20;
explanation for/response to 223–5;
introduction to 218–19; political context
of 232–3; requirements for, applying
230, 230–2, *231*; responses to unfair 225;
scale of impact of 222–3, *223*; solution
to 225–6; validity, validation and design
of 226–8; variation and, identifying/
managing 220–1, *221*, *222*
Horner, R.H. 238
Hoskyn, M. 241
Houchins, D.E. 43
Hudson, C. 69
Hultqvist, K. 159
Hursh, D. 32
Huxley, J. 143
hybrid circular narratives of
intersectionality 187–93
Hymes, D. 225

IDEA *see* Individuals with Disabilities
Education Act (IDEA)
impairment-disability binary 184
inclusive schooling 151–2
Individualized Educational Plan (IEP) 123
Individuals with Disabilities Education
Act (IDEA) 34, 124, 125, 177, 279;
disproportionality issues and 47–8;
racialization of disabilities and changes
to 178; Response to Intervention
and 48
Individuals with Disabilities Education
Improvement Act 239, 250–1
intellectual disability (ID) 47
Inter-Institutional Centre for Language
Development and Assessment
(ICELDA) 225
International Baccalaureate (IB)
programme 122
international comparative assessments and:
students with SEND and 36–40
intersectionality: characteristics of 185;
contrapuntal analysis of 180–1; cultural
model and 184–5; culture as dynamic
process and 249–50; hybrid circular
narratives of 187–93; political 185;
racialization of disability and 179–80;
structural 185; types of 185–6; unitary
approach to 186–7

Israel, standardised tests in 15–28;
accountability and 17–19; Beller and
21–2; Dovrat Committee and 19–21;
introduction to 15–17; Meitzav tests as
15–16, 19–27; power of numbers and
15–17, 27–8; purpose of 15; *see also*
Meitzav tests
Israeli Ministry of Education 15
Israeli Movement for Freedom of
Information 21
Israeli National Authority for Measurement
and Evaluation in Education (RAMA)
16, 19–20, 21
Israeli National Institute for Testing and
Evaluation 21

James, M. 202
Johnston, P. 48
Jolly, J.L. 127
Jurdak, M. 83

Kalberg, J. 238
Kane, M.T. 227
Kaplan, G. 140–1
Kidder-Ashley, P. 155
Kliewer, C. 152
Kliger, A. 23
Klinger, J. 3
Klingner, J. 47, 50, 58, 114, 267
knowledge production, cultural practice of
244–6
kotahitanga value 205, *207*, 213–14
Kourea, L. 49
Kuhn, T.S. 243
Kunnan, A.J. 227

labeling: political purpose of 3;
problematizing 149; special educational
services and 149
Ladson-Billings, G. 4, 94, 265
laissez-faire eugenics 146
Lane, K. 238
language assessment, design principles for
228–9
Lärarnas Riksförbund (teachers
union) 74
Lareau, A. 97
Larry P. v. Riles 125
Lather, P. 250
Latour, B. 246
Lau v. Nichols 124–5
league tables 18, 19
learning disabilities (LD) 149–50; role of 3;
RTI to identify 48

286 *Index*

'Learning Disabilities Eligibility in the 1990s: An Analysis of State Practices' (Kidder-Ashley et al.) 155
Leonardo, Z. 248
Lester, F.K. 71
Li, L. 208
likabehandling ('equal treatment') 83
Lingard, B. 18–19
Linn, R. L. 17
Livneh, I. 20
Llewellyn, A. 71
local educational agency (LEA) 48
Loeb, S. 34
Logan, J.R. 127
Lowe, R. 143
Lowrey, K.A. 36
low-stakes accountability system, Meitzav tests as 16, 19–27
Ludmerer, K.M. 139
Luke, A. 70
Lundahl, C. 77

Macartney, B. 202
McCall, L. 191
McDermott, R. 249
Macfarlane, A. 204
Macfarlane, S. 204
McMahon, B.T. 249
MacMillan, D. 187, 189–90
McSorley, K. 154–5
McWilliams, M. 132
mainstreaming 151–2
manaakitanga value 205, *207*, 209–11
manifestation review 131–2
Māori Curriculum Te Marautanga o Aotearoa 200
Markovich, D. 20
Marley, B. 278
mathematics education, quality and equity in *see* national testing
mathematics for all 71
mathematics testing, equity in 70–1
medical model, racialization of disability 179, 183
Meekosha, H. 2
'Meitzav Fever: Schools Lost Their Sanity, The' (Velner) 22
Meitzav tests 19–27; Beller and 22; components of 16, 19; described 15–16, 19; Dovrat Committee and 19–21; educational triage and 25–6; as low-stakes testing 22; negative consequences of, investigative data/methods used 23–4; policy borrowing and 16, 20;

resource diversion and 25; standardised tests logic and, acceptance/use of 26–7; teachers/principals and, pressure on 24–5; teaching to tests and 25
Mendick, H. 71
Messick, S. 4, 227
Mickelson, J.-R. 161, 162
Minca, E. 127
Minear, A. 187, 191
Mis-education of the Negro, The (Woodson) 165
Mismeasure of Man, The (Gould) 164
Mission Rebels 125
Mitchell, N. 179
moral panic 133
Morton, M. 202

narrative assessment: features of 198–9; *New Zealand Curriculum* and 204
National Assessment Program-Literacy and Numeracy (NAPLAN) 18
National Association of State Directors of Special Education (NASDSE) 48
National Center on Response to Intervention (NCRI) 50, 51
National Collaborating Centre for Mental Health 93
National Council on Disability 34
national degeneration, eugenics and 139
National Education Goals 2000 151
National Research Center on Learning Disabilities (NRCLD) 48, 50
National Senior Certificate (NSC) examinations 220, *221*
national testing 68–84; accountability and 17–19; discourse theory used in 68–9; equity in mathematics and 70–1; exclusion and 72; introduction to 68; quality in 69–70; in Sweden 72–84; *see also* Sweden, national testing in
Nation At Risk, A 151
new eugenics of assessment 3
Newman, L. 95–6
New Zealand *see* Aotearoa New Zealand, assessment in
New Zealand Curriculum (NZC) 200–1; key competencies of 201; narrative assessment and 204; *Te Whāriki* and 203
New Zealand Curriculum Exemplars for Learners with Special Education Needs 203–4
No Child Left Behind Act (NCLB) 4–5, 17–18, 34, 38, 251

nondominant communities, marginalization of 241–3

Obama, B. 278
O'Dowd, C. 98
Office of Civil Rights (OCR) 47
Office of Special Education Programs (OSEP) 47
Office of the Child and School Student Representative 73, 75
old eugenics: historiographical debates of 138–42; impact of, on education 143–5
O'Regan, F. 99
Orfield, G. 38
Organisation for Economic Cooperation and Development (OECD) 36, 40
Osborne, F. 143
O'Sullivan, D. 204
outlaw ontology, disability as 146–7
Ozga, J. 18, 27–8

Palmer, A.S. 227
Paperson, L. 94
paradigm expansion 243–4
pathology, as legitimizing device 94
Perryman, J. 18
Pettersson, D. 69
Phelps, A. 149
Pickens, D. 139
Piron, Shai 15, 22
PISA see Programme for International Student Assessment (PISA)
Plank, S.B. 83
Plessy v. Ferguson 121
Polesel, J. 19
policy as numbers logic 19
policy borrowing: Dovrat Committee and 20; Meitzav tests and 16, 20; transnational organisations and 20
political intersectionality 185
Poorer Children's Educational Attainment: How important are attitudes and behaviour? (Goodman and Gregg) 96
Porter, J. 99
positions of need 80
Powell, C. 278
power of numbers 15–17; Meitzav tests; comparisons and 27–8; dimensions of 27–8; Israeli Meitzav tests and 19–23; measurement of educational outcomes and 27; *see also* Israel, standardised tests in
precocious masturbators 144

President's Commission on Excellence in Special Education 48
Prewitt, K. 192
Programme for International Student Assessment (PISA) 36–40, 69; aims of 37; cycles for 36–7; defined 36; political influence of 37–8; student-based exclusion categories for 39–40; tests 1, 20; young people with SEND and, inclusion of 38–40, *41*
Project Based Learning (PBL) 122
PsycINFO 252
pumanawatnga value 205, *207*, 214–15

quality in testing 69–70
Quick, F. 143

race: disability and 105–8; psychopathologically related diagnosis and 91–5; spatializing 94–5
Race to the Top 251
racial disproportionality representation research 181–2; contrapuntal analysis of 189–91
racial imaginaries 142–3, 145
racialization of disabilities 177–93; African American learners and 177–8, 181; American Indian/Alaska Native students and 178, 181; concerns with 177; contrapuntal analysis of 180–1, 189–91; cultural model 184–5; disproportionate representation research on 181–2; future research for 191–3; hybrid circular narratives 187–93; IDEA and, changes in 178; intersectionality and 185–6; introduction to 177–81; Latino/a students and 178; medical model 183; scholarship on 178–9; social model 183–4; unitary approach to identity and 186–7
RAMA see Israeli National Authority for Measurement and Evaluation in Education (RAMA)
ranagtiratanga value 205, *207*, 211–13
Raymond, M.E. 34
reactive measures of human actions 17
relational equity 71, 83
repositioning 80–1
Repository for Germinal Choice 143
Reschly, D. 187, 189–90
Research Institute of Industrial Economics 74–5
Resnik, J. 21
Response to Intervention (RTI) 2–3, 47–64; to address disproportionality 56;

CLD learners and, inclusion of 53, *54–5*, 56, *57*; context specific CLD guidance case studies 58–62; core features of 48; culturally responsive instruction and 49–50, 58; data sources 50–1; defined 48; development levels by state *52–3*; disproportionate representation and 47; ELLs and 58–60, 63; ESOLs and 60–2; to identify learning disabilities 48; legal changes/tenets of 47–8; Model Screening Tool 51; overview of, in United States 50; policy implementation of 49; states use of, to address disproportionality 51, *52–3*, 53; study findings 62–4
responsible assessment design 228; conditions needed for 229
Rhodes, W. 160–1, 162
Rice, S. 19
Rizvi, F. 70
Rodwell, G. 144
Roe, M. 140, 166
Rohde, A. L. 93, 98
Rollock, N. 108
Ross, K. J. 133–4
RTI *see* Response to Intervention (RTI)

Sa'ar, Gideon 15–16
Said, E. 180
Samuels, C. 123
Sanford, J. 120
Sartor, D. 43
Sauder, M. 17, 28
Saunders, L. 50
Saunders, P. 50
scale of impact of language examinations 222–3, *223*
'School-to-Work Transition for Youth with Disabilities: A Review of Outcomes and Practices' (Phelps and Hanley-Maxwell) 149
Schram, S. F. 96, 97
Schraven, J. 127
scientific truth, defined 243
Scott, D. 127, 134, 182
Searle, G. R. 139
Searle, J. R. 226
Section 504 of Rehabilitation Act of 1973 120–34; Black students and 122–4; characteristics of 126; disability definition by 126; DisCrit, disproportionality and 129–33; disproportionality debate and 127–9; *Dred Scott v. Sandford* case and 120–2; major life activities definition by 126;

mitigating measures definition by 126; people eligible under 124–7; as right to exclude 133–4; supplementary/related aids and services definition by 126
'Section 504-Only Students National Incidence Data' (Zirkel and Weathers) 128
Selden, S. 144
self-fulfilling prophecies 17
SEN assessments 1, 2, 113–15
SEND *see* special educational needs and disability (SEND)
service-provision models, quality control and 157–60
Shaw, L. R. 249
Shepard, L. A. 4
Shepcaro, J. 238
Shippen, M. 43
Siebers, T. 183
situated knowledge, experimental research and 238–9
Sivenbring, J. 76
Skiba, R. 47
Skolverket 76–7
Skounti, M. 98
Sleeter, C. 3, 109, 115, 116
Smith, I. D. 95
Smith, R. 202
social model, racialization of disability 179, 183–4
sociocultural views of assessment, New Zealand 203–4
socio-economic striations, class and 95–8
soft governance 69
Soja, E. 91
spatialization 91; of race 94–5
special education: disproportionate representation in 47–64 (*see also* Response to Intervention (RTI)); minority students in 181–2; overrepresentation in, and testing bias 47–64
special educational needs and disability (SEND) 32–43; accountability-based reform and 34–6; balance and 43; cross-national comparisons and 40; international comparative assessments and students with 36–40; introduction to 32–3; PISA and 38–40, *41*; test- or standards-based accountability and education of students with 33–4; in UK, Tomlinson and 40, 42; *see also* Programme for International Student Assessment (PISA)

special education provision 160–7
special needs, assessing 110–13
standardised tests in American education system 17–18
standards-based accountability: described 32; education of students with SEND and 33–4; policies 33–4
Staples, M. 83
Star, S. L. 251
state designated handicapping condition 150
state education agencies (SEAs) 47
Stefancic, J. 115
Steiner-Khamsi, G. 20
sterilization 139
Stiker, H.-J. 150–1
Strand, S. 97
structural intersectionality 185
'Students with "504 plans" More Likely to Be White, Enrolled in Non-Title I Schools' (Samuels blog) 123–4
superiority effects 142
Swanson, H. L. 241
swarming effect 151–2
Sweden, national testing in 72–84; equity and quality in 79–82; future of 82–4; mistreatment cases 74; multilingual students and 75–7; organisation of 78; overview of 72–5; school for all concept and 72–3; students with special test-taking needs 78–9; Swedish school system, organisation of 75; third-grade mathematics tests 77–8
Sweden equity and quality *see* Sweden, national testing in
Swedish Discrimination Act 74
Swedish Schools Inspectorate 74; Office of the Child and School Student Representative 75
Symonds, B. 91

Taff, S. 203
Tamimi, S. 93
Taylor, E. 93
teaching to the tests 25
test-based accountability, education of students with SEND and 33–4
testing, exclusion and 72
Test of Advanced Language Ability (TALA) 230, 230–2
Te Whāriki 200, 203
third-grade national mathematics tests, Sweden 77–8
Third International Mathematics and Science Survey 151

Thomas, G. 153–4
Time for Education: Teachers Work With Support, Special Support and Individual Plans (Utbildnings departementet) 75
TIMSS *see* Trends in International Maths and Science Study (TIMSS)
Title VI of the Elementary and Secondary Education Act 150
Tomlinson, S. 40, 42, 96, 153, 155–6
Trends in International Maths and Science Study (TIMSS) 1, 36, 69
Tveit, S. 77

UH (Une Heure) materials 38
Umalusi 219–22; *see also* home languages assessment, South Africa
unitary approach to identity 186–7
United States: No Child left Behind 4–5; Response To Intervention in 2–3; RTI implementation in 50; school curricula in 2; standardised tests in 17–18
U.S. Department of Education 239; Office of Civil Rights 47, 239; Office of Special Education Programs 47, 50; RTI policy implementation and 49

Valero, P. 71
validity: components of 227–8; defined 226, 227; ecological, culture as dynamic process and 250; language tests and 227; unifying concept of 227
Varenne, H. 249
variation, identifying/managing in South Africa 220–1, *221, 222*
Vincent, C. 97, 108
Vygotsky, L. S. 244

Walker, C.J. 125
Walker, D. 93
Walkerdine, V. 69
Ward, K.J. 97
Ware, L. 157
Weathers, J. 123–4, 128, 130–1
Webber, M. 204
Weber, M.C. 125
Weier, G. 150
Welner, K.G. 4
whanaungatanga 205, 206, *207*, 208–9
White innocence 245
White logic 245–6
Wilkins, D. 226
Woodson, C.G. 165
Wrigley, T. 70

'Writing Eugenics: A History of Classifying Practices' (Garton) 141

Wundt, W. 244

Xi, X. 227

Yogev, A. 20

Yonah, Y. 20

Zirkel, P. 123–4, 128, 130–1

Zuberi, T. 245–6, 269